the AMAZING SPIDER-MAN

Life in the MAD DOG WARD

BOONE COUNTY LIBRARY
2040 9100 916 209 7

W9-AOH-990

SPIDER-MAN: LIFE IN THE MAD DOG WARD. Contains material originally published in magazine form as WEB OF SPIDER-MAN #33, AMAZING SPIDER-MAN #295, SPECTACULAR SPIDER-MAN #133 and SPIDER-MAN #29-31. First printing 2013. ISBN# 978-0-7851-8503-1. Published by MARVEL WORLDWIDE, INC., a subsidiary of MARVEL ENTERTAINMENT, LLC. OFFICE OF PUBLICATION: 135 West 50th Street, New York, NY 10020. Copyright © 1987, 1992, 1993 and 2013 Marvel Characters, Inc. All rights reserved. All characters featured in this issue and the distinctive names and likenesses thereof, and all related indicia are trademarks of Marvel Characters, Inc. No similarity between any of the names, characters, persons, and/or institutions in this magazine with those of any living or dead person or institution is intended, and any such similarity which may exist is purely coincidental. **Printed in the U.S.A.** ALAN FINE, EVP - Office of the President, Marvel Worldwide, Inc. and EVP & CMO Marvel Characters B.V.; DAN BUCKLEY, Publisher & President - Print, Animation & Digital Divisions; JOE QUESADA, Chief Creative Officer; TOM BREVOORT, SVP of Publishing; DAVID BOGART, SVP of Operations & Procurement, Publishing; C.B. CEBULSKI, SVP of Creator & Content Development; DAVID GABRIEL, SVP of Print & Digital Publishing Sales; JIM O'KEEFE, ...ing Technology; SUSAN CRESPI, Editorial Operations Manager; ALEX MORALES, Publishing Operations Manager; STAN LEE, Chairman Emeritus. ...m, please contact Niza Disla, Director of Marvel Partnerships, at ndisla@marvel. com. For Marvel subscription inquiries, please call 800-217-915... ...LLEY, INC., SALEM, VA, USA.

BOONE COUNTY PUBLIC LIBRARY
BURLINGTON, KY 41005

WRITER:
Ann Nocenti
PENCILERS:
Cynthia Martin & Chris Marrinan
INKERS:
Steve Leialoha, Kyle Baker,
Josef Rubinstein & Sam de la Rosa
with Don Hudson
COLORISTS:
Janet Jackson, Marie Javins
& Kevin Tinsley
LETTERERS:
Rick Parker & Chris Eliopoulos
ASSISTANT EDITOR:
Mike Lackey
EDITORS:
Jim Salicrup & Danny Fingeroth

FRONT COVER ARTIST:
Bill Sienkiewicz
BACK COVER ARTISTS:
Chris Marrinan, Sam de la Rosa
& Tom Smith

the AMAZING SPIDER-MAN

Life in the MAD DOG Ward

COLLECTION EDITOR & DESIGN: Nelson Ribeiro

ASSISTANT EDITOR: Alex Starbuck

EDITORS, SPECIAL PROJECTS:
Mark D. Beazley & Jennifer Grünwald

SENIOR EDITOR, SPECIAL PROJECTS:
Jeff Youngquist

RESEARCH: Jess Harrold

LAYOUT: Jeph York   PRODUCTION: Colortek

SVP OF PRINT & DIGITAL PUBLISHING SALES:
David Gabriel

EDITOR IN CHIEF: Axel Alonso

CHIEF CREATIVE OFFICER: Joe Quesada

PUBLISHER: Dan Buckley

EXECUTIVE PRODUCER: Alan Fine

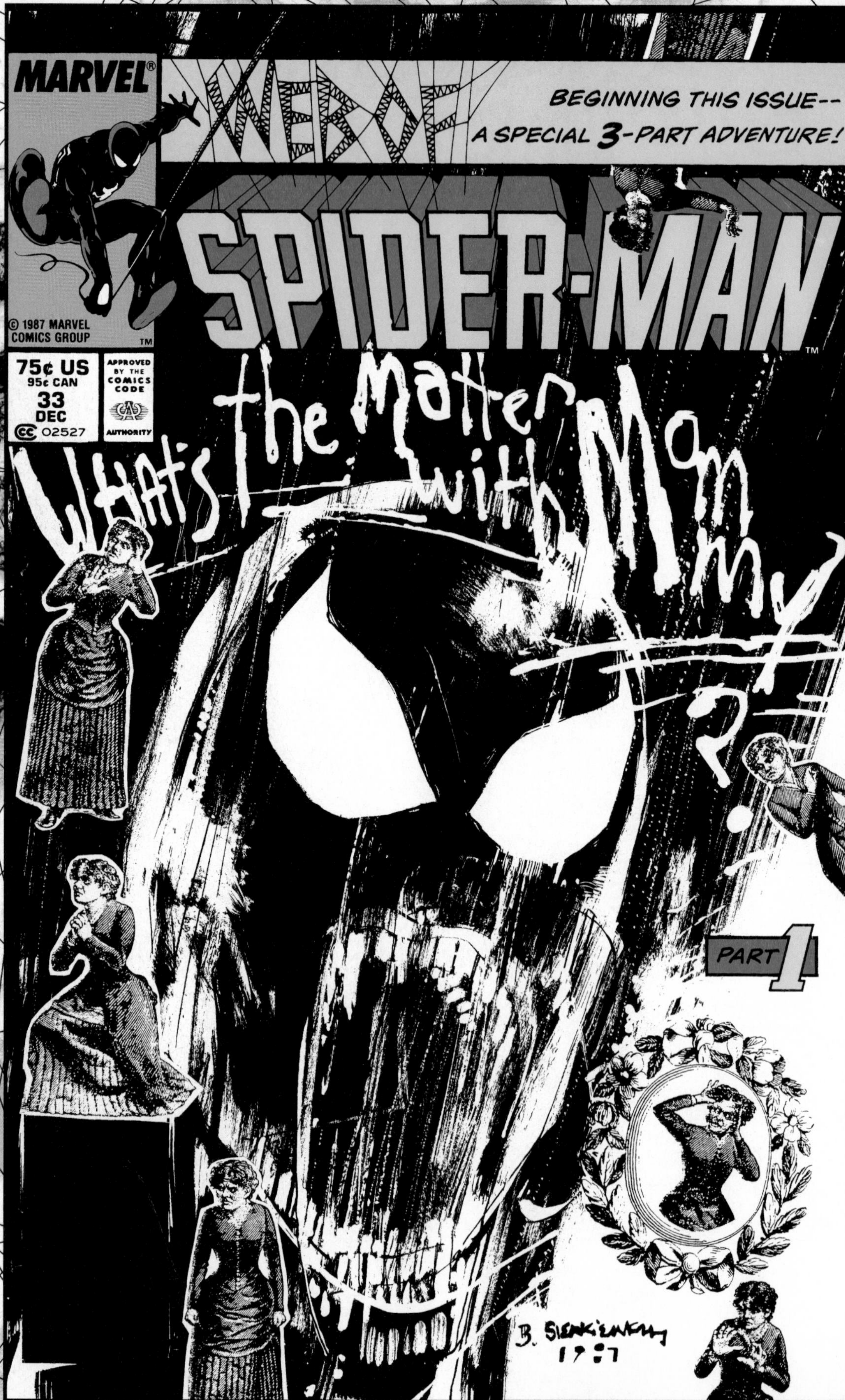
MARVEL®
WEB OF SPIDER-MAN™
BEGINNING THIS ISSUE--
A SPECIAL 3-PART ADVENTURE!
© 1987 MARVEL COMICS GROUP
75¢ US
95¢ CAN
33
DEC
02527
APPROVED BY THE COMICS CODE AUTHORITY
What's the Matter with My Mom?
PART 1
B. SIENKIEWICZ

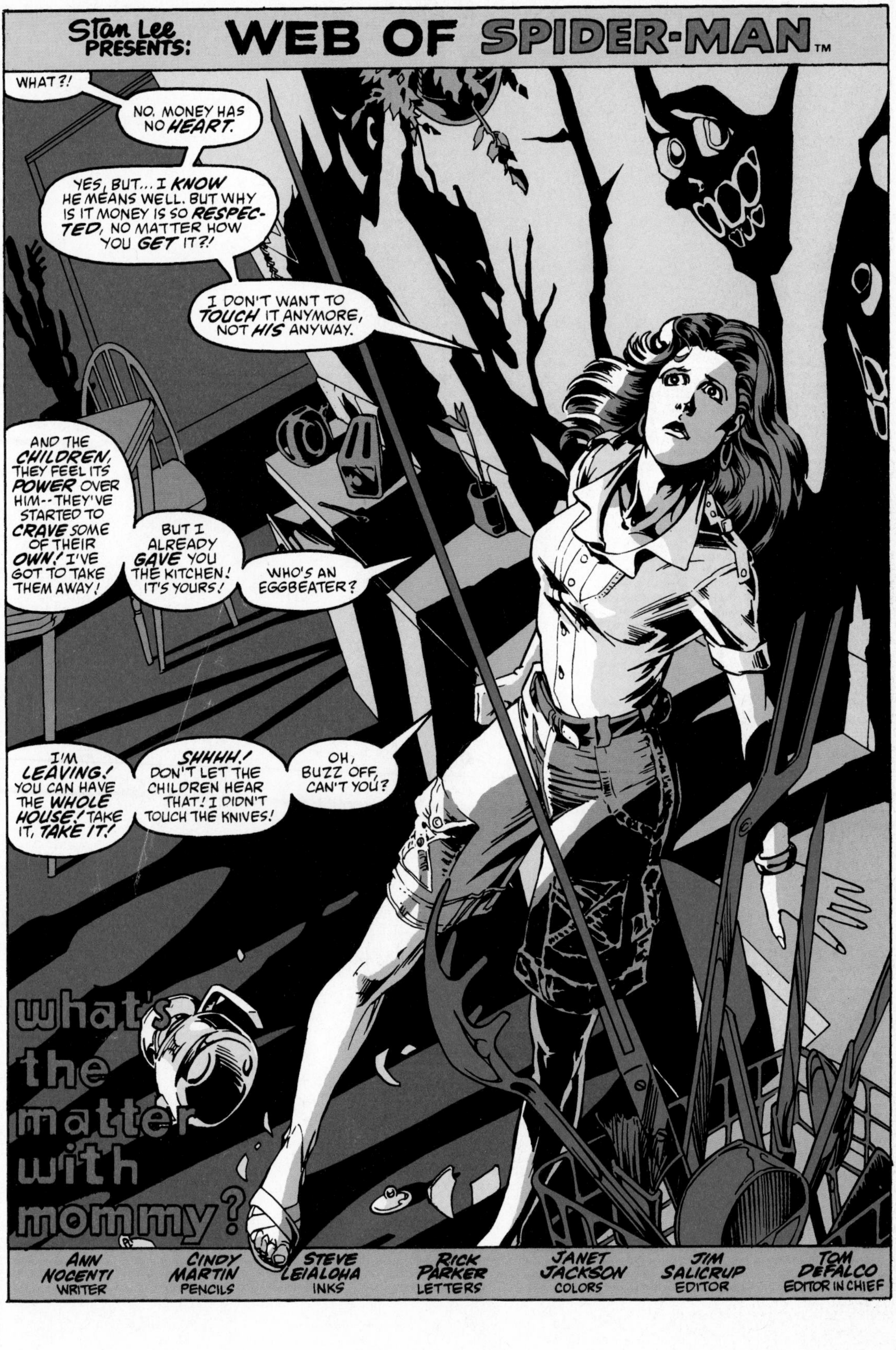
Stan Lee PRESENTS: WEB OF SPIDER-MAN™
WHAT?!
NO. MONEY HAS NO HEART.
YES, BUT... I KNOW HE MEANS WELL. BUT WHY IS IT MONEY IS SO RESPECTED, NO MATTER HOW YOU GET IT?!
I DON'T WANT TO TOUCH IT ANYMORE, NOT HIS ANYWAY.
AND THE CHILDREN, THEY FEEL ITS POWER OVER HIM--THEY'VE STARTED TO CRAVE SOME OF THEIR OWN! I'VE GOT TO TAKE THEM AWAY!
BUT I ALREADY GAVE YOU THE KITCHEN! IT'S YOURS!
WHO'S AN EGGBEATER?
I'M LEAVING! YOU CAN HAVE THE WHOLE HOUSE! TAKE IT, TAKE IT!
SHHHH! DON'T LET THE CHILDREN HEAR THAT! I DIDN'T TOUCH THE KNIVES!
OH, BUZZ OFF, CAN'T YOU?
what's the matter with mommy?
ANN NOCENTI WRITER
CINDY MARTIN PENCILS
STEVE LEIALOHA INKS
RICK PARKER LETTERS
JANET JACKSON COLORS
JIM SALICRUP EDITOR
TOM DEFALCO EDITOR IN CHIEF

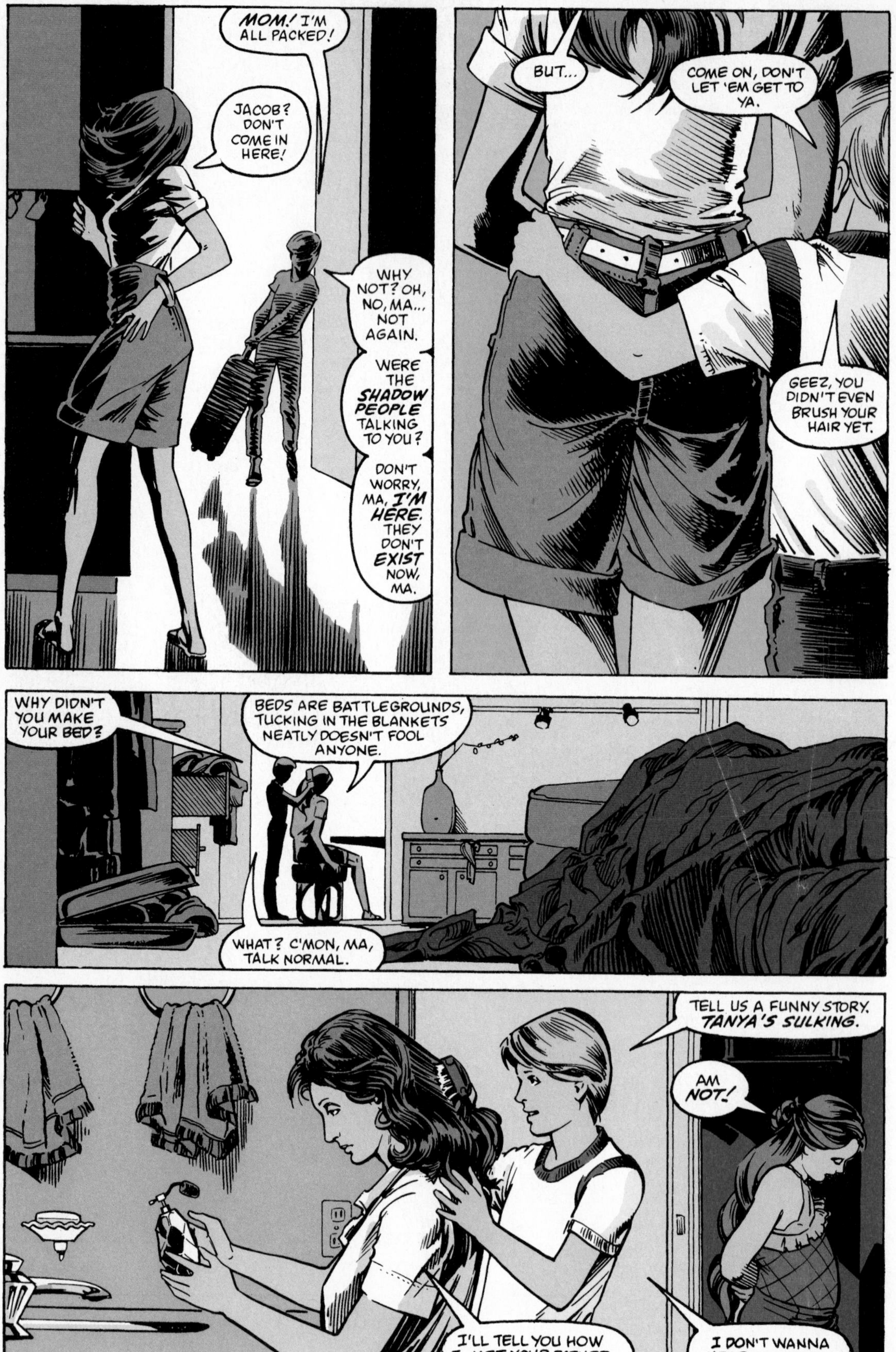
MOM! I'M ALL PACKED!
JACOB? DON'T COME IN HERE!
WHY NOT? OH, NO, MA... NOT AGAIN.
WERE THE SHADOW PEOPLE TALKING TO YOU?
DON'T WORRY, MA, I'M HERE. THEY DON'T EXIST NOW, MA.
BUT...
COME ON, DON'T LET 'EM GET TO YA.
GEEZ, YOU DIDN'T EVEN BRUSH YOUR HAIR YET.
WHY DIDN'T YOU MAKE YOUR BED?
BEDS ARE BATTLEGROUNDS, TUCKING IN THE BLANKETS NEATLY DOESN'T FOOL ANYONE.
WHAT? C'MON, MA, TALK NORMAL.
TELL US A FUNNY STORY. TANYA'S SULKING.
AM NOT!
I'LL TELL YOU HOW I MET YOUR FATHER...
I DON'T WANNA HEAR ABOUT HIM.

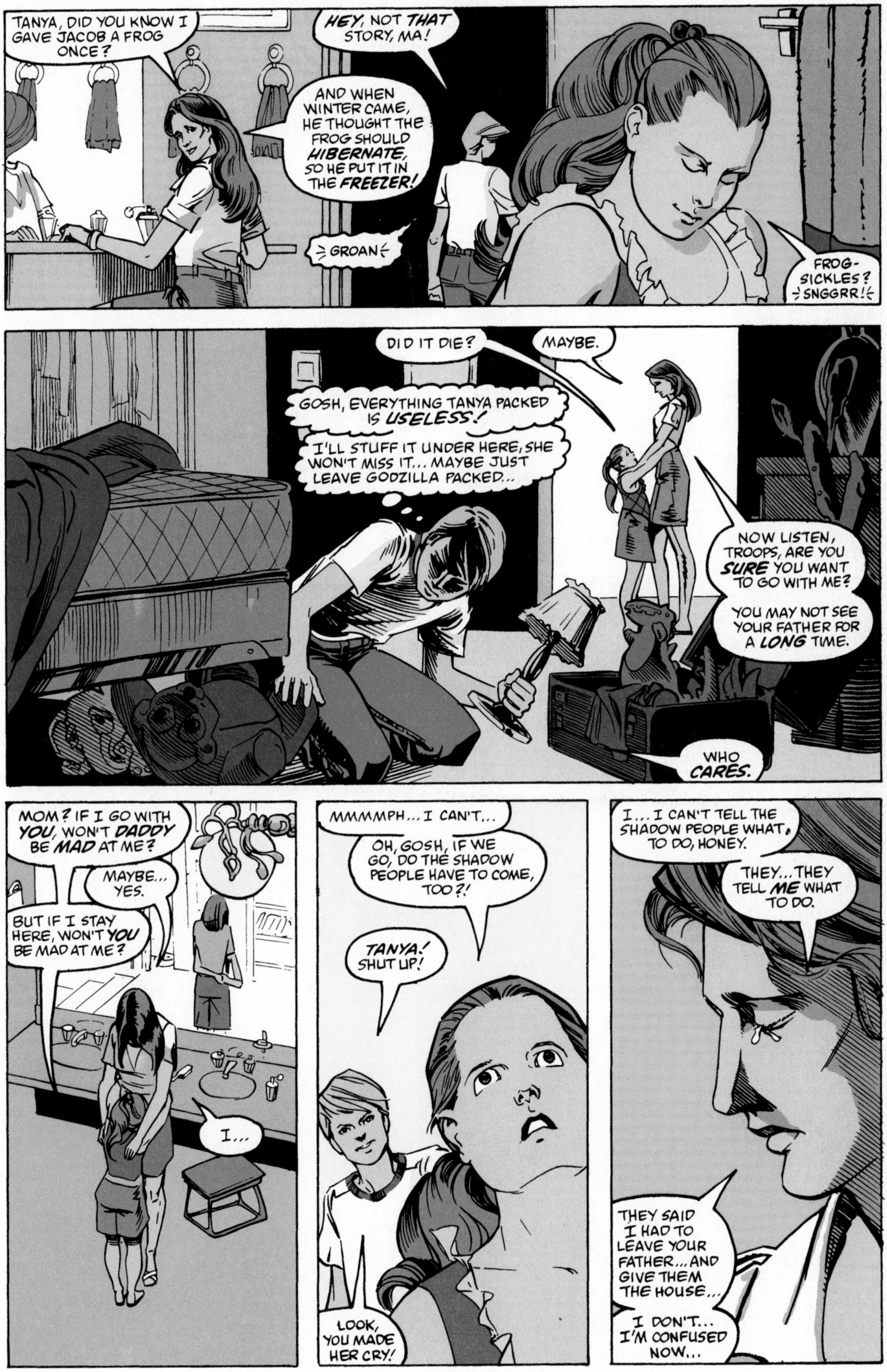
TANYA, DID YOU KNOW I GAVE JACOB A FROG ONCE?
HEY, NOT THAT STORY, MA!
AND WHEN WINTER CAME, HE THOUGHT THE FROG SHOULD HIBERNATE, SO HE PUT IT IN THE FREEZER!
GROAN
FROG-SICKLES? SNGGRR!
DID IT DIE?
MAYBE.
GOSH, EVERYTHING TANYA PACKED IS USELESS!
I'LL STUFF IT UNDER HERE, SHE WON'T MISS IT... MAYBE JUST LEAVE GODZILLA PACKED...
NOW LISTEN, TROOPS, ARE YOU SURE YOU WANT TO GO WITH ME?
YOU MAY NOT SEE YOUR FATHER FOR A LONG TIME.
WHO CARES.
MOM? IF I GO WITH YOU, WON'T DADDY BE MAD AT ME?
MAYBE... YES.
BUT IF I STAY HERE, WON'T YOU BE MAD AT ME?
I...
MMMMPH... I CAN'T...
OH, GOSH, IF WE GO, DO THE SHADOW PEOPLE HAVE TO COME, TOO?!
TANYA! SHUT UP!
LOOK, YOU MADE HER CRY!
I... I CAN'T TELL THE SHADOW PEOPLE WHAT TO DO, HONEY.
THEY... THEY TELL ME WHAT TO DO.
THEY SAID I HAD TO LEAVE YOUR FATHER... AND GIVE THEM THE HOUSE...
I DON'T... I'M CONFUSED NOW...

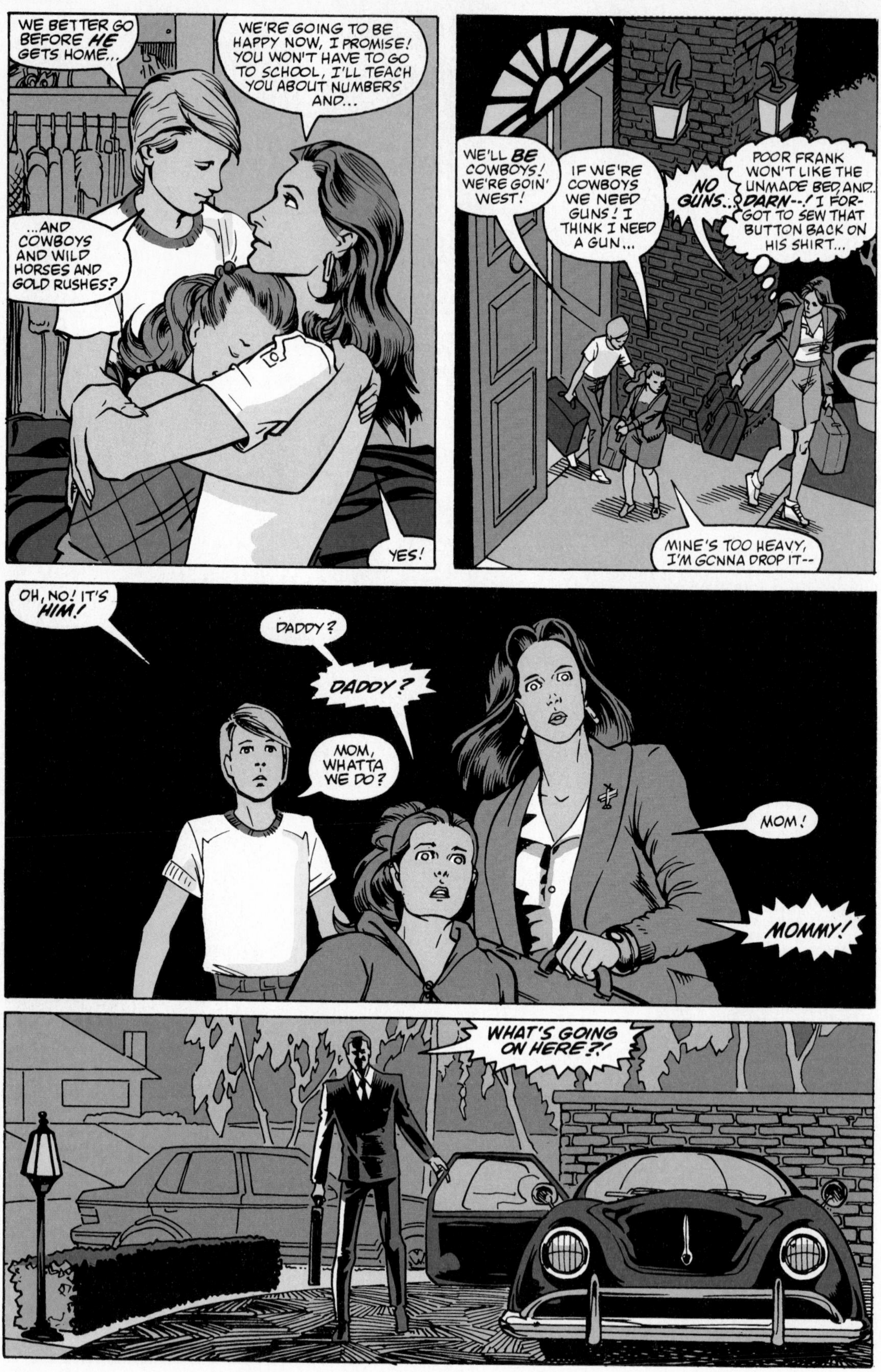

WE BETTER GO BEFORE HE GETS HOME...
WE'RE GOING TO BE HAPPY NOW, I PROMISE! YOU WON'T HAVE TO GO TO SCHOOL, I'LL TEACH YOU ABOUT NUMBERS AND...
...AND COWBOYS AND WILD HORSES AND GOLD RUSHES?
YES!
WE'LL BE COWBOYS! WE'RE GOIN' WEST!
IF WE'RE COWBOYS WE NEED GUNS! I THINK I NEED A GUN...
NO GUNS...
POOR FRANK WON'T LIKE THE UNMADE BED AND... DARN--! I FORGOT TO SEW THAT BUTTON BACK ON HIS SHIRT...
MINE'S TOO HEAVY, I'M GONNA DROP IT--
OH, NO! IT'S HIM!
DADDY?
DADDY?
MOM, WHATTA WE DO?
MOM!
MOMMY!
WHAT'S GOING ON HERE?!

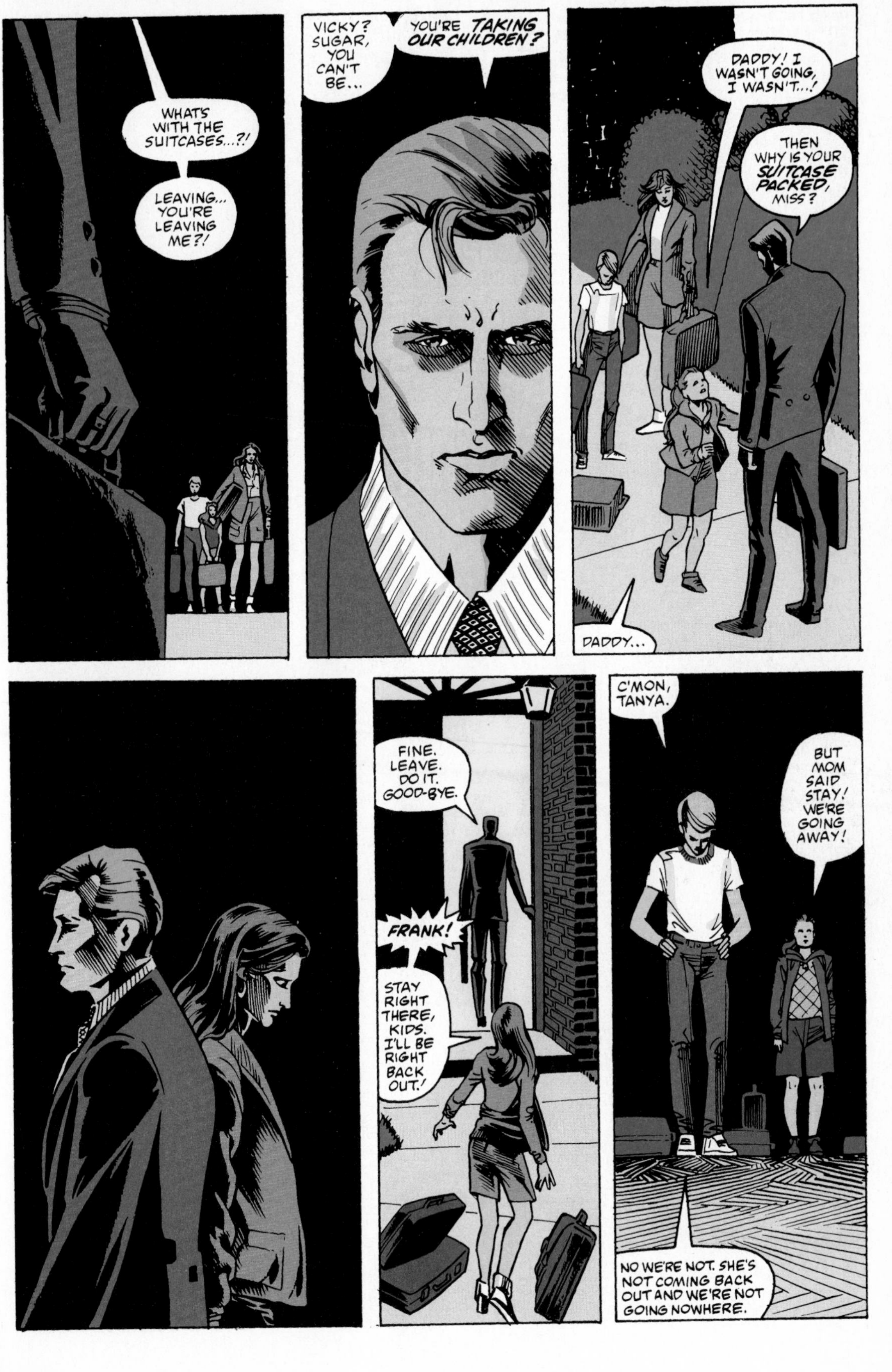
WHAT'S WITH THE SUITCASES...?!
LEAVING... YOU'RE LEAVING ME?!
VICKY? SUGAR, YOU CAN'T BE...
YOU'RE TAKING OUR CHILDREN?
DADDY! I WASN'T GOING, I WASN'T...!
THEN WHY IS YOUR SUITCASE PACKED, MISS?
DADDY...
FINE. LEAVE. DO IT. GOOD-BYE.
FRANK!
STAY RIGHT THERE, KIDS. I'LL BE RIGHT BACK OUT!
C'MON, TANYA.
BUT MOM SAID STAY! WE'RE GOING AWAY!
NO WE'RE NOT. SHE'S NOT COMING BACK OUT AND WE'RE NOT GOING NOWHERE.

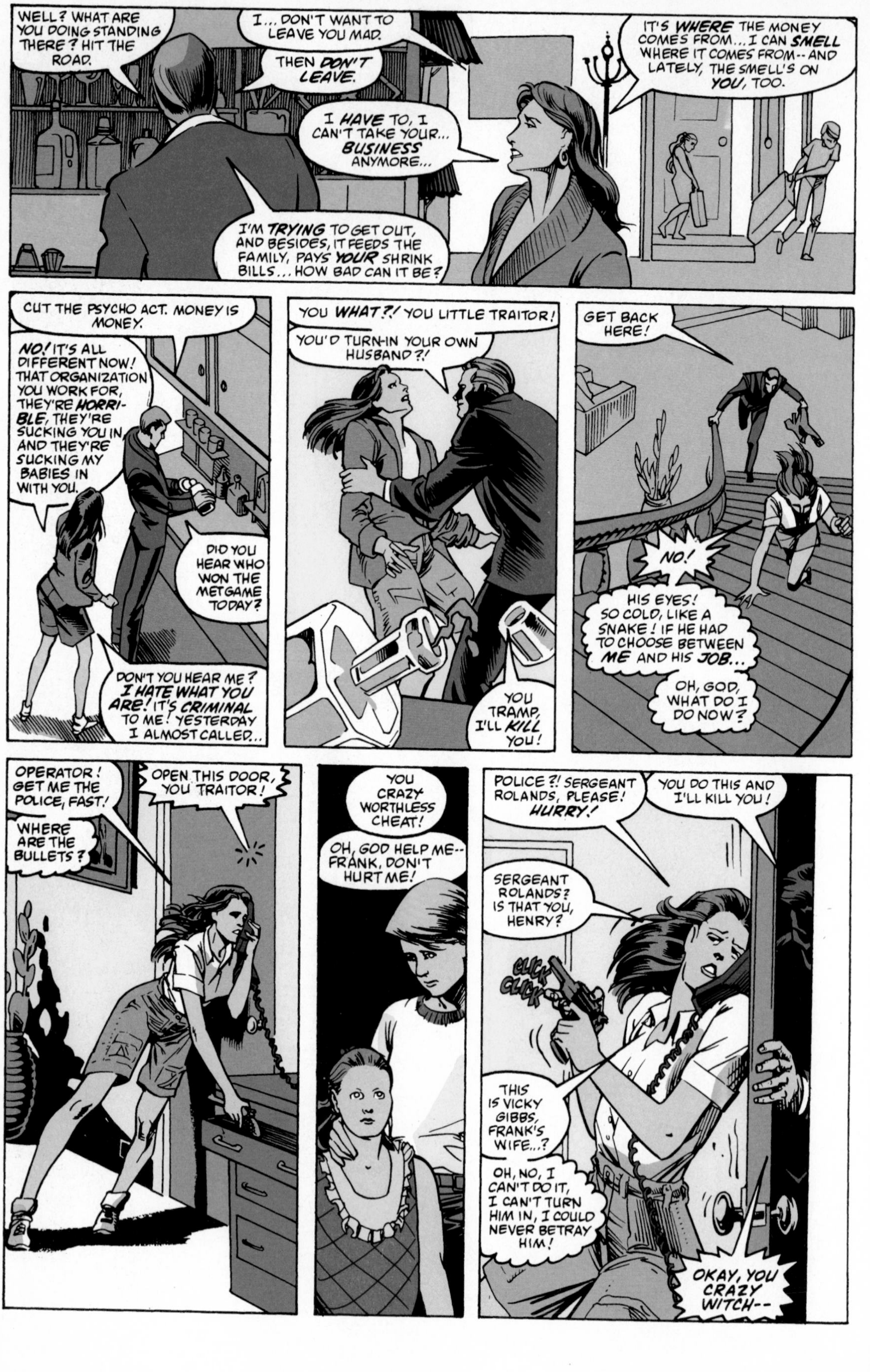
WELL? WHAT ARE YOU DOING STANDING THERE? HIT THE ROAD.
I... DON'T WANT TO LEAVE YOU MAD.
THEN DON'T LEAVE.
I HAVE TO, I CAN'T TAKE YOUR... BUSINESS ANYMORE...
IT'S WHERE THE MONEY COMES FROM... I CAN SMELL WHERE IT COMES FROM-- AND LATELY, THE SMELL'S ON YOU, TOO.
I'M TRYING TO GET OUT, AND BESIDES, IT FEEDS THE FAMILY, PAYS YOUR SHRINK BILLS... HOW BAD CAN IT BE?
CUT THE PSYCHO ACT. MONEY IS MONEY.
NO! IT'S ALL DIFFERENT NOW! THAT ORGANIZATION YOU WORK FOR, THEY'RE HORRIBLE, THEY'RE SUCKING YOU IN, AND THEY'RE SUCKING MY BABIES IN WITH YOU.
DID YOU HEAR WHO WON THE MET GAME TODAY?
DON'T YOU HEAR ME? I HATE WHAT YOU ARE! IT'S CRIMINAL TO ME! YESTERDAY I ALMOST CALLED...
YOU WHAT?! YOU LITTLE TRAITOR!
YOU'D TURN-IN YOUR OWN HUSBAND?!
YOU TRAMP, I'LL KILL YOU!
GET BACK HERE!
NO!
HIS EYES! SO COLD, LIKE A SNAKE! IF HE HAD TO CHOOSE BETWEEN ME AND HIS JOB...
OH, GOD, WHAT DO I DO NOW?
OPERATOR! GET ME THE POLICE, FAST!
OPEN THIS DOOR, YOU TRAITOR!
WHERE ARE THE BULLETS?
YOU CRAZY WORTHLESS CHEAT!
OH, GOD HELP ME-- FRANK, DON'T HURT ME!
POLICE?! SERGEANT ROLANDS, PLEASE! HURRY!
YOU DO THIS AND I'LL KILL YOU!
SERGEANT ROLANDS? IS THAT YOU, HENRY?
CLICK CLICK
THIS IS VICKY GIBBS, FRANK'S WIFE...?
OH, NO, I CAN'T DO IT, I CAN'T TURN HIM IN, I COULD NEVER BETRAY HIM!
OKAY, YOU CRAZY WITCH--

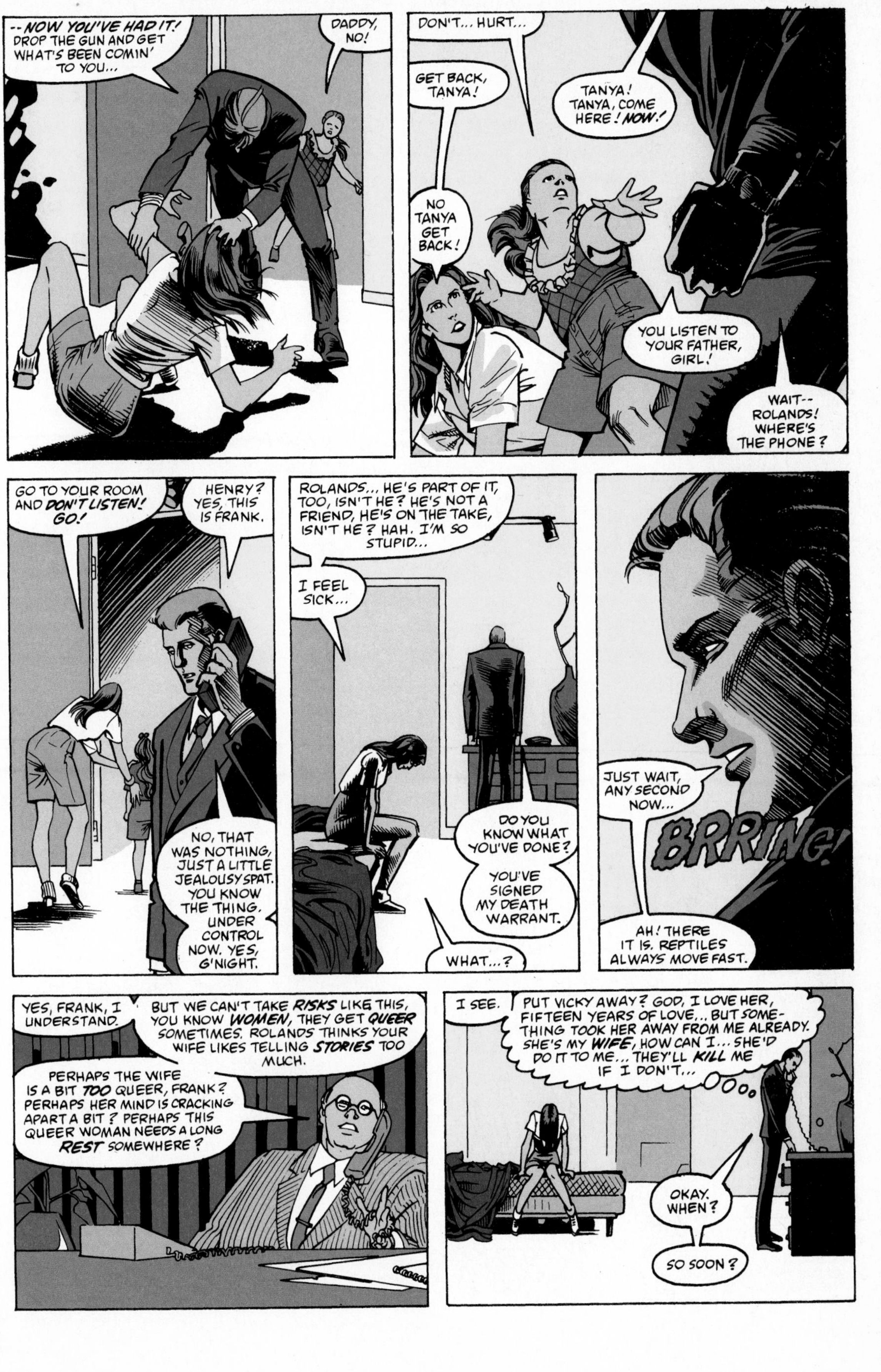
--NOW YOU'VE HAD IT! DROP THE GUN AND GET WHAT'S BEEN COMIN' TO YOU...
DADDY, NO!
DON'T... HURT...
GET BACK, TANYA!
TANYA! TANYA, COME HERE! NOW!
NO TANYA GET BACK!
YOU LISTEN TO YOUR FATHER, GIRL!
WAIT-- ROLANDS! WHERE'S THE PHONE?
GO TO YOUR ROOM AND DON'T LISTEN! GO!
HENRY? YES, THIS IS FRANK.
NO, THAT WAS NOTHING, JUST A LITTLE JEALOUSY SPAT. YOU KNOW THE THING. UNDER CONTROL NOW. YES, G'NIGHT.
ROLANDS... HE'S PART OF IT, TOO, ISN'T HE? HE'S NOT A FRIEND, HE'S ON THE TAKE, ISN'T HE? HAH. I'M SO STUPID...
I FEEL SICK...
DO YOU KNOW WHAT YOU'VE DONE?
YOU'VE SIGNED MY DEATH WARRANT.
WHAT...?
JUST WAIT, ANY SECOND NOW...
BRRING!
AH! THERE IT IS. REPTILES ALWAYS MOVE FAST.
YES, FRANK, I UNDERSTAND.
BUT WE CAN'T TAKE RISKS LIKE THIS, YOU KNOW WOMEN, THEY GET QUEER SOMETIMES. ROLANDS THINKS YOUR WIFE LIKES TELLING STORIES TOO MUCH.
PERHAPS THE WIFE IS A BIT TOO QUEER, FRANK? PERHAPS HER MIND IS CRACKING APART A BIT? PERHAPS THIS QUEER WOMAN NEEDS A LONG REST SOMEWHERE?
I SEE.
PUT VICKY AWAY? GOD, I LOVE HER, FIFTEEN YEARS OF LOVE... BUT SOMETHING TOOK HER AWAY FROM ME ALREADY. SHE'S MY WIFE, HOW CAN I... SHE'D DO IT TO ME... THEY'LL KILL ME IF I DON'T...
OKAY. WHEN?
SO SOON?

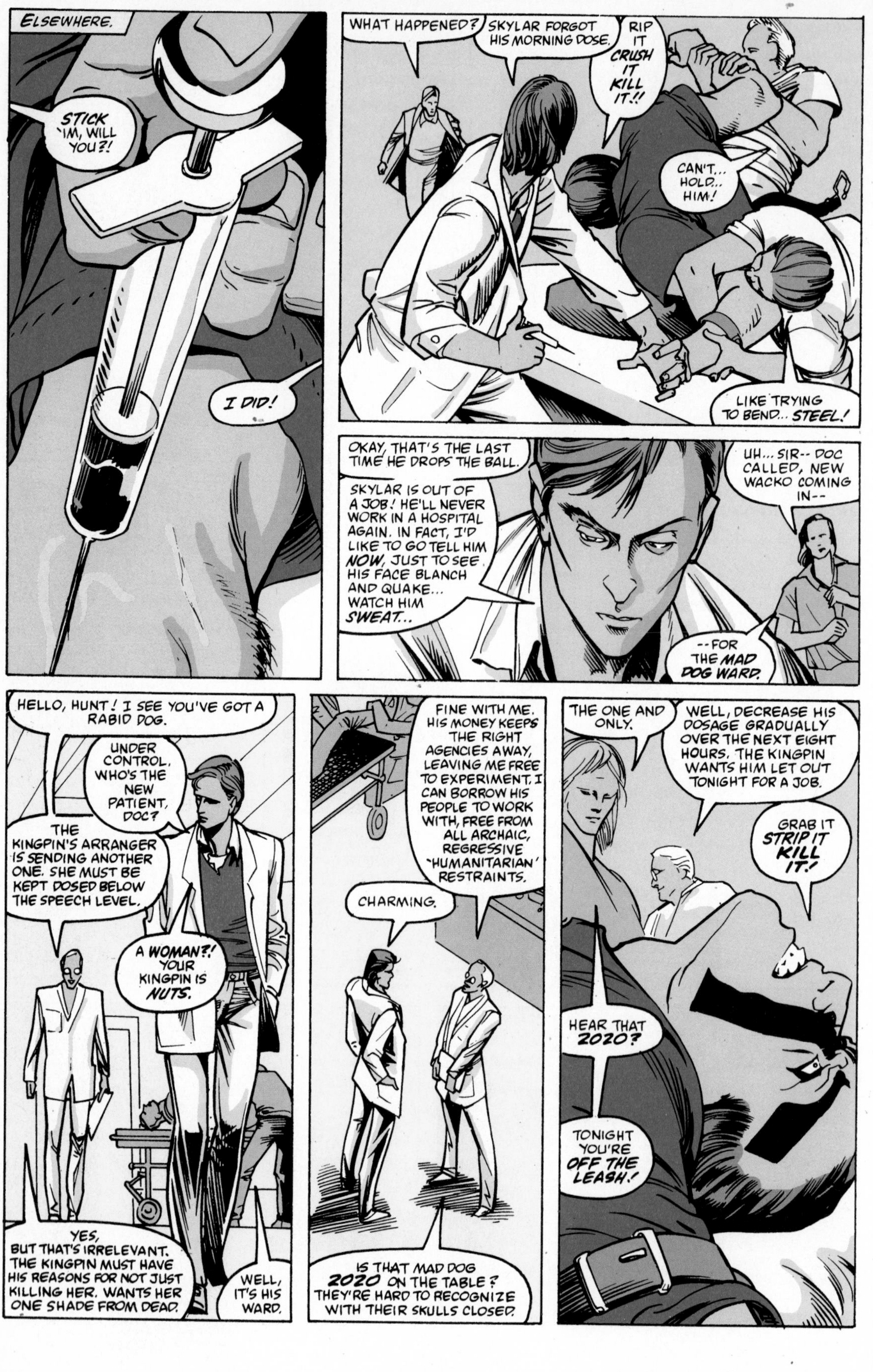
ELSEWHERE.
STICK 'IM, WILL YOU?!
I DID!
WHAT HAPPENED?
SKYLAR FORGOT HIS MORNING DOSE.
RIP IT CRUSH IT KILL IT!!
CAN'T... HOLD... HIM!
LIKE TRYING TO BEND... STEEL!
OKAY, THAT'S THE LAST TIME HE DROPS THE BALL.
SKYLAR IS OUT OF A JOB! HE'LL NEVER WORK IN A HOSPITAL AGAIN. IN FACT, I'D LIKE TO GO TELL HIM NOW, JUST TO SEE HIS FACE BLANCH AND QUAKE... WATCH HIM SWEAT...
UH... SIR-- DOC CALLED, NEW WACKO COMING IN--
--FOR THE MAD DOG WARD.
HELLO, HUNT! I SEE YOU'VE GOT A RABID DOG.
UNDER CONTROL. WHO'S THE NEW PATIENT, DOC?
THE KINGPIN'S ARRANGER IS SENDING ANOTHER ONE. SHE MUST BE KEPT DOSED BELOW THE SPEECH LEVEL.
A WOMAN?! YOUR KINGPIN IS NUTS.
YES, BUT THAT'S IRRELEVANT. THE KINGPIN MUST HAVE HIS REASONS FOR NOT JUST KILLING HER. WANTS HER ONE SHADE FROM DEAD.
WELL, IT'S HIS WARD.
FINE WITH ME. HIS MONEY KEEPS THE RIGHT AGENCIES AWAY, LEAVING ME FREE TO EXPERIMENT. I CAN BORROW HIS PEOPLE TO WORK WITH, FREE FROM ALL ARCHAIC, REGRESSIVE 'HUMANITARIAN' RESTRAINTS.
CHARMING.
IS THAT MAD DOG 2020 ON THE TABLE? THEY'RE HARD TO RECOGNIZE WITH THEIR SKULLS CLOSED.
THE ONE AND ONLY.
WELL, DECREASE HIS DOSAGE GRADUALLY OVER THE NEXT EIGHT HOURS. THE KINGPIN WANTS HIM LET OUT TONIGHT FOR A JOB.
GRAB IT STRIP IT KILL IT!
HEAR THAT 2020?
TONIGHT YOU'RE OFF THE LEASH!

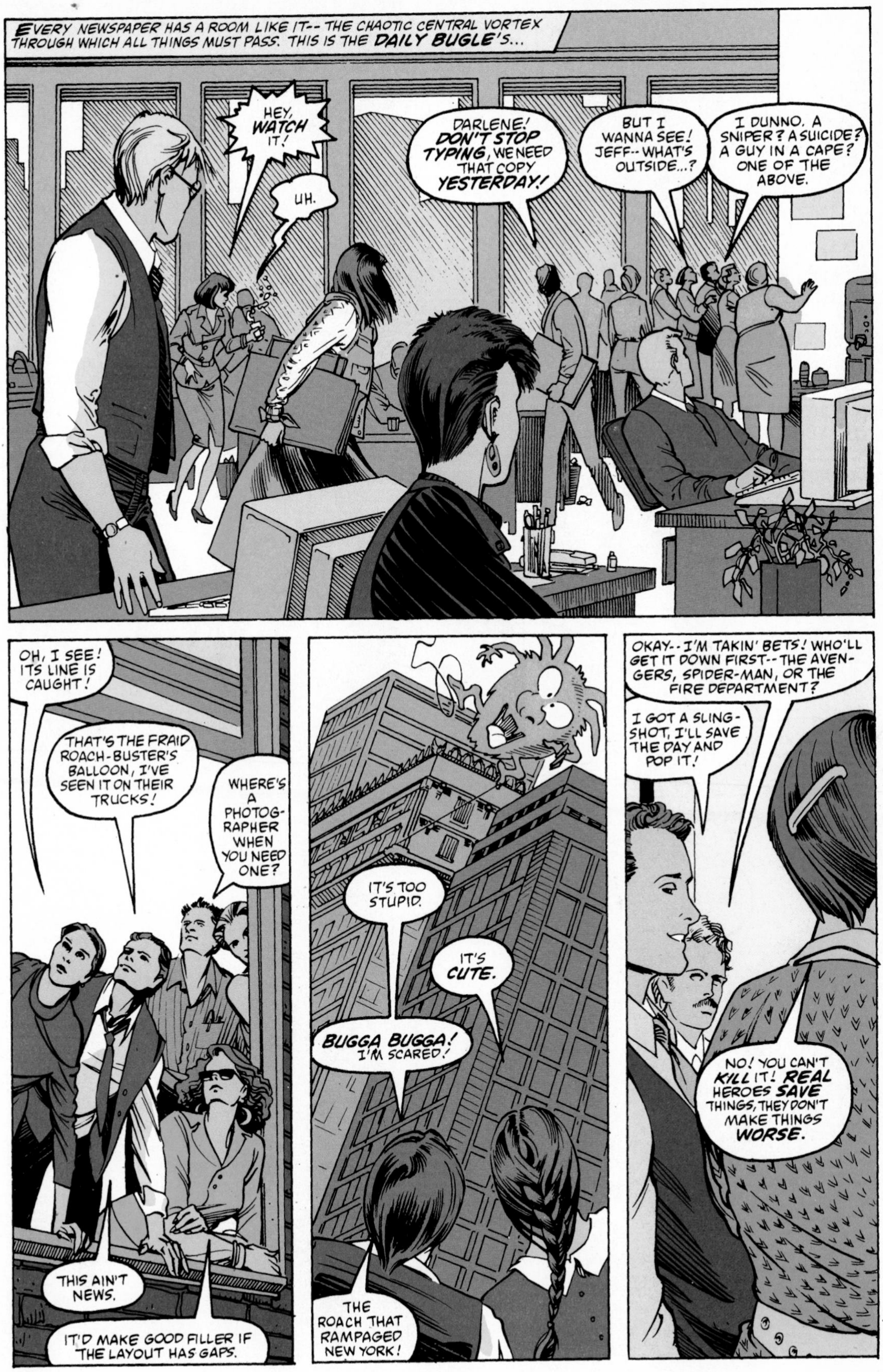
EVERY NEWSPAPER HAS A ROOM LIKE IT-- THE CHAOTIC CENTRAL VORTEX THROUGH WHICH ALL THINGS MUST PASS. THIS IS THE DAILY BUGLE'S...
HEY, WATCH IT!
UH.
DARLENE! DON'T STOP TYPING, WE NEED THAT COPY YESTERDAY!
BUT I WANNA SEE! JEFF-- WHAT'S OUTSIDE...?
I DUNNO. A SNIPER? A SUICIDE? A GUY IN A CAPE? ONE OF THE ABOVE.
OH, I SEE! ITS LINE IS CAUGHT!
THAT'S THE FRAID ROACH-BUSTER'S BALLOON, I'VE SEEN IT ON THEIR TRUCKS!
WHERE'S A PHOTOGRAPHER WHEN YOU NEED ONE?
THIS AIN'T NEWS.
IT'D MAKE GOOD FILLER IF THE LAYOUT HAS GAPS.
IT'S TOO STUPID.
IT'S CUTE.
BUGGA BUGGA! I'M SCARED!
THE ROACH THAT RAMPAGED NEW YORK!
OKAY-- I'M TAKIN' BETS! WHO'LL GET IT DOWN FIRST-- THE AVENGERS, SPIDER-MAN, OR THE FIRE DEPARTMENT?
I GOT A SLING-SHOT, I'LL SAVE THE DAY AND POP IT!
NO! YOU CAN'T KILL IT! REAL HEROES SAVE THINGS, THEY DON'T MAKE THINGS WORSE.

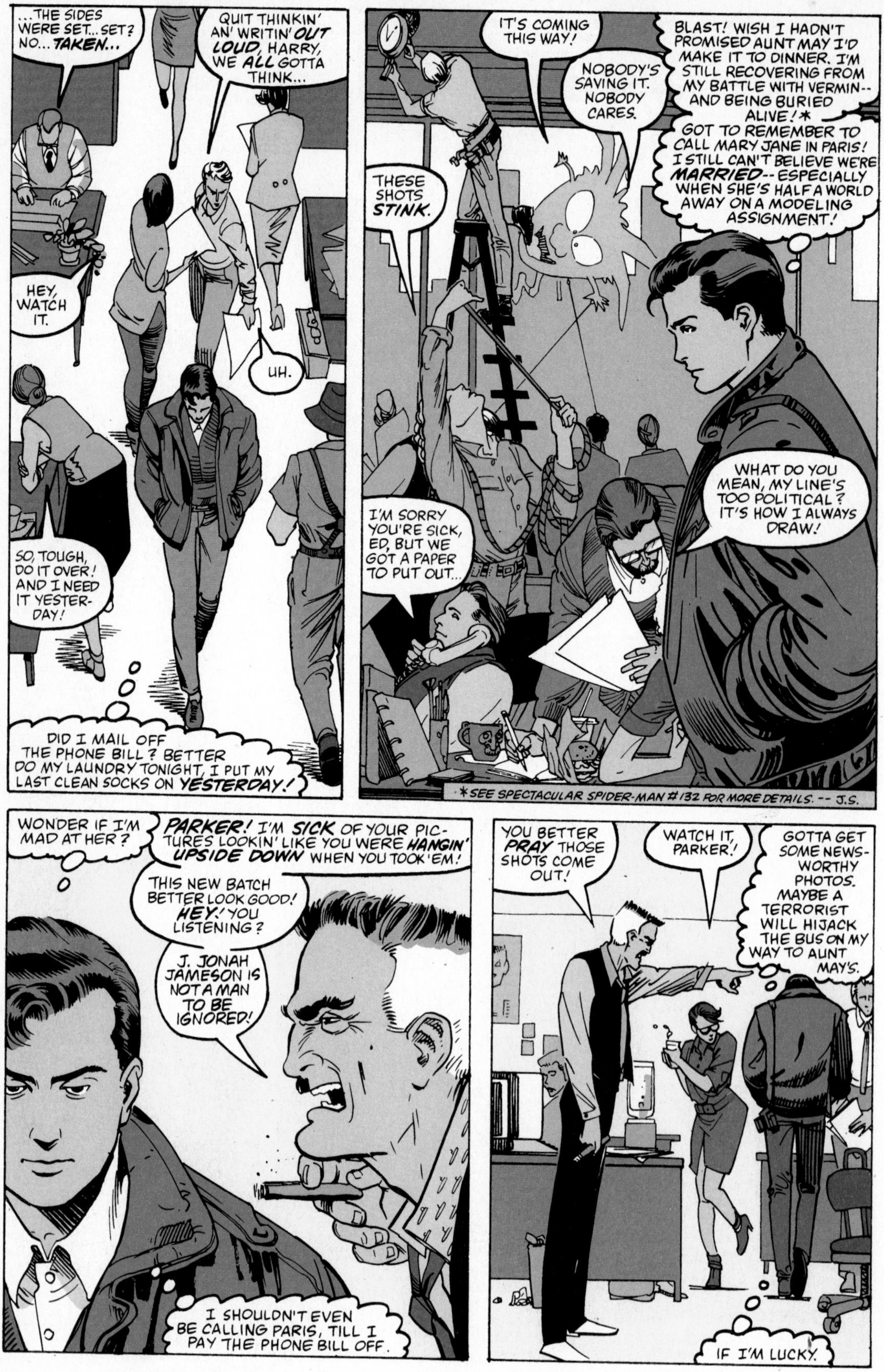

...THE SIDES WERE SET... SET? NO... TAKEN...
QUIT THINKIN' AN' WRITIN' OUT LOUD, HARRY, WE ALL GOTTA THINK...
HEY, WATCH IT.
UH.
SO, TOUGH, DO IT OVER! AND I NEED IT YESTER-DAY!
DID I MAIL OFF THE PHONE BILL? BETTER DO MY LAUNDRY TONIGHT, I PUT MY LAST CLEAN SOCKS ON YESTERDAY!
IT'S COMING THIS WAY!
NOBODY'S SAVING IT. NOBODY CARES.
BLAST! WISH I HADN'T PROMISED AUNT MAY I'D MAKE IT TO DINNER. I'M STILL RECOVERING FROM MY BATTLE WITH VERMIN-- AND BEING BURIED ALIVE!* GOT TO REMEMBER TO CALL MARY JANE IN PARIS! I STILL CAN'T BELIEVE WE'RE MARRIED-- ESPECIALLY WHEN SHE'S HALF A WORLD AWAY ON A MODELING ASSIGNMENT!
THESE SHOTS STINK.
WHAT DO YOU MEAN, MY LINE'S TOO POLITICAL? IT'S HOW I ALWAYS DRAW!
I'M SORRY YOU'RE SICK, ED, BUT WE GOT A PAPER TO PUT OUT...
*SEE SPECTACULAR SPIDER-MAN #132 FOR MORE DETAILS. -- J.S.
WONDER IF I'M MAD AT HER?
PARKER! I'M SICK OF YOUR PIC-TURES LOOKIN' LIKE YOU WERE HANGIN' UPSIDE DOWN WHEN YOU TOOK 'EM!
THIS NEW BATCH BETTER LOOK GOOD! HEY! YOU LISTENING?
J. JONAH JAMESON IS NOT A MAN TO BE IGNORED!
I SHOULDN'T EVEN BE CALLING PARIS, TILL I PAY THE PHONE BILL OFF.
YOU BETTER PRAY THOSE SHOTS COME OUT!
WATCH IT, PARKER!
GOTTA GET SOME NEWS-WORTHY PHOTOS. MAYBE A TERRORIST WILL HIJACK THE BUS ON MY WAY TO AUNT MAY'S.
IF I'M LUCKY.

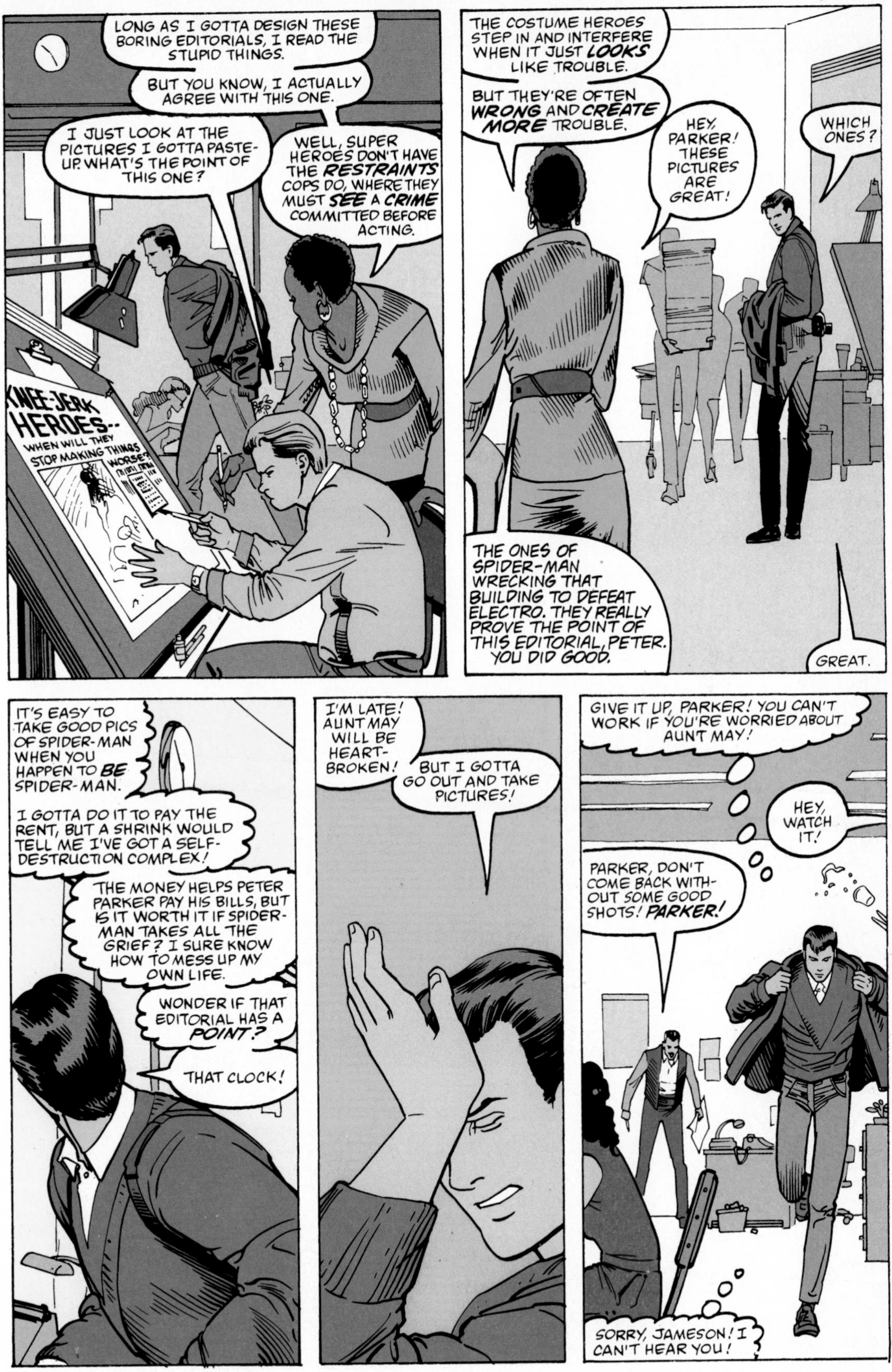
LONG AS I GOTTA DESIGN THESE BORING EDITORIALS, I READ THE STUPID THINGS.
BUT YOU KNOW, I ACTUALLY AGREE WITH THIS ONE.
I JUST LOOK AT THE PICTURES I GOTTA PASTE-UP. WHAT'S THE POINT OF THIS ONE?
WELL, SUPER HEROES DON'T HAVE THE RESTRAINTS COPS DO, WHERE THEY MUST SEE A CRIME COMMITTED BEFORE ACTING.
KNEE-JERK HEROES-- WHEN WILL THEY STOP MAKING THINGS WORSE?
THE COSTUME HEROES STEP IN AND INTERFERE WHEN IT JUST LOOKS LIKE TROUBLE.
BUT THEY'RE OFTEN WRONG AND CREATE MORE TROUBLE.
HEY, PARKER! THESE PICTURES ARE GREAT!
WHICH ONES?
THE ONES OF SPIDER-MAN WRECKING THAT BUILDING TO DEFEAT ELECTRO. THEY REALLY PROVE THE POINT OF THIS EDITORIAL, PETER. YOU DID GOOD.
GREAT.
IT'S EASY TO TAKE GOOD PICS OF SPIDER-MAN WHEN YOU HAPPEN TO BE SPIDER-MAN.
I GOTTA DO IT TO PAY THE RENT, BUT A SHRINK WOULD TELL ME I'VE GOT A SELF-DESTRUCTION COMPLEX!
THE MONEY HELPS PETER PARKER PAY HIS BILLS, BUT IS IT WORTH IT IF SPIDER-MAN TAKES ALL THE GRIEF? I SURE KNOW HOW TO MESS UP MY OWN LIFE.
WONDER IF THAT EDITORIAL HAS A POINT?
THAT CLOCK!
I'M LATE! AUNT MAY WILL BE HEART-BROKEN!
BUT I GOTTA GO OUT AND TAKE PICTURES!
GIVE IT UP, PARKER! YOU CAN'T WORK IF YOU'RE WORRIED ABOUT AUNT MAY!
HEY, WATCH IT!
PARKER, DON'T COME BACK WITH-OUT SOME GOOD SHOTS! PARKER!
SORRY, JAMESON! I CAN'T HEAR YOU!

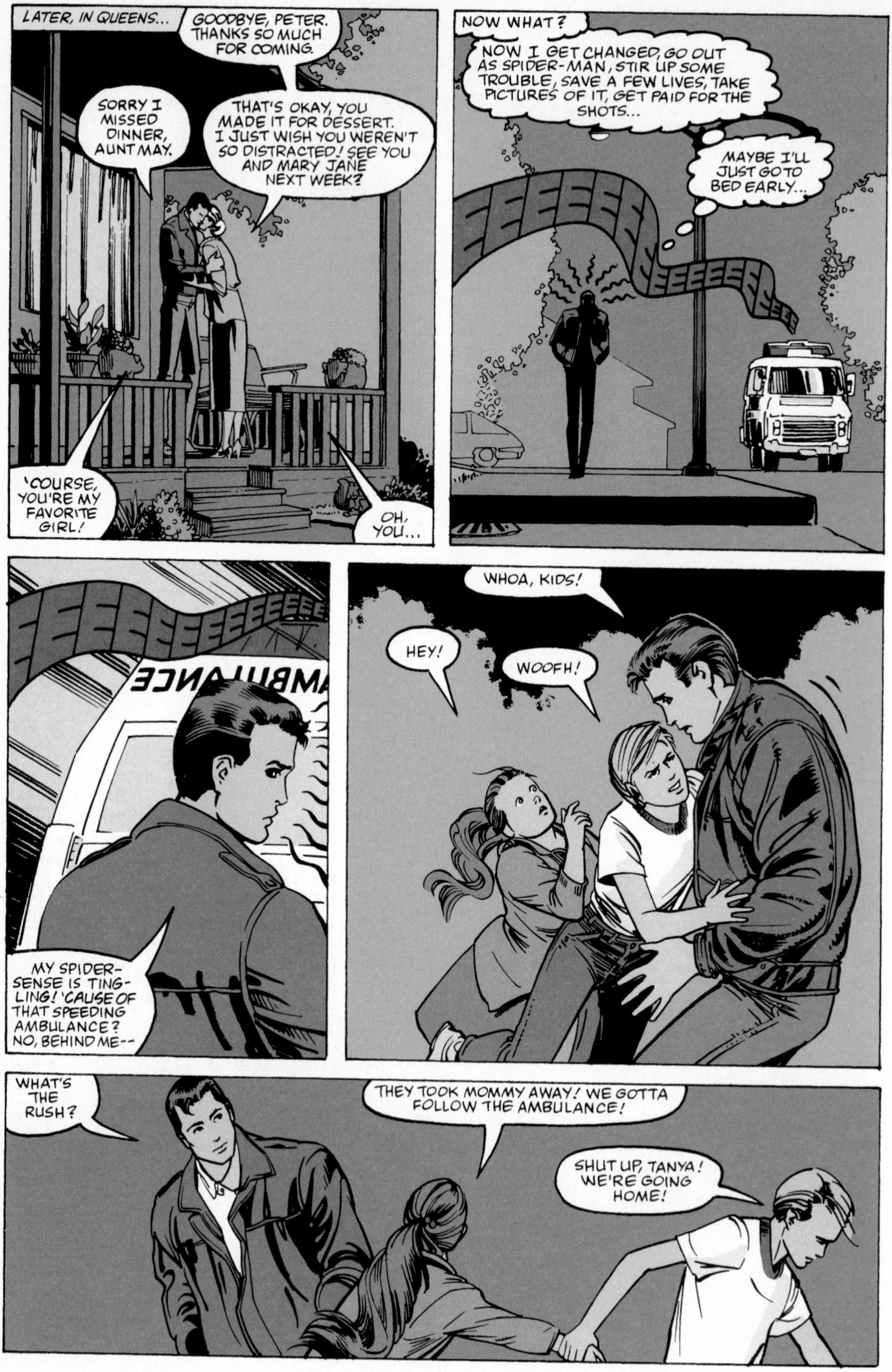
LATER, IN QUEENS...
GOODBYE, PETER. THANKS SO MUCH FOR COMING.
SORRY I MISSED DINNER, AUNT MAY.
THAT'S OKAY, YOU MADE IT FOR DESSERT. I JUST WISH YOU WEREN'T SO DISTRACTED! SEE YOU AND MARY JANE NEXT WEEK?
'COURSE, YOU'RE MY FAVORITE GIRL!
OH, YOU...
NOW WHAT?
NOW I GET CHANGED, GO OUT AS SPIDER-MAN, STIR UP SOME TROUBLE, SAVE A FEW LIVES, TAKE PICTURES OF IT, GET PAID FOR THE SHOTS...
MAYBE I'LL JUST GO TO BED EARLY...
MY SPIDER-SENSE IS TINGLING! 'CAUSE OF THAT SPEEDING AMBULANCE? NO, BEHIND ME--
WHOA, KIDS!
HEY!
WOOFH!
WHAT'S THE RUSH?
THEY TOOK MOMMY AWAY! WE GOTTA FOLLOW THE AMBULANCE!
SHUT UP, TANYA! WE'RE GOING HOME!

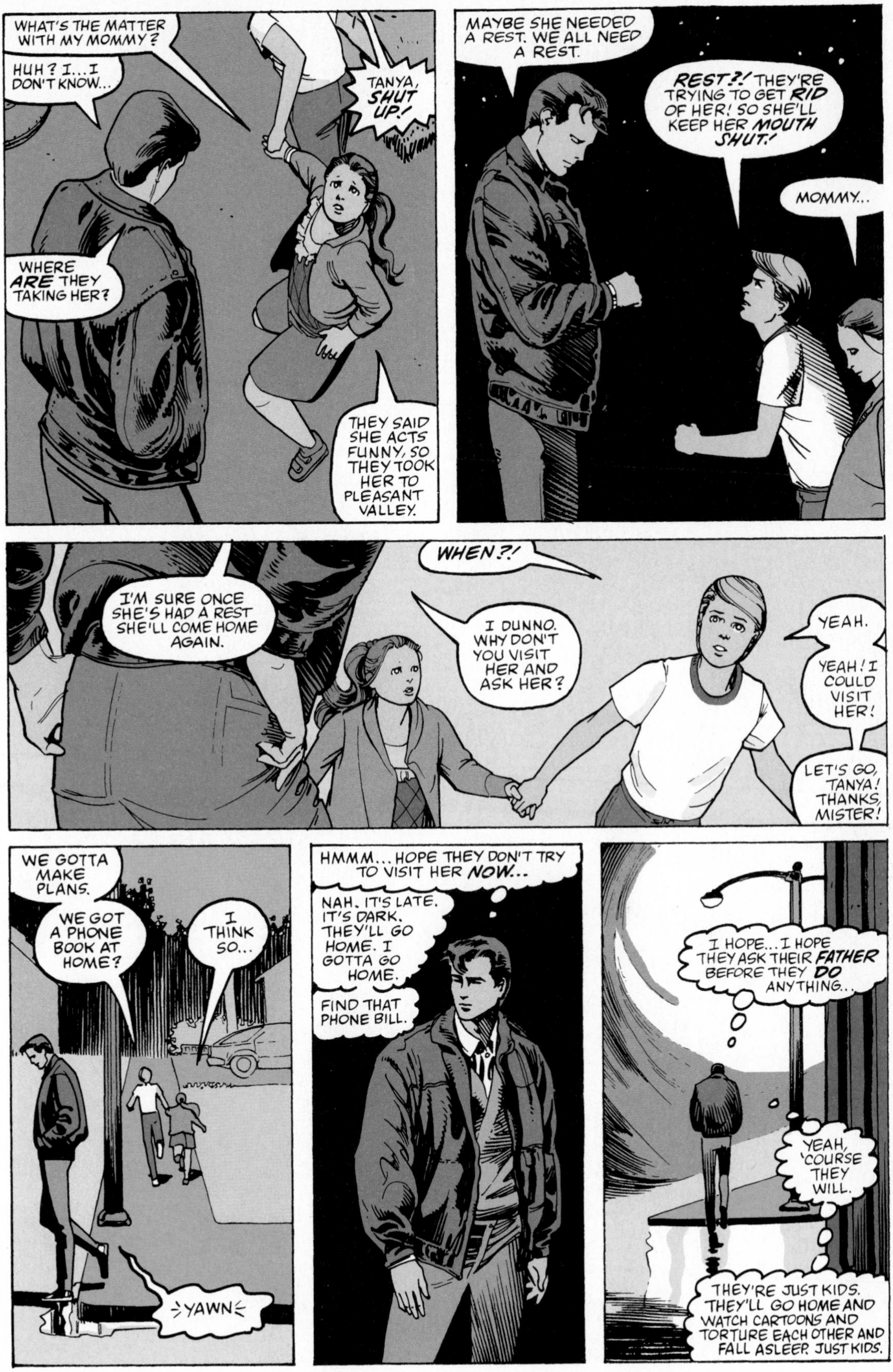
WHAT'S THE MATTER WITH MY MOMMY?
HUH? I...I DON'T KNOW...
TANYA, SHUT UP!
WHERE ARE THEY TAKING HER?
THEY SAID SHE ACTS FUNNY, SO THEY TOOK HER TO PLEASANT VALLEY.
MAYBE SHE NEEDED A REST. WE ALL NEED A REST.
REST?! THEY'RE TRYING TO GET RID OF HER! SO SHE'LL KEEP HER MOUTH SHUT!
MOMMY...
I'M SURE ONCE SHE'S HAD A REST SHE'LL COME HOME AGAIN.
WHEN?!
I DUNNO. WHY DON'T YOU VISIT HER AND ASK HER?
YEAH.
YEAH! I COULD VISIT HER!
LET'S GO, TANYA! THANKS, MISTER!
WE GOTTA MAKE PLANS.
WE GOT A PHONE BOOK AT HOME?
I THINK SO...
YAWN
HMMM... HOPE THEY DON'T TRY TO VISIT HER NOW...
NAH. IT'S LATE. IT'S DARK. THEY'LL GO HOME. I GOTTA GO HOME.
FIND THAT PHONE BILL.
I HOPE... I HOPE THEY ASK THEIR FATHER BEFORE THEY DO ANYTHING...
YEAH, 'COURSE THEY WILL.
THEY'RE JUST KIDS. THEY'LL GO HOME AND WATCH CARTOONS AND TORTURE EACH OTHER AND FALL ASLEEP. JUST KIDS.

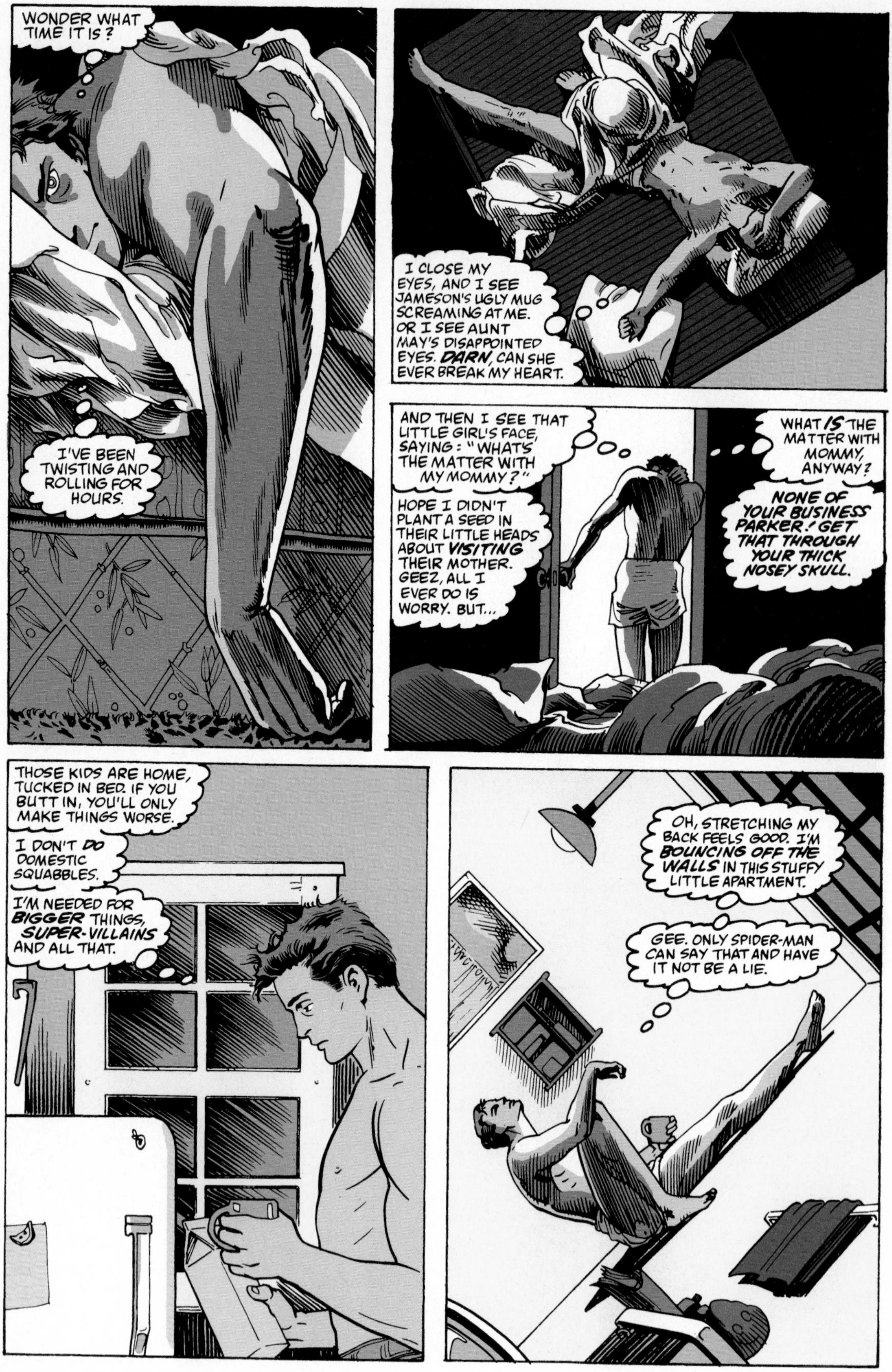
WONDER WHAT TIME IT IS?
I'VE BEEN TWISTING AND ROLLING FOR HOURS.
I CLOSE MY EYES, AND I SEE JAMESON'S UGLY MUG SCREAMING AT ME. OR I SEE AUNT MAY'S DISAPPOINTED EYES. DARN, CAN SHE EVER BREAK MY HEART.
AND THEN I SEE THAT LITTLE GIRL'S FACE, SAYING: "WHAT'S THE MATTER WITH MY MOMMY?"
HOPE I DIDN'T PLANT A SEED IN THEIR LITTLE HEADS ABOUT VISITING THEIR MOTHER. GEEZ, ALL I EVER DO IS WORRY. BUT...
WHAT IS THE MATTER WITH MOMMY, ANYWAY?
NONE OF YOUR BUSINESS PARKER! GET THAT THROUGH YOUR THICK NOSEY SKULL.
THOSE KIDS ARE HOME, TUCKED IN BED. IF YOU BUTT IN, YOU'LL ONLY MAKE THINGS WORSE.
I DON'T DO DOMESTIC SQUABBLES.
I'M NEEDED FOR BIGGER THINGS, SUPER-VILLAINS AND ALL THAT.
OH, STRETCHING MY BACK FEELS GOOD. I'M BOUNCING OFF THE WALLS IN THIS STUFFY LITTLE APARTMENT.
GEE. ONLY SPIDER-MAN CAN SAY THAT AND HAVE IT NOT BE A LIE.

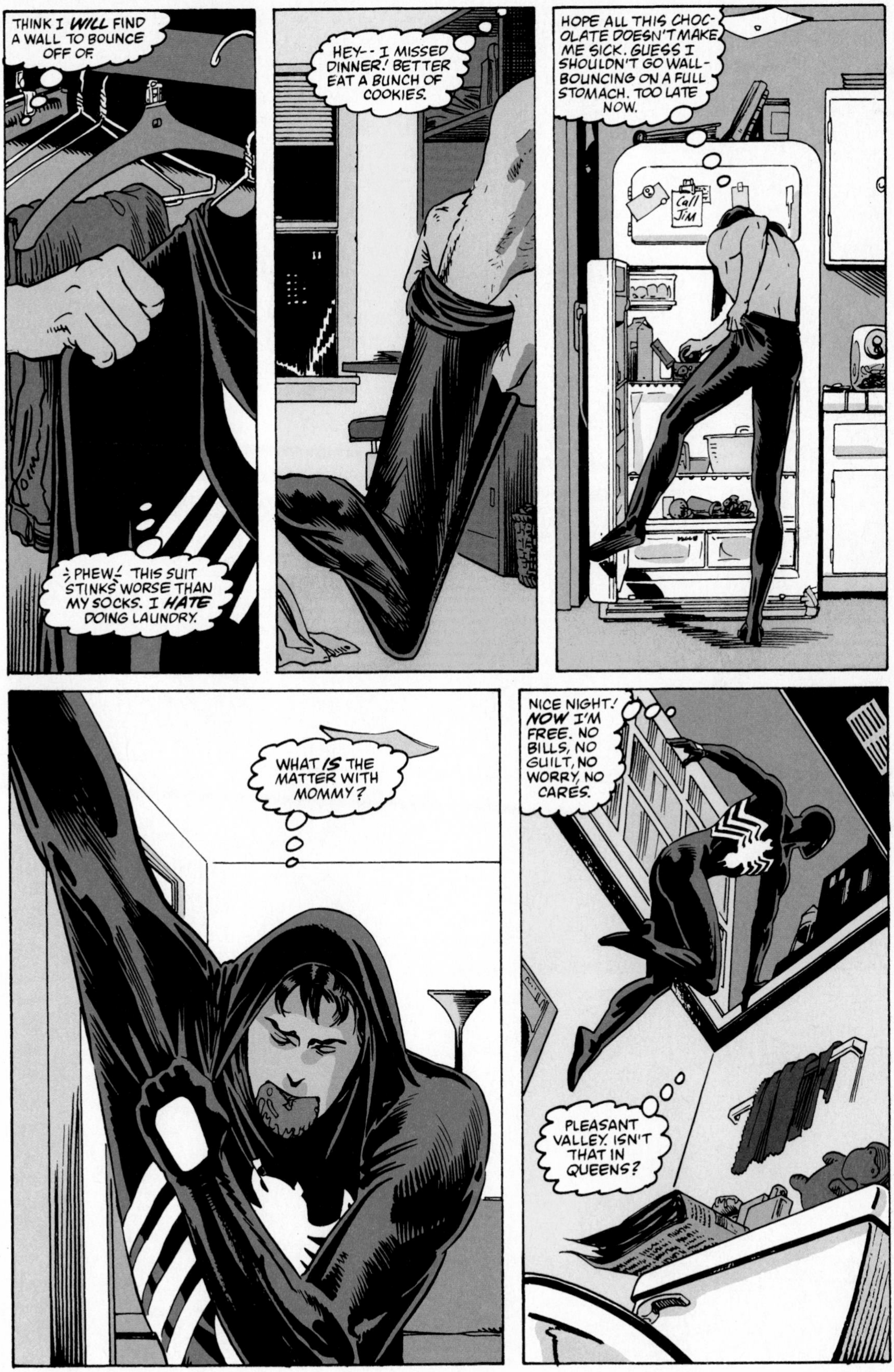
THINK I WILL FIND A WALL TO BOUNCE OFF OF.
PHEW! THIS SUIT STINKS WORSE THAN MY SOCKS. I HATE DOING LAUNDRY.
HEY-- I MISSED DINNER! BETTER EAT A BUNCH OF COOKIES.
HOPE ALL THIS CHOCOLATE DOESN'T MAKE ME SICK. GUESS I SHOULDN'T GO WALL-BOUNCING ON A FULL STOMACH. TOO LATE NOW.
Call Jim
WHAT IS THE MATTER WITH MOMMY?
NICE NIGHT! NOW I'M FREE. NO BILLS, NO GUILT, NO WORRY, NO CARES.
PLEASANT VALLEY. ISN'T THAT IN QUEENS?

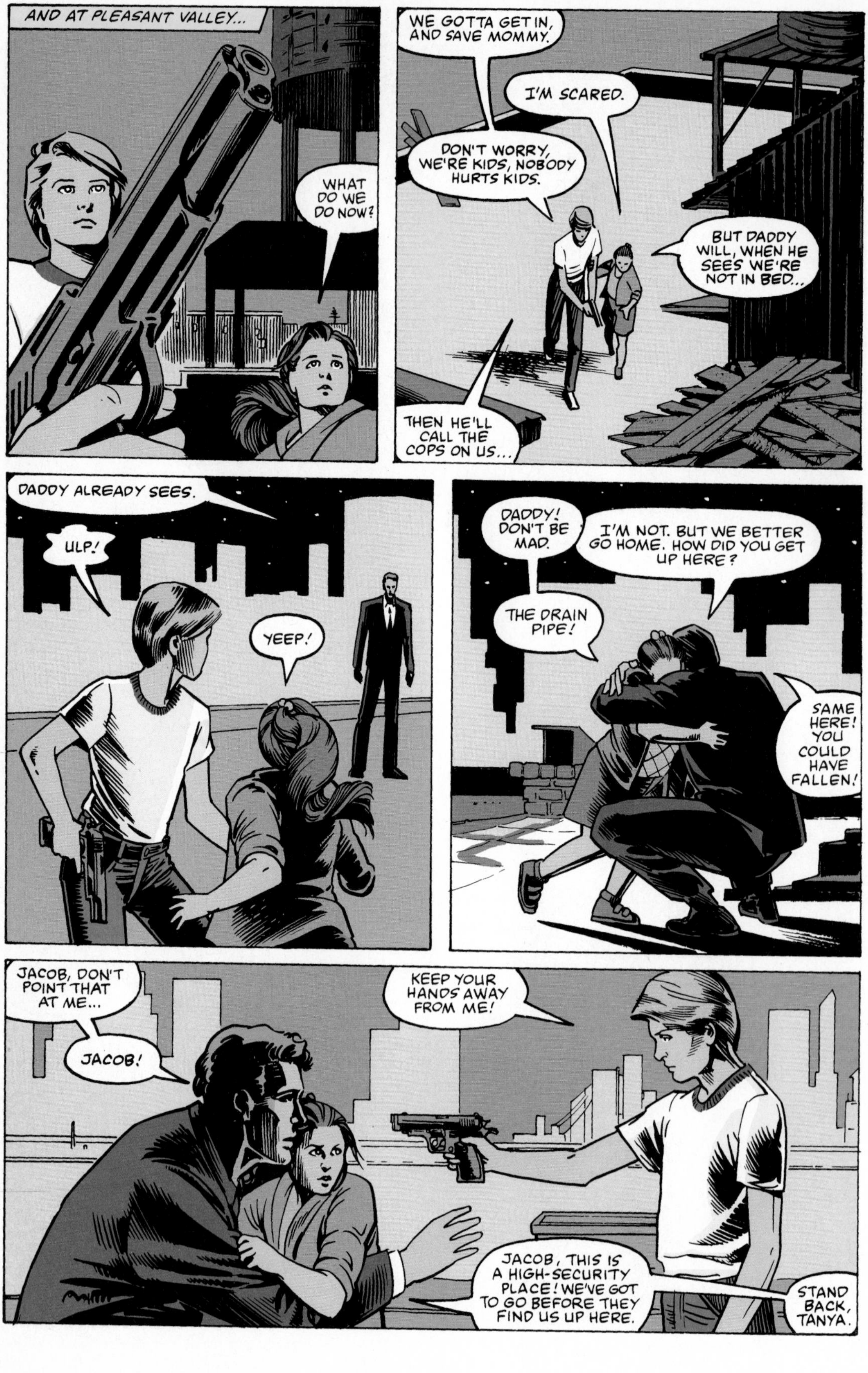
AND AT PLEASANT VALLEY...
WHAT DO WE DO NOW?
WE GOTTA GET IN, AND SAVE MOMMY.
I'M SCARED.
DON'T WORRY, WE'RE KIDS, NOBODY HURTS KIDS.
BUT DADDY WILL, WHEN HE SEES WE'RE NOT IN BED...
THEN HE'LL CALL THE COPS ON US...
DADDY ALREADY SEES.
ULP!
YEEP!
DADDY! DON'T BE MAD.
I'M NOT. BUT WE BETTER GO HOME. HOW DID YOU GET UP HERE?
THE DRAIN PIPE!
SAME HERE! YOU COULD HAVE FALLEN!
JACOB, DON'T POINT THAT AT ME...
JACOB!
KEEP YOUR HANDS AWAY FROM ME!
JACOB, THIS IS A HIGH-SECURITY PLACE! WE'VE GOT TO GO BEFORE THEY FIND US UP HERE.
STAND BACK, TANYA.

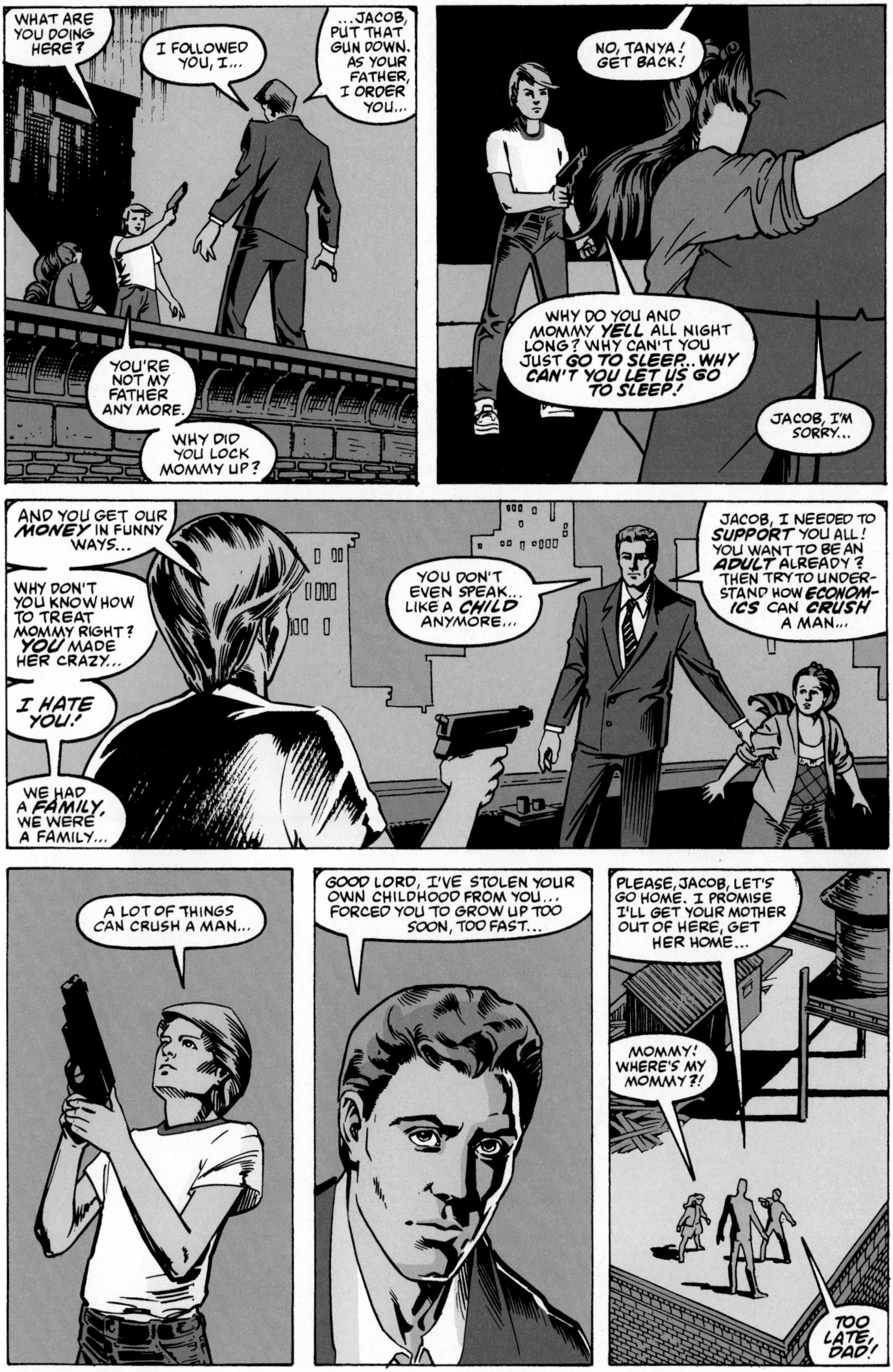

WHAT ARE YOU DOING HERE?
I FOLLOWED YOU, I...
...JACOB, PUT THAT GUN DOWN. AS YOUR FATHER, I ORDER YOU...
YOU'RE NOT MY FATHER ANY MORE.
WHY DID YOU LOCK MOMMY UP?
NO, TANYA! GET BACK!
WHY DO YOU AND MOMMY YELL ALL NIGHT LONG? WHY CAN'T YOU JUST GO TO SLEEP.. WHY CAN'T YOU LET US GO TO SLEEP!
JACOB, I'M SORRY...
AND YOU GET OUR MONEY IN FUNNY WAYS...
WHY DON'T YOU KNOW HOW TO TREAT MOMMY RIGHT? YOU MADE HER CRAZY...
I HATE YOU!
WE HAD A FAMILY, WE WERE A FAMILY...
YOU DON'T EVEN SPEAK... LIKE A CHILD ANYMORE...
JACOB, I NEEDED TO SUPPORT YOU ALL! YOU WANT TO BE AN ADULT ALREADY? THEN TRY TO UNDERSTAND HOW ECONOMICS CAN CRUSH A MAN...
A LOT OF THINGS CAN CRUSH A MAN...
GOOD LORD, I'VE STOLEN YOUR OWN CHILDHOOD FROM YOU... FORCED YOU TO GROW UP TOO SOON, TOO FAST...
PLEASE, JACOB, LET'S GO HOME. I PROMISE I'LL GET YOUR MOTHER OUT OF HERE, GET HER HOME...
MOMMY! WHERE'S MY MOMMY?!
TOO LATE, DAD!

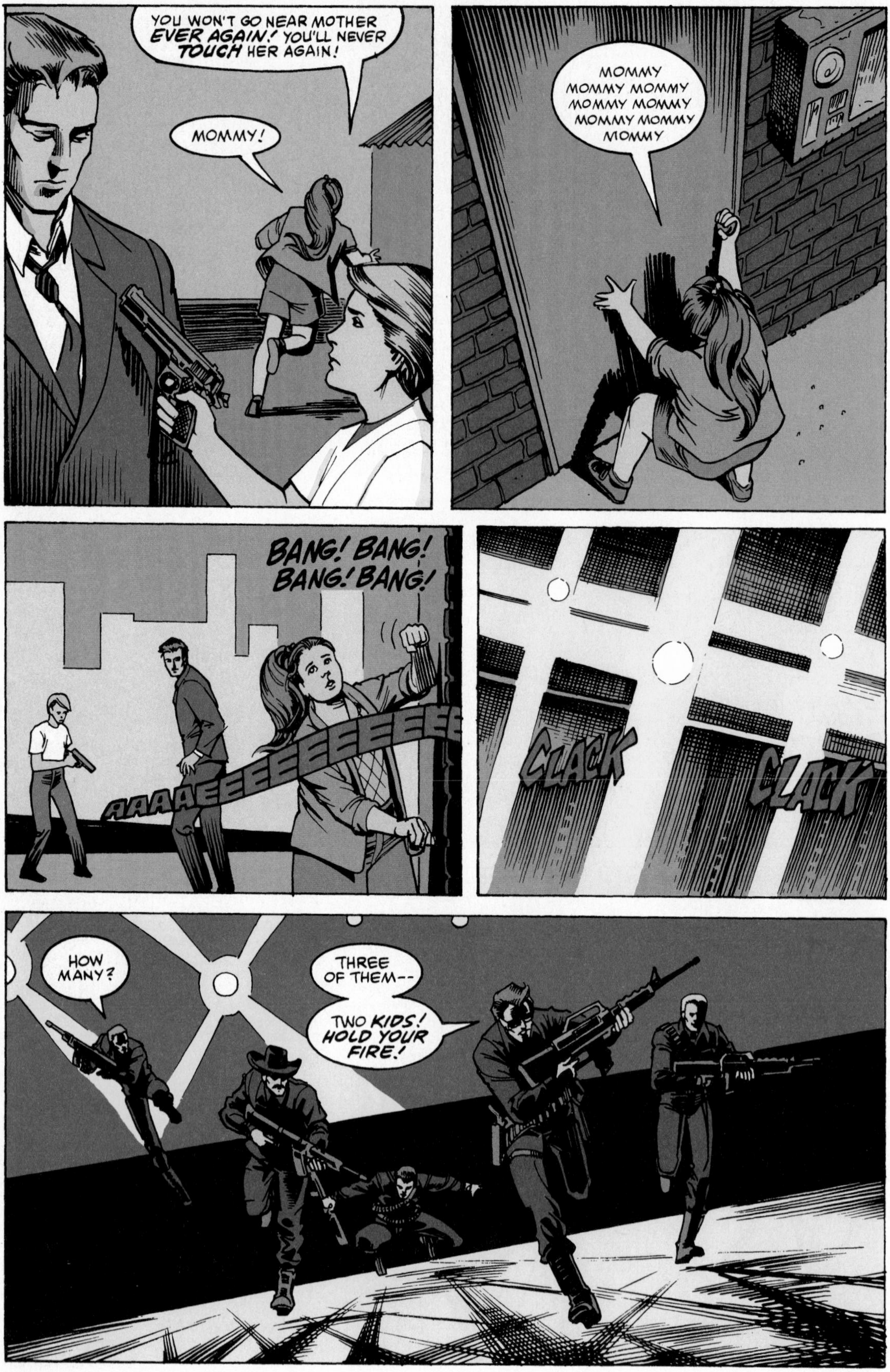
YOU WON'T GO NEAR MOTHER EVER AGAIN! YOU'LL NEVER TOUCH HER AGAIN!
MOMMY!
MOMMY MOMMY MOMMY MOMMY MOMMY MOMMY MOMMY MOMMY
BANG! BANG! BANG! BANG!
AAAAEEEEEEEEEEEEEE
CLACK
CLACK
HOW MANY?
THREE OF THEM--
TWO KIDS! HOLD YOUR FIRE!

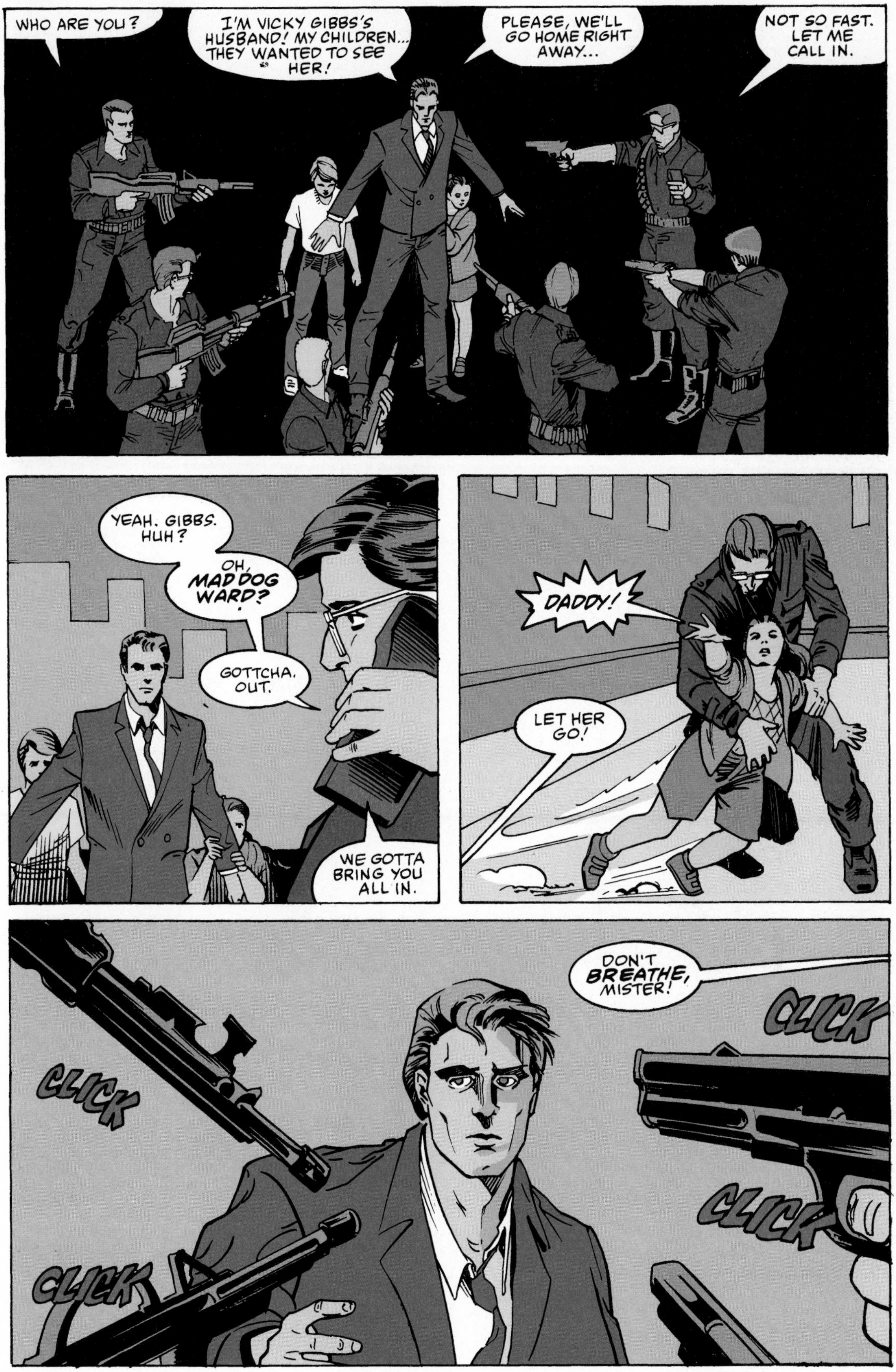
WHO ARE YOU?
I'M VICKY GIBBS'S HUSBAND! MY CHILDREN... THEY WANTED TO SEE HER!
PLEASE, WE'LL GO HOME RIGHT AWAY...
NOT SO FAST. LET ME CALL IN.
YEAH. GIBBS. HUH?
OH, MAD DOG WARD?
GOTTCHA. OUT.
WE GOTTA BRING YOU ALL IN.
DADDY!
LET HER GO!
DON'T BREATHE, MISTER!
CLICK
CLICK
CLICK
CLICK

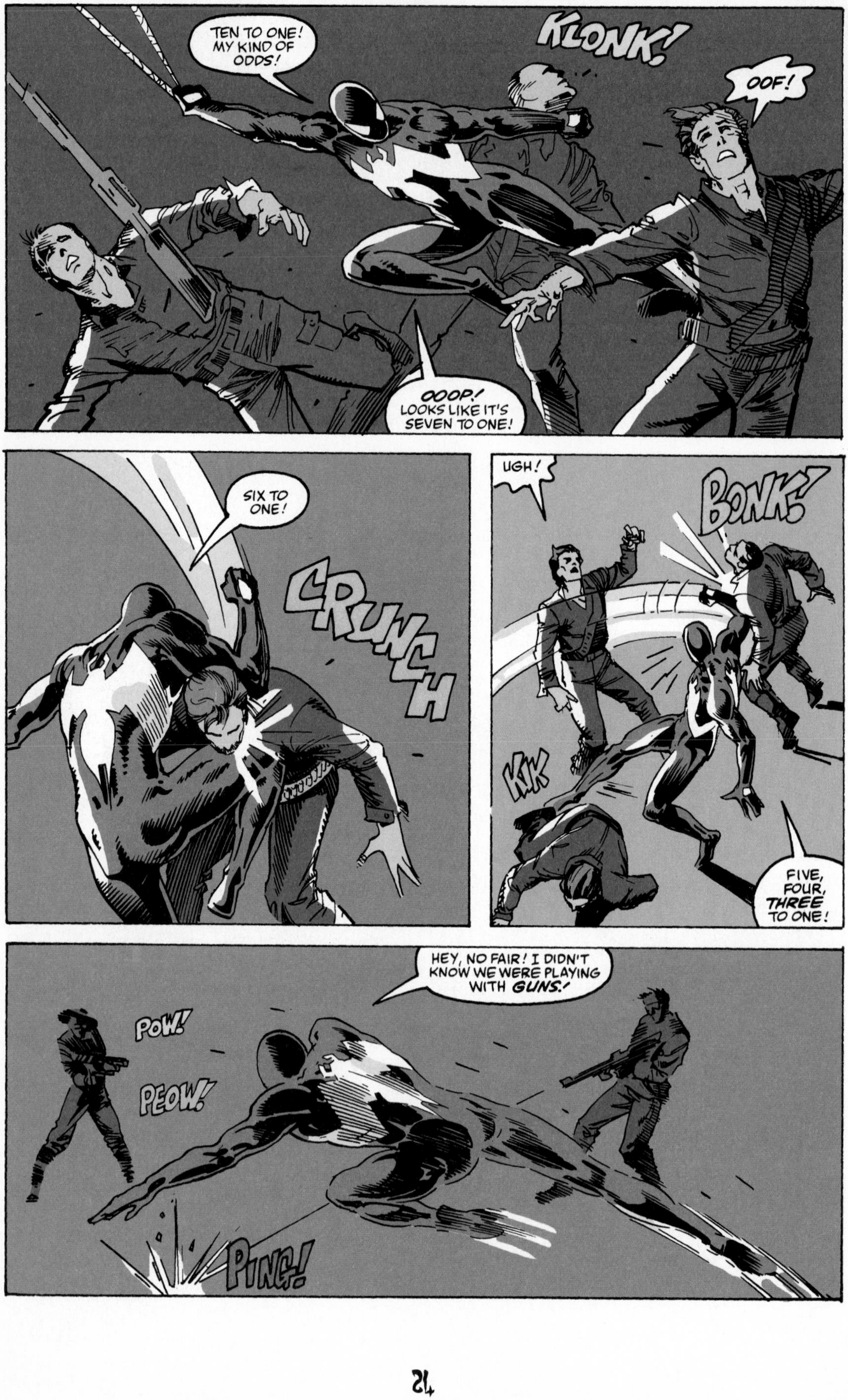
TEN TO ONE! MY KIND OF ODDS!
KLONK!
OOF!
OOOP! LOOKS LIKE IT'S SEVEN TO ONE!
SIX TO ONE!
CRUNCH
UGH!
BONK!
KIK
FIVE, FOUR, THREE TO ONE!
HEY, NO FAIR! I DIDN'T KNOW WE WERE PLAYING WITH GUNS!
POW!
PEOW!
PING!

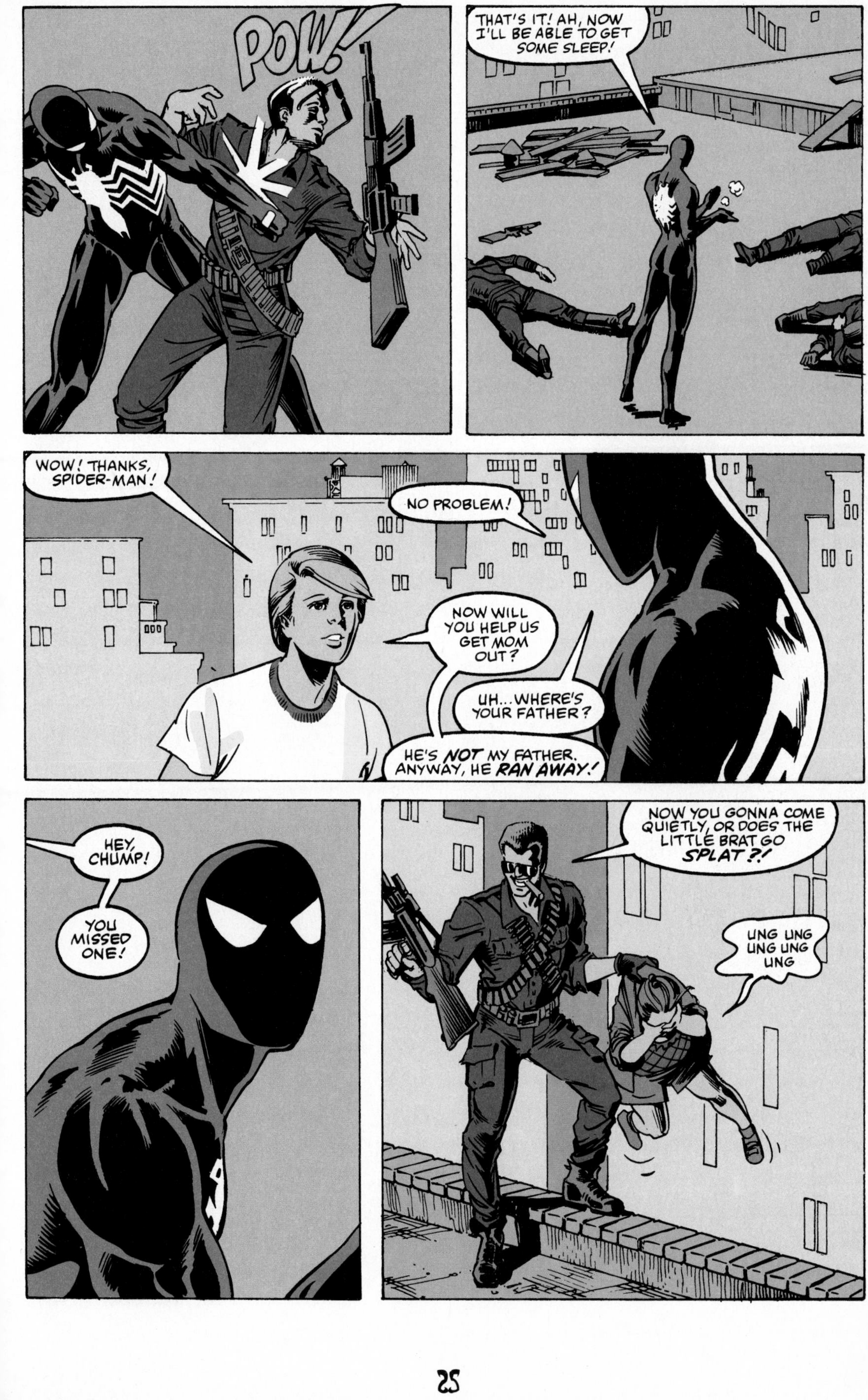
POW!
THAT'S IT! AH, NOW I'LL BE ABLE TO GET SOME SLEEP!
WOW! THANKS, SPIDER-MAN!
NO PROBLEM!
NOW WILL YOU HELP US GET MOM OUT?
UH... WHERE'S YOUR FATHER?
HE'S NOT MY FATHER. ANYWAY, HE RAN AWAY!
HEY, CHUMP!
YOU MISSED ONE!
NOW YOU GONNA COME QUIETLY, OR DOES THE LITTLE BRAT GO SPLAT?!
UNG UNG UNG UNG UNG

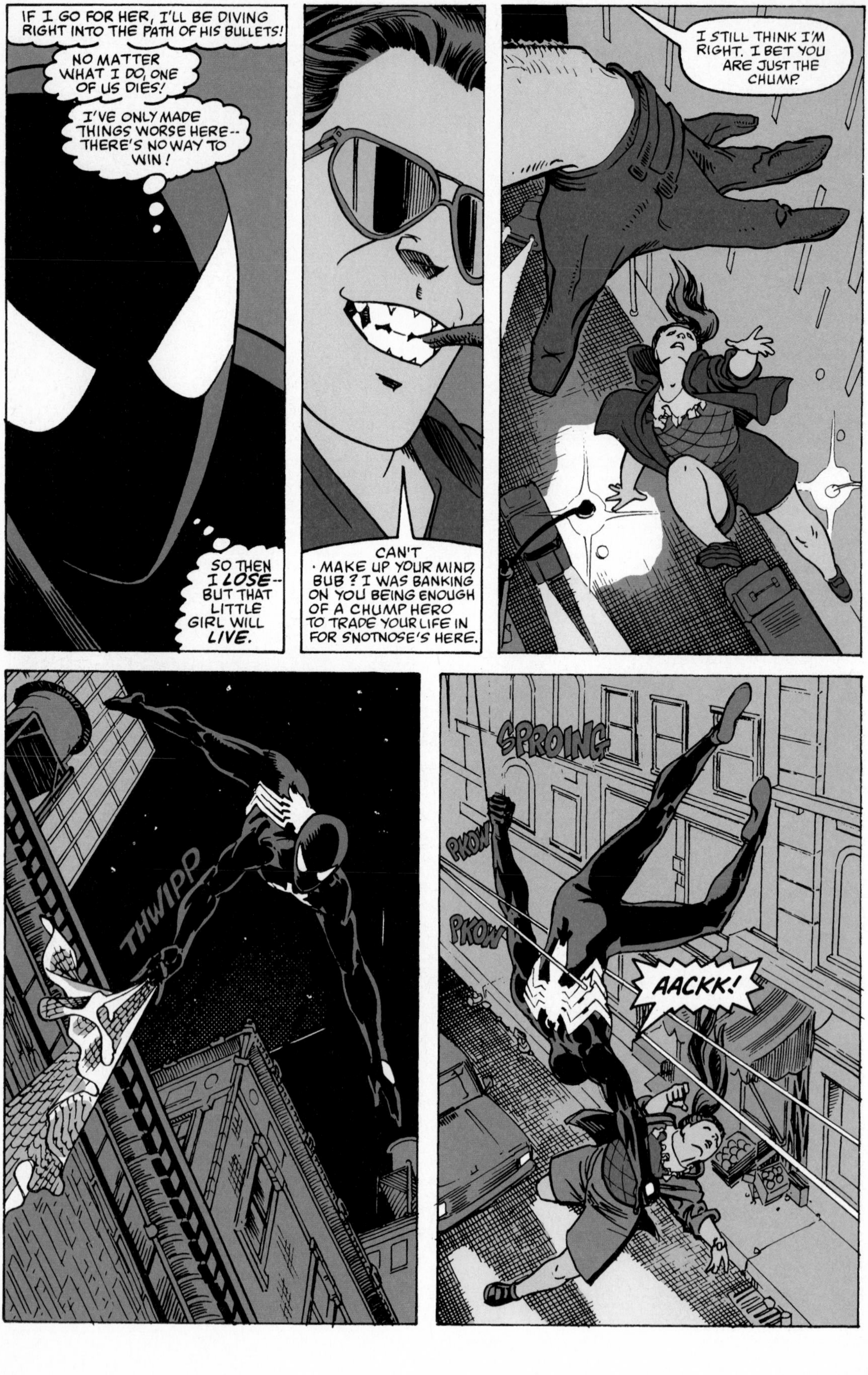

IF I GO FOR HER, I'LL BE DIVING RIGHT INTO THE PATH OF HIS BULLETS!
NO MATTER WHAT I DO, ONE OF US DIES!
I'VE ONLY MADE THINGS WORSE HERE-- THERE'S NO WAY TO WIN!
SO THEN I LOSE-- BUT THAT LITTLE GIRL WILL LIVE.
CAN'T MAKE UP YOUR MIND, BUB? I WAS BANKING ON YOU BEING ENOUGH OF A CHUMP HERO TO TRADE YOUR LIFE IN FOR SNOTNOSE'S HERE.
I STILL THINK I'M RIGHT. I BET YOU ARE JUST THE CHUMP.
THWIPP
SPROING
PKOW
PKOW
AACKK!

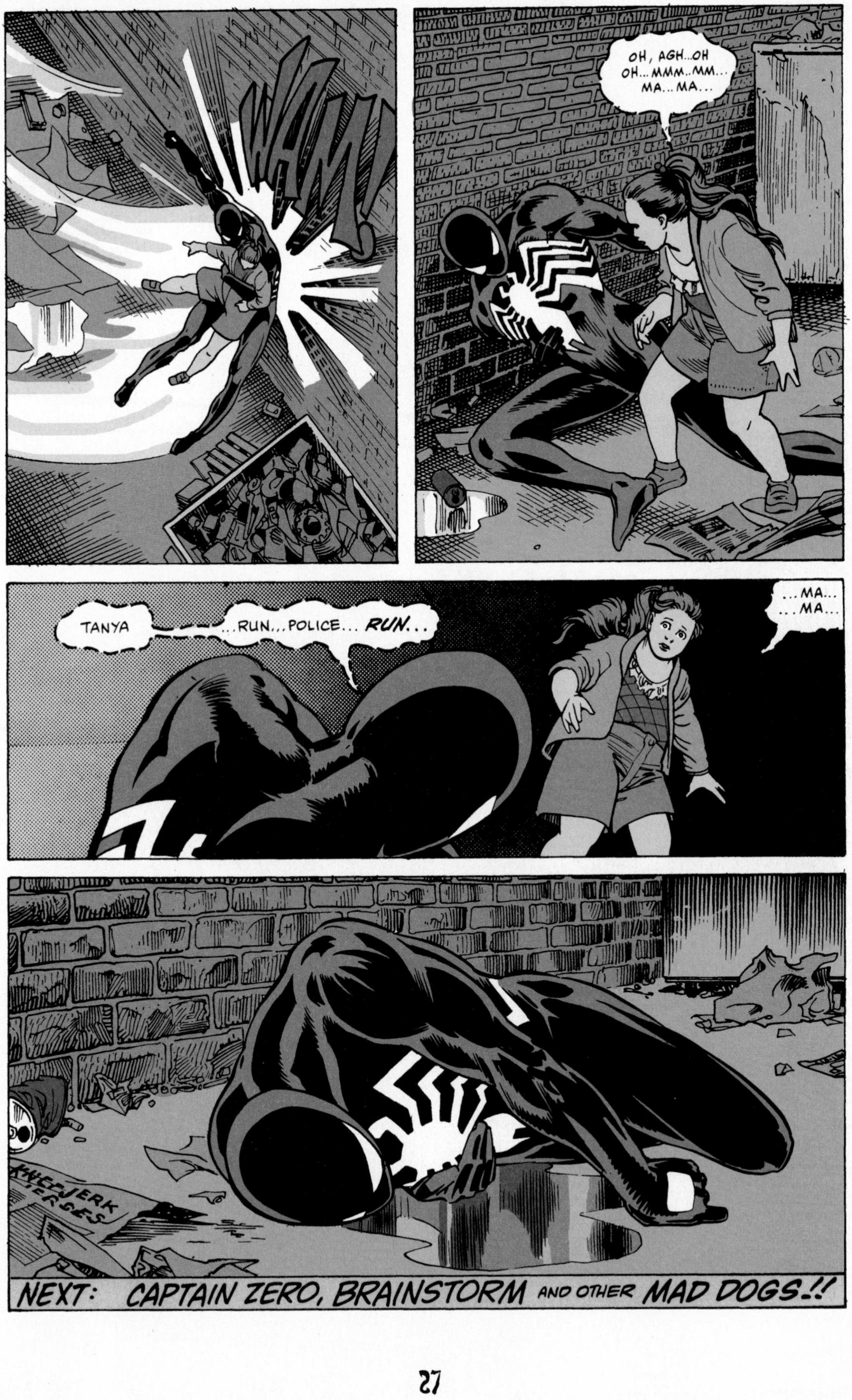
WAM!
OH, AGH...OH OH... MMM...MM... MA... MA...
TANYA ...RUN... POLICE... RUN...
...MA... ...MA...
NEXT: CAPTAIN ZERO, BRAINSTORM AND OTHER MAD DOGS!!

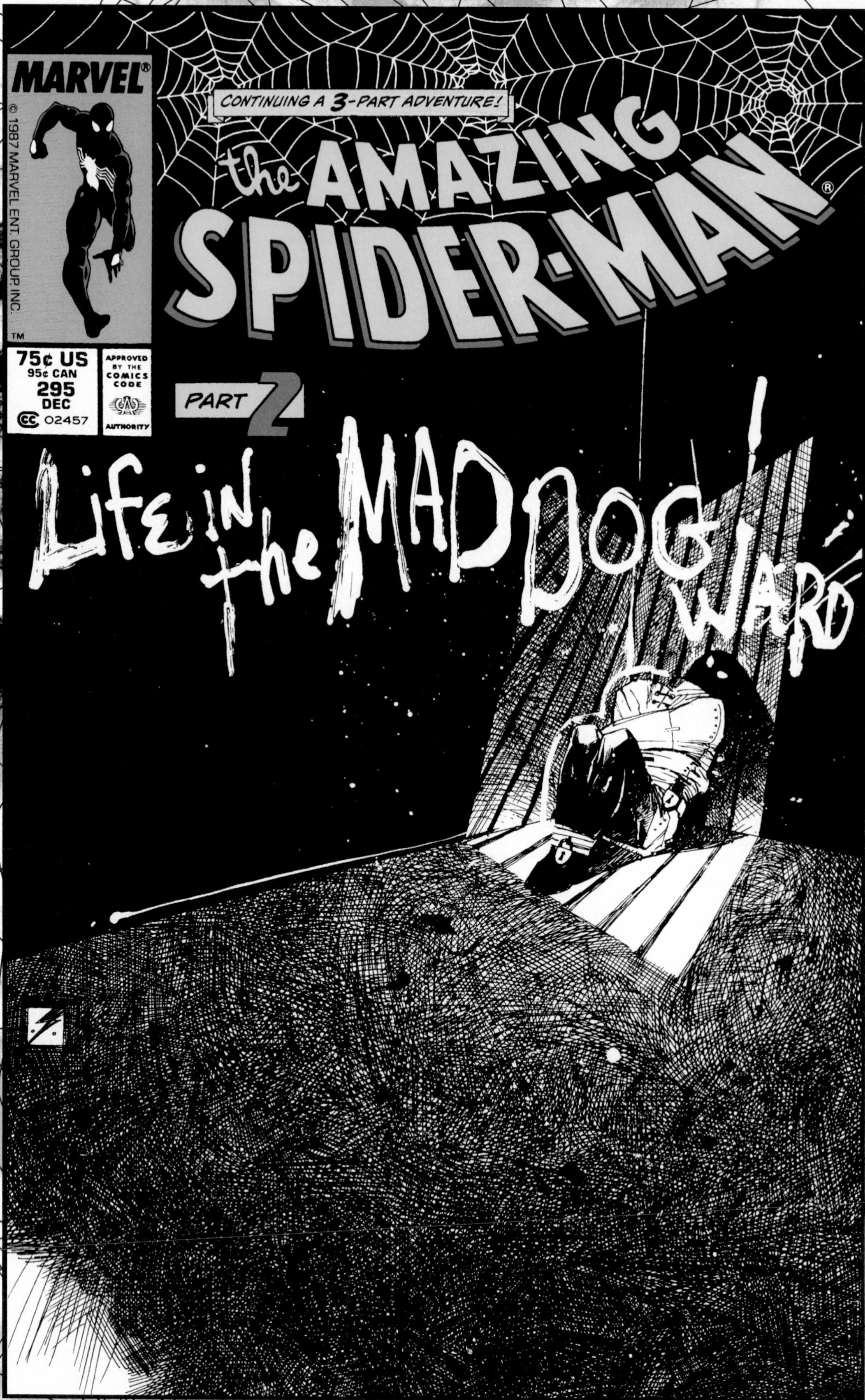
MARVEL
© 1987 MARVEL ENT. GROUP, INC.
75¢ US
95¢ CAN
295
DEC
02457
APPROVED BY THE COMICS CODE AUTHORITY
CONTINUING A 3-PART ADVENTURE!
the AMAZING SPIDER-MAN
PART 2
Life in the MAD DOG WARD

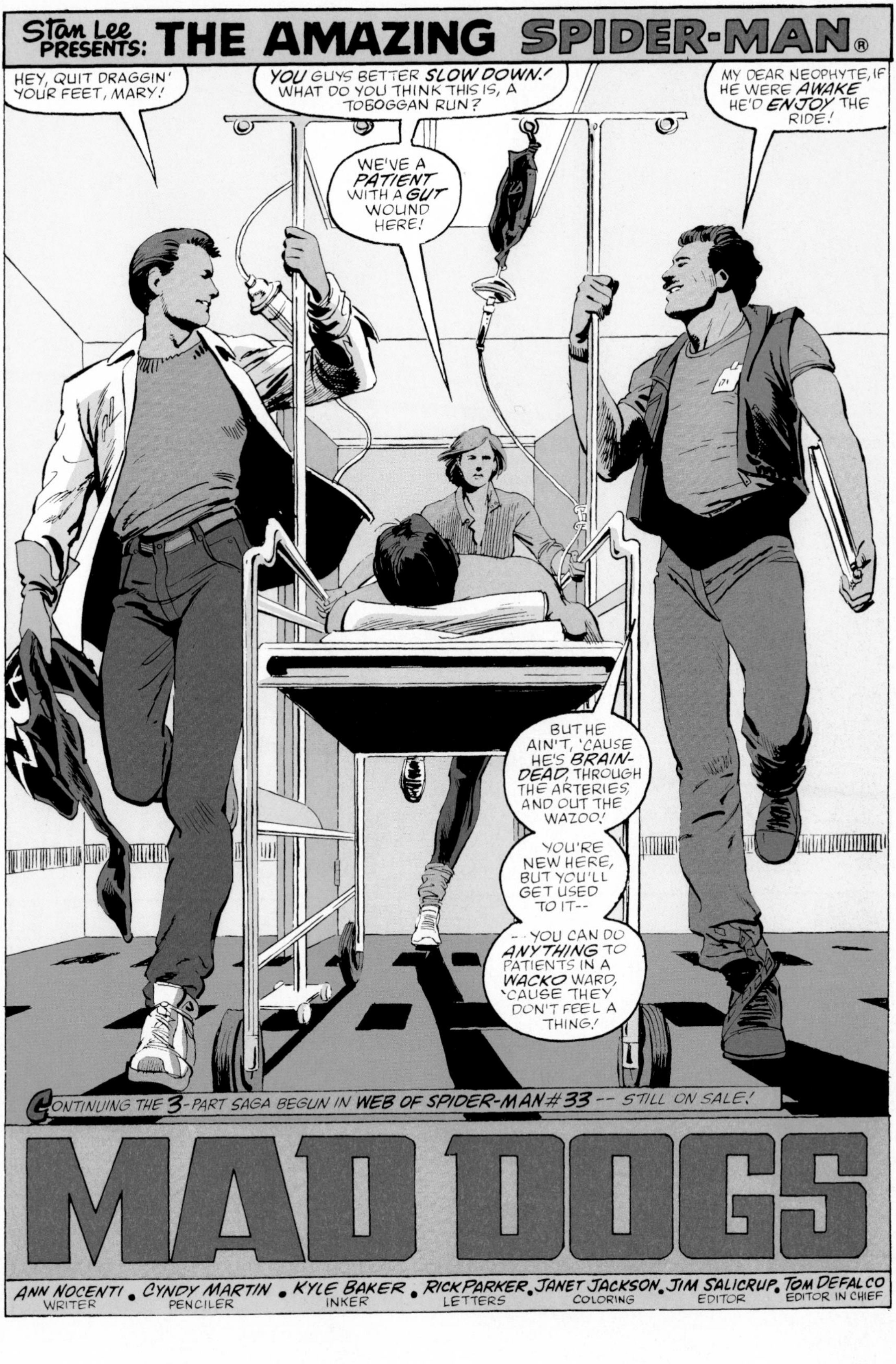

Stan Lee PRESENTS: THE AMAZING SPIDER-MAN®
HEY, QUIT DRAGGIN' YOUR FEET, MARY!
YOU GUYS BETTER SLOW DOWN! WHAT DO YOU THINK THIS IS, A TOBOGGAN RUN?
WE'VE A PATIENT WITH A GUT WOUND HERE!
MY DEAR NEOPHYTE, IF HE WERE AWAKE HE'D ENJOY THE RIDE!
BUT HE AIN'T, 'CAUSE HE'S BRAIN-DEAD, THROUGH THE ARTERIES, AND OUT THE WAZOO!
YOU'RE NEW HERE, BUT YOU'LL GET USED TO IT--
--YOU CAN DO ANYTHING TO PATIENTS IN A WACKO WARD, 'CAUSE THEY DON'T FEEL A THING!
CONTINUING THE 3-PART SAGA BEGUN IN WEB OF SPIDER-MAN #33 -- STILL ON SALE!
MAD DOGS
ANN NOCENTI WRITER • CYNDY MARTIN PENCILER • KYLE BAKER INKER • RICK PARKER LETTERS • JANET JACKSON COLORING • JIM SALICRUP EDITOR • TOM DEFALCO EDITOR IN CHIEF

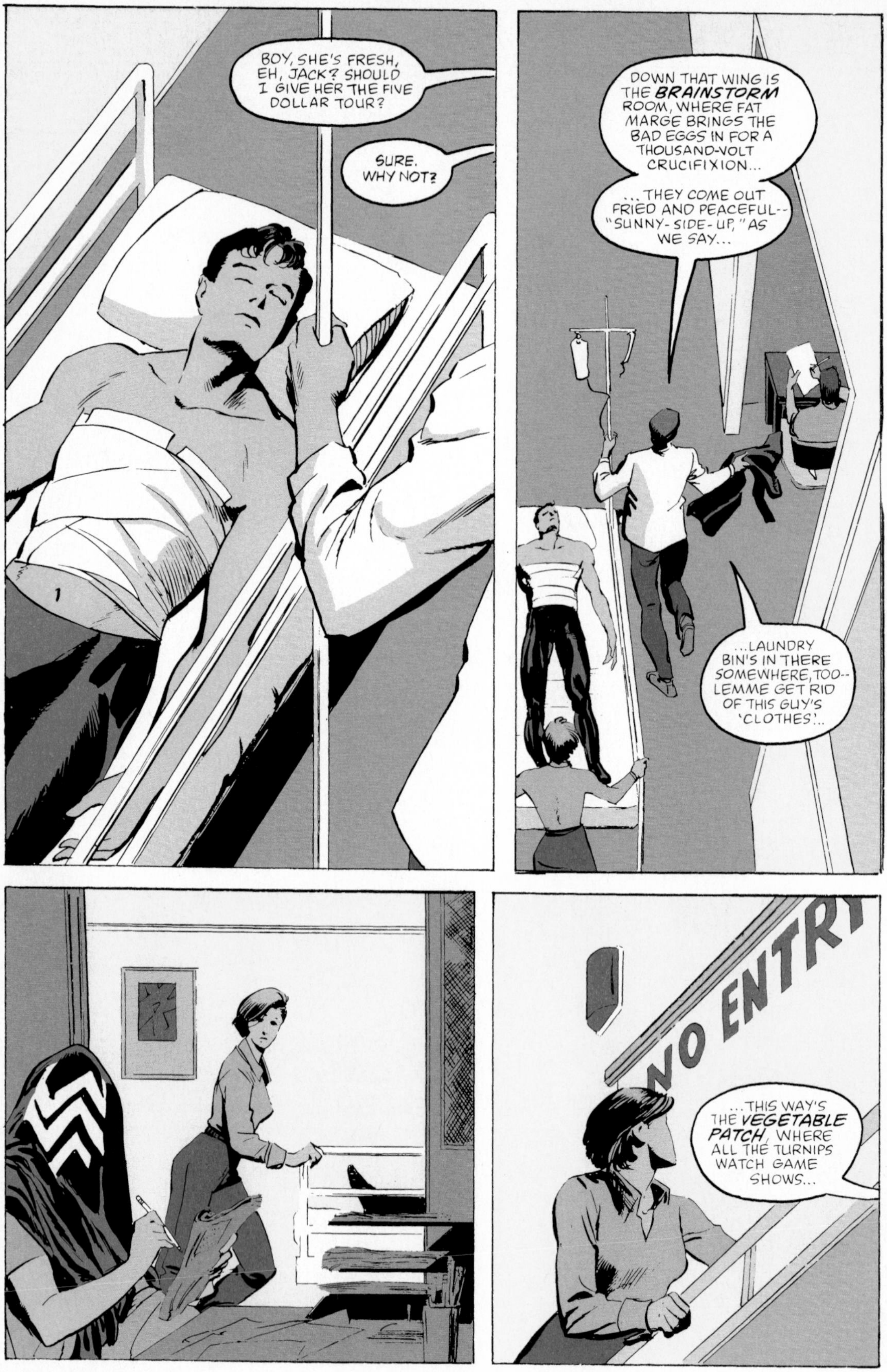
BOY, SHE'S FRESH, EH, JACK? SHOULD I GIVE HER THE FIVE DOLLAR TOUR?
SURE. WHY NOT?
DOWN THAT WING IS THE BRAINSTORM ROOM, WHERE FAT MARGE BRINGS THE BAD EGGS IN FOR A THOUSAND-VOLT CRUCIFIXION...
...THEY COME OUT FRIED AND PEACEFUL-- "SUNNY-SIDE-UP," AS WE SAY...
...LAUNDRY BIN'S IN THERE SOMEWHERE, TOO-- LEMME GET RID OF THIS GUY'S 'CLOTHES'...
NO ENTRY
...THIS WAY'S THE VEGETABLE PATCH, WHERE ALL THE TURNIPS WATCH GAME SHOWS...

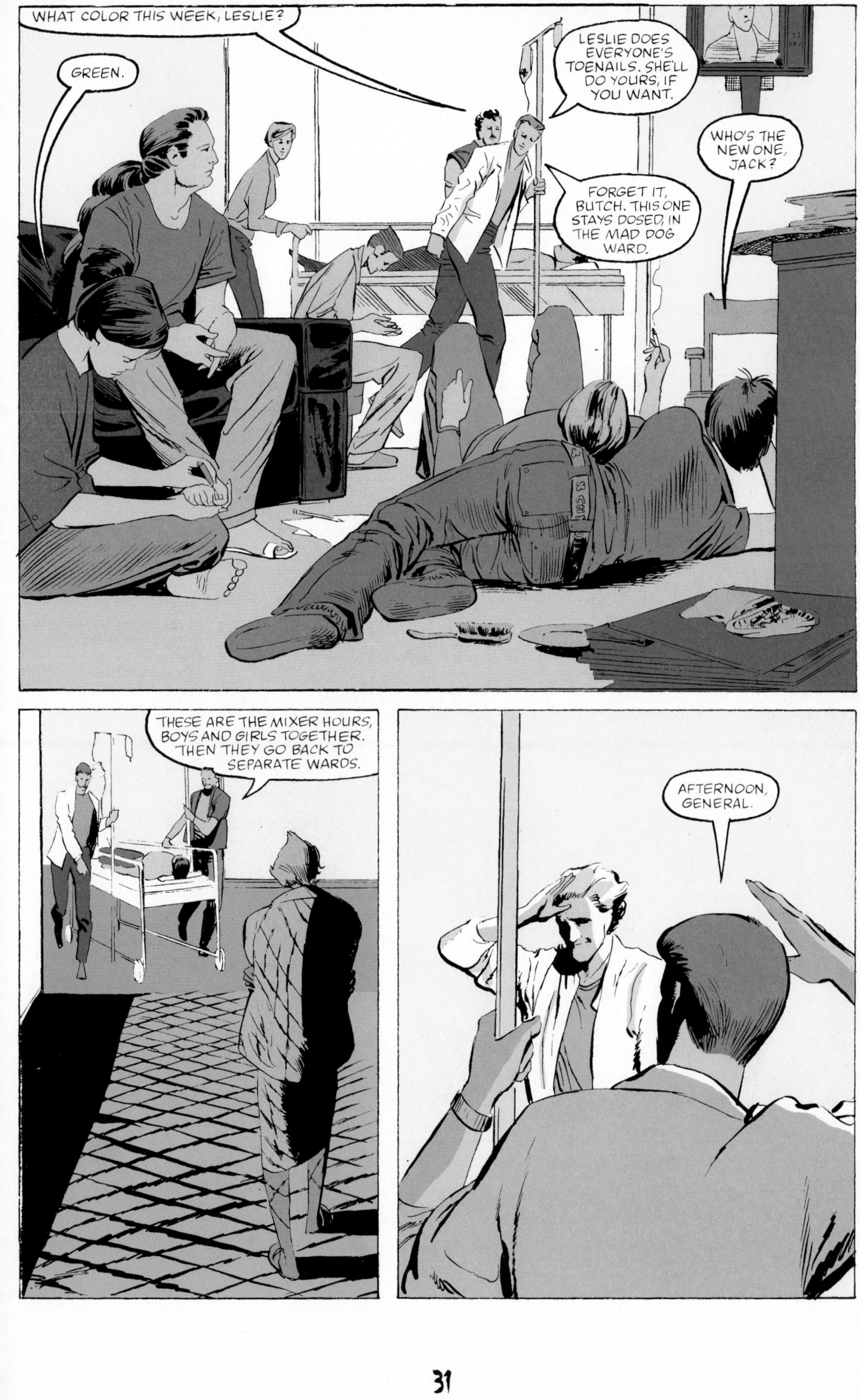
WHAT COLOR THIS WEEK, LESLIE?
GREEN.
LESLIE DOES EVERYONE'S TOENAILS. SHE'LL DO YOURS, IF YOU WANT.
WHO'S THE NEW ONE, JACK?
FORGET IT, BUTCH. THIS ONE STAYS DOSED, IN THE MAD DOG WARD.
THESE ARE THE MIXER HOURS, BOYS AND GIRLS TOGETHER. THEN THEY GO BACK TO SEPARATE WARDS.
AFTERNOON, GENERAL.

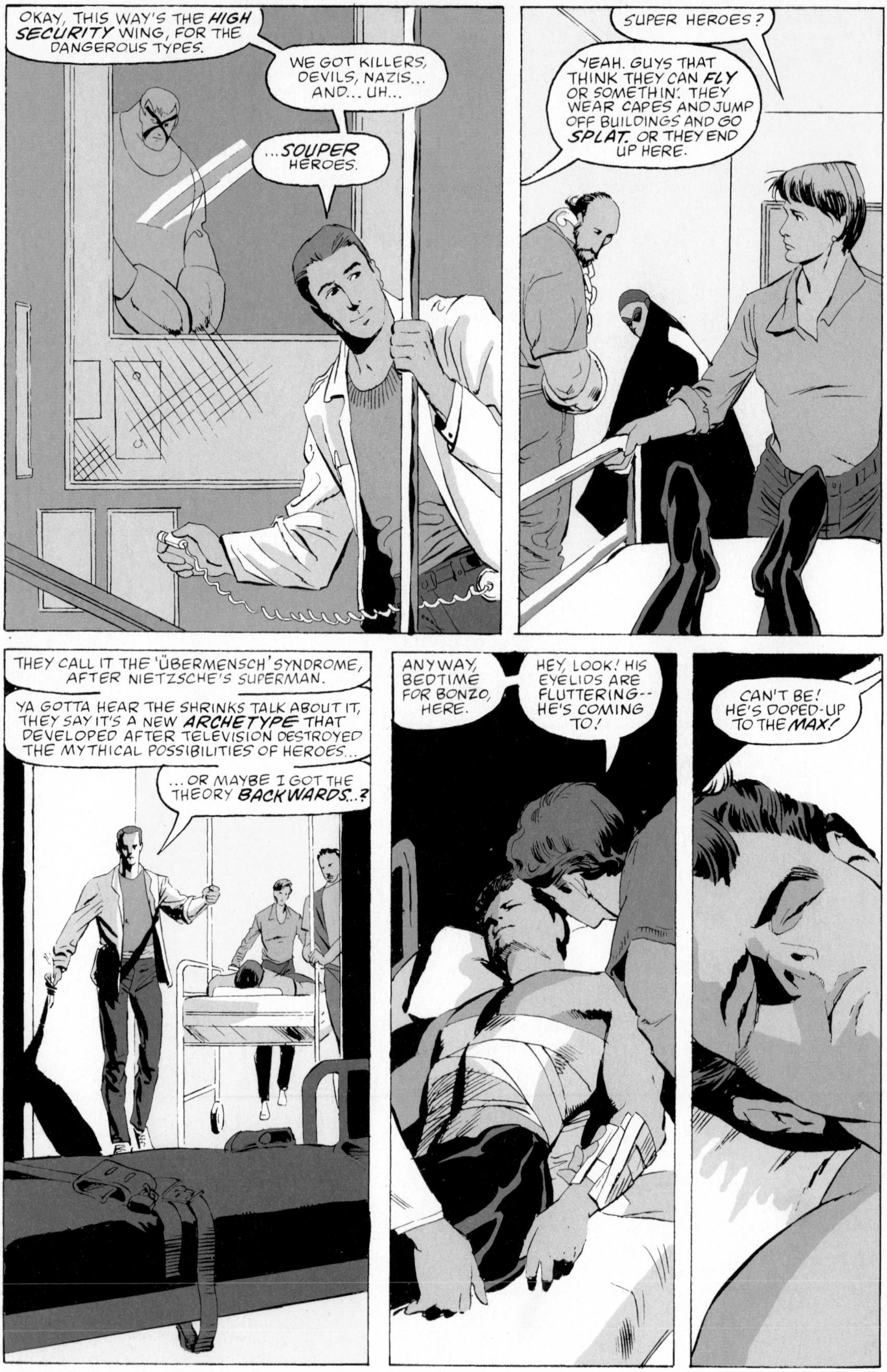
OKAY, THIS WAY'S THE HIGH SECURITY WING, FOR THE DANGEROUS TYPES.
WE GOT KILLERS, DEVILS, NAZIS... AND... UH...
...SOUPER HEROES.
SUPER HEROES?
YEAH. GUYS THAT THINK THEY CAN FLY OR SOMETHIN'. THEY WEAR CAPES AND JUMP OFF BUILDINGS AND GO SPLAT. OR THEY END UP HERE.
THEY CALL IT THE 'ÜBERMENSCH' SYNDROME, AFTER NIETZSCHE'S SUPERMAN.
YA GOTTA HEAR THE SHRINKS TALK ABOUT IT, THEY SAY IT'S A NEW ARCHETYPE THAT DEVELOPED AFTER TELEVISION DESTROYED THE MYTHICAL POSSIBILITIES OF HEROES...
...OR MAYBE I GOT THE THEORY BACKWARDS...?
ANYWAY, BEDTIME FOR BONZO, HERE.
HEY, LOOK! HIS EYELIDS ARE FLUTTERING-- HE'S COMING TO!
CAN'T BE! HE'S DOPED-UP TO THE MAX!

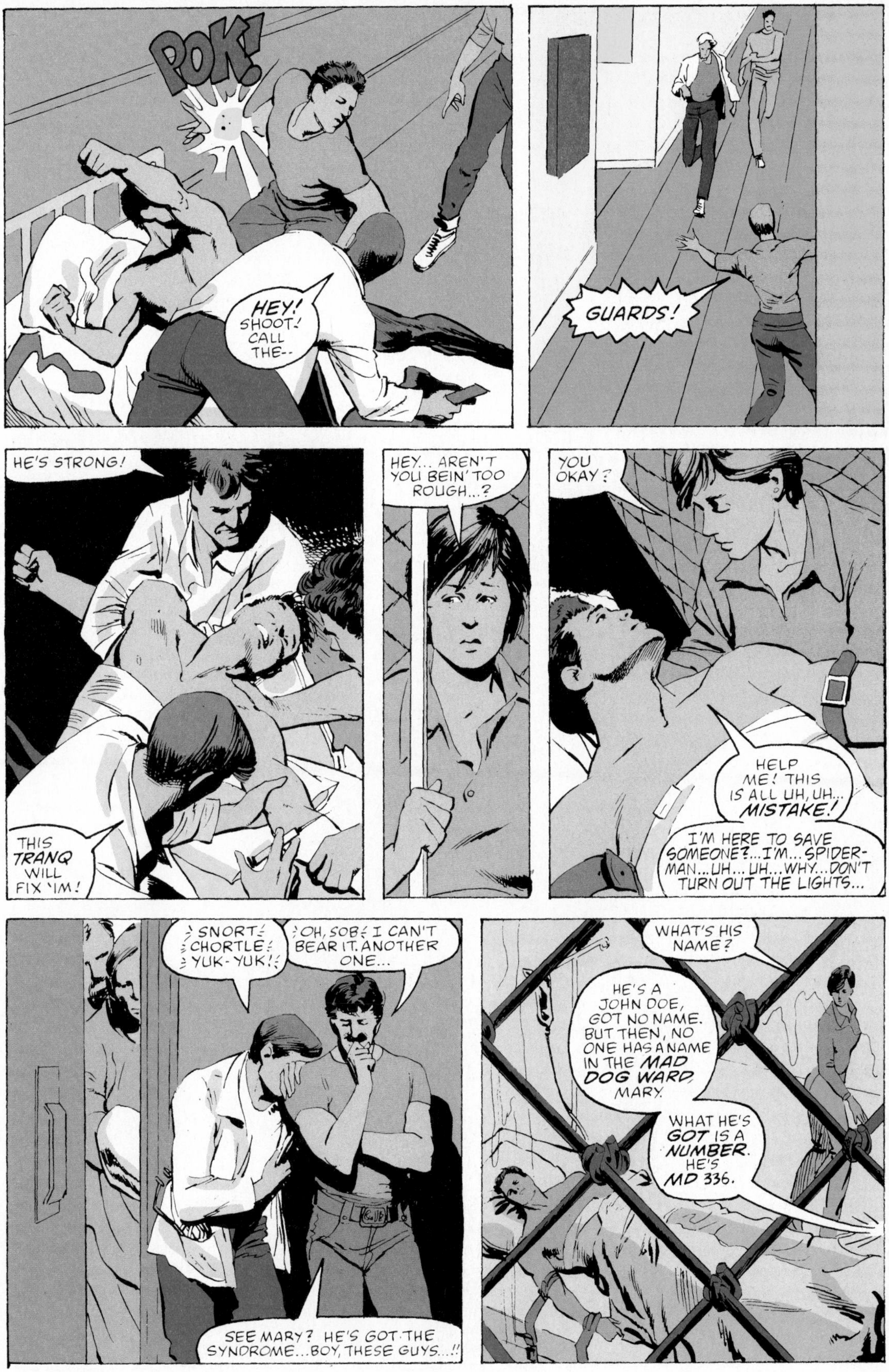
POK!
HEY! SHOOT! CALL THE--
GUARDS!
HE'S STRONG!
THIS TRANQ WILL FIX 'IM!
HEY... AREN'T YOU BEIN' TOO ROUGH...?
YOU OKAY?
HELP ME! THIS IS ALL UH, UH... MISTAKE!
I'M HERE TO SAVE SOMEONE?...I'M... SPIDER-MAN...UH... UH...WHY...DON'T TURN OUT THE LIGHTS...
SNORT CHORTLE YUK-YUK!
OH, SOB I CAN'T BEAR IT. ANOTHER ONE...
SEE MARY? HE'S GOT THE SYNDROME...BOY, THESE GUYS...!!
WHAT'S HIS NAME?
HE'S A JOHN DOE, GOT NO NAME. BUT THEN, NO ONE HAS A NAME IN THE MAD DOG WARD, MARY.
WHAT HE'S GOT IS A NUMBER. HE'S MD 336.

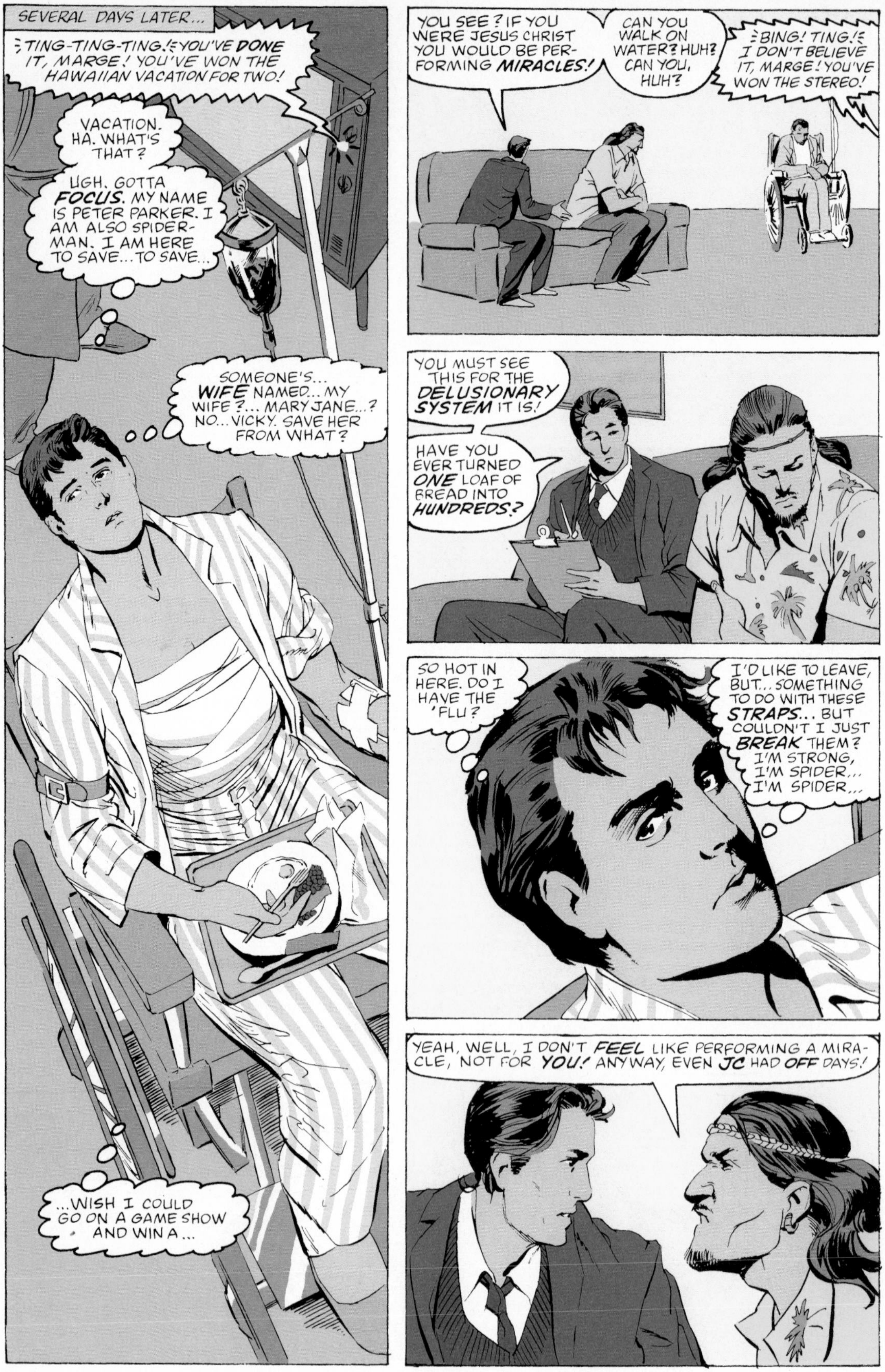

SEVERAL DAYS LATER...
≈TING-TING-TING!≈ YOU'VE DONE IT, MARGE! YOU'VE WON THE HAWAIIAN VACATION FOR TWO!
VACATION. HA. WHAT'S THAT?
UGH. GOTTA FOCUS. MY NAME IS PETER PARKER. I AM ALSO SPIDER-MAN. I AM HERE TO SAVE... TO SAVE...
SOMEONE'S... WIFE NAMED... MY WIFE?... MARY JANE...? NO... VICKY. SAVE HER FROM WHAT?
...WISH I COULD GO ON A GAME SHOW AND WIN A...
YOU SEE? IF YOU WERE JESUS CHRIST YOU WOULD BE PERFORMING MIRACLES!
CAN YOU WALK ON WATER? HUH? CAN YOU, HUH?
≈BING! TING!≈ I DON'T BELIEVE IT, MARGE! YOU'VE WON THE STEREO!
YOU MUST SEE THIS FOR THE DELUSIONARY SYSTEM IT IS!
HAVE YOU EVER TURNED ONE LOAF OF BREAD INTO HUNDREDS?
SO HOT IN HERE. DO I HAVE THE 'FLU?
I'D LIKE TO LEAVE, BUT... SOMETHING TO DO WITH THESE STRAPS... BUT COULDN'T I JUST BREAK THEM? I'M STRONG, I'M SPIDER... I'M SPIDER...
YEAH, WELL, I DON'T FEEL LIKE PERFORMING A MIRACLE, NOT FOR YOU! ANYWAY, EVEN JC HAD OFF DAYS!

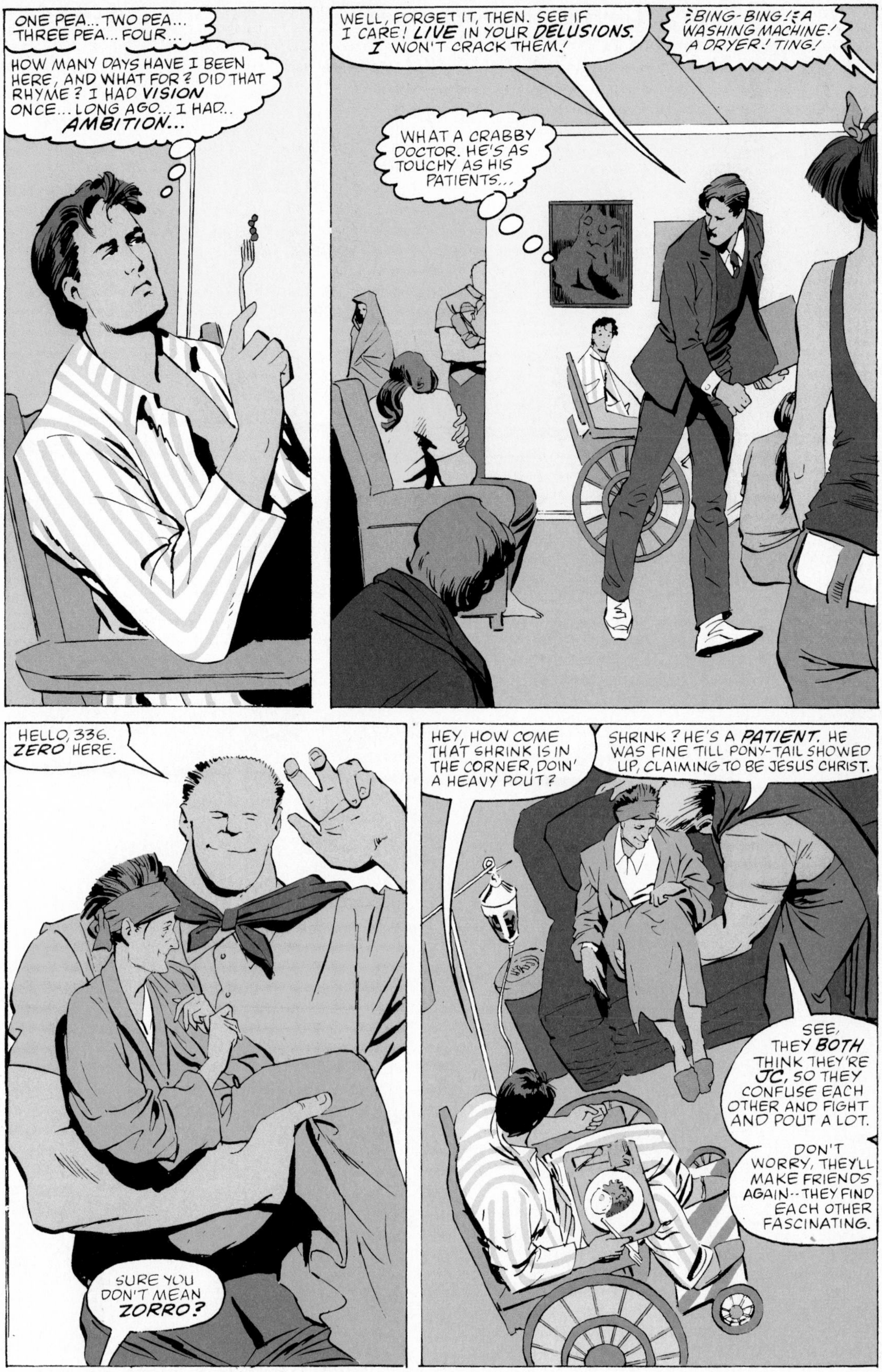
ONE PEA... TWO PEA... THREE PEA... FOUR...
HOW MANY DAYS HAVE I BEEN HERE, AND WHAT FOR? DID THAT RHYME? I HAD VISION ONCE... LONG AGO... I HAD... AMBITION...
WELL, FORGET IT, THEN. SEE IF I CARE! LIVE IN YOUR DELUSIONS. I WON'T CRACK THEM!
BING-BING! A WASHING MACHINE! A DRYER! TING!
WHAT A CRABBY DOCTOR. HE'S AS TOUCHY AS HIS PATIENTS...
HELLO, 336. ZERO HERE.
SURE YOU DON'T MEAN ZORRO?
HEY, HOW COME THAT SHRINK IS IN THE CORNER, DOIN' A HEAVY POUT?
SHRINK? HE'S A PATIENT. HE WAS FINE TILL PONY-TAIL SHOWED UP, CLAIMING TO BE JESUS CHRIST.
SEE, THEY BOTH THINK THEY'RE JC, SO THEY CONFUSE EACH OTHER AND FIGHT AND POUT A LOT.
DON'T WORRY, THEY'LL MAKE FRIENDS AGAIN--THEY FIND EACH OTHER FASCINATING.

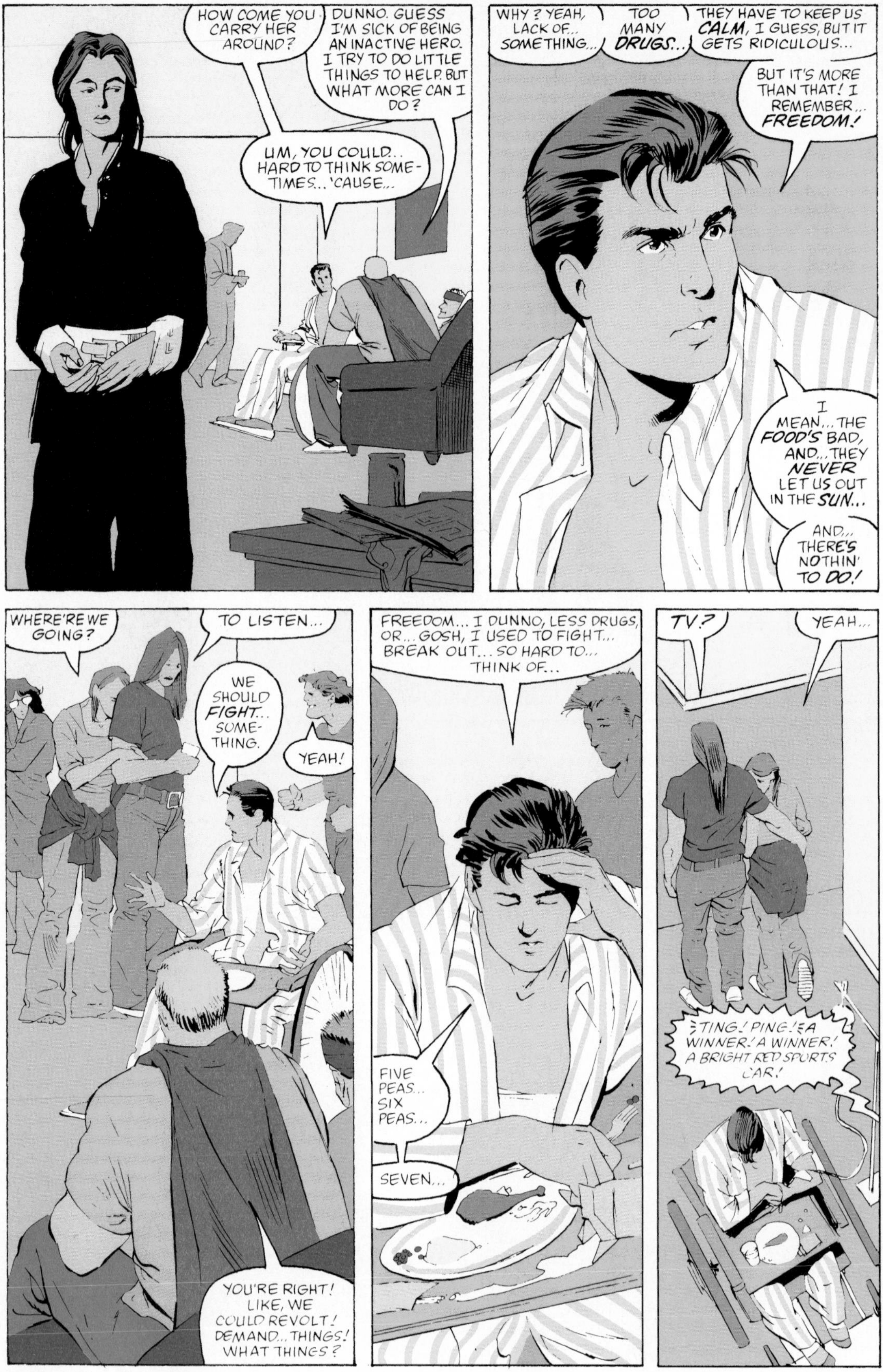
HOW COME YOU CARRY HER AROUND?
DUNNO. GUESS I'M SICK OF BEING AN INACTIVE HERO. I TRY TO DO LITTLE THINGS TO HELP. BUT WHAT MORE CAN I DO?
UM, YOU COULD... HARD TO THINK SOMETIMES... 'CAUSE...
WHY? YEAH, LACK OF... SOMETHING...
TOO MANY DRUGS...
THEY HAVE TO KEEP US CALM, I GUESS, BUT IT GETS RIDICULOUS...
BUT IT'S MORE THAN THAT! I REMEMBER... FREEDOM!
I MEAN... THE FOOD'S BAD, AND... THEY NEVER LET US OUT IN THE SUN...
AND... THERE'S NOTHIN' TO DO!
WHERE'RE WE GOING?
TO LISTEN...
WE SHOULD FIGHT... SOMETHING.
YEAH!
YOU'RE RIGHT! LIKE, WE COULD REVOLT! DEMAND... THINGS! WHAT THINGS?
FREEDOM... I DUNNO, LESS DRUGS, OR... GOSH, I USED TO FIGHT... BREAK OUT... SO HARD TO... THINK OF...
FIVE PEAS... SIX PEAS...
SEVEN...
TV?
YEAH...
TING! PING! A WINNER! A WINNER! A BRIGHT RED SPORTS CAR!

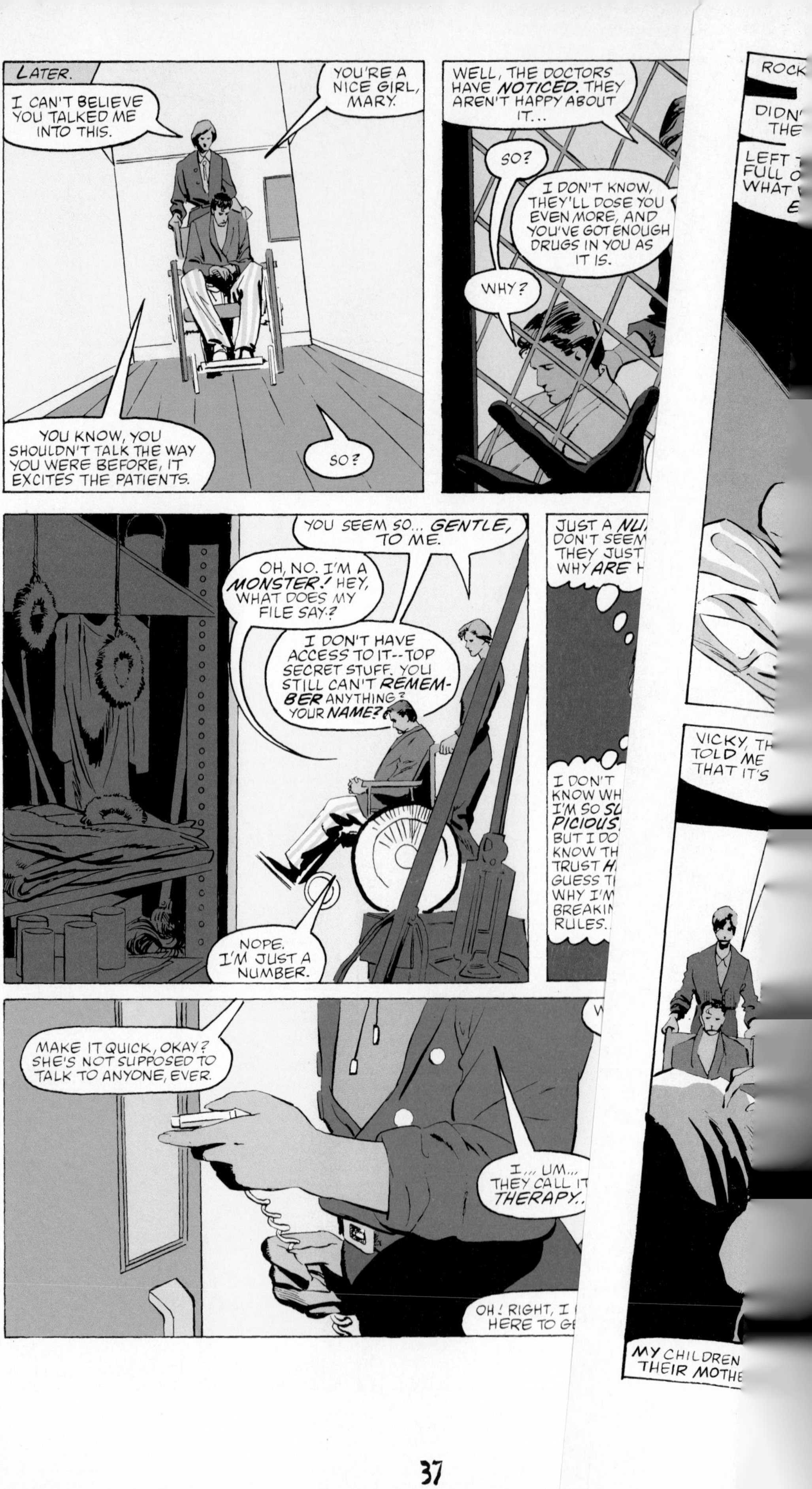
LATER.
I CAN'T BELIEVE YOU TALKED ME INTO THIS.
YOU'RE A NICE GIRL, MARY.
YOU KNOW, YOU SHOULDN'T TALK THE WAY YOU WERE BEFORE, IT EXCITES THE PATIENTS.
SO?
WELL, THE DOCTORS HAVE NOTICED. THEY AREN'T HAPPY ABOUT IT...
SO?
I DON'T KNOW, THEY'LL DOSE YOU EVEN MORE, AND YOU'VE GOT ENOUGH DRUGS IN YOU AS IT IS.
WHY?
YOU SEEM SO... GENTLE, TO ME.
OH, NO. I'M A MONSTER! HEY, WHAT DOES MY FILE SAY?
I DON'T HAVE ACCESS TO IT--TOP SECRET STUFF. YOU STILL CAN'T REMEMBER ANYTHING? YOUR NAME?
NOPE. I'M JUST A NUMBER.
MAKE IT QUICK, OKAY? SHE'S NOT SUPPOSED TO TALK TO ANYONE, EVER.
I... UM... THEY CALL IT THERAPY.
MY CHILDREN

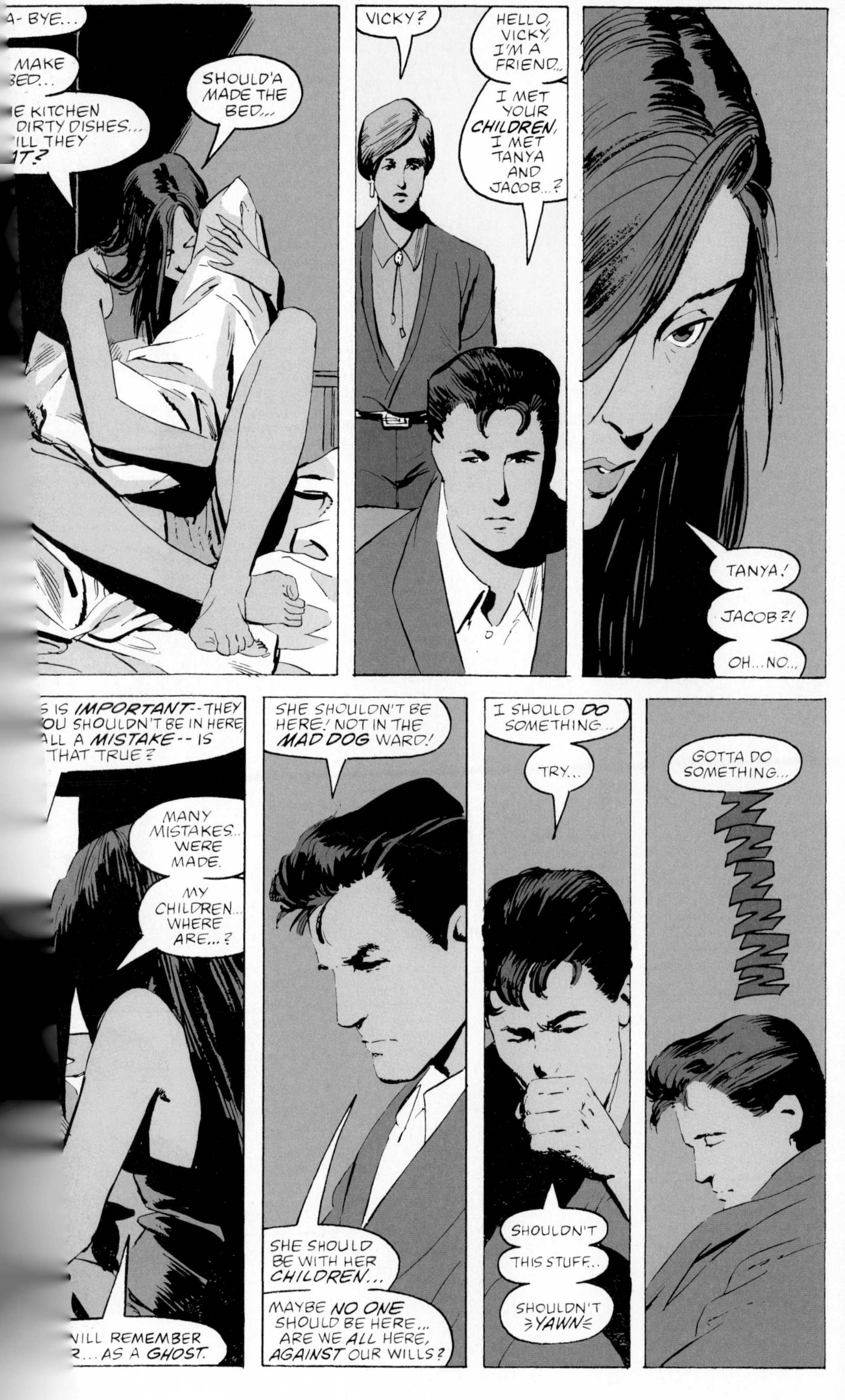

A- BYE...
MAKE BED...
E KITCHEN DIRTY DISHES... ILL THEY IT?
SHOULD'A MADE THE BED...
VICKY?
HELLO, VICKY, I'M A FRIEND...
I MET YOUR CHILDREN, I MET TANYA AND JACOB...?
TANYA!
JACOB?!
OH... NO...
S IS IMPORTANT--THEY OU SHOULDN'T BE IN HERE, ALL A MISTAKE--IS THAT TRUE?
MANY MISTAKES... WERE MADE.
MY CHILDREN... WHERE ARE...?
NILL REMEMBER R... AS A GHOST.
SHE SHOULDN'T BE HERE! NOT IN THE MAD DOG WARD!
SHE SHOULD BE WITH HER CHILDREN...
MAYBE NO ONE SHOULD BE HERE... ARE WE ALL HERE, AGAINST OUR WILLS?
I SHOULD DO SOMETHING...
TRY...
SHOULDN'T
THIS STUFF...
SHOULDN'T
YAWN
GOTTA DO SOMETHING...
ZZZZZZZ

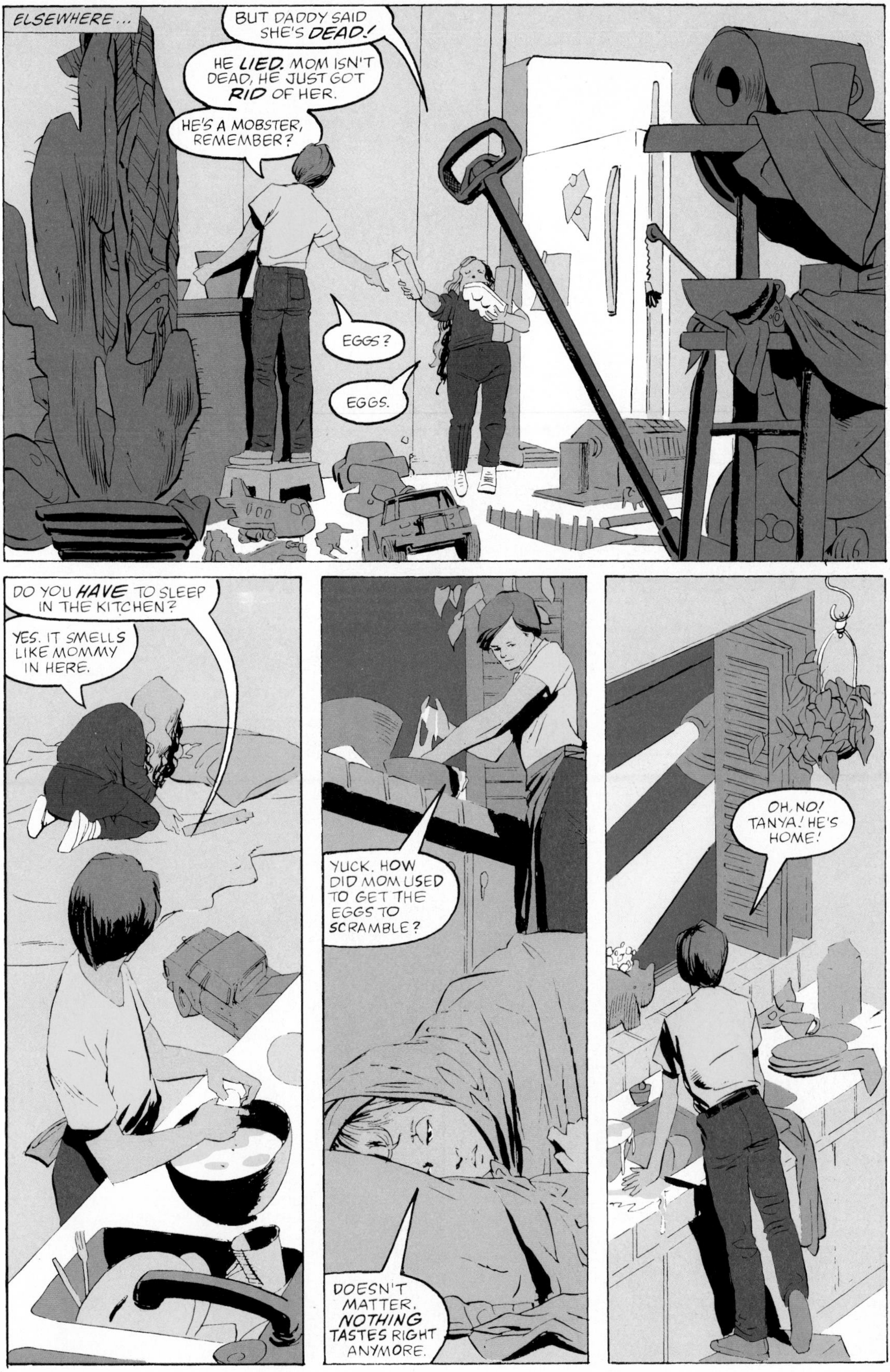
ELSEWHERE...
BUT DADDY SAID SHE'S DEAD!
HE LIED. MOM ISN'T DEAD, HE JUST GOT RID OF HER.
HE'S A MOBSTER, REMEMBER?
EGGS?
EGGS.
DO YOU HAVE TO SLEEP IN THE KITCHEN?
YES. IT SMELLS LIKE MOMMY IN HERE.
YUCK. HOW DID MOM USED TO GET THE EGGS TO SCRAMBLE?
DOESN'T MATTER. NOTHING TASTES RIGHT ANYMORE.
OH, NO! TANYA! HE'S HOME!

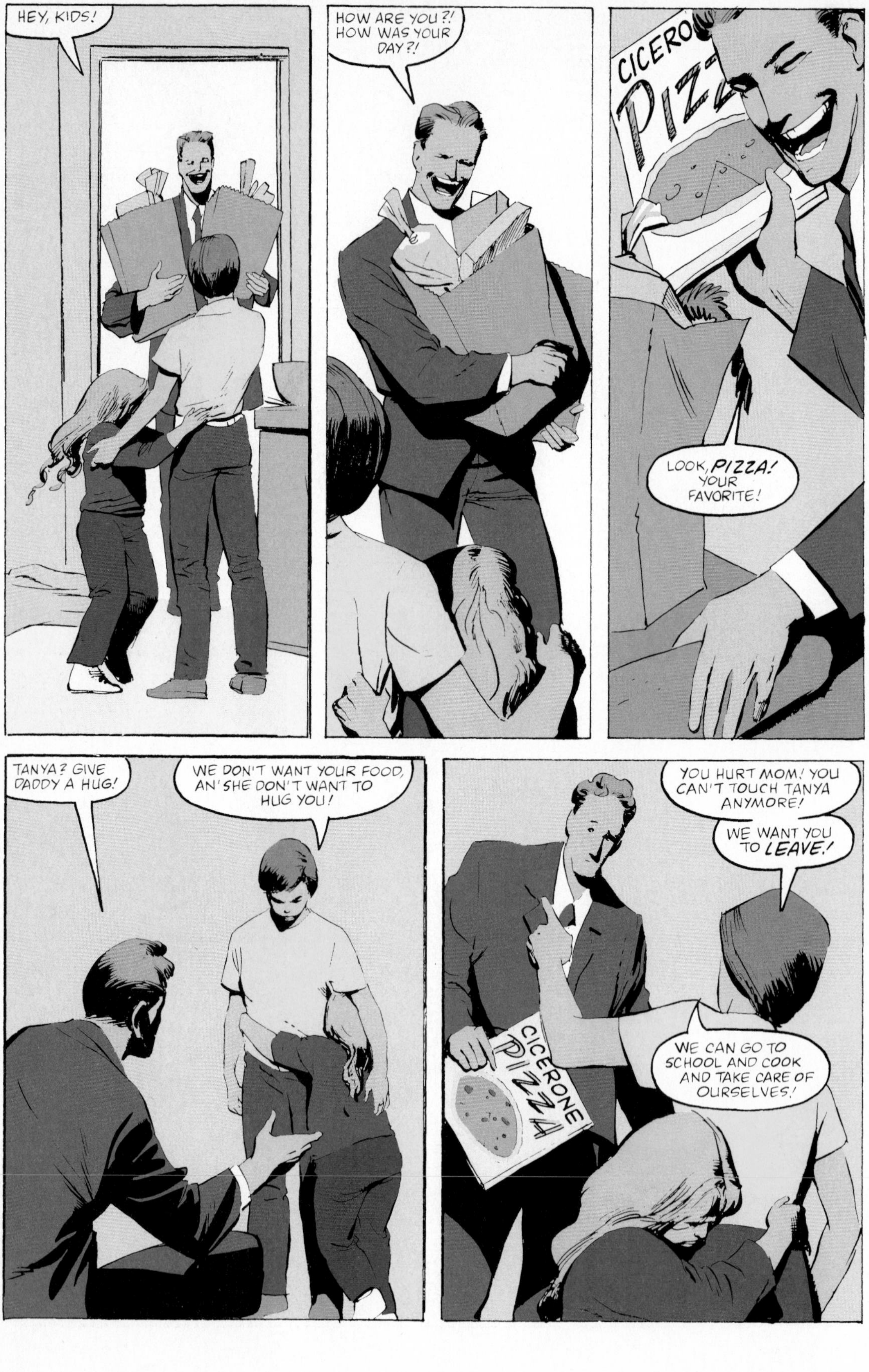
HEY, KIDS!
HOW ARE YOU?! HOW WAS YOUR DAY?!
CICERO
PIZZ
LOOK, PIZZA! YOUR FAVORITE!
TANYA? GIVE DADDY A HUG!
WE DON'T WANT YOUR FOOD, AN' SHE DON'T WANT TO HUG YOU!
YOU HURT MOM! YOU CAN'T TOUCH TANYA ANYMORE!
WE WANT YOU TO LEAVE!
CICERONE PIZZA
WE CAN GO TO SCHOOL AND COOK AND TAKE CARE OF OURSELVES!

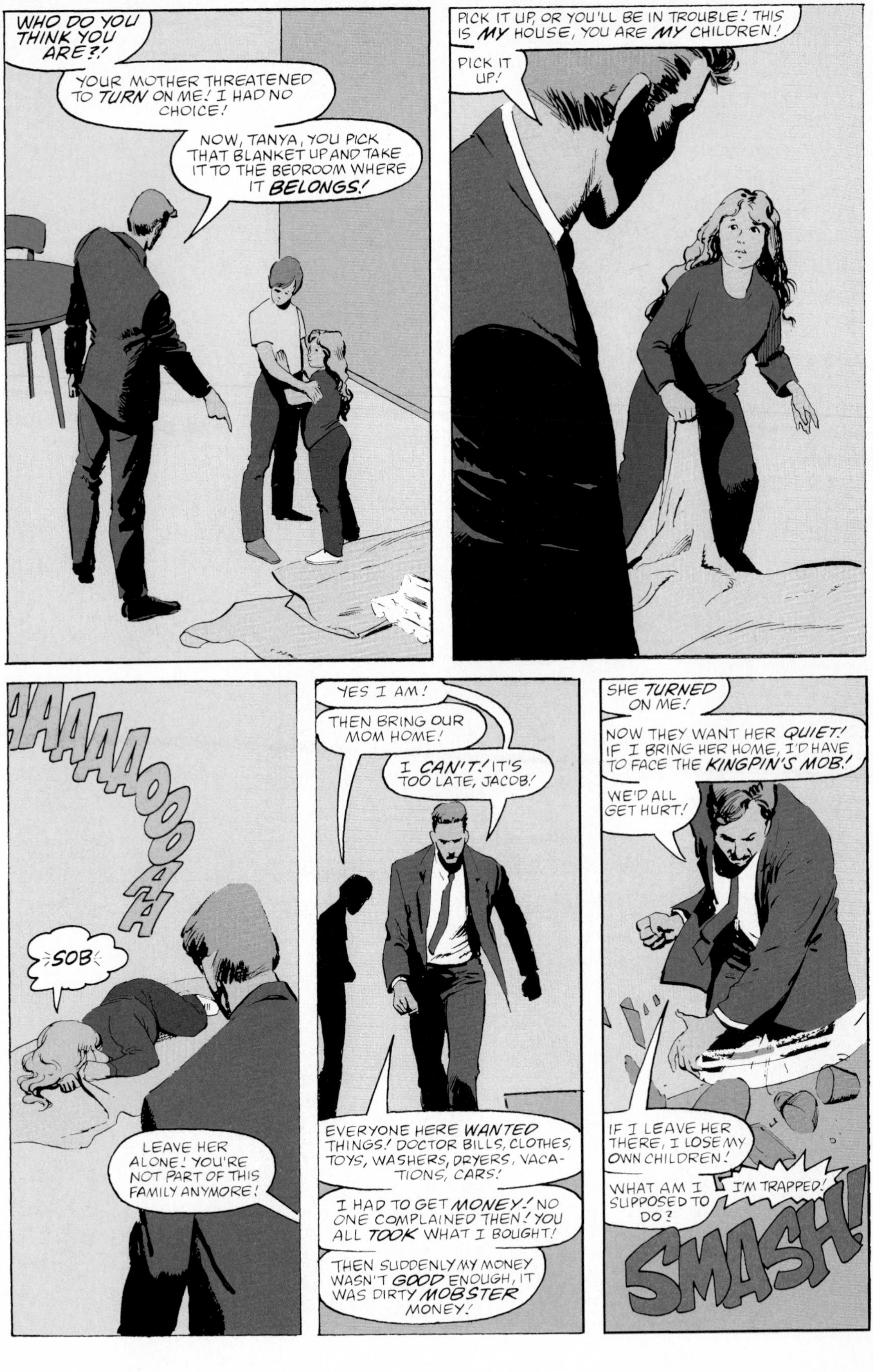

WHO DO YOU THINK YOU ARE?!
YOUR MOTHER THREATENED TO TURN ON ME! I HAD NO CHOICE!
NOW, TANYA, YOU PICK THAT BLANKET UP AND TAKE IT TO THE BEDROOM WHERE IT BELONGS!
PICK IT UP, OR YOU'LL BE IN TROUBLE! THIS IS MY HOUSE, YOU ARE MY CHILDREN!
PICK IT UP!
AAAAAAOOOOAAA
SOB
LEAVE HER ALONE! YOU'RE NOT PART OF THIS FAMILY ANYMORE!
YES I AM!
THEN BRING OUR MOM HOME!
I CAN'T! IT'S TOO LATE, JACOB!
EVERYONE HERE WANTED THINGS! DOCTOR BILLS, CLOTHES, TOYS, WASHERS, DRYERS, VACATIONS, CARS!
I HAD TO GET MONEY! NO ONE COMPLAINED THEN! YOU ALL TOOK WHAT I BOUGHT!
THEN SUDDENLY MY MONEY WASN'T GOOD ENOUGH, IT WAS DIRTY MOBSTER MONEY!
SHE TURNED ON ME!
NOW THEY WANT HER QUIET! IF I BRING HER HOME, I'D HAVE TO FACE THE KINGPIN'S MOB!
WE'D ALL GET HURT!
IF I LEAVE HER THERE, I LOSE MY OWN CHILDREN!
WHAT AM I SUPPOSED TO DO?
I'M TRAPPED!
SMASH!

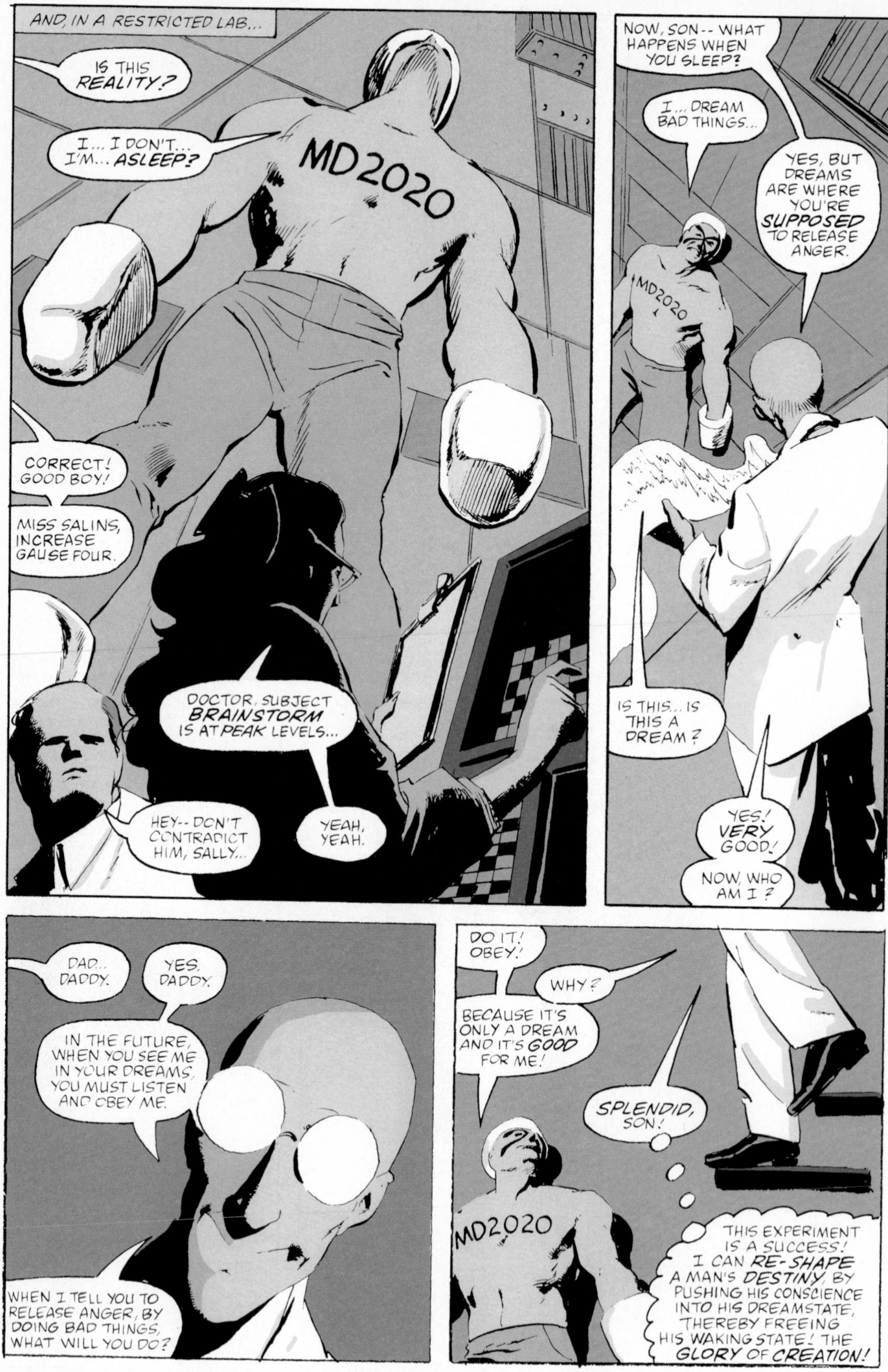

AND, IN A RESTRICTED LAB...
IS THIS REALITY?
I... I DON'T... I'M... ASLEEP?
MD2020
CORRECT! GOOD BOY!
MISS SALINS, INCREASE GAUSE FOUR.
DOCTOR, SUBJECT BRAINSTORM IS AT PEAK LEVELS...
HEY-- DON'T CONTRADICT HIM, SALLY...
YEAH, YEAH.
NOW, SON-- WHAT HAPPENS WHEN YOU SLEEP?
I... DREAM BAD THINGS...
YES, BUT DREAMS ARE WHERE YOU'RE SUPPOSED TO RELEASE ANGER.
MD2020
IS THIS... IS THIS A DREAM?
YES! VERY GOOD!
NOW, WHO AM I?
DAD... DADDY.
YES, DADDY.
IN THE FUTURE, WHEN YOU SEE ME IN YOUR DREAMS, YOU MUST LISTEN AND OBEY ME.
WHEN I TELL YOU TO RELEASE ANGER, BY DOING BAD THINGS, WHAT WILL YOU DO?
DO IT! OBEY!
WHY?
BECAUSE IT'S ONLY A DREAM AND IT'S GOOD FOR ME!
SPLENDID, SON!
MD2020
THIS EXPERIMENT IS A SUCCESS! I CAN RE-SHAPE A MAN'S DESTINY, BY PUSHING HIS CONSCIENCE INTO HIS DREAMSTATE, THEREBY FREEING HIS WAKING STATE! THE GLORY OF CREATION!

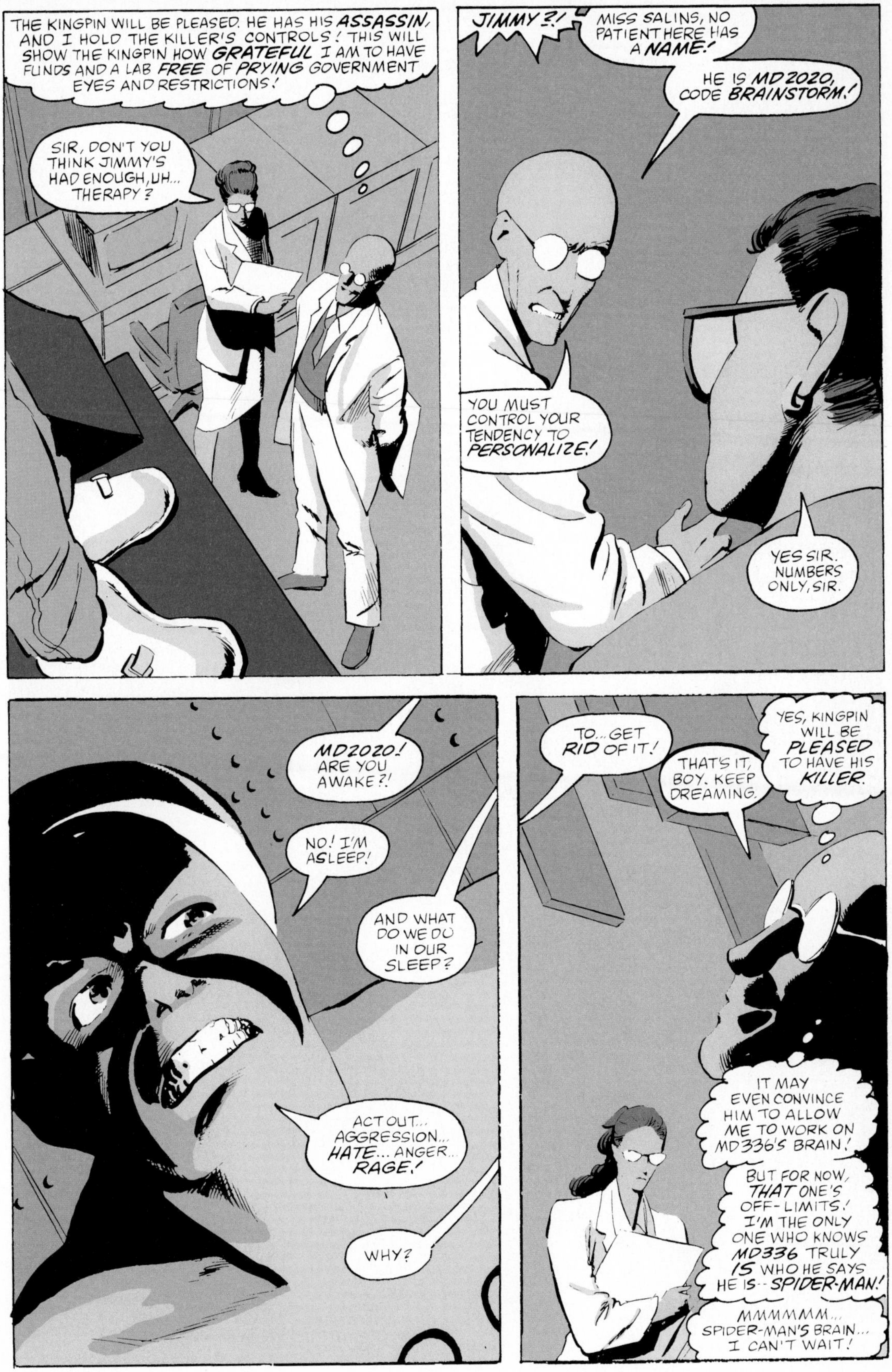
THE KINGPIN WILL BE PLEASED. HE HAS HIS ASSASSIN, AND I HOLD THE KILLER'S CONTROLS! THIS WILL SHOW THE KINGPIN HOW GRATEFUL I AM TO HAVE FUNDS AND A LAB FREE OF PRYING GOVERNMENT EYES AND RESTRICTIONS!
SIR, DON'T YOU THINK JIMMY'S HAD ENOUGH, UH... THERAPY?
JIMMY?!
MISS SALINS, NO PATIENT HERE HAS A NAME!
HE IS MD2020, CODE BRAINSTORM!
YOU MUST CONTROL YOUR TENDENCY TO PERSONALIZE!
YES SIR. NUMBERS ONLY, SIR.
MD2020! ARE YOU AWAKE?!
NO! I'M ASLEEP!
AND WHAT DO WE DO IN OUR SLEEP?
ACT OUT... AGGRESSION... HATE... ANGER... RAGE!
WHY?
TO... GET RID OF IT!
THAT'S IT, BOY. KEEP DREAMING.
YES, KINGPIN WILL BE PLEASED TO HAVE HIS KILLER.
IT MAY EVEN CONVINCE HIM TO ALLOW ME TO WORK ON MD336'S BRAIN!
BUT FOR NOW, THAT ONE'S OFF-LIMITS! I'M THE ONLY ONE WHO KNOWS MD336 TRULY IS WHO HE SAYS HE IS--SPIDER-MAN!
MMMMMM... SPIDER-MAN'S BRAIN... I CAN'T WAIT!

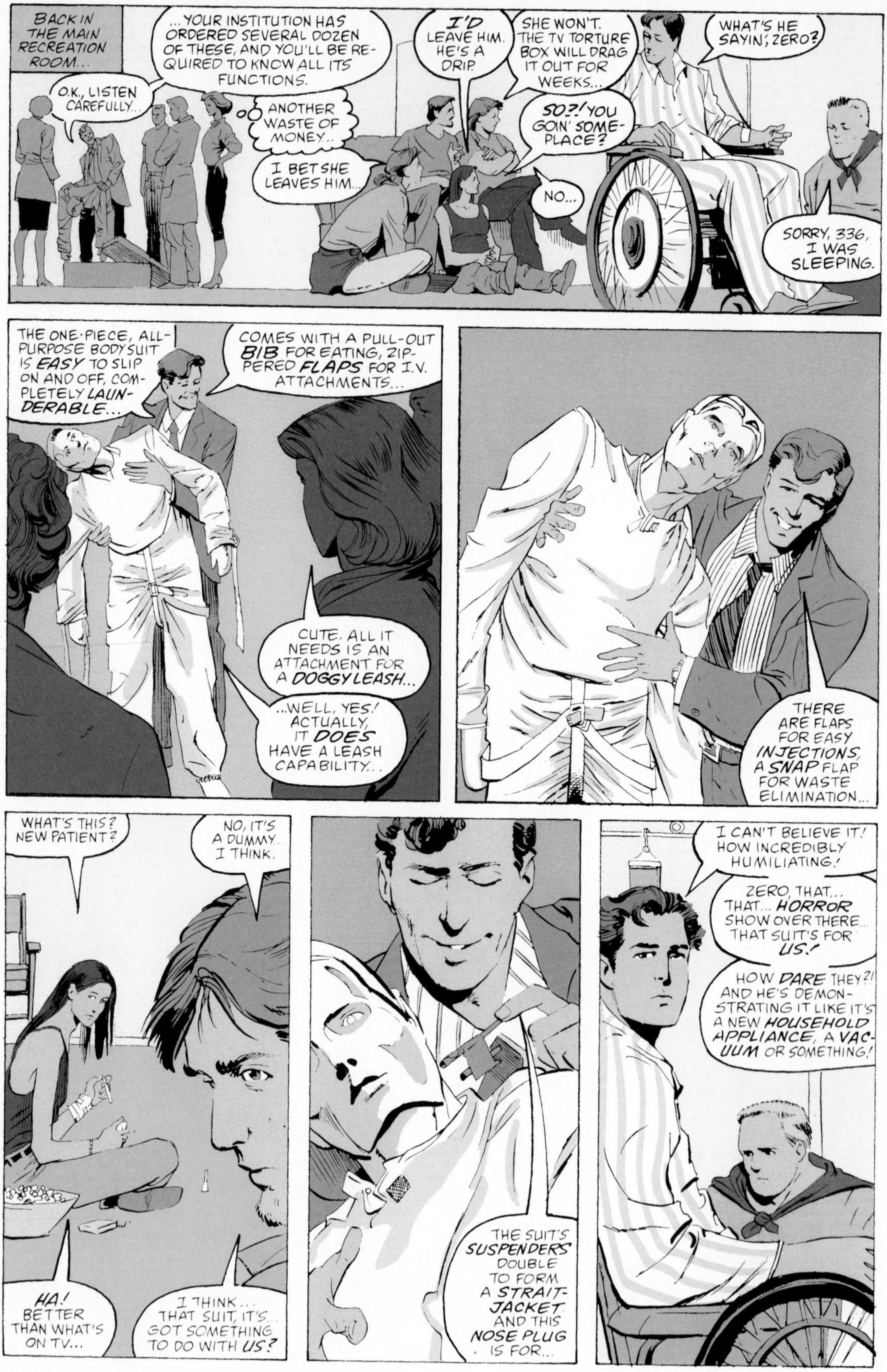
BACK IN THE MAIN RECREATION ROOM...
...YOUR INSTITUTION HAS ORDERED SEVERAL DOZEN OF THESE, AND YOU'LL BE REQUIRED TO KNOW ALL ITS FUNCTIONS.
O.K., LISTEN CAREFULLY...
ANOTHER WASTE OF MONEY...
I BET SHE LEAVES HIM...
I'D LEAVE HIM. HE'S A DRIP.
SHE WON'T. THE TV TORTURE BOX WILL DRAG IT OUT FOR WEEKS...
SO?! YOU GOIN' SOMEPLACE?
NO...
WHAT'S HE SAYIN', ZERO?
SORRY, 336, I WAS SLEEPING.
THE ONE-PIECE, ALL-PURPOSE BODYSUIT IS EASY TO SLIP ON AND OFF, COMPLETELY LAUNDERABLE...
COMES WITH A PULL-OUT BIB FOR EATING, ZIPPERED FLAPS FOR I.V. ATTACHMENTS...
CUTE. ALL IT NEEDS IS AN ATTACHMENT FOR A DOGGY LEASH...
...WELL, YES! ACTUALLY, IT DOES HAVE A LEASH CAPABILITY...
THERE ARE FLAPS FOR EASY INJECTIONS, A SNAP FLAP FOR WASTE ELIMINATION...
WHAT'S THIS? NEW PATIENT?
NO, IT'S A DUMMY... I THINK.
HA! BETTER THAN WHAT'S ON TV...
I THINK... THAT SUIT, IT'S... GOT SOMETHING TO DO WITH US?
THE SUIT'S SUSPENDERS DOUBLE TO FORM A STRAIT-JACKET. AND THIS NOSE PLUG IS FOR...
I CAN'T BELIEVE IT! HOW INCREDIBLY HUMILIATING!
ZERO, THAT... THAT... HORROR SHOW OVER THERE... THAT SUIT'S FOR US!
HOW DARE THEY?! AND HE'S DEMONSTRATING IT LIKE IT'S A NEW HOUSEHOLD APPLIANCE, A VACUUM OR SOMETHING!

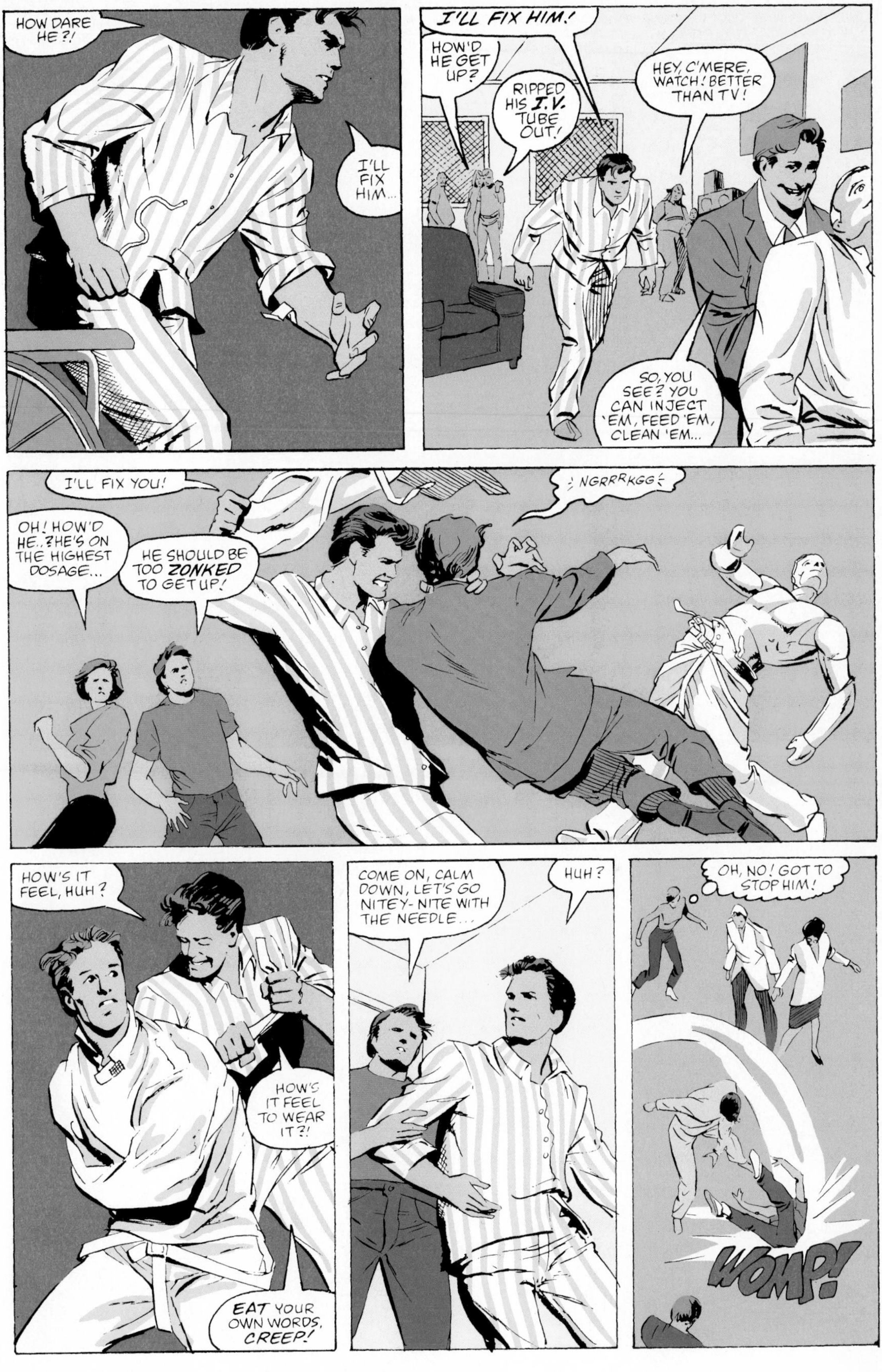
HOW DARE HE?!
I'LL FIX HIM...
I'LL FIX HIM!
HOW'D HE GET UP?
RIPPED HIS I.V. TUBE OUT!
HEY, C'MERE, WATCH! BETTER THAN TV!
SO, YOU SEE? YOU CAN INJECT 'EM, FEED 'EM, CLEAN 'EM...
I'LL FIX YOU!
NGRRRKGG
OH! HOW'D HE..?HE'S ON THE HIGHEST DOSAGE...
HE SHOULD BE TOO ZONKED TO GET UP!
HOW'S IT FEEL, HUH?
HOW'S IT FEEL TO WEAR IT?!
EAT YOUR OWN WORDS, CREEP!
COME ON, CALM DOWN, LET'S GO NITEY-NITE WITH THE NEEDLE...
HUH?
OH, NO! GOT TO STOP HIM!
WOMP!

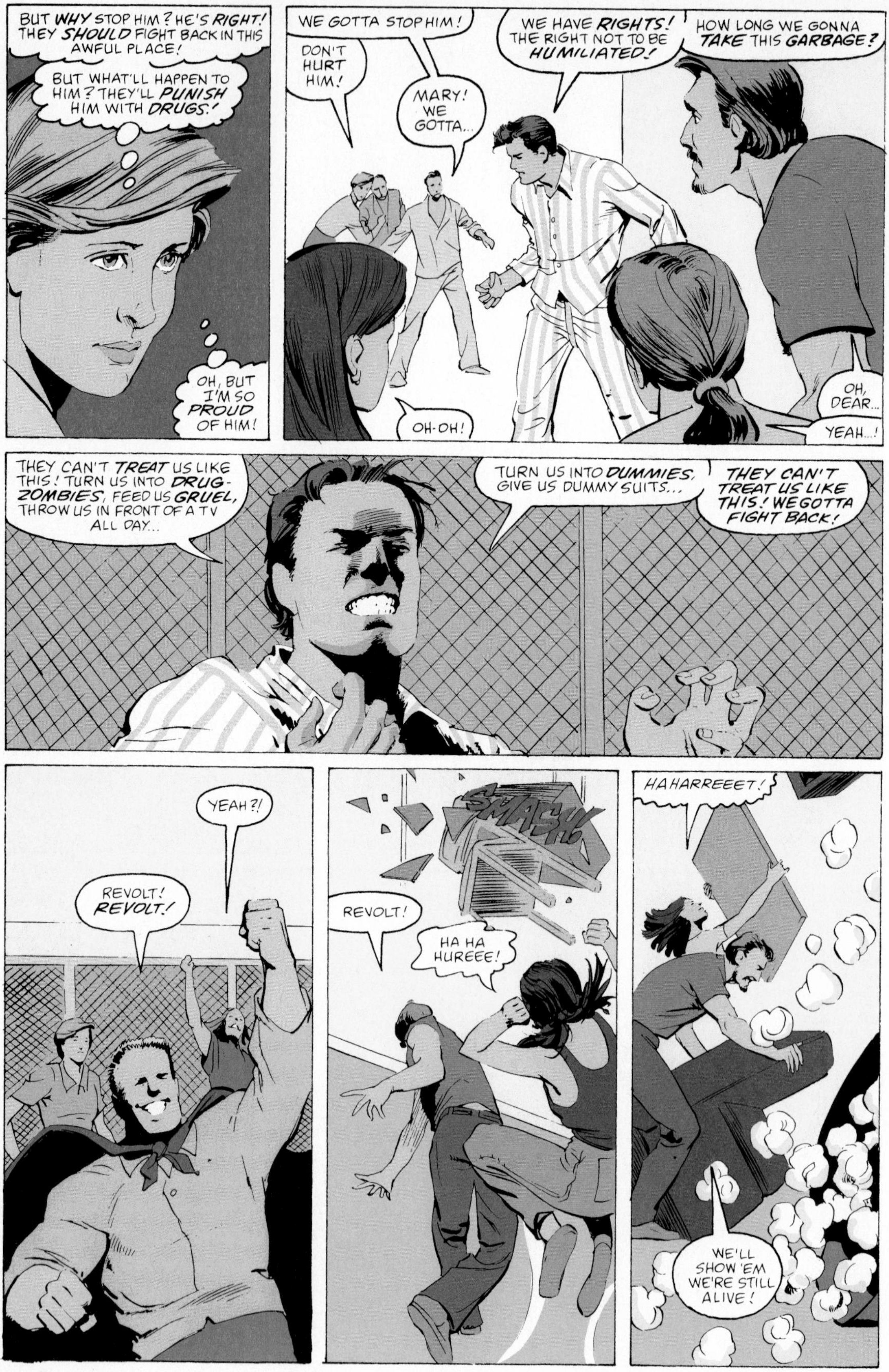
BUT WHY STOP HIM? HE'S RIGHT! THEY SHOULD FIGHT BACK IN THIS AWFUL PLACE!
BUT WHAT'LL HAPPEN TO HIM? THEY'LL PUNISH HIM WITH DRUGS!
OH, BUT I'M SO PROUD OF HIM!
WE GOTTA STOP HIM!
DON'T HURT HIM!
MARY! WE GOTTA...
WE HAVE RIGHTS! THE RIGHT NOT TO BE HUMILIATED!
HOW LONG WE GONNA TAKE THIS GARBAGE?
OH-OH!
OH, DEAR...
YEAH...!
THEY CAN'T TREAT US LIKE THIS! TURN US INTO DRUG-ZOMBIES, FEED US GRUEL, THROW US IN FRONT OF A TV ALL DAY...
TURN US INTO DUMMIES, GIVE US DUMMY SUITS...
THEY CAN'T TREAT US LIKE THIS! WE GOTTA FIGHT BACK!
YEAH?!
REVOLT! REVOLT!
SMASH!
REVOLT!
HA HA HUREEE!
HA HA HARREEET!
WE'LL SHOW 'EM WE'RE STILL ALIVE!

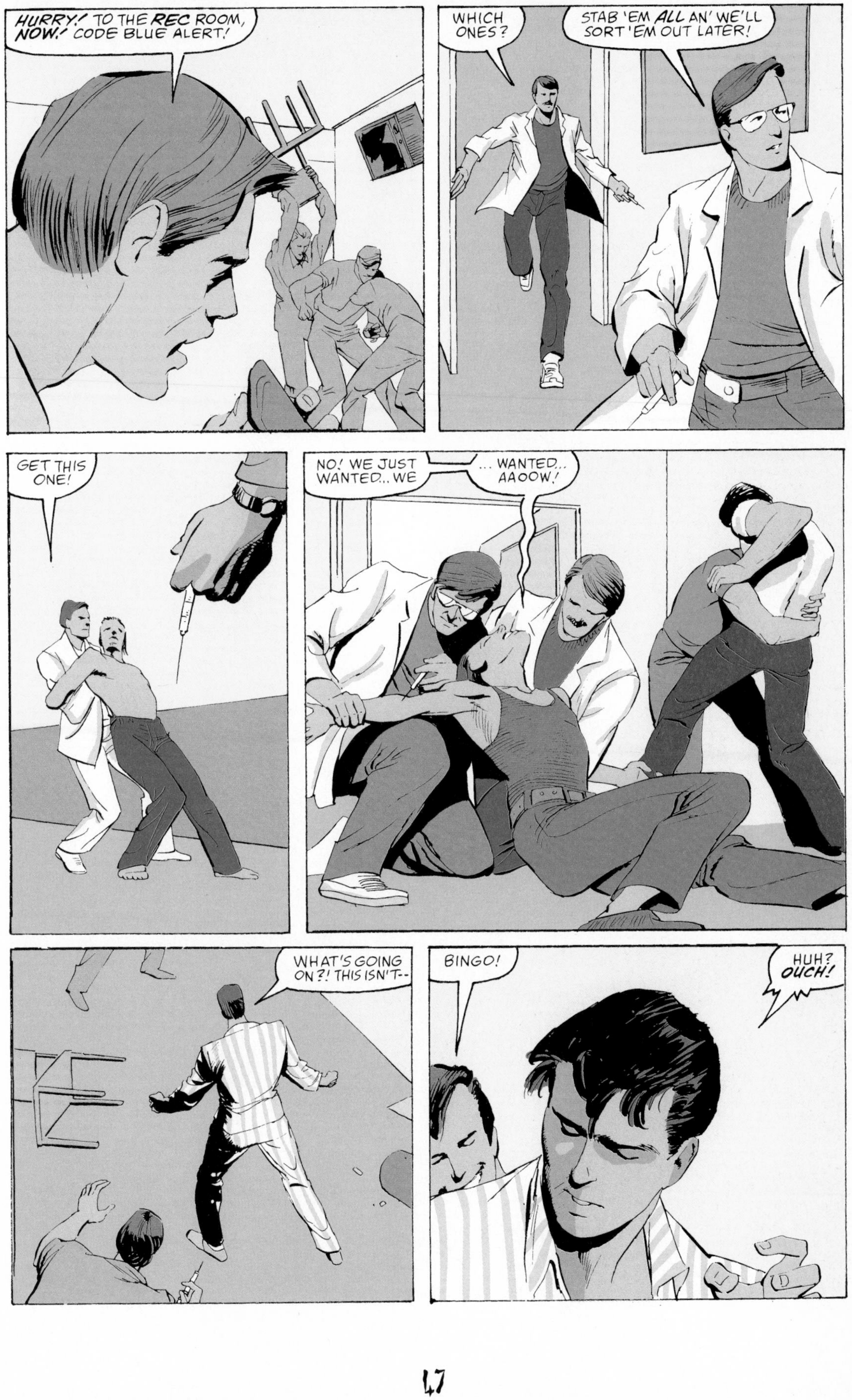
HURRY! TO THE REC ROOM, NOW! CODE BLUE ALERT!
WHICH ONES?
STAB 'EM ALL AN' WE'LL SORT 'EM OUT LATER!
GET THIS ONE!
NO! WE JUST WANTED... WE
... WANTED... AAOOW!
WHAT'S GOING ON?! THIS ISN'T--
BINGO!
HUH? OUCH!

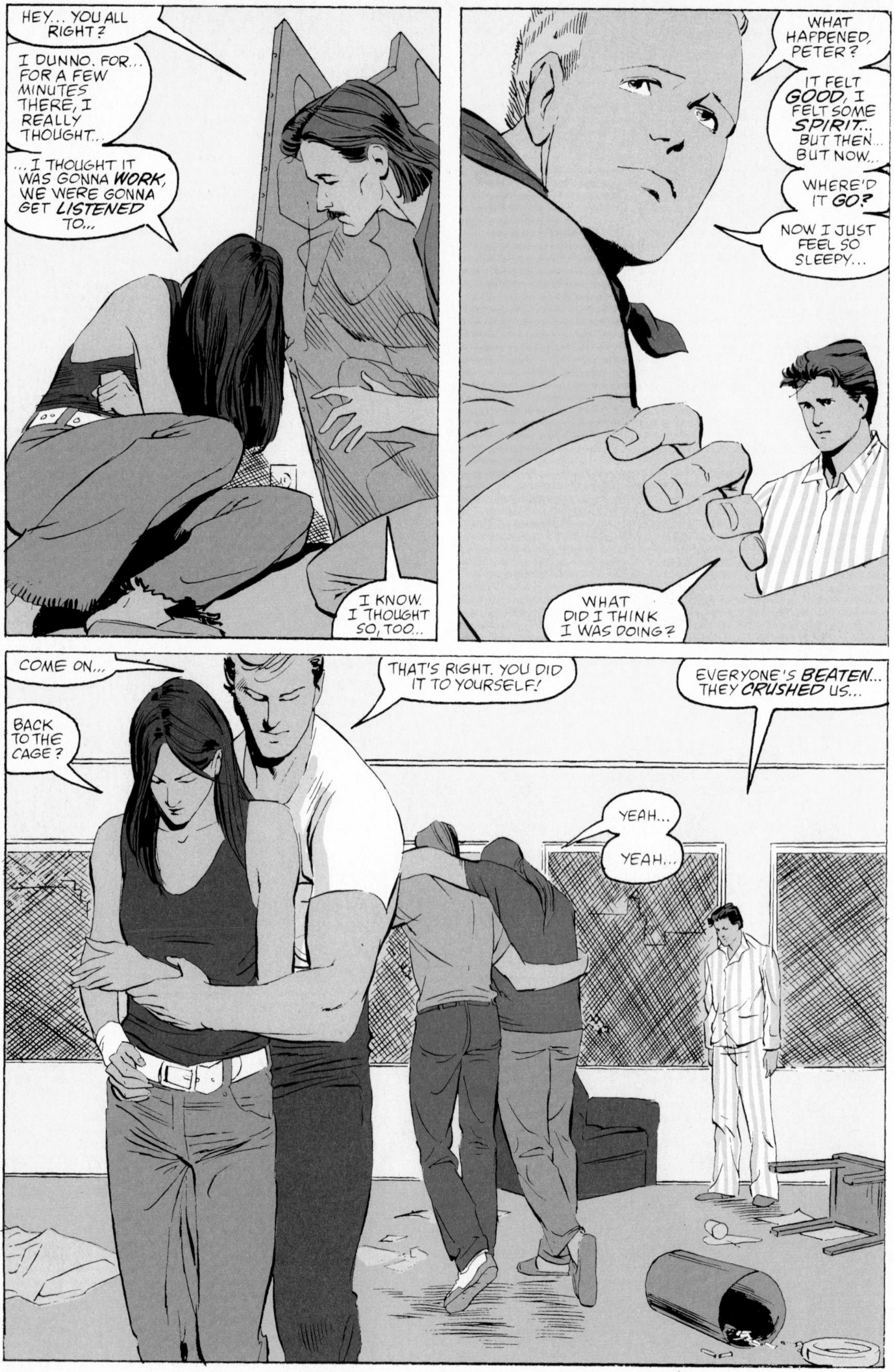
HEY... YOU ALL RIGHT?
I DUNNO. FOR... FOR A FEW MINUTES THERE, I REALLY THOUGHT...
...I THOUGHT IT WAS GONNA **WORK**, WE WERE GONNA GET **LISTENED** TO...
I KNOW. I THOUGHT SO, TOO...
WHAT HAPPENED, PETER?
IT FELT **GOOD**, I FELT SOME **SPIRIT**... BUT THEN... BUT NOW...
WHERE'D IT **GO?**
NOW I JUST FEEL SO SLEEPY...
WHAT DID I THINK I WAS DOING?
COME ON...
BACK TO THE CAGE?
THAT'S RIGHT. YOU DID IT TO YOURSELF!
EVERYONE'S **BEATEN**... THEY **CRUSHED** US...
YEAH...
YEAH...

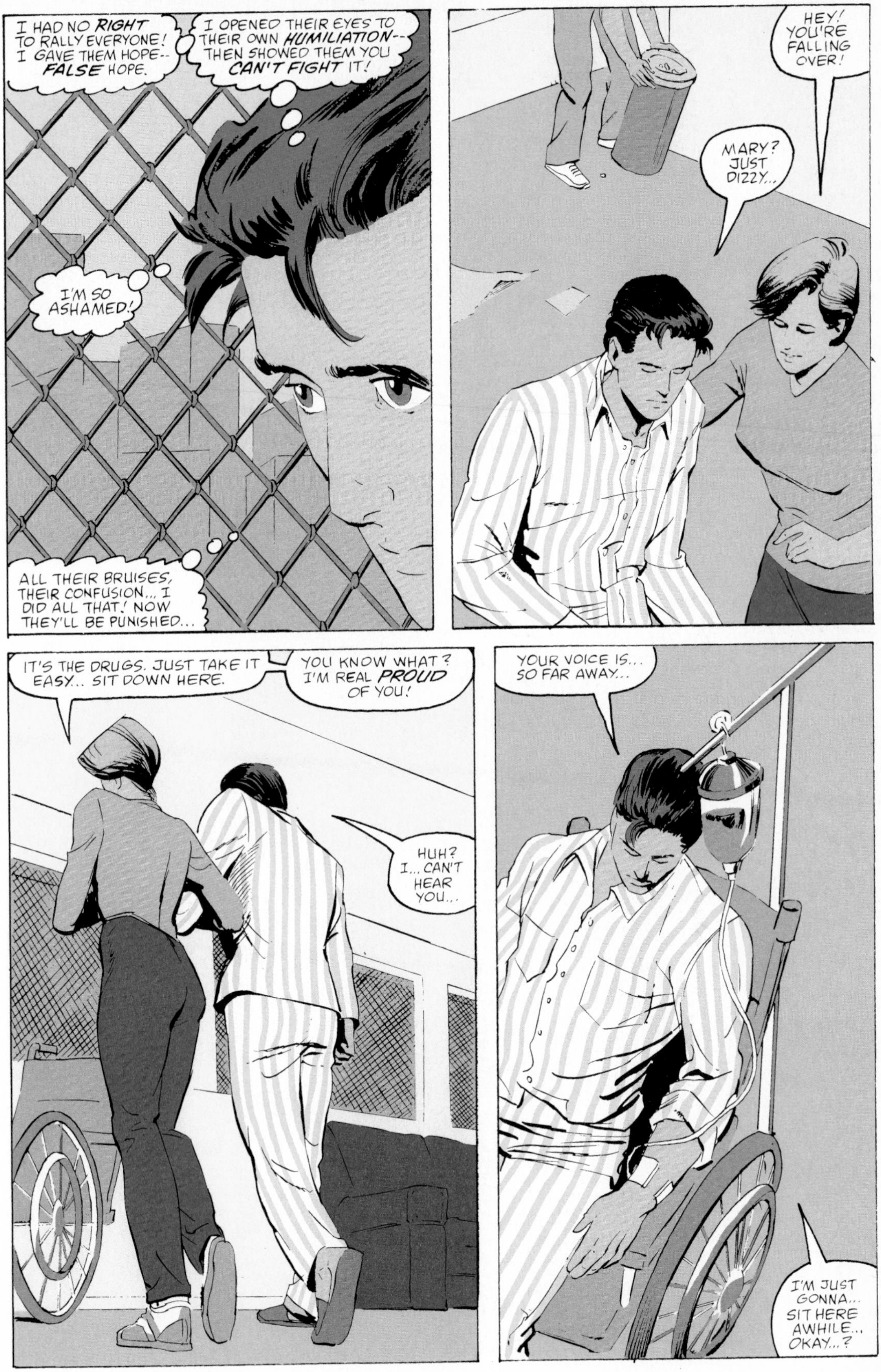
I HAD NO RIGHT TO RALLY EVERYONE! I GAVE THEM HOPE-- FALSE HOPE.
I OPENED THEIR EYES TO THEIR OWN HUMILIATION-- THEN SHOWED THEM YOU CAN'T FIGHT IT!
I'M SO ASHAMED!
ALL THEIR BRUISES, THEIR CONFUSION... I DID ALL THAT! NOW THEY'LL BE PUNISHED...
HEY! YOU'RE FALLING OVER!
MARY? JUST DIZZY...
IT'S THE DRUGS. JUST TAKE IT EASY... SIT DOWN HERE.
YOU KNOW WHAT? I'M REAL PROUD OF YOU!
HUH? I... CAN'T HEAR YOU...
YOUR VOICE IS... SO FAR AWAY...
I'M JUST GONNA... SIT HERE AWHILE... OKAY...?

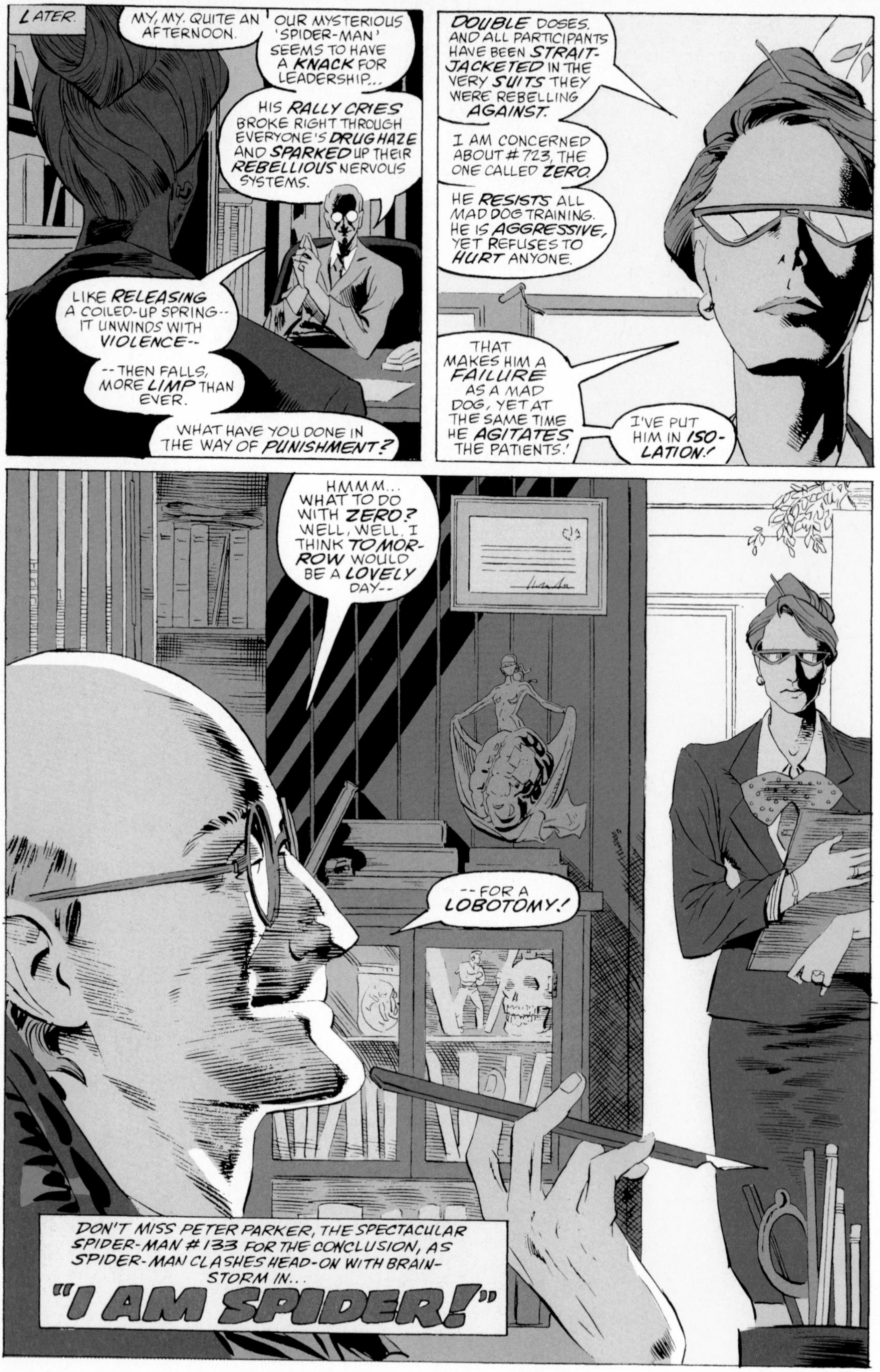
LATER.
MY, MY. QUITE AN AFTERNOON.
OUR MYSTERIOUS 'SPIDER-MAN' SEEMS TO HAVE A KNACK FOR LEADERSHIP...
HIS RALLY CRIES BROKE RIGHT THROUGH EVERYONE'S DRUG HAZE AND SPARKED UP THEIR REBELLIOUS NERVOUS SYSTEMS.
LIKE RELEASING A COILED-UP SPRING-- IT UNWINDS WITH VIOLENCE--
--THEN FALLS, MORE LIMP THAN EVER.
WHAT HAVE YOU DONE IN THE WAY OF PUNISHMENT?
DOUBLE DOSES. AND ALL PARTICIPANTS HAVE BEEN STRAIT-JACKETED IN THE VERY SUITS THEY WERE REBELLING AGAINST.
I AM CONCERNED ABOUT #723, THE ONE CALLED ZERO.
HE RESISTS ALL MAD DOG TRAINING. HE IS AGGRESSIVE, YET REFUSES TO HURT ANYONE.
THAT MAKES HIM A FAILURE AS A MAD DOG, YET AT THE SAME TIME HE AGITATES THE PATIENTS.'
I'VE PUT HIM IN ISO-LATION!
HMMM... WHAT TO DO WITH ZERO? WELL, WELL. I THINK TOMOR-ROW WOULD BE A LOVELY DAY--
--FOR A LOBOTOMY!
DON'T MISS PETER PARKER, THE SPECTACULAR SPIDER-MAN #133 FOR THE CONCLUSION, AS SPIDER-MAN CLASHES HEAD-ON WITH BRAIN-STORM IN...
"I AM SPIDER!"

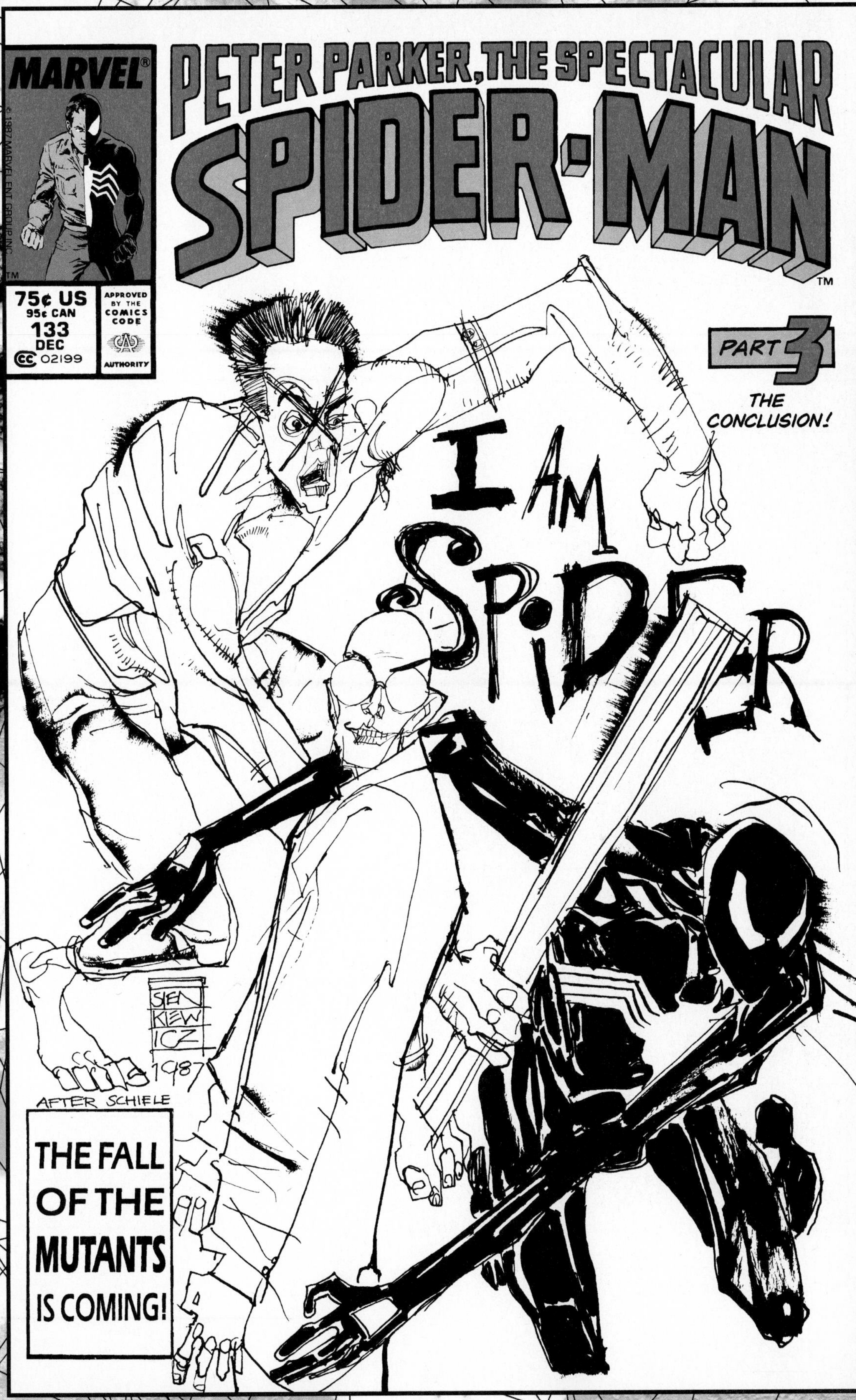
MARVEL®
© 1987 MARVEL ENT. GROUP INC.
PETER PARKER, THE SPECTACULAR
SPIDER-MAN
TM
75¢ US
95¢ CAN
133
DEC
CC 02199
APPROVED BY THE COMICS CODE AUTHORITY
PART 3
THE CONCLUSION!
I AM SPIDER
SIEN KIEW ICZ 1987
AFTER SCHIELE
THE FALL OF THE MUTANTS IS COMING!

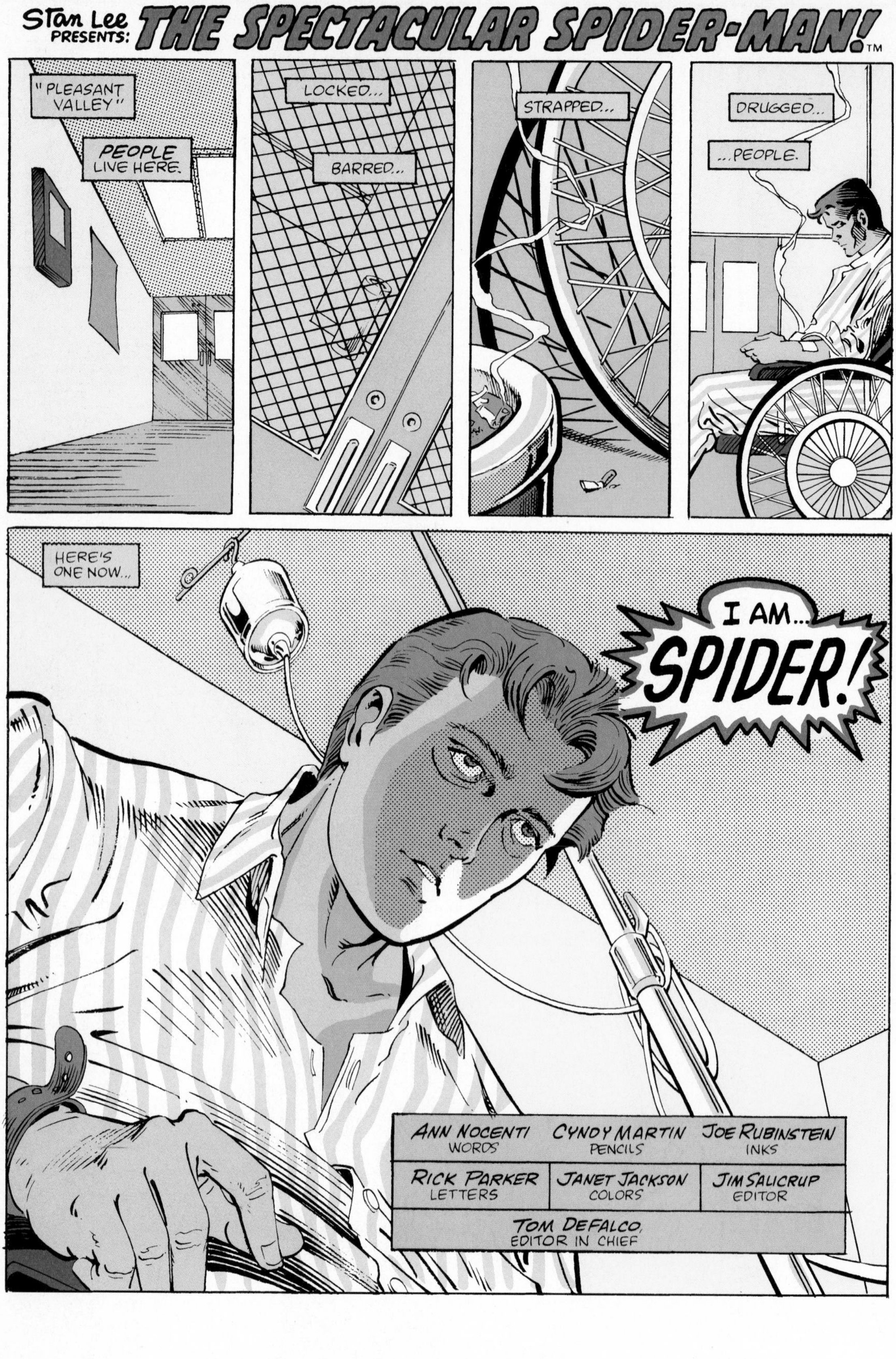
Stan Lee PRESENTS: THE SPECTACULAR SPIDER-MAN!™
"PLEASANT VALLEY"
PEOPLE LIVE HERE.
LOCKED...
BARRED...
STRAPPED...
DRUGGED...
...PEOPLE.
HERE'S ONE NOW...
I AM... SPIDER!
ANN NOCENTI WORDS
CYNDY MARTIN PENCILS
JOE RUBINSTEIN INKS
RICK PARKER LETTERS
JANET JACKSON COLORS
JIM SALICRUP EDITOR
TOM DEFALCO, EDITOR IN CHIEF

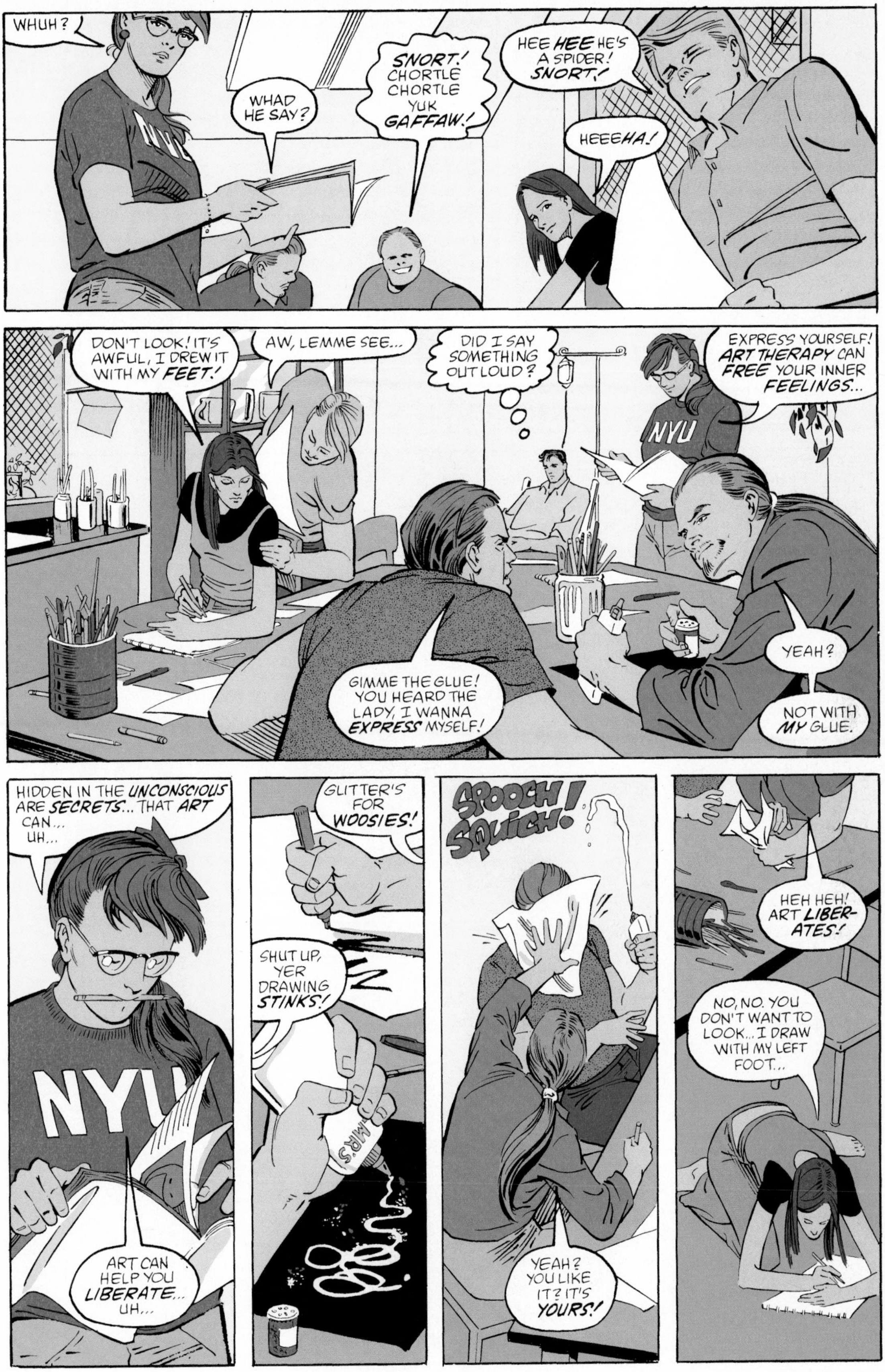
WHUH?
WHAD HE SAY?
SNORT! CHORTLE CHORTLE YUK GAFFAW!
HEE HEE HE'S A SPIDER! SNORT!
HEEEHA!
DON'T LOOK! IT'S AWFUL, I DREW IT WITH MY FEET!
AW, LEMME SEE...
DID I SAY SOMETHING OUT LOUD?
EXPRESS YOURSELF! ART THERAPY CAN FREE YOUR INNER FEELINGS...
GIMME THE GLUE! YOU HEARD THE LADY, I WANNA EXPRESS MYSELF!
YEAH?
NOT WITH MY GLUE.
HIDDEN IN THE UNCONSCIOUS ARE SECRETS... THAT ART CAN... UH...
ART CAN HELP YOU LIBERATE... UH...
GLITTER'S FOR WOOSIES!
SHUT UP, YER DRAWING STINKS!
SPOOCH! SQUICH!
YEAH? YOU LIKE IT? IT'S YOURS!
HEH HEH! ART LIBERATES!
NO, NO. YOU DON'T WANT TO LOOK... I DRAW WITH MY LEFT FOOT...

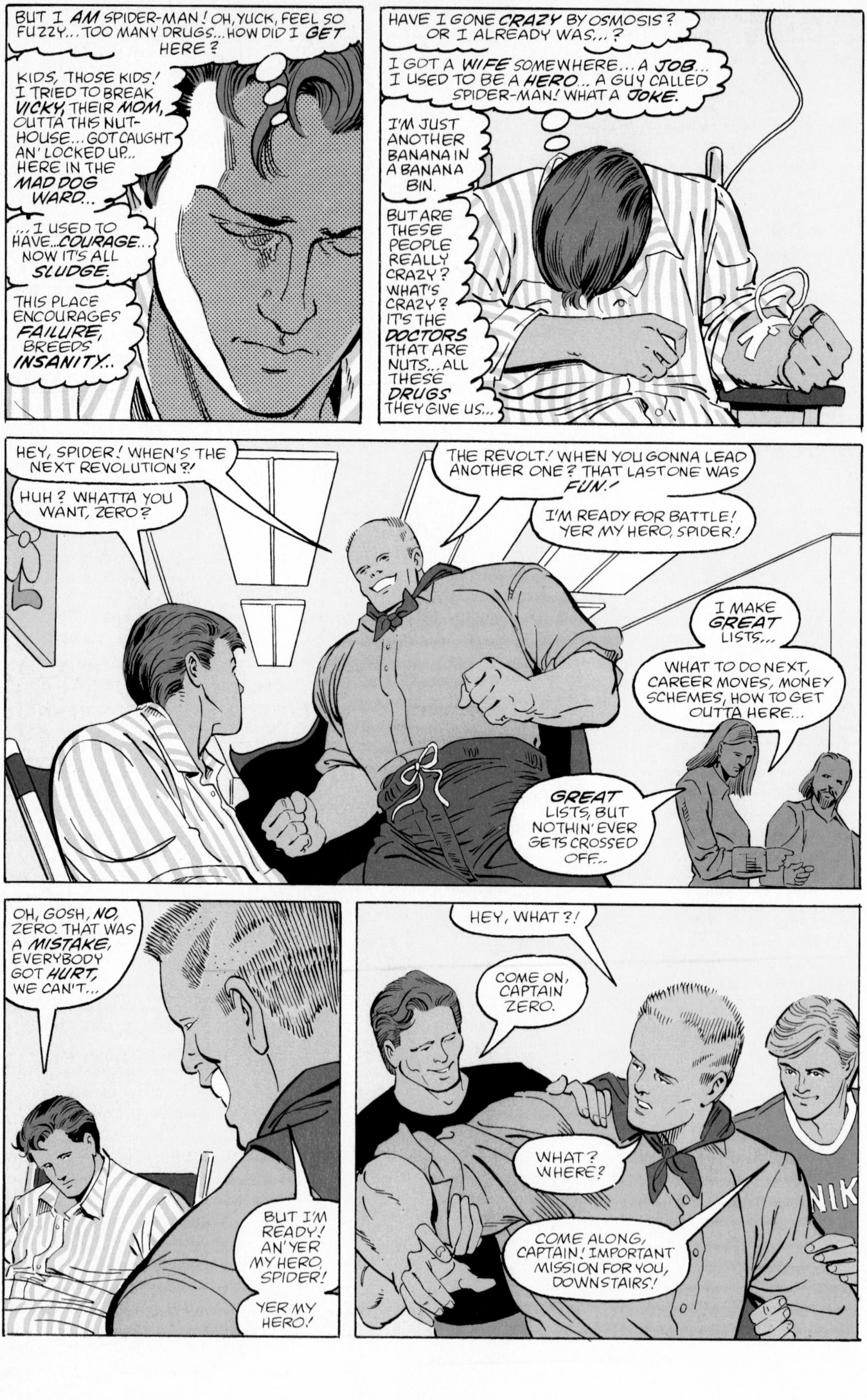

BUT I AM SPIDER-MAN! OH, YUCK, FEEL SO FUZZY... TOO MANY DRUGS... HOW DID I GET HERE?
KIDS, THOSE KIDS! I TRIED TO BREAK VICKY, THEIR MOM, OUTTA THIS NUT-HOUSE... GOT CAUGHT AN' LOCKED UP... HERE IN THE MAD DOG WARD...
... I USED TO HAVE... COURAGE... NOW IT'S ALL SLUDGE.
THIS PLACE ENCOURAGES FAILURE, BREEDS INSANITY...
HAVE I GONE CRAZY BY OSMOSIS? OR I ALREADY WAS...?
I GOT A WIFE SOMEWHERE... A JOB... I USED TO BE A HERO... A GUY CALLED SPIDER-MAN! WHAT A JOKE.
I'M JUST ANOTHER BANANA IN A BANANA BIN.
BUT ARE THESE PEOPLE REALLY CRAZY? WHAT'S CRAZY? IT'S THE DOCTORS THAT ARE NUTS... ALL THESE DRUGS THEY GIVE US...
HEY, SPIDER! WHEN'S THE NEXT REVOLUTION?!
HUH? WHATTA YOU WANT, ZERO?
THE REVOLT! WHEN YOU GONNA LEAD ANOTHER ONE? THAT LAST ONE WAS FUN!
I'M READY FOR BATTLE! YER MY HERO, SPIDER!
I MAKE GREAT LISTS...
WHAT TO DO NEXT, CAREER MOVES, MONEY SCHEMES, HOW TO GET OUTTA HERE...
GREAT LISTS, BUT NOTHIN' EVER GETS CROSSED OFF...
OH, GOSH, NO, ZERO. THAT WAS A MISTAKE, EVERYBODY GOT HURT, WE CAN'T...
BUT I'M READY! AN' YER MY HERO, SPIDER!
YER MY HERO!
HEY, WHAT?!
COME ON, CAPTAIN ZERO.
WHAT? WHERE?
COME ALONG, CAPTAIN! IMPORTANT MISSION FOR YOU, DOWNSTAIRS!
NIK

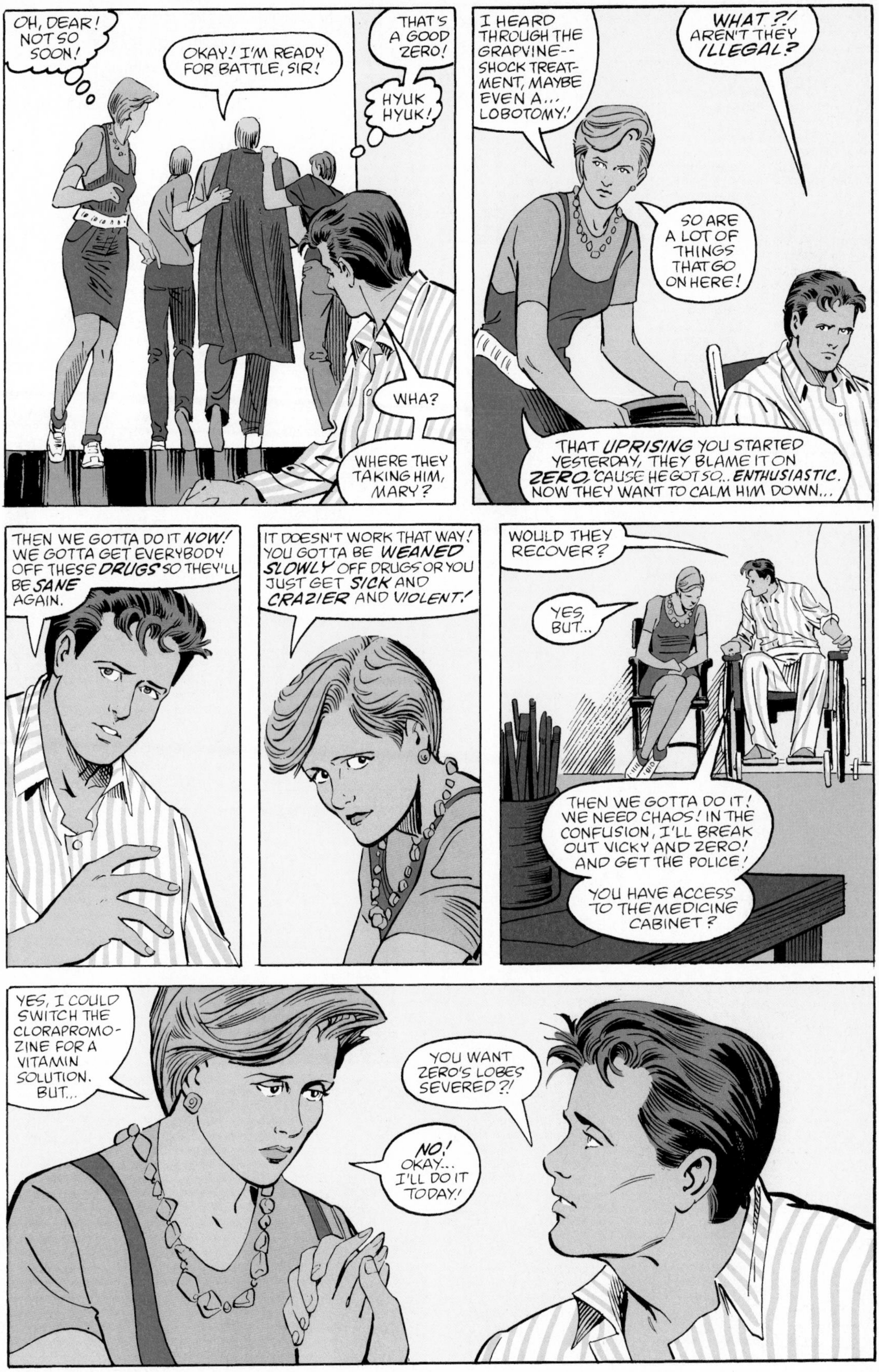
OH, DEAR! NOT SO SOON!
OKAY! I'M READY FOR BATTLE, SIR!
THAT'S A GOOD ZERO!
HYUK HYUK!
WHA?
WHERE THEY TAKING HIM, MARY?
I HEARD THROUGH THE GRAPVINE-- SHOCK TREATMENT, MAYBE EVEN A... LOBOTOMY!
WHAT?! AREN'T THEY ILLEGAL?
SO ARE A LOT OF THINGS THAT GO ON HERE!
THAT UPRISING YOU STARTED YESTERDAY, THEY BLAME IT ON ZERO. 'CAUSE HE GOT SO... ENTHUSIASTIC. NOW THEY WANT TO CALM HIM DOWN...
THEN WE GOTTA DO IT NOW! WE GOTTA GET EVERYBODY OFF THESE DRUGS SO THEY'LL BE SANE AGAIN.
IT DOESN'T WORK THAT WAY! YOU GOTTA BE WEANED SLOWLY OFF DRUGS OR YOU JUST GET SICK AND CRAZIER AND VIOLENT!
WOULD THEY RECOVER?
YES, BUT...
THEN WE GOTTA DO IT! WE NEED CHAOS! IN THE CONFUSION, I'LL BREAK OUT VICKY AND ZERO! AND GET THE POLICE!
YOU HAVE ACCESS TO THE MEDICINE CABINET?
YES, I COULD SWITCH THE CLORAPROMOZINE FOR A VITAMIN SOLUTION. BUT...
YOU WANT ZERO'S LOBES SEVERED?!
NO! OKAY... I'LL DO IT TODAY!

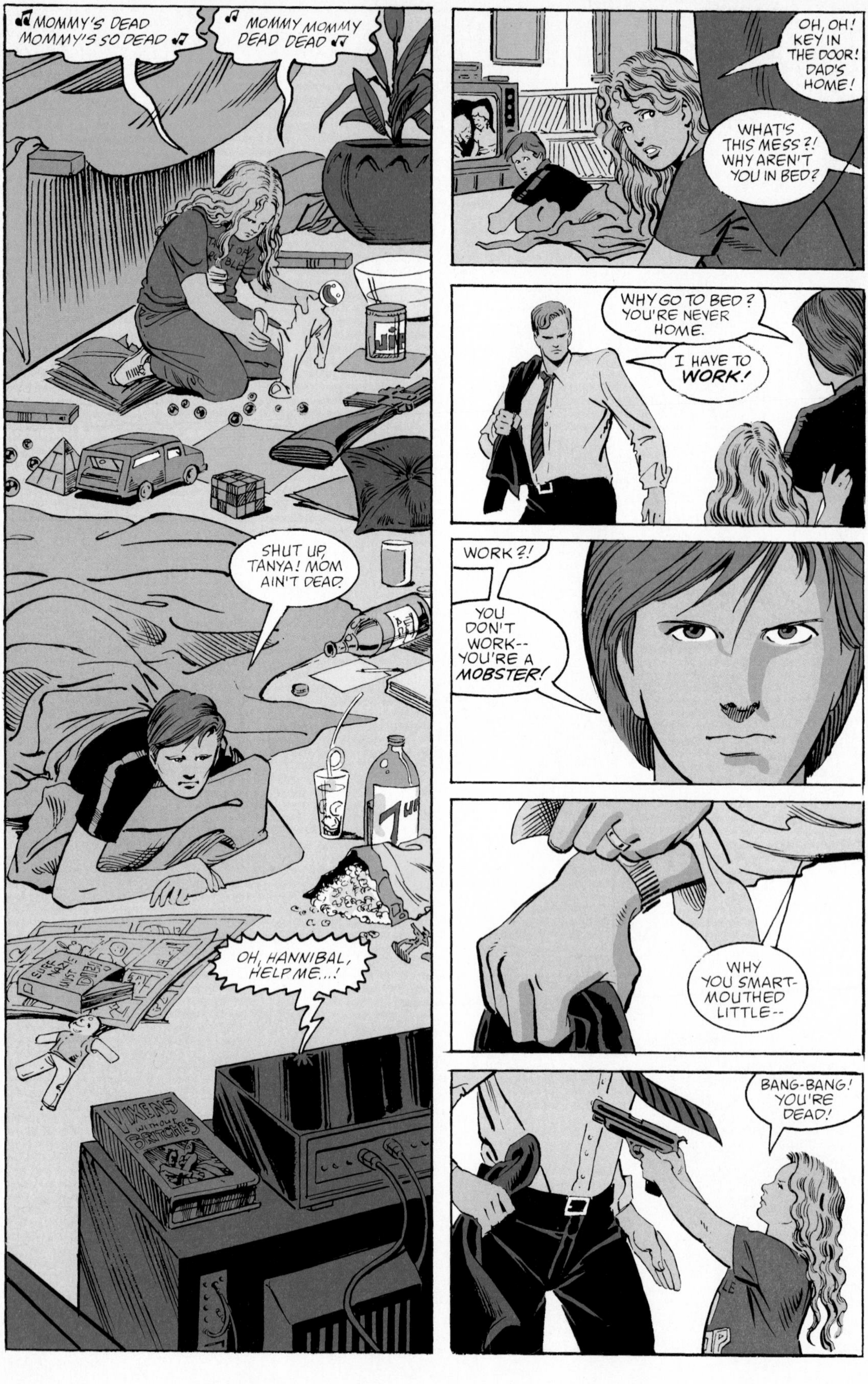
MOMMY'S DEAD MOMMY'S SO DEAD
MOMMY MOMMY DEAD DEAD
SHUT UP, TANYA! MOM AIN'T DEAD.
OH, HANNIBAL, HELP ME...!
VIXENS WITHOUT BRITCHES
OH, OH! KEY IN THE DOOR! DAD'S HOME!
WHAT'S THIS MESS?! WHY AREN'T YOU IN BED?
WHY GO TO BED? YOU'RE NEVER HOME.
I HAVE TO WORK!
WORK?!
YOU DON'T WORK-- YOU'RE A MOBSTER!
WHY YOU SMART-MOUTHED LITTLE--
BANG-BANG! YOU'RE DEAD!

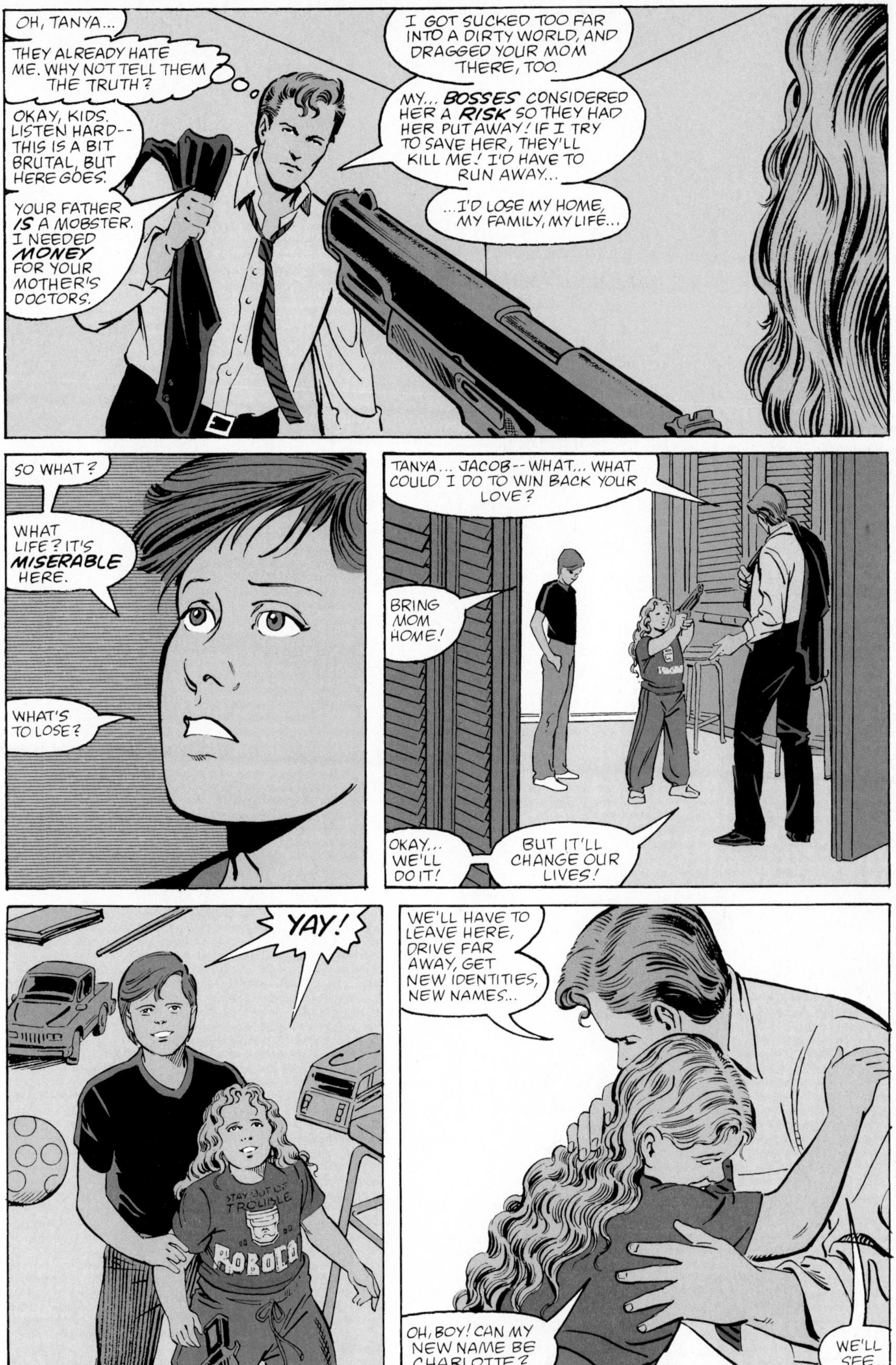
OH, TANYA...
THEY ALREADY HATE ME. WHY NOT TELL THEM THE TRUTH?
OKAY, KIDS. LISTEN HARD-- THIS IS A BIT BRUTAL, BUT HERE GOES.
YOUR FATHER IS A MOBSTER. I NEEDED MONEY FOR YOUR MOTHER'S DOCTORS.
I GOT SUCKED TOO FAR INTO A DIRTY WORLD, AND DRAGGED YOUR MOM THERE, TOO.
MY... BOSSES CONSIDERED HER A RISK SO THEY HAD HER PUT AWAY! IF I TRY TO SAVE HER, THEY'LL KILL ME! I'D HAVE TO RUN AWAY...
...I'D LOSE MY HOME, MY FAMILY, MY LIFE...
SO WHAT?
WHAT LIFE? IT'S MISERABLE HERE.
WHAT'S TO LOSE?
TANYA... JACOB-- WHAT... WHAT COULD I DO TO WIN BACK YOUR LOVE?
BRING MOM HOME!
OKAY... WE'LL DO IT!
BUT IT'LL CHANGE OUR LIVES!
YAY!
STAY OUT OF TROUBLE
ROBOCO
WE'LL HAVE TO LEAVE HERE, DRIVE FAR AWAY, GET NEW IDENTITIES, NEW NAMES...
OH, BOY! CAN MY NEW NAME BE CHARLOTTE?
WE'LL SEE...

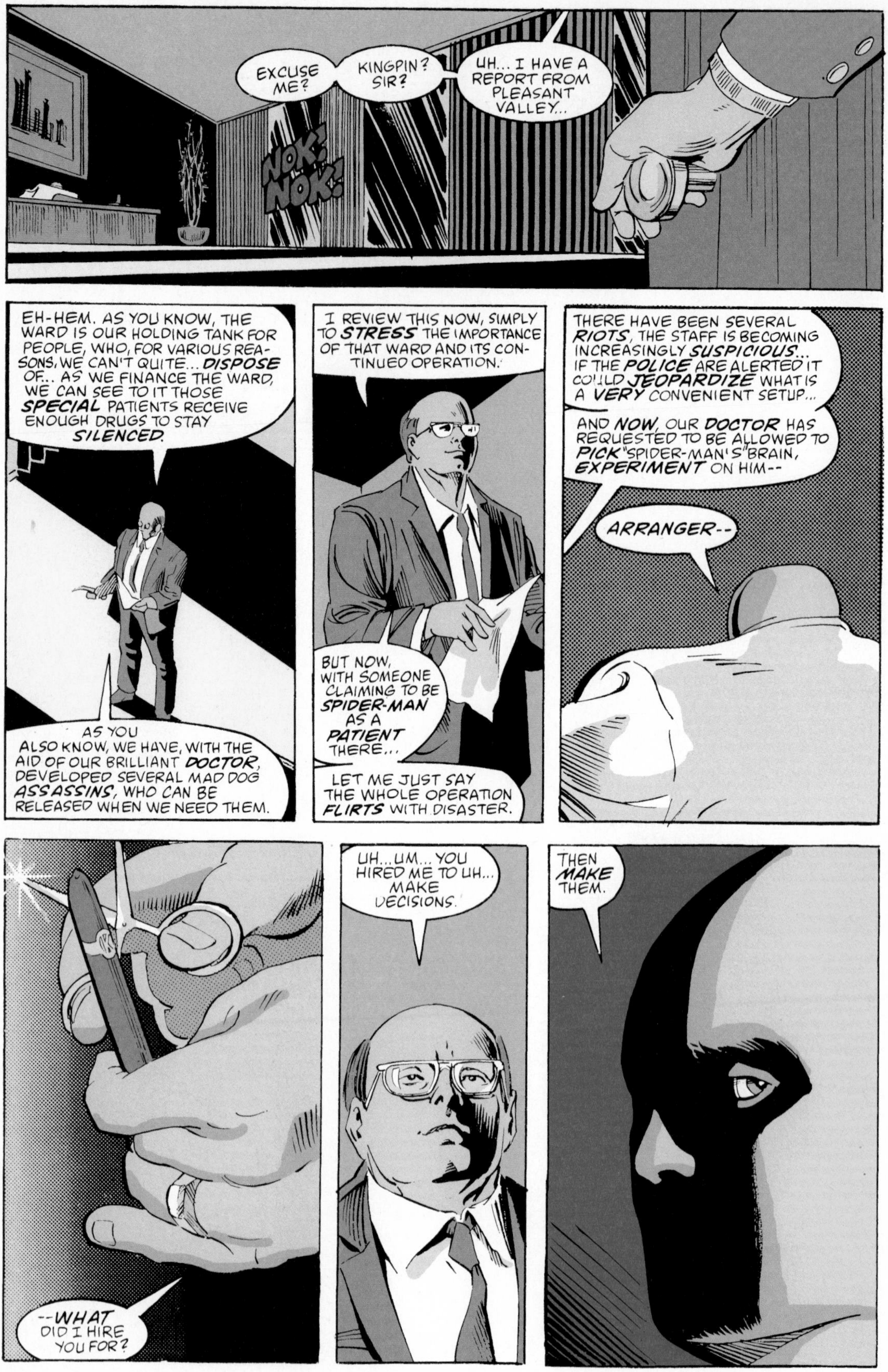
EXCUSE ME?
KINGPIN? SIR?
UH... I HAVE A REPORT FROM PLEASANT VALLEY...
NOK! NOK!
EH-HEM. AS YOU KNOW, THE WARD IS OUR HOLDING TANK FOR PEOPLE, WHO, FOR VARIOUS REASONS, WE CAN'T QUITE... DISPOSE OF... AS WE FINANCE THE WARD, WE CAN SEE TO IT THOSE SPECIAL PATIENTS RECEIVE ENOUGH DRUGS TO STAY SILENCED.
AS YOU ALSO KNOW, WE HAVE, WITH THE AID OF OUR BRILLIANT DOCTOR, DEVELOPED SEVERAL MAD DOG ASSASSINS, WHO CAN BE RELEASED WHEN WE NEED THEM.
I REVIEW THIS NOW, SIMPLY TO STRESS THE IMPORTANCE OF THAT WARD AND ITS CONTINUED OPERATION.
BUT NOW, WITH SOMEONE CLAIMING TO BE SPIDER-MAN AS A PATIENT THERE...
LET ME JUST SAY THE WHOLE OPERATION FLIRTS WITH DISASTER.
THERE HAVE BEEN SEVERAL RIOTS, THE STAFF IS BECOMING INCREASINGLY SUSPICIOUS... IF THE POLICE ARE ALERTED IT COULD JEOPARDIZE WHAT IS A VERY CONVENIENT SETUP...
AND NOW, OUR DOCTOR HAS REQUESTED TO BE ALLOWED TO PICK "SPIDER-MAN'S" BRAIN, EXPERIMENT ON HIM--
ARRANGER--
--WHAT DID I HIRE YOU FOR?
UH...UM... YOU HIRED ME TO UH... MAKE DECISIONS.
THEN MAKE THEM.

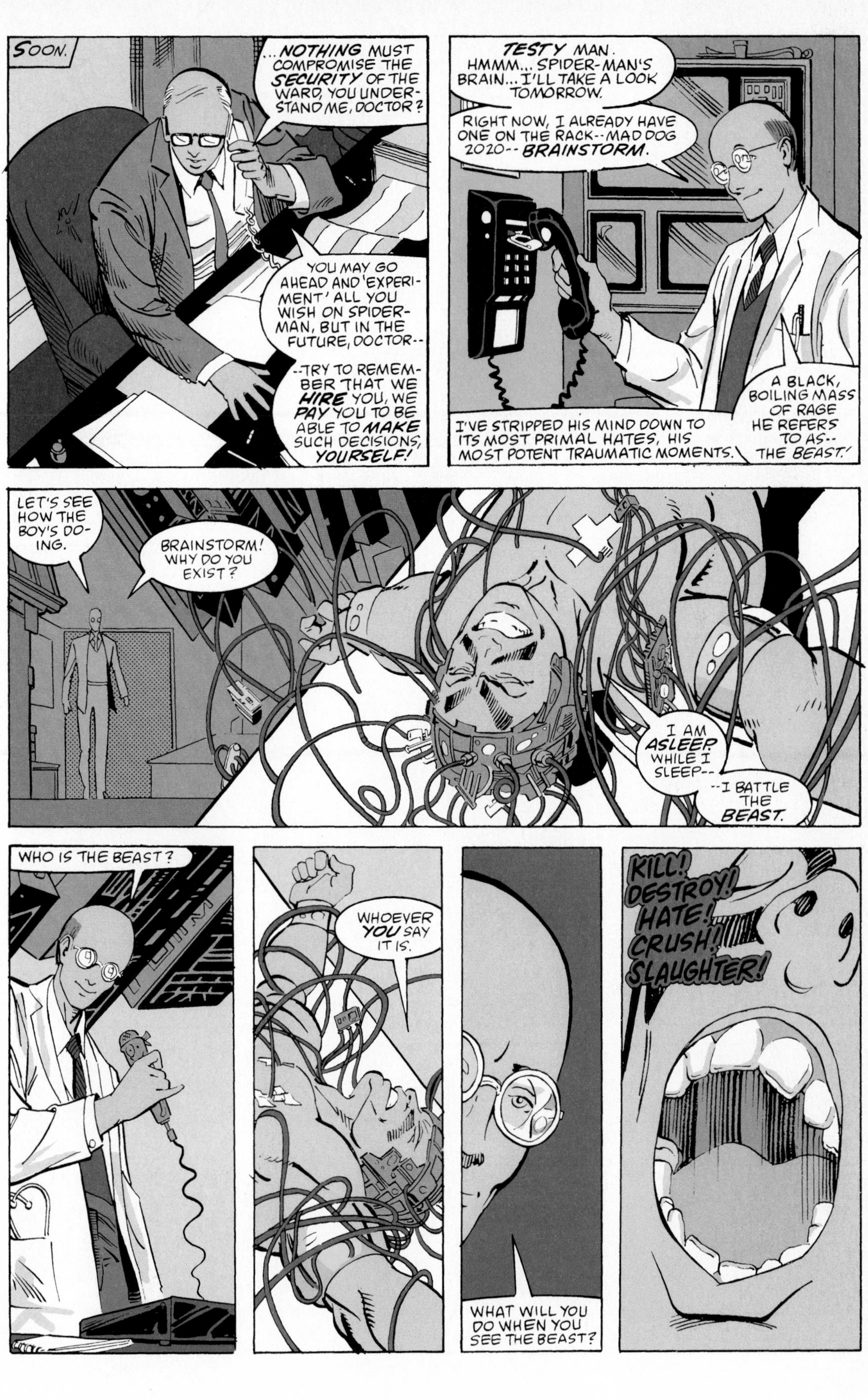
SOON.
...NOTHING MUST COMPROMISE THE SECURITY OF THE WARD, YOU UNDERSTAND ME, DOCTOR?
YOU MAY GO AHEAD AND 'EXPERIMENT' ALL YOU WISH ON SPIDER-MAN, BUT IN THE FUTURE, DOCTOR--
--TRY TO REMEMBER THAT WE HIRE YOU, WE PAY YOU TO BE ABLE TO MAKE SUCH DECISIONS, YOURSELF!
TESTY MAN. HMMM... SPIDER-MAN'S BRAIN... I'LL TAKE A LOOK TOMORROW.
RIGHT NOW, I ALREADY HAVE ONE ON THE RACK--MAD DOG 2020--BRAINSTORM.
I'VE STRIPPED HIS MIND DOWN TO ITS MOST PRIMAL HATES, HIS MOST POTENT TRAUMATIC MOMENTS.
A BLACK, BOILING MASS OF RAGE HE REFERS TO AS--THE BEAST.'
LET'S SEE HOW THE BOY'S DOING.
BRAINSTORM! WHY DO YOU EXIST?
I AM ASLEEP. WHILE I SLEEP--
--I BATTLE THE BEAST.
WHO IS THE BEAST?
WHOEVER YOU SAY IT IS.
WHAT WILL YOU DO WHEN YOU SEE THE BEAST?
KILL! DESTROY! HATE! CRUSH! SLAUGHTER!

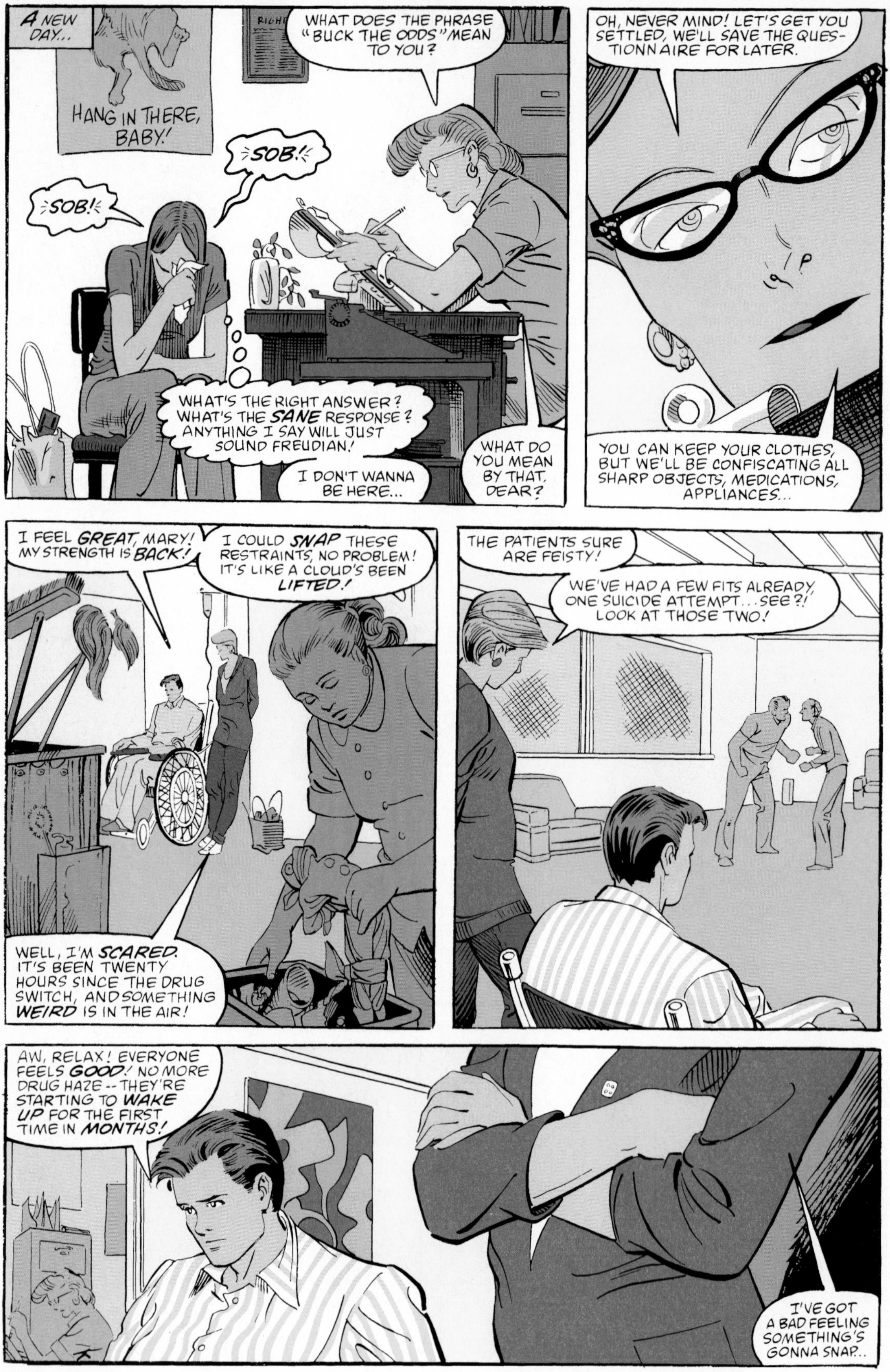
A NEW DAY...
HANG IN THERE, BABY!
WHAT DOES THE PHRASE "BUCK THE ODDS" MEAN TO YOU?
SOB!
SOB!
WHAT'S THE RIGHT ANSWER? WHAT'S THE SANE RESPONSE? ANYTHING I SAY WILL JUST SOUND FREUDIAN!
I DON'T WANNA BE HERE...
WHAT DO YOU MEAN BY THAT, DEAR?
OH, NEVER MIND! LET'S GET YOU SETTLED, WE'LL SAVE THE QUESTIONNAIRE FOR LATER.
YOU CAN KEEP YOUR CLOTHES, BUT WE'LL BE CONFISCATING ALL SHARP OBJECTS, MEDICATIONS, APPLIANCES...
I FEEL GREAT, MARY! MY STRENGTH IS BACK!
I COULD SNAP THESE RESTRAINTS, NO PROBLEM! IT'S LIKE A CLOUD'S BEEN LIFTED!
WELL, I'M SCARED. IT'S BEEN TWENTY HOURS SINCE THE DRUG SWITCH, AND SOMETHING WEIRD IS IN THE AIR!
THE PATIENTS SURE ARE FEISTY!
WE'VE HAD A FEW FITS ALREADY, ONE SUICIDE ATTEMPT... SEE?! LOOK AT THOSE TWO!
AW, RELAX! EVERYONE FEELS GOOD! NO MORE DRUG HAZE -- THEY'RE STARTING TO WAKE UP FOR THE FIRST TIME IN MONTHS!
I'VE GOT A BAD FEELING SOMETHING'S GONNA SNAP...

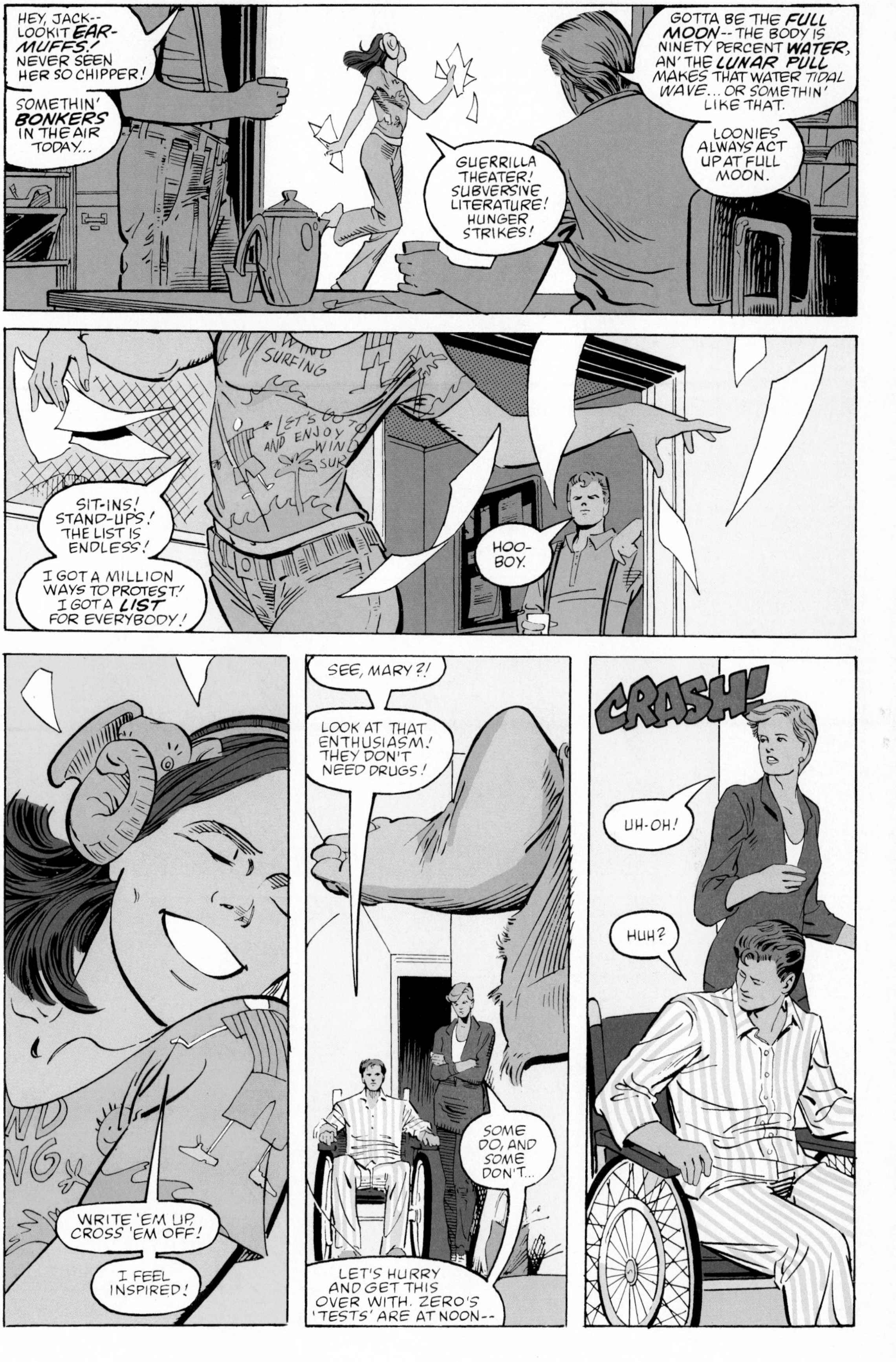
HEY, JACK-- LOOKIT EAR-MUFFS! NEVER SEEN HER SO CHIPPER!
SOMETHIN' BONKERS IN THE AIR TODAY...
GOTTA BE THE FULL MOON-- THE BODY IS NINETY PERCENT WATER, AN' THE LUNAR PULL MAKES THAT WATER TIDAL WAVE... OR SOMETHIN' LIKE THAT.
LOONIES ALWAYS ACT UP AT FULL MOON.
GUERRILLA THEATER! SUBVERSIVE LITERATURE! HUNGER STRIKES!
SIT-INS! STAND-UPS! THE LIST IS ENDLESS!
I GOT A MILLION WAYS TO PROTEST! I GOT A LIST FOR EVERYBODY!
HOO-BOY.
WRITE 'EM UP, CROSS 'EM OFF!
I FEEL INSPIRED!
SEE, MARY?!
LOOK AT THAT ENTHUSIASM! THEY DON'T NEED DRUGS!
SOME DO, AND SOME DON'T...
LET'S HURRY AND GET THIS OVER WITH. ZERO'S 'TESTS' ARE AT NOON--
CRASH!
UH-OH!
HUH?

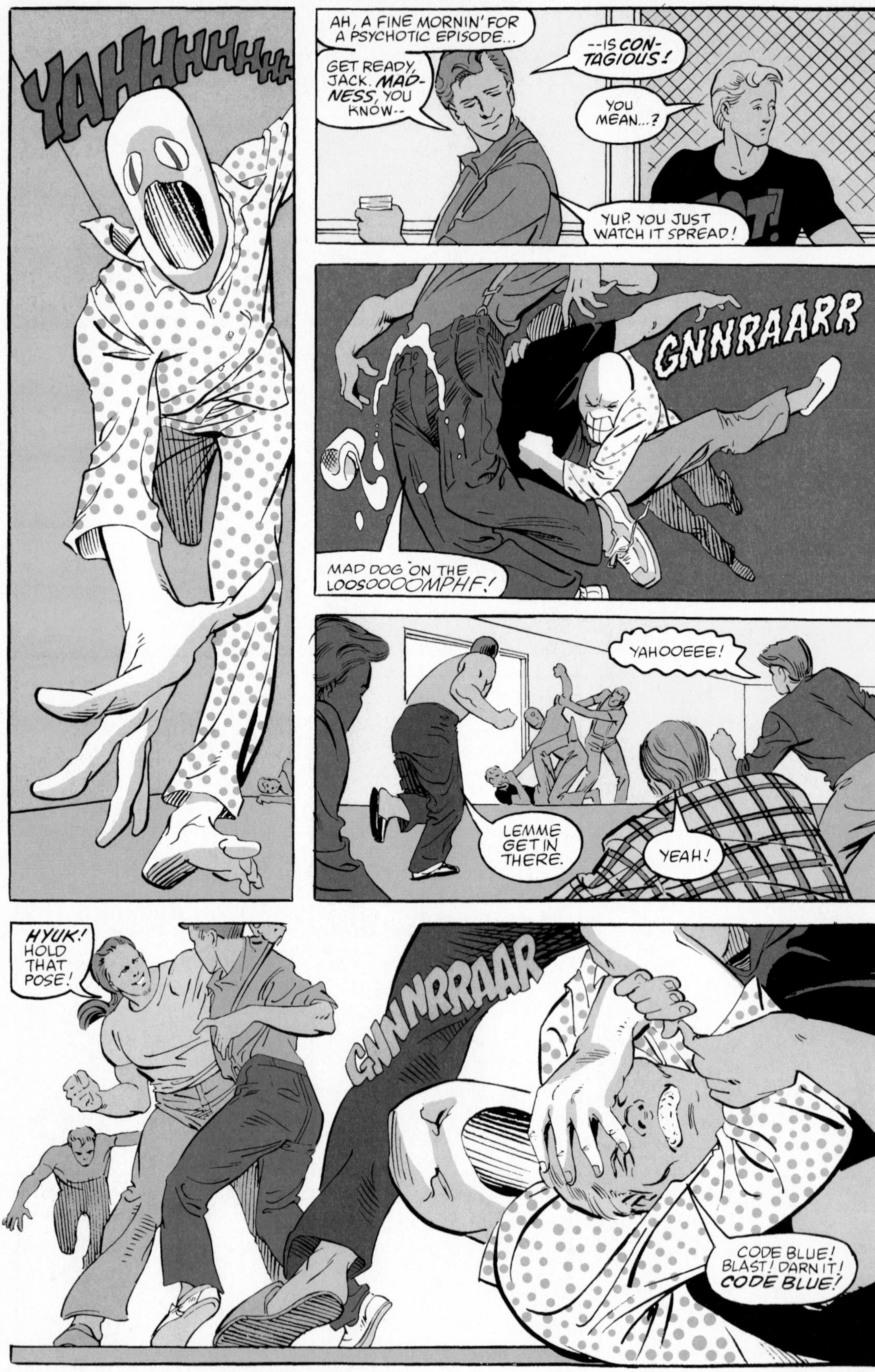
YAHHHHHhhh
AH, A FINE MORNIN' FOR A PSYCHOTIC EPISODE...
GET READY, JACK. MADNESS, YOU KNOW--
--IS CONTAGIOUS!
YOU MEAN...?
YUP. YOU JUST WATCH IT SPREAD!
GNNRAARR
MAD DOG ON THE LOOSOOOOMPHF!
YAHOOEEE!
LEMME GET IN THERE.
YEAH!
HYUK! HOLD THAT POSE!
GNNRRAAR
CODE BLUE! BLAST! DARN IT! CODE BLUE!

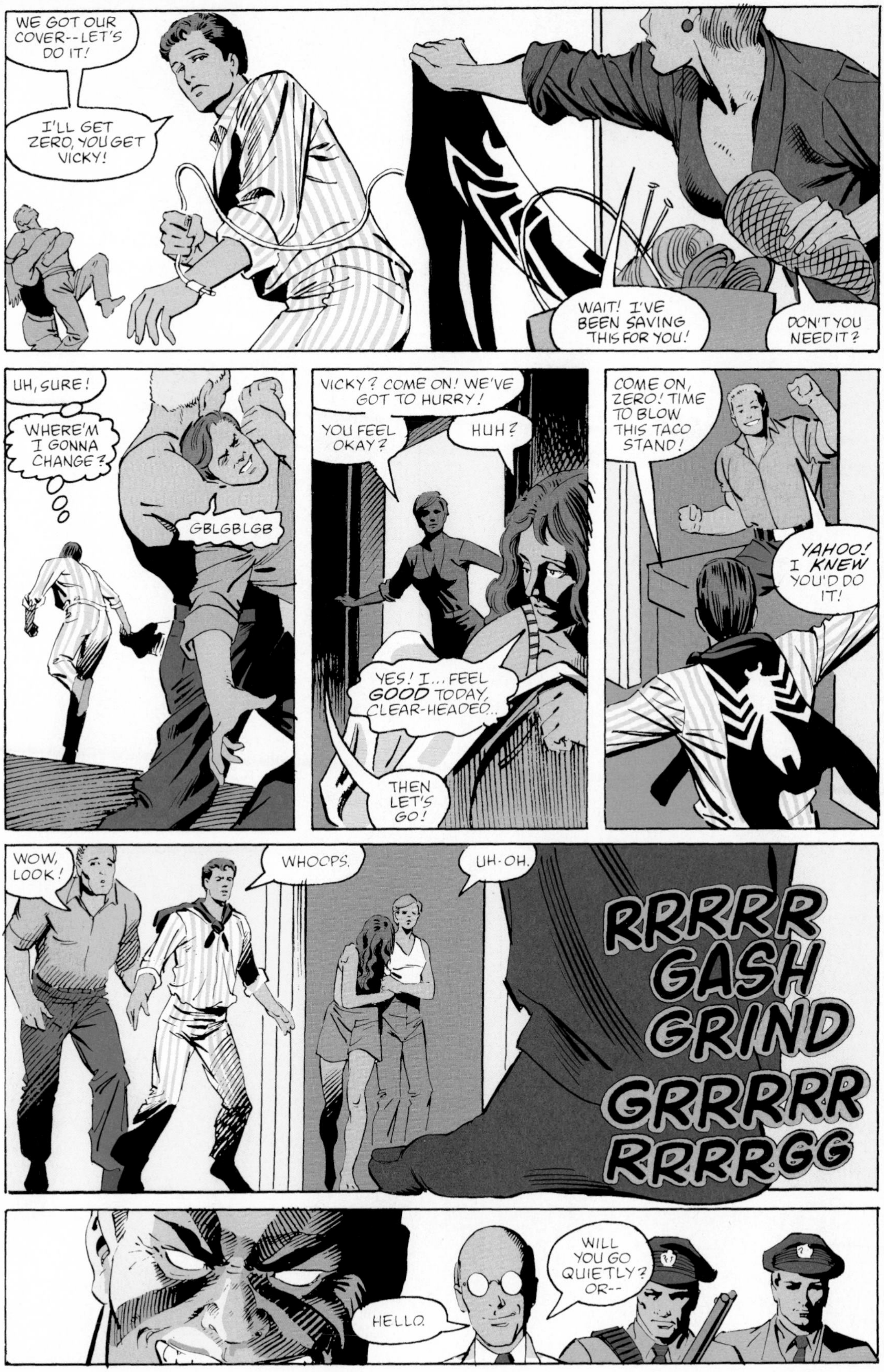
WE GOT OUR COVER--LET'S DO IT!
I'LL GET ZERO, YOU GET VICKY!
WAIT! I'VE BEEN SAVING THIS FOR YOU!
DON'T YOU NEED IT?
UH, SURE!
WHERE'M I GONNA CHANGE?
GBLGBLGB
VICKY? COME ON! WE'VE GOT TO HURRY!
YOU FEEL OKAY?
HUH?
YES! I... FEEL GOOD TODAY, CLEAR-HEADED...
THEN LET'S GO!
COME ON, ZERO! TIME TO BLOW THIS TACO STAND!
YAHOO! I KNEW YOU'D DO IT!
WOW, LOOK!
WHOOPS.
UH-OH.
RRRRR GASH GRIND GRRRRR RRRRGG
WILL YOU GO QUIETLY? OR--
HELLO.

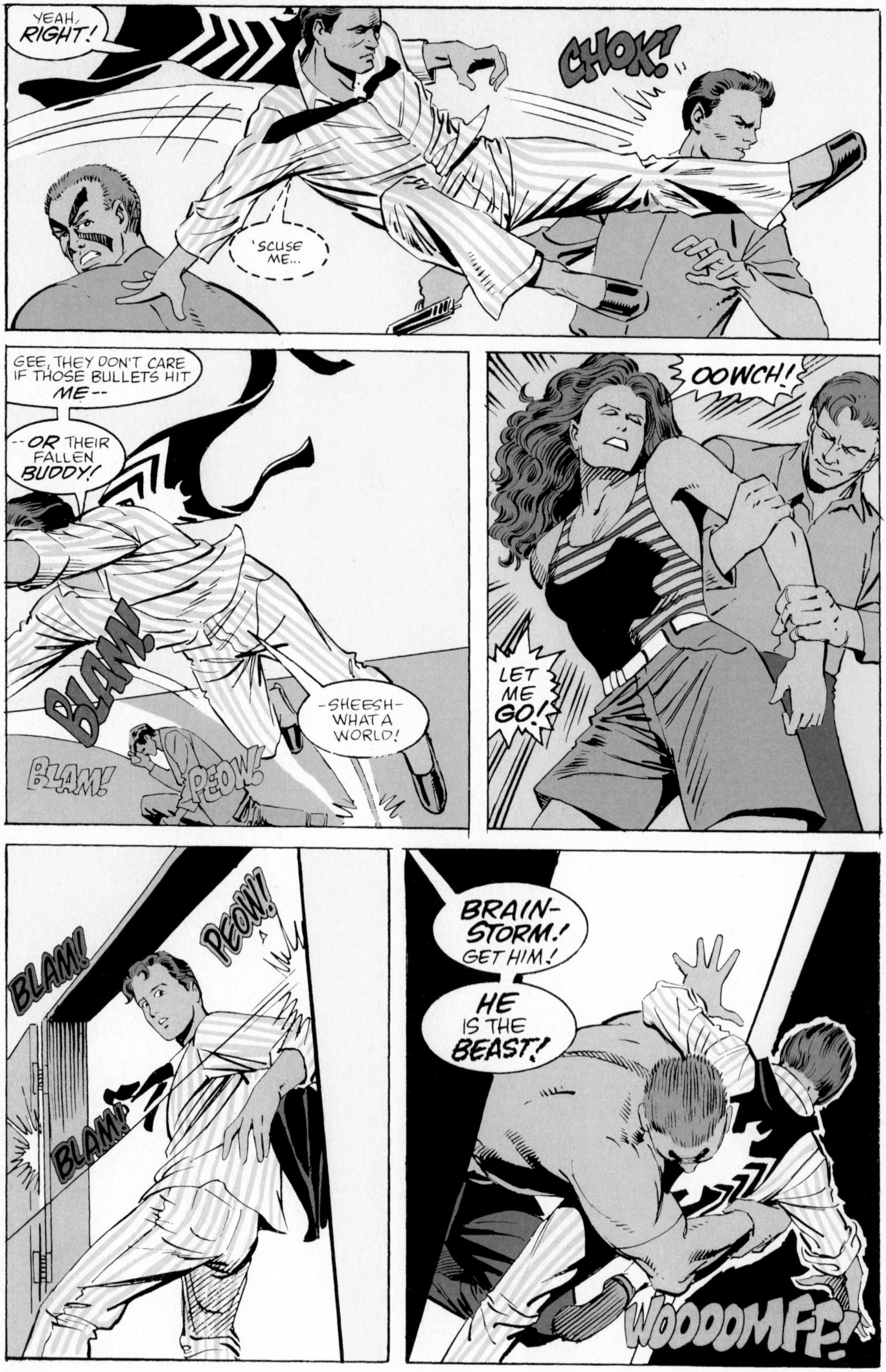
YEAH, RIGHT!
CHOK!
'SCUSE ME...
GEE, THEY DON'T CARE IF THOSE BULLETS HIT ME--
--OR THEIR FALLEN BUDDY!
BLAM!
BLAM!
PEOW!
-SHEESH- WHAT A WORLD!
OOWCH!
LET ME GO!
BLAM!
PEOW!
BLAM!
BLAM!
BRAIN-STORM! GET HIM!
HE IS THE BEAST!
WOOOOMFF!

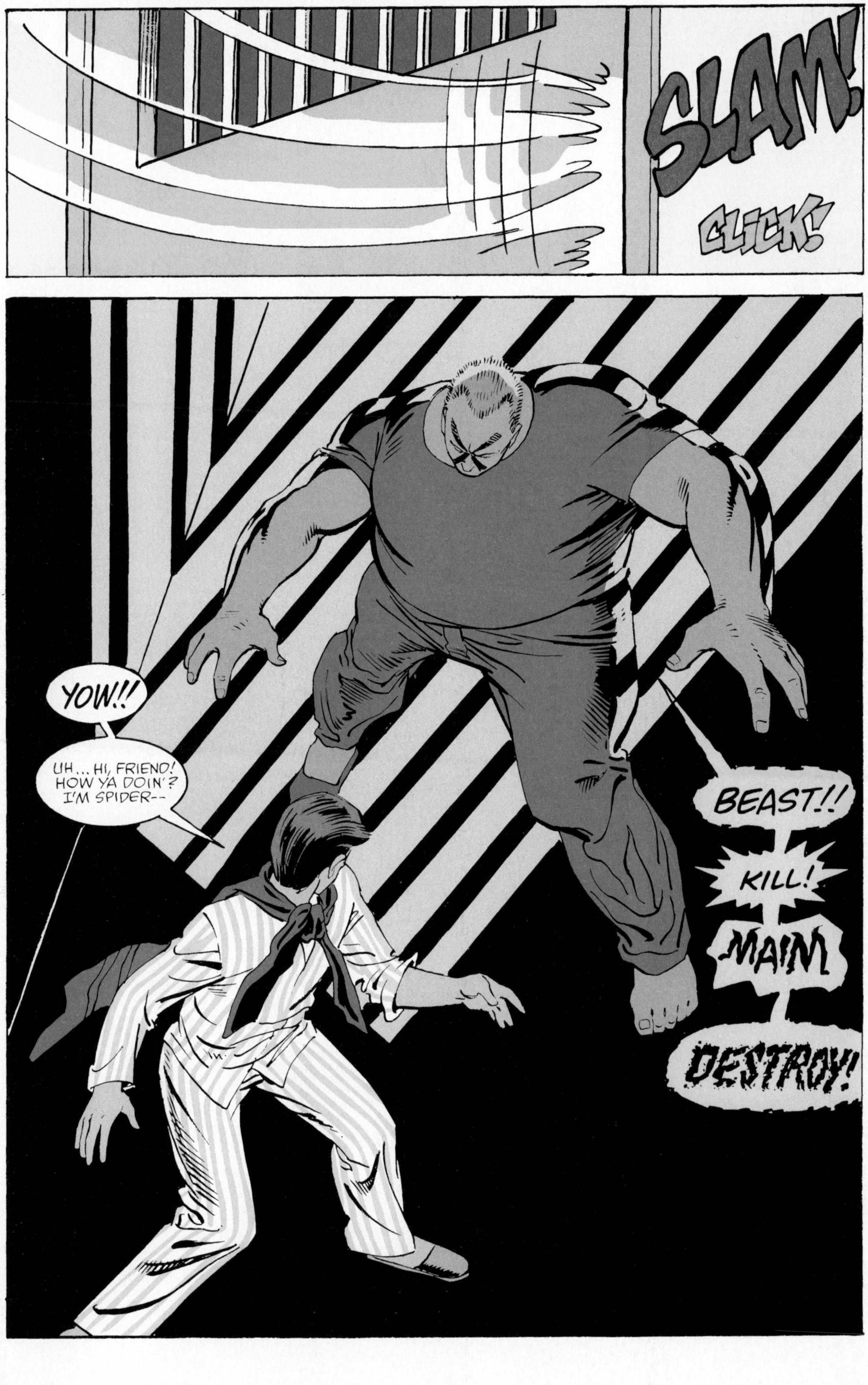
SLAM!
CLICK!
YOW!!
UH... HI, FRIEND! HOW YA DOIN'? I'M SPIDER--
BEAST!!
KILL!
MAIM
DESTROY!

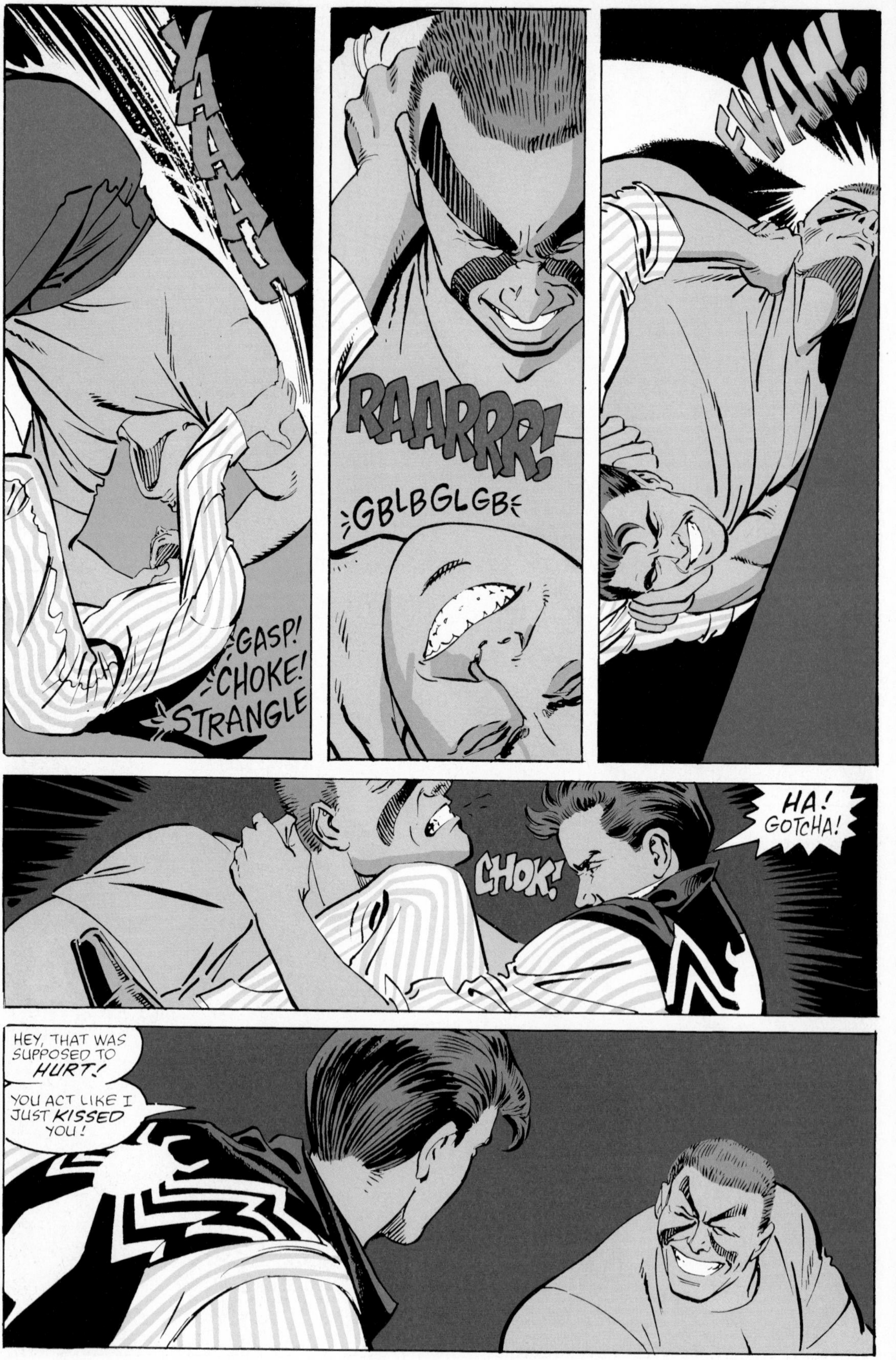
YAAAAH
GASP! CHOKE! STRANGLE
RAARRR!
GBLBGLGB
FWAM!
CHOK!
HA! GOTCHA!
HEY, THAT WAS SUPPOSED TO HURT!
YOU ACT LIKE I JUST KISSED YOU!

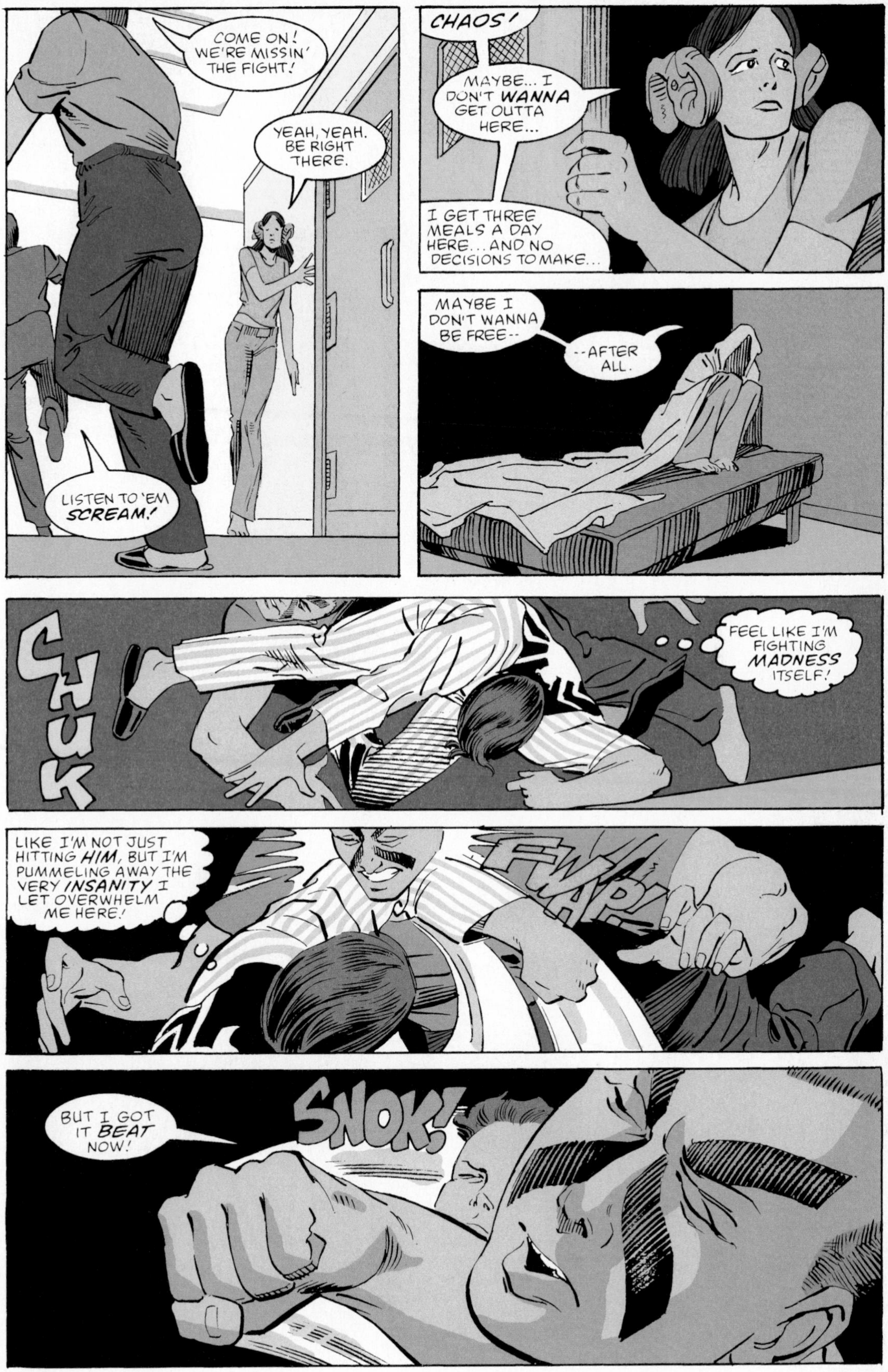

COME ON! WE'RE MISSIN' THE FIGHT!
YEAH, YEAH. BE RIGHT THERE.
LISTEN TO 'EM SCREAM!
CHAOS!
MAYBE... I DON'T WANNA GET OUTTA HERE...
I GET THREE MEALS A DAY HERE... AND NO DECISIONS TO MAKE...
MAYBE I DON'T WANNA BE FREE--
--AFTER ALL.
CHUK
FEEL LIKE I'M FIGHTING MADNESS ITSELF!
LIKE I'M NOT JUST HITTING HIM, BUT I'M PUMMELING AWAY THE VERY INSANITY I LET OVERWHELM ME HERE!
FWAP!
SNOK!
BUT I GOT IT BEAT NOW!

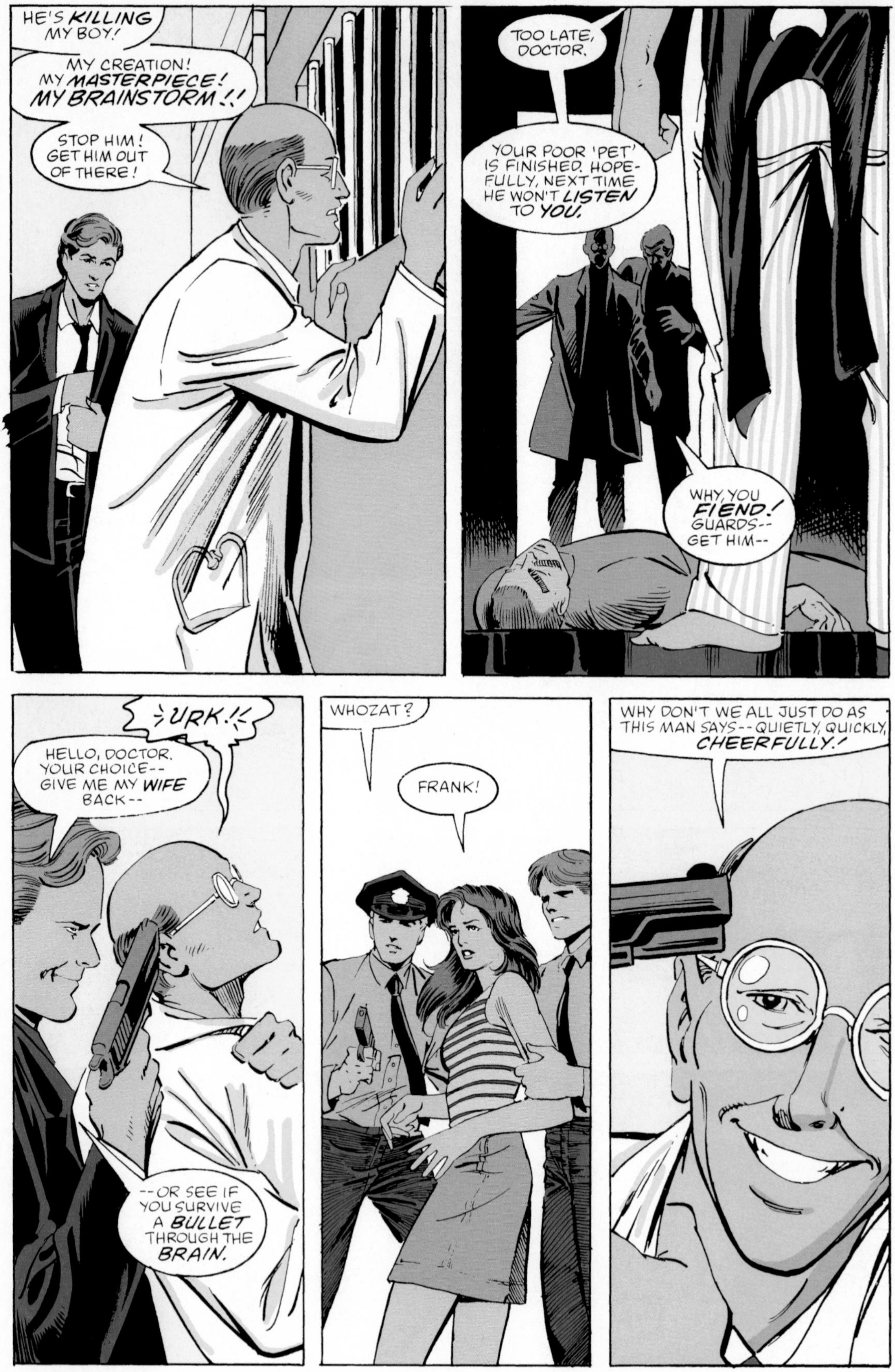
HE'S KILLING MY BOY!
MY CREATION! MY MASTERPIECE! MY BRAINSTORM!!
STOP HIM! GET HIM OUT OF THERE!
TOO LATE, DOCTOR.
YOUR POOR 'PET' IS FINISHED. HOPE-FULLY, NEXT TIME HE WON'T LISTEN TO YOU.
WHY, YOU FIEND! GUARDS-- GET HIM--
URK!!
HELLO, DOCTOR. YOUR CHOICE-- GIVE ME MY WIFE BACK--
--OR SEE IF YOU SURVIVE A BULLET THROUGH THE BRAIN.
WHOZAT?
FRANK!
WHY DON'T WE ALL JUST DO AS THIS MAN SAYS--QUIETLY, QUICKLY, CHEERFULLY!

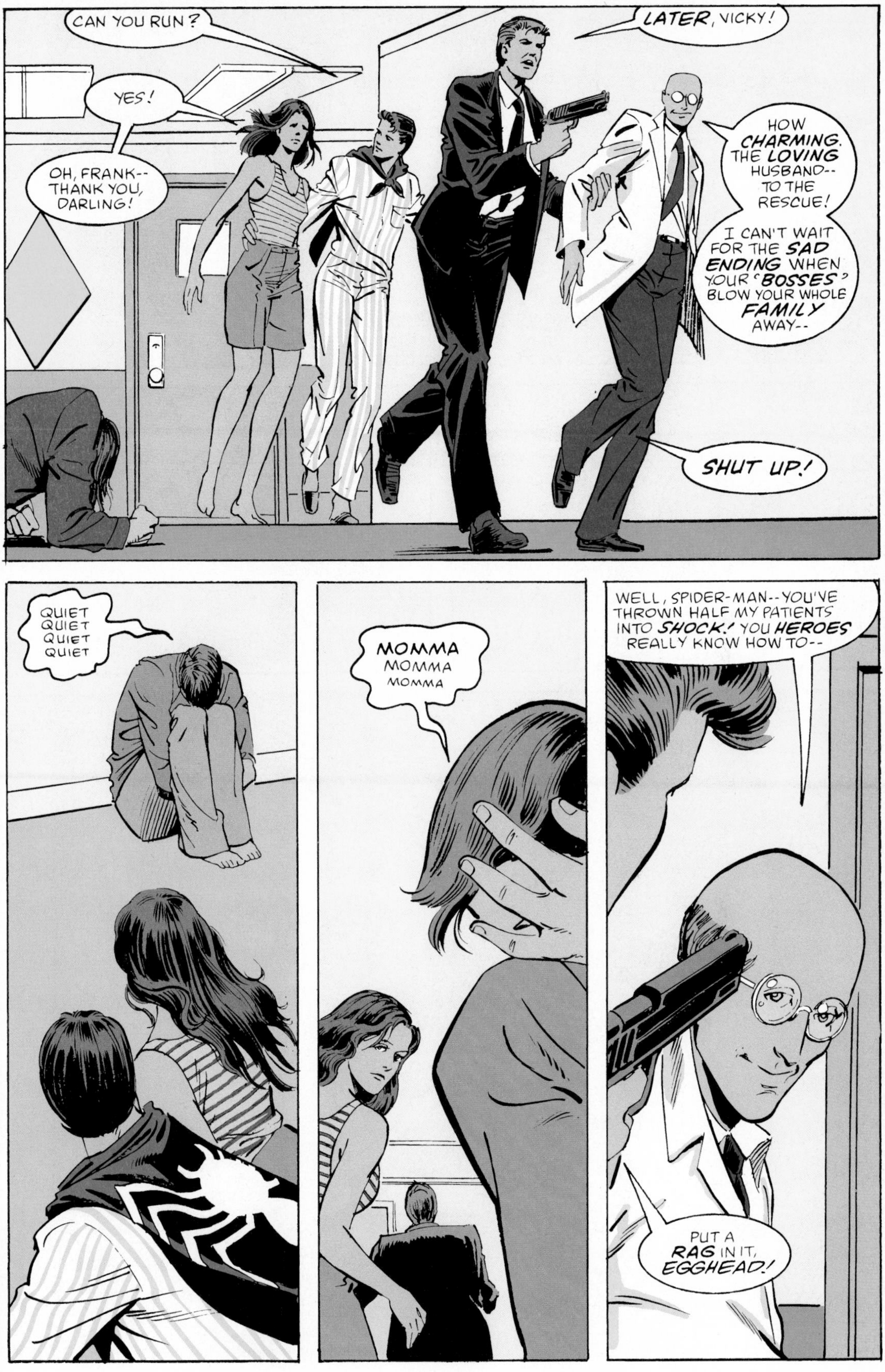
CAN YOU RUN?
YES!
OH, FRANK-- THANK YOU, DARLING!
LATER, VICKY!
HOW CHARMING. THE LOVING HUSBAND-- TO THE RESCUE!
I CAN'T WAIT FOR THE SAD ENDING WHEN YOUR 'BOSSES' BLOW YOUR WHOLE FAMILY AWAY--
SHUT UP!
QUIET QUIET QUIET QUIET
MOMMA MOMMA MOMMA
WELL, SPIDER-MAN--YOU'VE THROWN HALF MY PATIENTS INTO SHOCK! YOU HEROES REALLY KNOW HOW TO--
PUT A RAG IN IT, EGGHEAD!

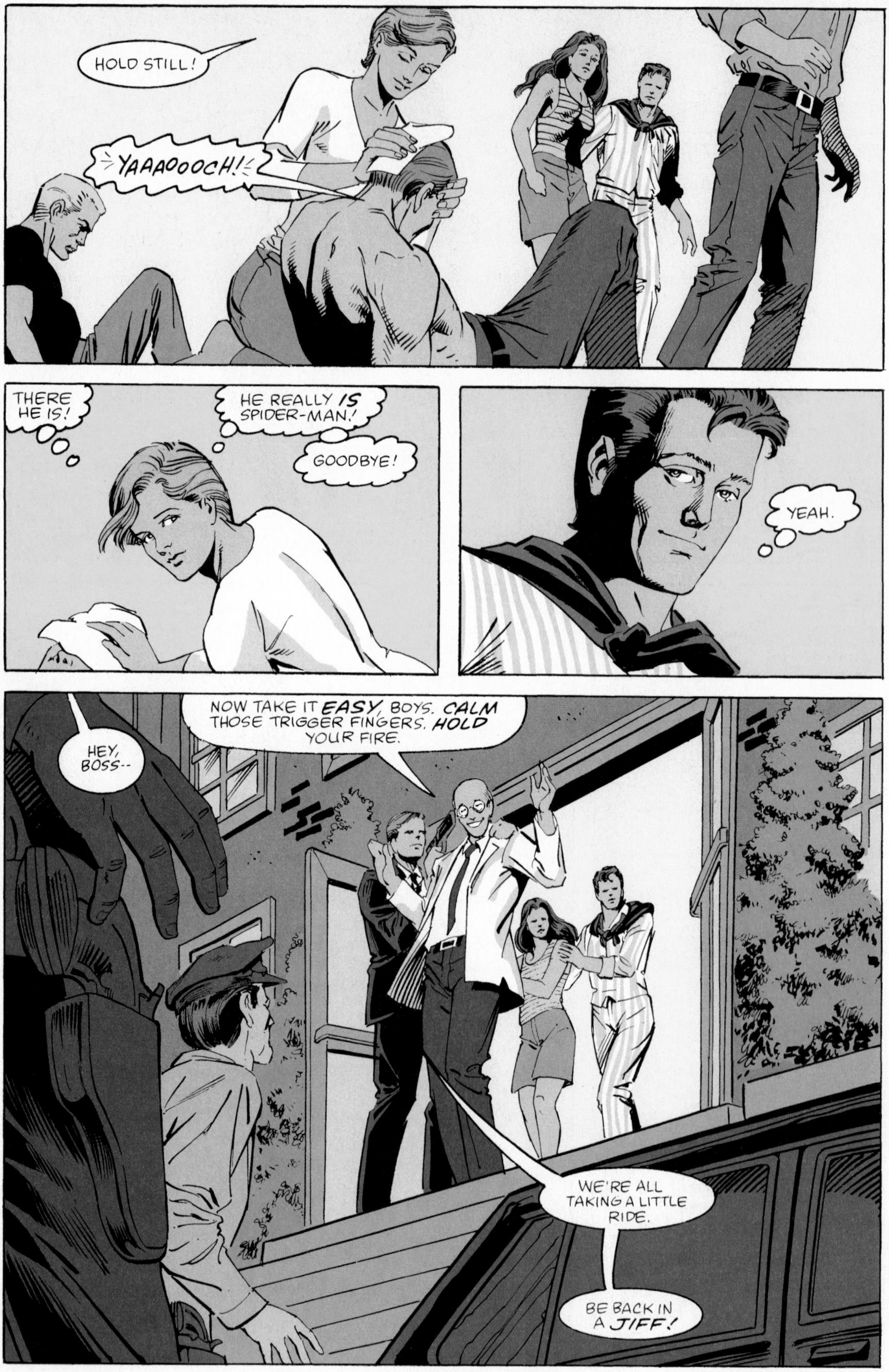
HOLD STILL!
YAAAOOOCH!
THERE HE IS!
HE REALLY IS SPIDER-MAN!
GOODBYE!
YEAH.
HEY, BOSS--
NOW TAKE IT EASY, BOYS. CALM THOSE TRIGGER FINGERS. HOLD YOUR FIRE.
WE'RE ALL TAKING A LITTLE RIDE.
BE BACK IN A JIFF!

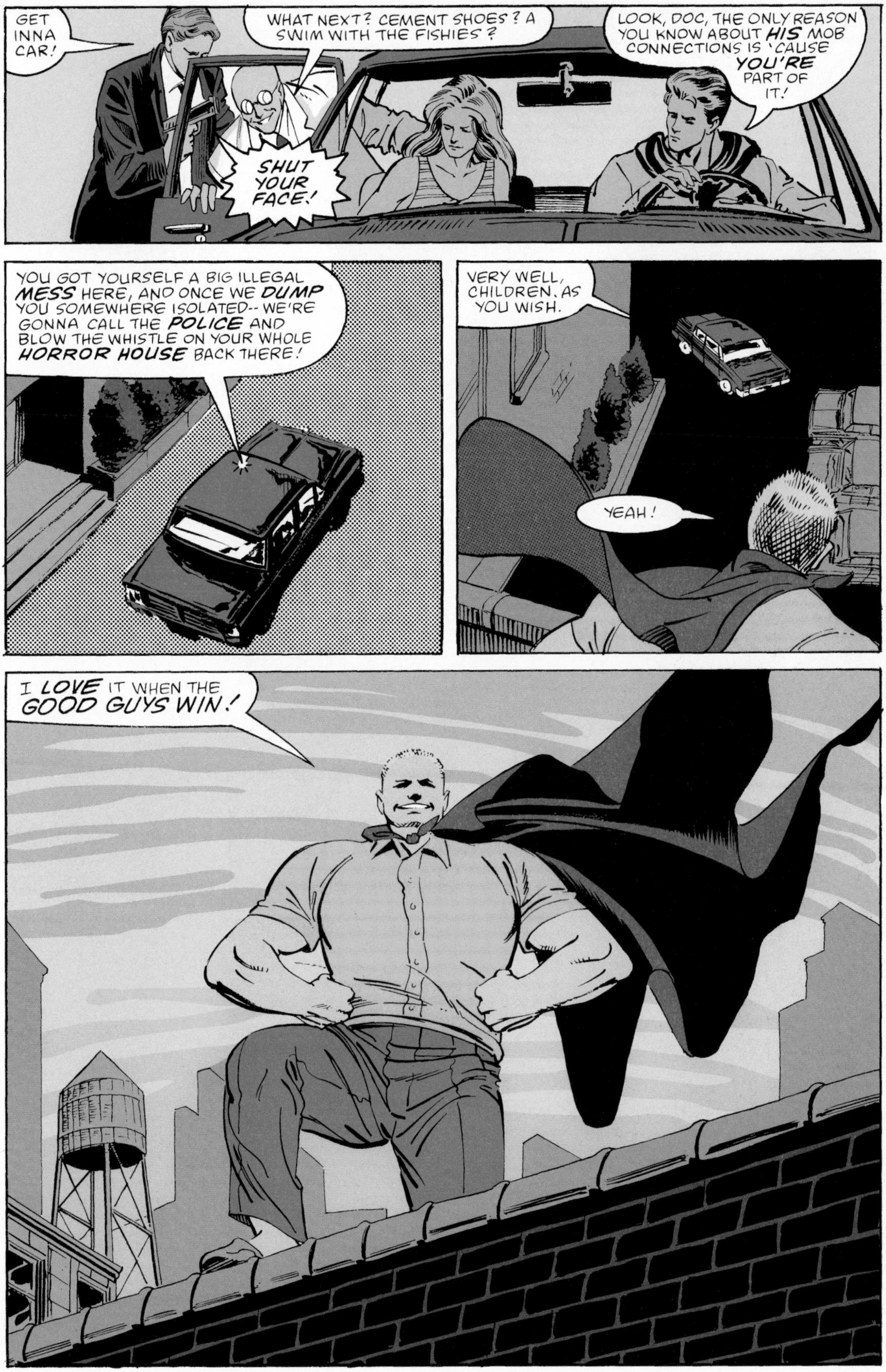
GET INNA CAR!
WHAT NEXT? CEMENT SHOES? A SWIM WITH THE FISHIES?
SHUT YOUR FACE!
LOOK, DOC, THE ONLY REASON YOU KNOW ABOUT HIS MOB CONNECTIONS IS 'CAUSE YOU'RE PART OF IT!
YOU GOT YOURSELF A BIG ILLEGAL MESS HERE, AND ONCE WE DUMP YOU SOMEWHERE ISOLATED-- WE'RE GONNA CALL THE POLICE AND BLOW THE WHISTLE ON YOUR WHOLE HORROR HOUSE BACK THERE!
VERY WELL, CHILDREN. AS YOU WISH.
YEAH!
I LOVE IT WHEN THE GOOD GUYS WIN!

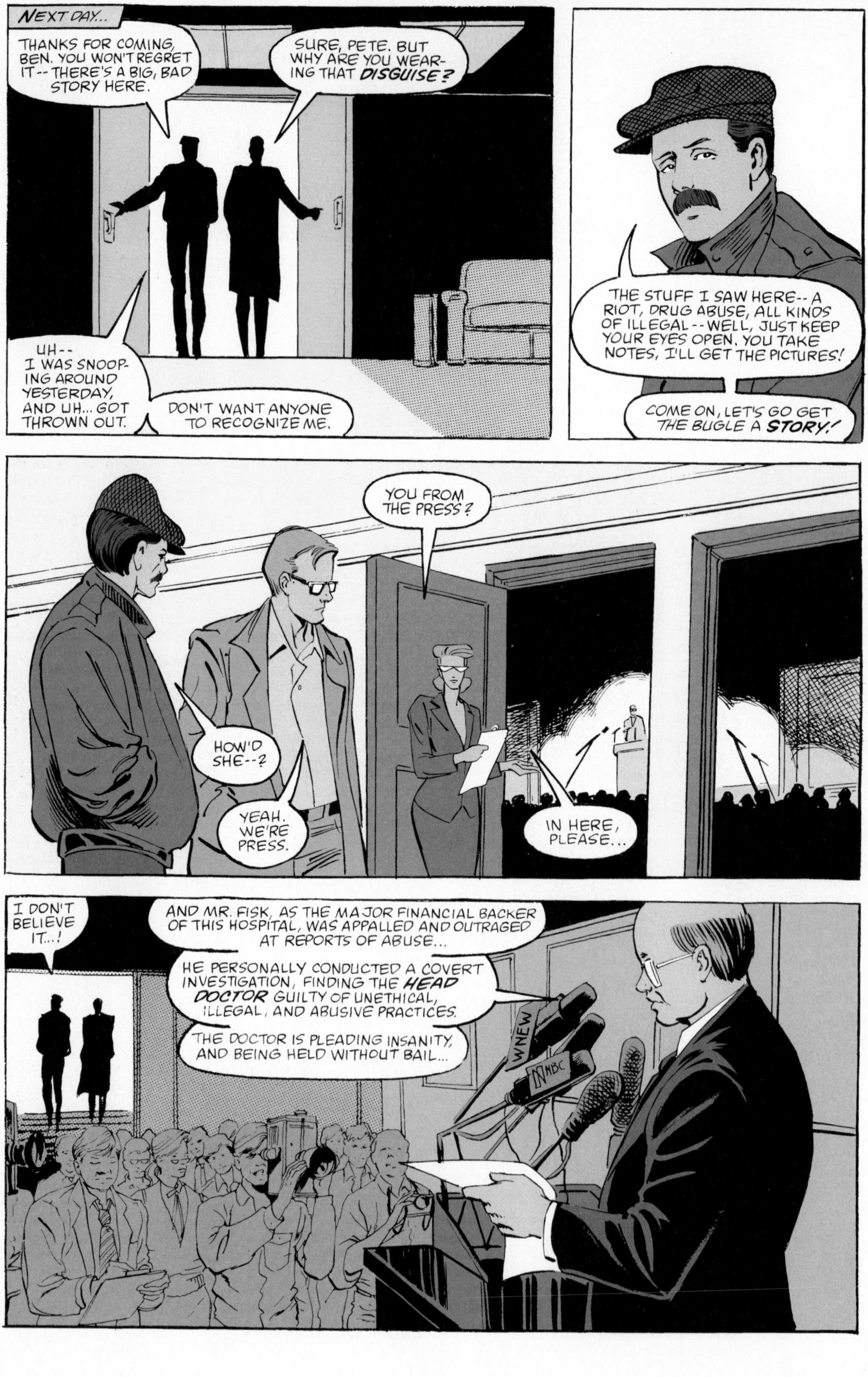
NEXT DAY...
THANKS FOR COMING, BEN. YOU WON'T REGRET IT -- THERE'S A BIG, BAD STORY HERE.
SURE, PETE. BUT WHY ARE YOU WEARING THAT DISGUISE?
UH-- I WAS SNOOPING AROUND YESTERDAY, AND UH... GOT THROWN OUT.
DON'T WANT ANYONE TO RECOGNIZE ME.
THE STUFF I SAW HERE-- A RIOT, DRUG ABUSE, ALL KINDS OF ILLEGAL -- WELL, JUST KEEP YOUR EYES OPEN. YOU TAKE NOTES, I'LL GET THE PICTURES!
COME ON, LET'S GO GET THE BUGLE A STORY!
YOU FROM THE PRESS?
HOW'D SHE--?
YEAH. WE'RE PRESS.
IN HERE, PLEASE...
I DON'T BELIEVE IT...!
AND MR. FISK, AS THE MAJOR FINANCIAL BACKER OF THIS HOSPITAL, WAS APPALLED AND OUTRAGED AT REPORTS OF ABUSE...
HE PERSONALLY CONDUCTED A COVERT INVESTIGATION, FINDING THE HEAD DOCTOR GUILTY OF UNETHICAL, ILLEGAL, AND ABUSIVE PRACTICES.
THE DOCTOR IS PLEADING INSANITY, AND BEING HELD WITHOUT BAIL...
WNEW
MBC

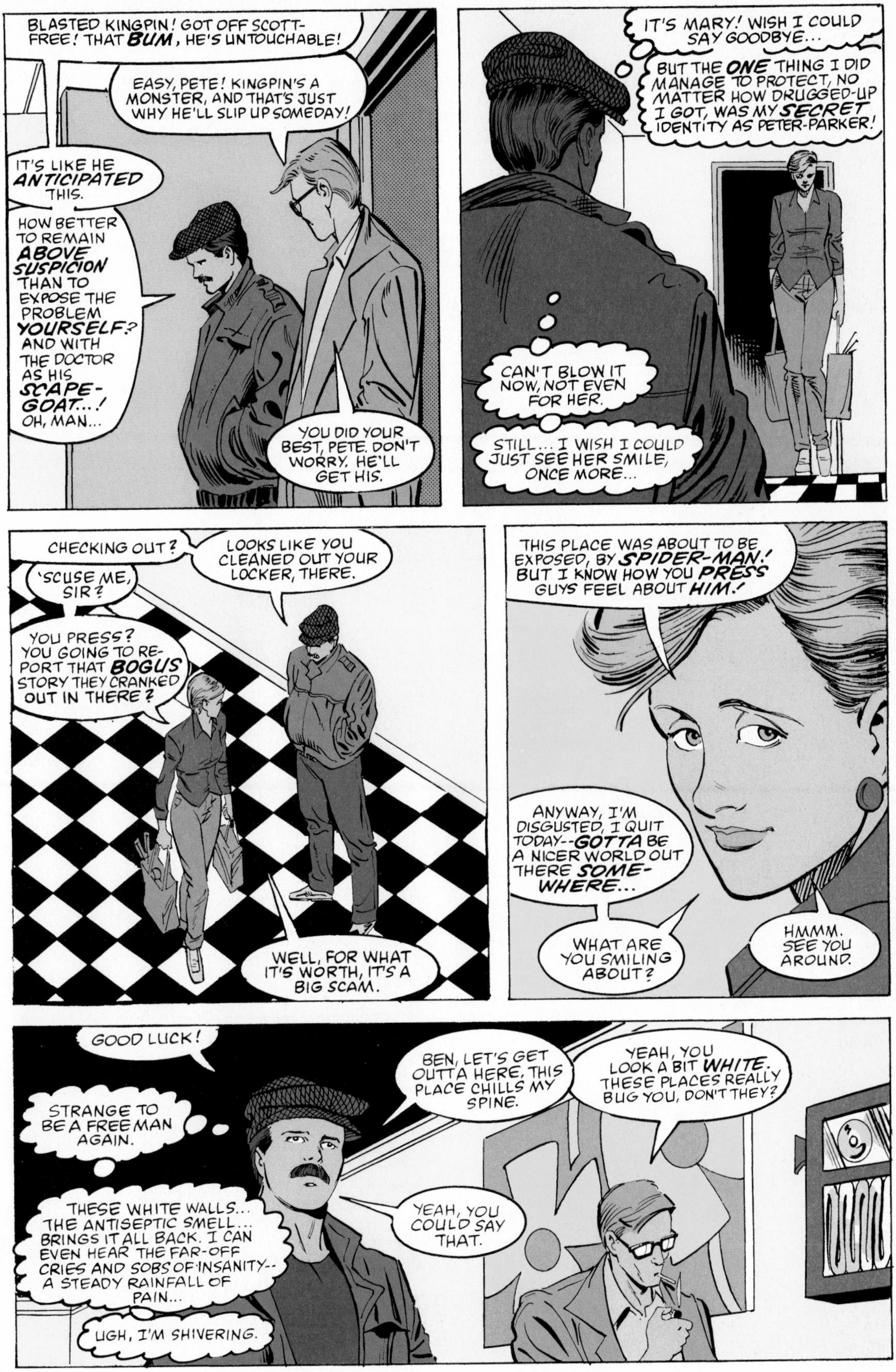
BLASTED KINGPIN! GOT OFF SCOTT-FREE! THAT BUM, HE'S UNTOUCHABLE!
EASY, PETE! KINGPIN'S A MONSTER, AND THAT'S JUST WHY HE'LL SLIP UP SOMEDAY!
IT'S LIKE HE ANTICIPATED THIS.
HOW BETTER TO REMAIN ABOVE SUSPICION THAN TO EXPOSE THE PROBLEM YOURSELF? AND WITH THE DOCTOR AS HIS SCAPE-GOAT...! OH, MAN...
YOU DID YOUR BEST, PETE. DON'T WORRY. HE'LL GET HIS.
IT'S MARY! WISH I COULD SAY GOODBYE...
BUT THE ONE THING I DID MANAGE TO PROTECT, NO MATTER HOW DRUGGED-UP I GOT, WAS MY SECRET IDENTITY AS PETER-PARKER!
CAN'T BLOW IT NOW, NOT EVEN FOR HER.
STILL... I WISH I COULD JUST SEE HER SMILE, ONCE MORE...
CHECKING OUT?
'SCUSE ME, SIR?
LOOKS LIKE YOU CLEANED OUT YOUR LOCKER, THERE.
YOU PRESS? YOU GOING TO REPORT THAT BOGUS STORY THEY CRANKED OUT IN THERE?
WELL, FOR WHAT IT'S WORTH, IT'S A BIG SCAM.
THIS PLACE WAS ABOUT TO BE EXPOSED, BY SPIDER-MAN! BUT I KNOW HOW YOU PRESS GUYS FEEL ABOUT HIM!
ANYWAY, I'M DISGUSTED, I QUIT TODAY--GOTTA BE A NICER WORLD OUT THERE SOME-WHERE...
WHAT ARE YOU SMILING ABOUT?
HMMM. SEE YOU AROUND.
GOOD LUCK!
STRANGE TO BE A FREE MAN AGAIN.
BEN, LET'S GET OUTTA HERE, THIS PLACE CHILLS MY SPINE.
YEAH, YOU LOOK A BIT WHITE. THESE PLACES REALLY BUG YOU, DON'T THEY?
THESE WHITE WALLS... THE ANTISEPTIC SMELL... BRINGS IT ALL BACK. I CAN EVEN HEAR THE FAR-OFF CRIES AND SOBS OF INSANITY-- A STEADY RAINFALL OF PAIN...
YEAH, YOU COULD SAY THAT.
UGH, I'M SHIVERING.

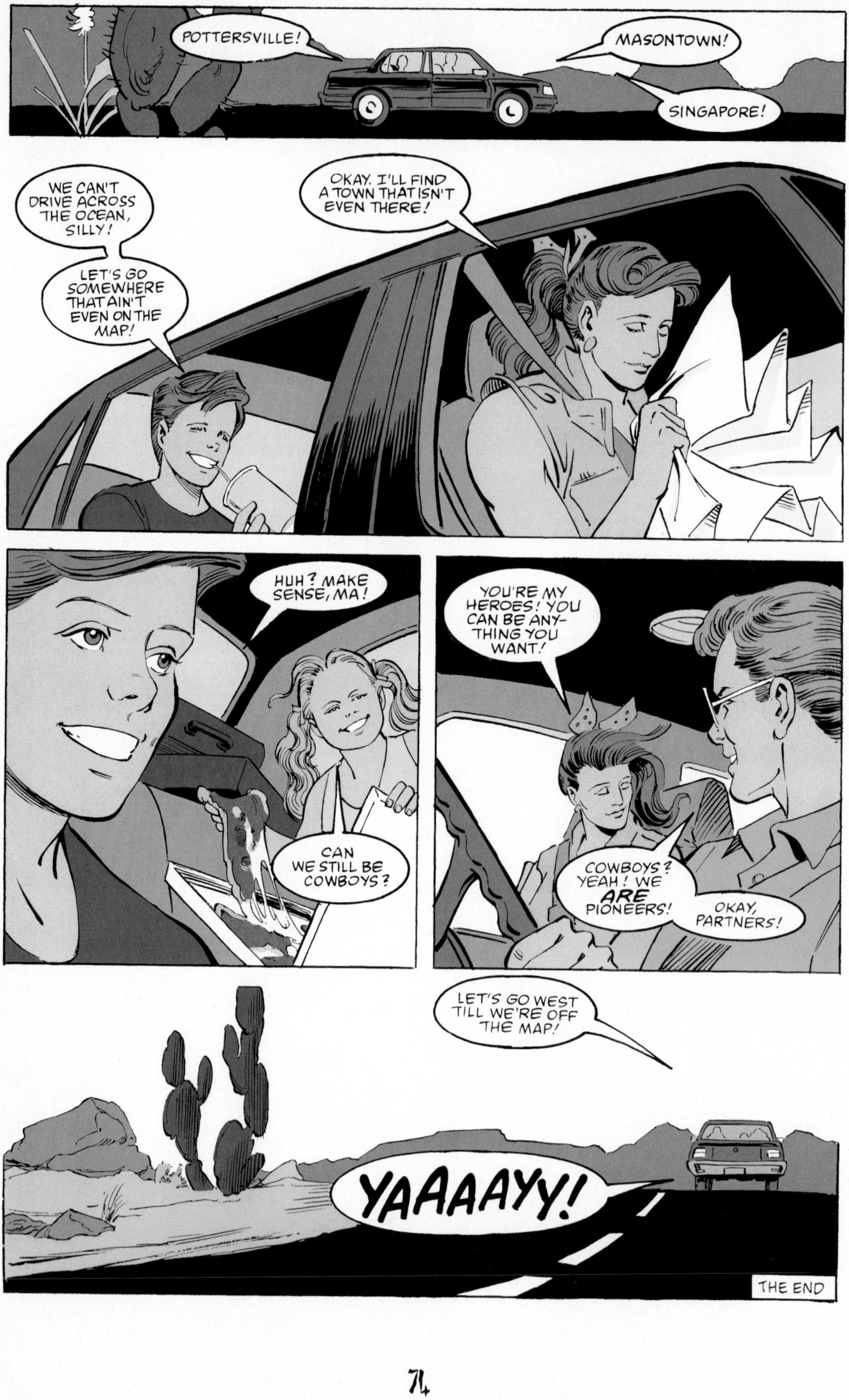
POTTERSVILLE!
MASONTOWN!
SINGAPORE!
WE CAN'T DRIVE ACROSS THE OCEAN, SILLY!
LET'S GO SOMEWHERE THAT AIN'T EVEN ON THE MAP!
OKAY. I'LL FIND A TOWN THAT ISN'T EVEN THERE!
HUH? MAKE SENSE, MA!
CAN WE STILL BE COWBOYS?
YOU'RE MY HEROES! YOU CAN BE ANYTHING YOU WANT!
COWBOYS? YEAH! WE ARE PIONEERS!
OKAY, PARTNERS!
LET'S GO WEST TILL WE'RE OFF THE MAP!
YAAAAYY!
THE END

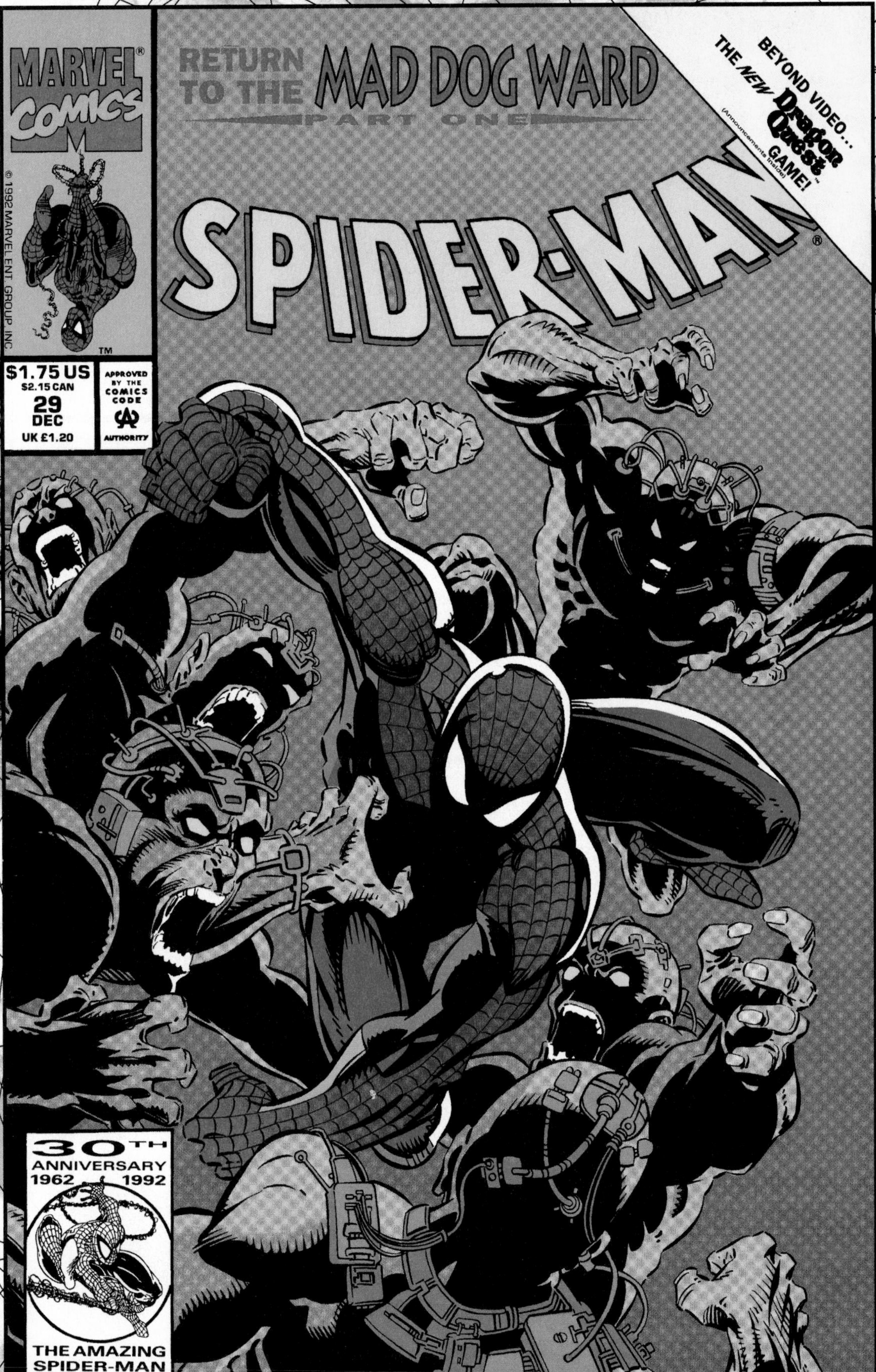
MARVEL® COMICS
RETURN TO THE MAD DOG WARD
PART ONE
BEYOND VIDEO...
THE NEW Dragon Quest™ GAME!
(Announcements inside)
SPIDER-MAN®
© 1992 MARVEL ENT. GROUP, INC.
$1.75 US
$2.15 CAN
29
DEC
UK £1.20
APPROVED BY THE COMICS CODE AUTHORITY
30TH ANNIVERSARY
1962 1992
THE AMAZING SPIDER-MAN

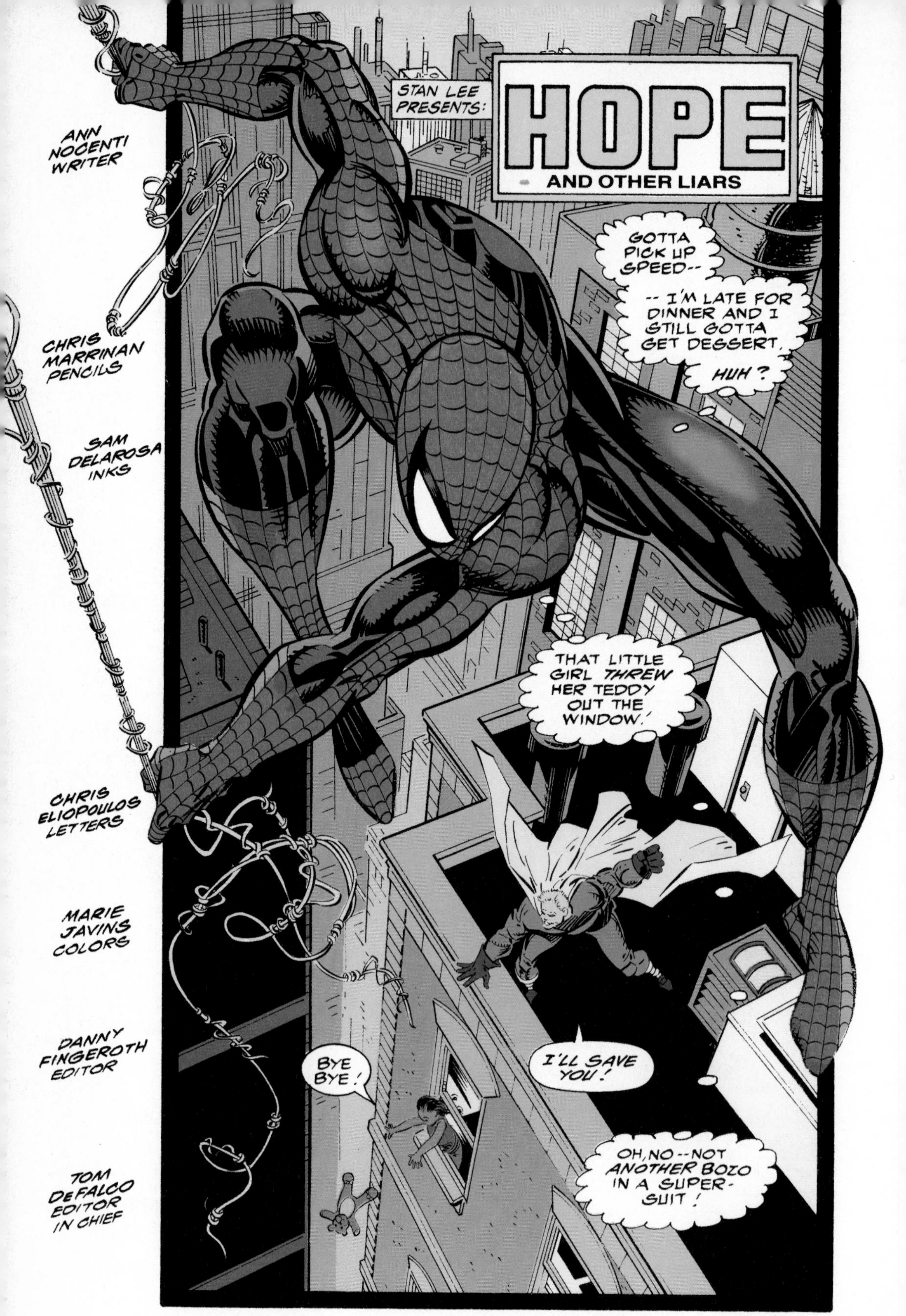
STAN LEE PRESENTS:
HOPE
AND OTHER LIARS
ANN NOCENTI WRITER
CHRIS MARRINAN PENCILS
SAM DELAROSA INKS
CHRIS ELIOPOULOS LETTERS
MARIE JAVINS COLORS
DANNY FINGEROTH EDITOR
TOM DEFALCO EDITOR IN CHIEF
GOTTA PICK UP SPEED--
-- I'M LATE FOR DINNER AND I STILL GOTTA GET DESSERT.
HUH ?
THAT LITTLE GIRL THREW HER TEDDY OUT THE WINDOW!
BYE BYE!
I'LL SAVE YOU!
OH, NO--NOT ANOTHER BOZO IN A SUPER-SUIT!

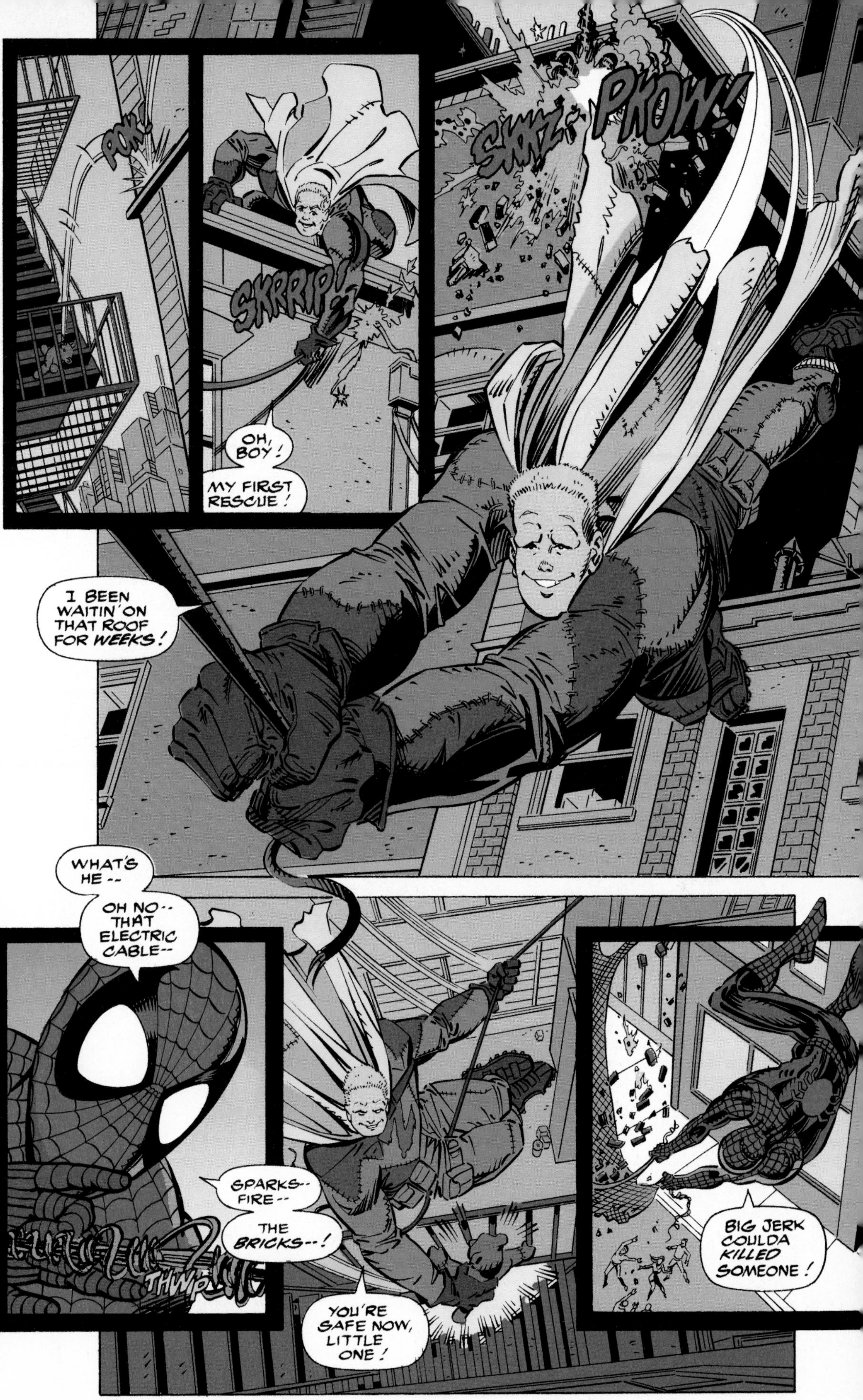
POK!
SKRRIP!
OH, BOY!
MY FIRST RESCUE!
SKKZ
PKOW!
I BEEN WAITIN' ON THAT ROOF FOR WEEKS!
WHAT'S HE --
OH NO-- THAT ELECTRIC CABLE--
SPARKS-- FIRE--
THE BRICKS--!
THWIP
YOU'RE SAFE NOW, LITTLE ONE!
BIG JERK COULDA KILLED SOMEONE!

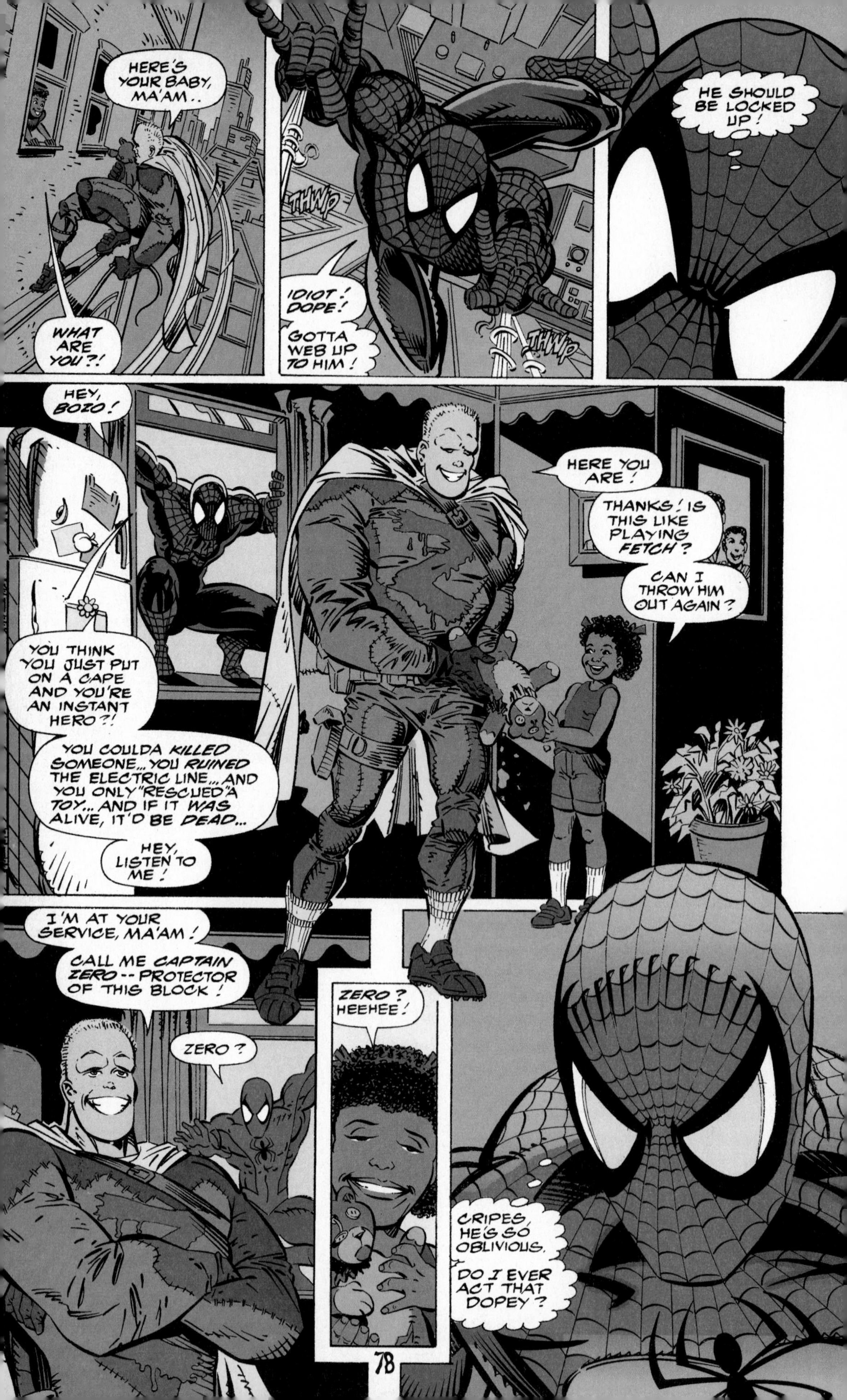
HERE'S YOUR BABY, MA'AM..
WHAT ARE YOU?!
THWIP
IDIOT! DOPE!
GOTTA WEB UP TO HIM!
THWIP
HE SHOULD BE LOCKED UP!
HEY, BOZO!
HERE YOU ARE!
THANKS! IS THIS LIKE PLAYING FETCH?
CAN I THROW HIM OUT AGAIN?
YOU THINK YOU JUST PUT ON A CAPE AND YOU'RE AN INSTANT HERO?!
YOU COULDA KILLED SOMEONE... YOU RUINED THE ELECTRIC LINE... AND YOU ONLY "RESCUED" A TOY... AND IF IT WAS ALIVE, IT'D BE DEAD...
HEY, LISTEN TO ME!
I'M AT YOUR SERVICE, MA'AM!
CALL ME CAPTAIN ZERO -- PROTECTOR OF THIS BLOCK!
ZERO?
ZERO? HEEHEE!
CRIPES, HE'S SO OBLIVIOUS.
DO I EVER ACT THAT DOPEY?

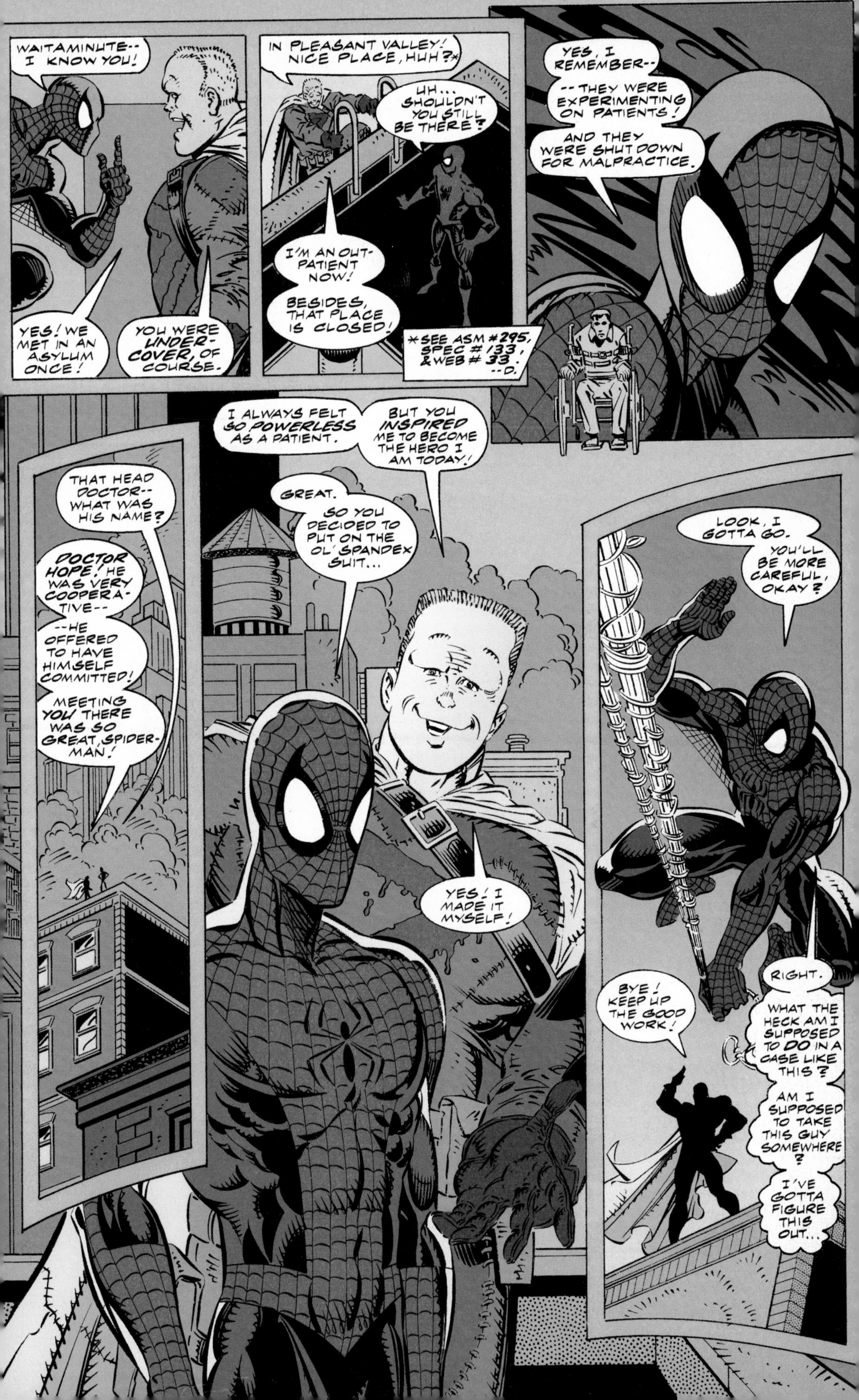
WAITAMINUTE-- I KNOW YOU!
YES! WE MET IN AN ASYLUM ONCE!
YOU WERE UNDER-COVER, OF COURSE.
IN PLEASANT VALLEY! NICE PLACE, HUH?*
UH... SHOULDN'T YOU STILL BE THERE?
I'M AN OUT-PATIENT NOW!
BESIDES, THAT PLACE IS CLOSED!
*SEE ASM #295, SPEC #133, & WEB #33. --D.
YES, I REMEMBER--
--THEY WERE EXPERIMENTING ON PATIENTS!
AND THEY WERE SHUT DOWN FOR MALPRACTICE.
THAT HEAD DOCTOR-- WHAT WAS HIS NAME?
DOCTOR HOPE! HE WAS VERY COOPERA-TIVE--
--HE OFFERED TO HAVE HIMSELF COMMITTED!
MEETING YOU THERE WAS SO GREAT, SPIDER-MAN!
I ALWAYS FELT SO POWERLESS AS A PATIENT.
BUT YOU INSPIRED ME TO BECOME THE HERO I AM TODAY!
GREAT.
SO YOU DECIDED TO PUT ON THE OL' SPANDEX SUIT...
YES! I MADE IT MYSELF!
LOOK, I GOTTA GO.
YOU'LL BE MORE CAREFUL, OKAY?
BYE! KEEP UP THE GOOD WORK!
RIGHT.
WHAT THE HECK AM I SUPPOSED TO DO IN A CASE LIKE THIS?
AM I SUPPOSED TO TAKE THIS GUY SOMEWHERE?
I'VE GOTTA FIGURE THIS OUT...

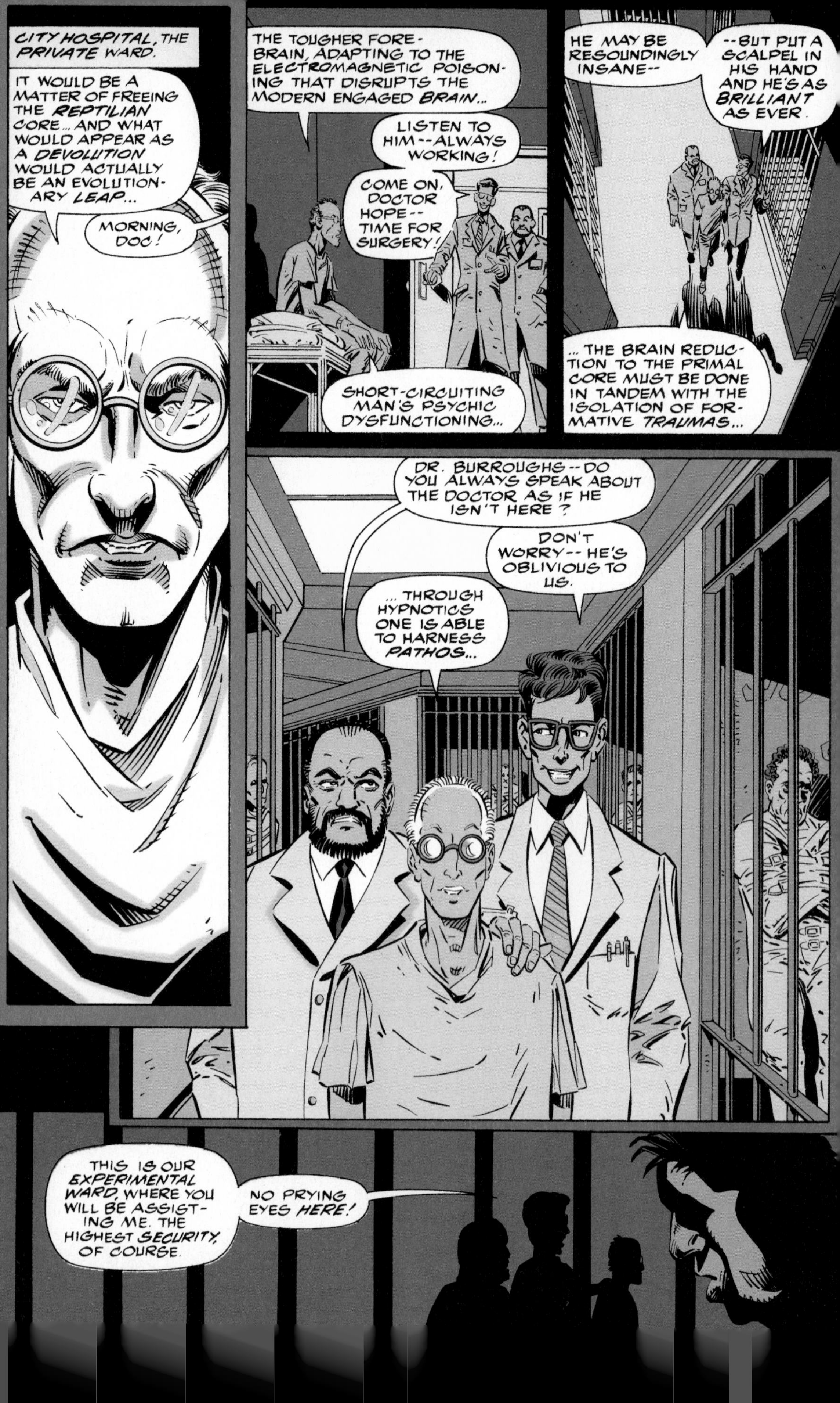
CITY HOSPITAL, THE PRIVATE WARD.
IT WOULD BE A MATTER OF FREEING THE REPTILIAN CORE... AND WHAT WOULD APPEAR AS A DEVOLUTION WOULD ACTUALLY BE AN EVOLUTIONARY LEAP...
MORNING, DOC!
THE TOUGHER FORE-BRAIN, ADAPTING TO THE ELECTROMAGNETIC POISONING THAT DISRUPTS THE MODERN ENGAGED BRAIN...
LISTEN TO HIM--ALWAYS WORKING!
COME ON, DOCTOR HOPE--TIME FOR SURGERY!
SHORT-CIRCUITING MAN'S PSYCHIC DYSFUNCTIONING...
HE MAY BE RESOUNDINGLY INSANE--
--BUT PUT A SCALPEL IN HIS HAND AND HE'S AS BRILLIANT AS EVER.
... THE BRAIN REDUCTION TO THE PRIMAL CORE MUST BE DONE IN TANDEM WITH THE ISOLATION OF FORMATIVE TRAUMAS...
DR. BURROUGHS--DO YOU ALWAYS SPEAK ABOUT THE DOCTOR AS IF HE ISN'T HERE?
DON'T WORRY--HE'S OBLIVIOUS TO US.
... THROUGH HYPNOTICS ONE IS ABLE TO HARNESS PATHOS...
THIS IS OUR EXPERIMENTAL WARD, WHERE YOU WILL BE ASSISTING ME. THE HIGHEST SECURITY, OF COURSE.
NO PRYING EYES HERE!

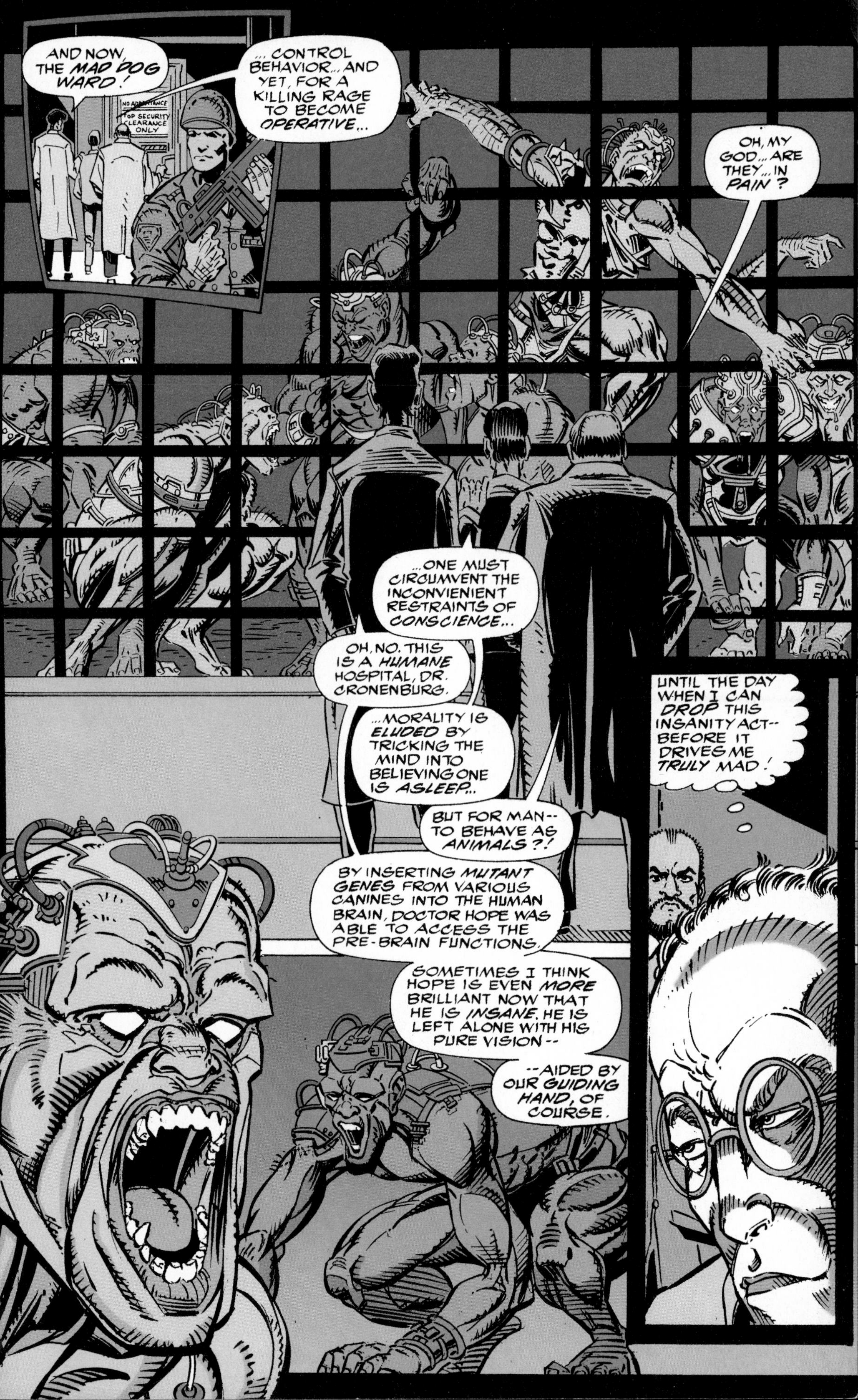
AND NOW, THE MAD DOG WARD!
...CONTROL BEHAVIOR... AND YET, FOR A KILLING RAGE TO BECOME OPERATIVE...
NO ADMITTANCE
TOP SECURITY CLEARANCE ONLY
OH, MY GOD... ARE THEY... IN PAIN?
...ONE MUST CIRCUMVENT THE INCONVIENIENT RESTRAINTS OF CONSCIENCE...
OH, NO. THIS IS A HUMANE HOSPITAL, DR. CRONENBURG.
...MORALITY IS ELUDED BY TRICKING THE MIND INTO BELIEVING ONE IS ASLEEP...
BUT FOR MAN-- TO BEHAVE AS ANIMALS?!
BY INSERTING MUTANT GENES FROM VARIOUS CANINES INTO THE HUMAN BRAIN, DOCTOR HOPE WAS ABLE TO ACCESS THE PRE-BRAIN FUNCTIONS.
SOMETIMES I THINK HOPE IS EVEN MORE BRILLIANT NOW THAT HE IS INSANE. HE IS LEFT ALONE WITH HIS PURE VISION--
--AIDED BY OUR GUIDING HAND, OF COURSE.
UNTIL THE DAY WHEN I CAN DROP THIS INSANITY ACT-- BEFORE IT DRIVES ME TRULY MAD!

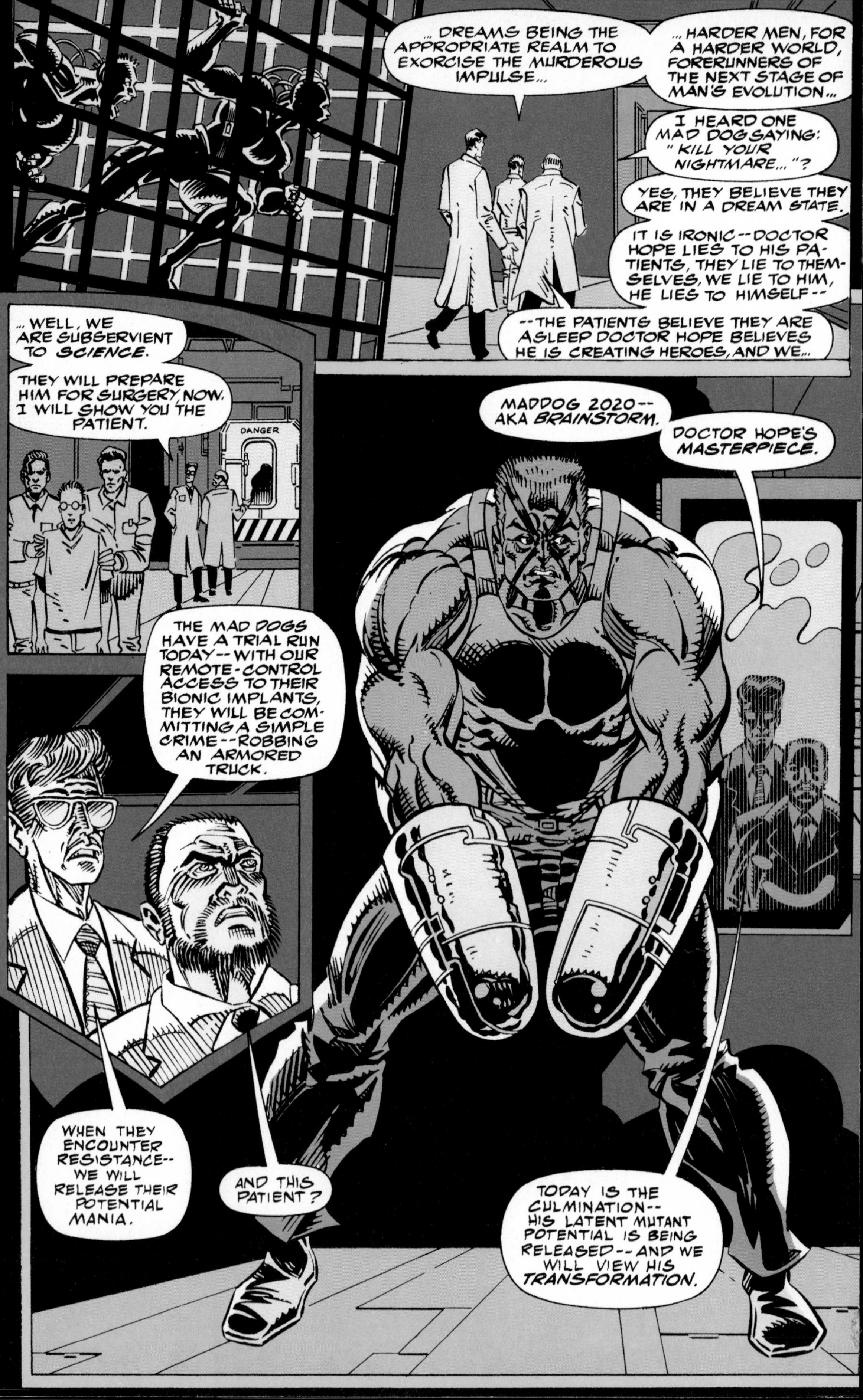
...DREAMS BEING THE APPROPRIATE REALM TO EXORCISE THE MURDEROUS IMPULSE...
...HARDER MEN, FOR A HARDER WORLD, FORERUNNERS OF THE NEXT STAGE OF MAN'S EVOLUTION...
I HEARD ONE MAD DOG SAYING: "KILL YOUR NIGHTMARE..."?
YES, THEY BELIEVE THEY ARE IN A DREAM STATE.
IT IS IRONIC--DOCTOR HOPE LIES TO HIS PATIENTS, THEY LIE TO THEMSELVES, WE LIE TO HIM, HE LIES TO HIMSELF--
--THE PATIENTS BELIEVE THEY ARE ASLEEP DOCTOR HOPE BELIEVES HE IS CREATING HEROES, AND WE...
...WELL, WE ARE SUBSERVIENT TO SCIENCE.
THEY WILL PREPARE HIM FOR SURGERY NOW. I WILL SHOW YOU THE PATIENT.
DANGER
THE MAD DOGS HAVE A TRIAL RUN TODAY--WITH OUR REMOTE-CONTROL ACCESS TO THEIR BIONIC IMPLANTS, THEY WILL BE COMMITTING A SIMPLE CRIME--ROBBING AN ARMORED TRUCK.
WHEN THEY ENCOUNTER RESISTANCE--WE WILL RELEASE THEIR POTENTIAL MANIA.
AND THIS PATIENT?
MADDOG 2020--AKA BRAINSTORM.
DOCTOR HOPE'S MASTERPIECE.
TODAY IS THE CULMINATION--HIS LATENT MUTANT POTENTIAL IS BEING RELEASED--AND WE WILL VIEW HIS TRANSFORMATION.

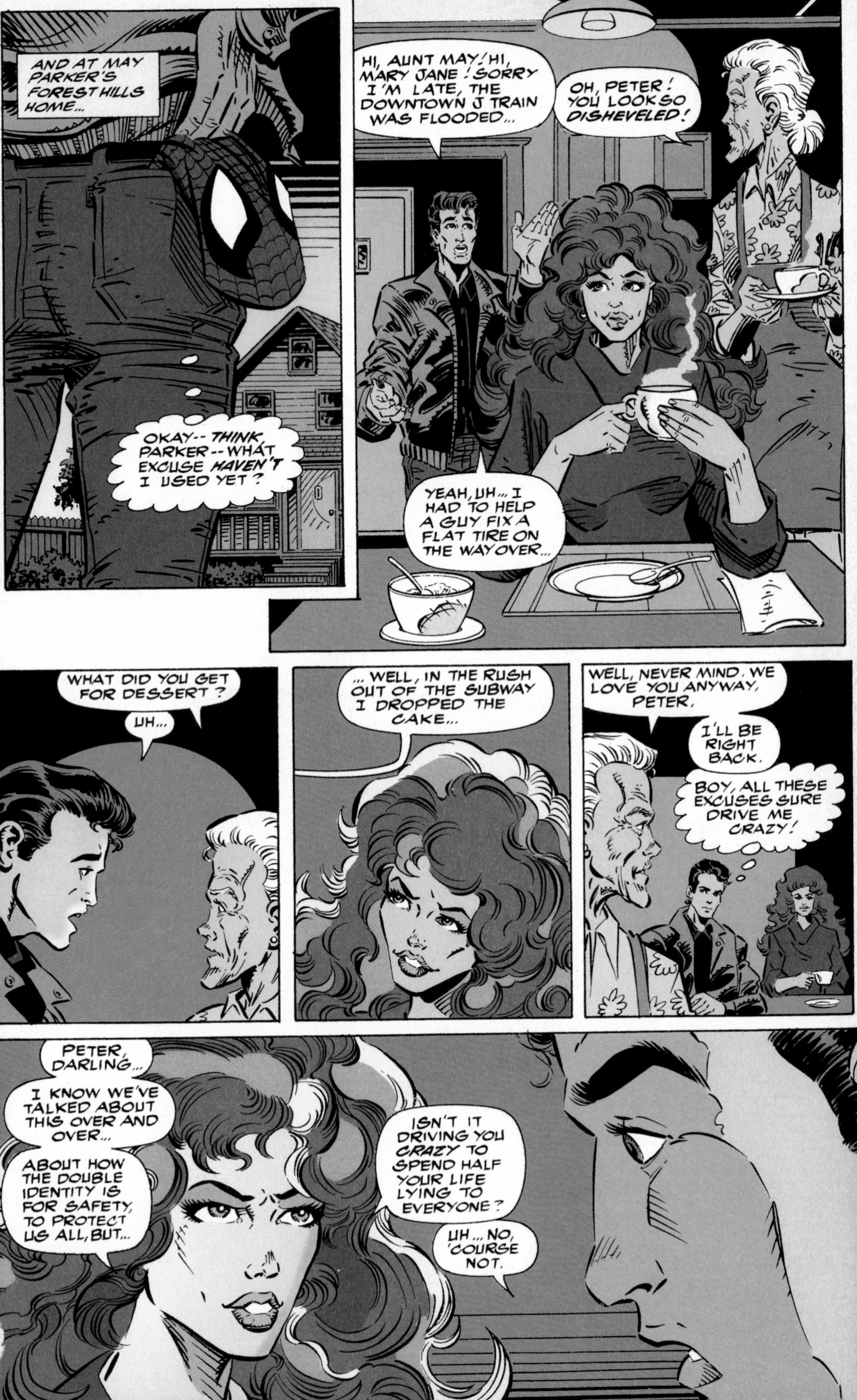
AND AT MAY PARKER'S FOREST HILLS HOME...
OKAY-- THINK, PARKER--WHAT EXCUSE HAVEN'T I USED YET?
HI, AUNT MAY! HI, MARY JANE! SORRY I'M LATE, THE DOWNTOWN J TRAIN WAS FLOODED...
OH, PETER! YOU LOOK SO DISHEVELED!
YEAH, UH... I HAD TO HELP A GUY FIX A FLAT TIRE ON THE WAY OVER...
WHAT DID YOU GET FOR DESSERT?
UH...
...WELL, IN THE RUSH OUT OF THE SUBWAY I DROPPED THE CAKE...
WELL, NEVER MIND. WE LOVE YOU ANYWAY, PETER.
I'LL BE RIGHT BACK.
BOY, ALL THESE EXCUSES SURE DRIVE ME CRAZY!
PETER, DARLING...
I KNOW WE'VE TALKED ABOUT THIS OVER AND OVER...
ABOUT HOW THE DOUBLE IDENTITY IS FOR SAFETY, TO PROTECT US ALL, BUT...
ISN'T IT DRIVING YOU CRAZY TO SPEND HALF YOUR LIFE LYING TO EVERYONE?
UH... NO, 'COURSE NOT.

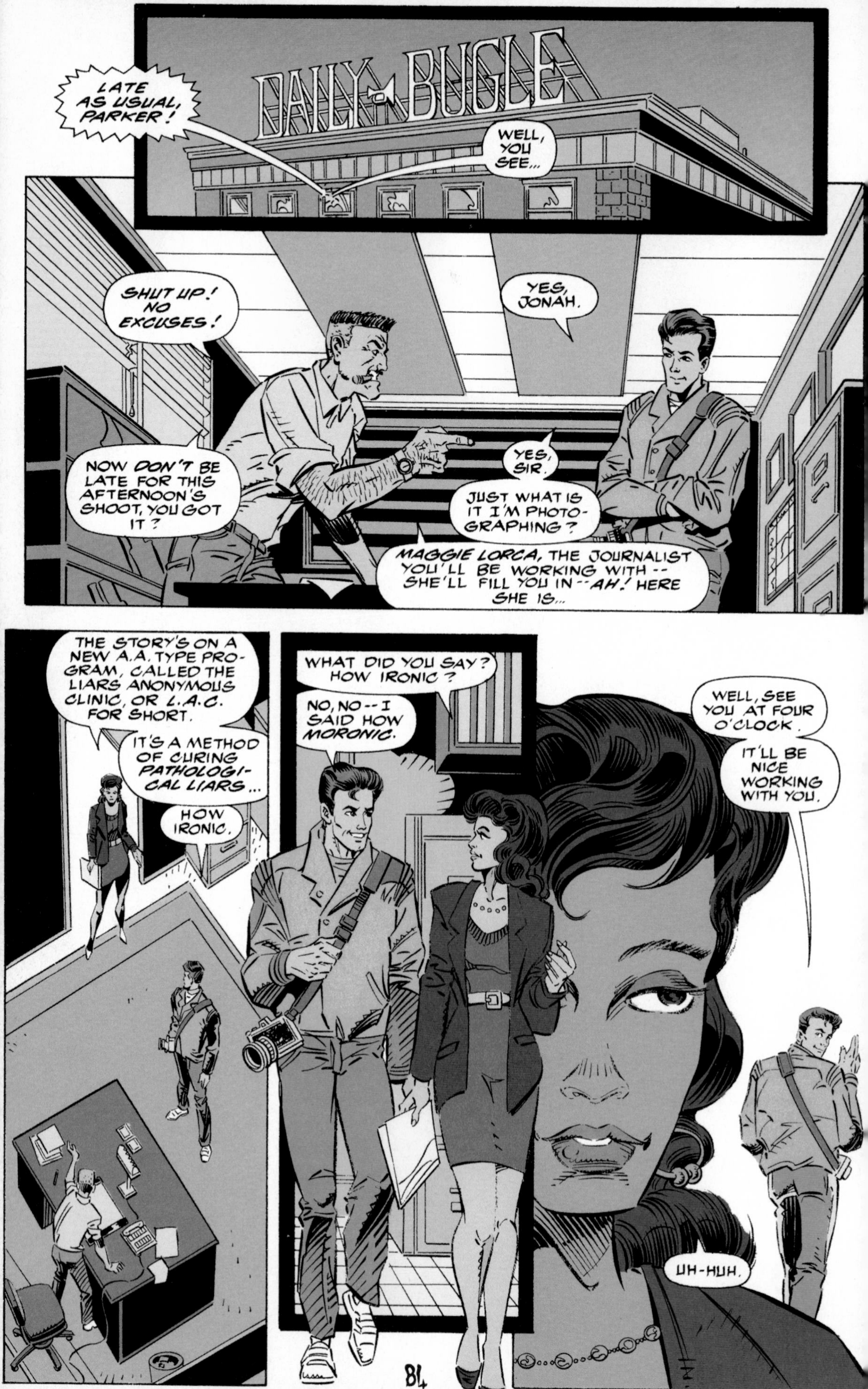
DAILY BUGLE
LATE AS USUAL, PARKER!
WELL, YOU SEE...
SHUT UP! NO EXCUSES!
YES, JONAH.
NOW DON'T BE LATE FOR THIS AFTERNOON'S SHOOT, YOU GOT IT?
YES, SIR.
JUST WHAT IS IT I'M PHOTOGRAPHING?
MAGGIE LORCA, THE JOURNALIST YOU'LL BE WORKING WITH -- SHE'LL FILL YOU IN -- AH! HERE SHE IS...
THE STORY'S ON A NEW A.A. TYPE PROGRAM, CALLED THE LIARS ANONYMOUS CLINIC, OR L.A.C. FOR SHORT.
IT'S A METHOD OF CURING PATHOLOGICAL LIARS...
HOW IRONIC.
WHAT DID YOU SAY? HOW IRONIC?
NO, NO -- I SAID HOW MORONIC.
WELL, SEE YOU AT FOUR O'CLOCK.
IT'LL BE NICE WORKING WITH YOU.
UH-HUH.

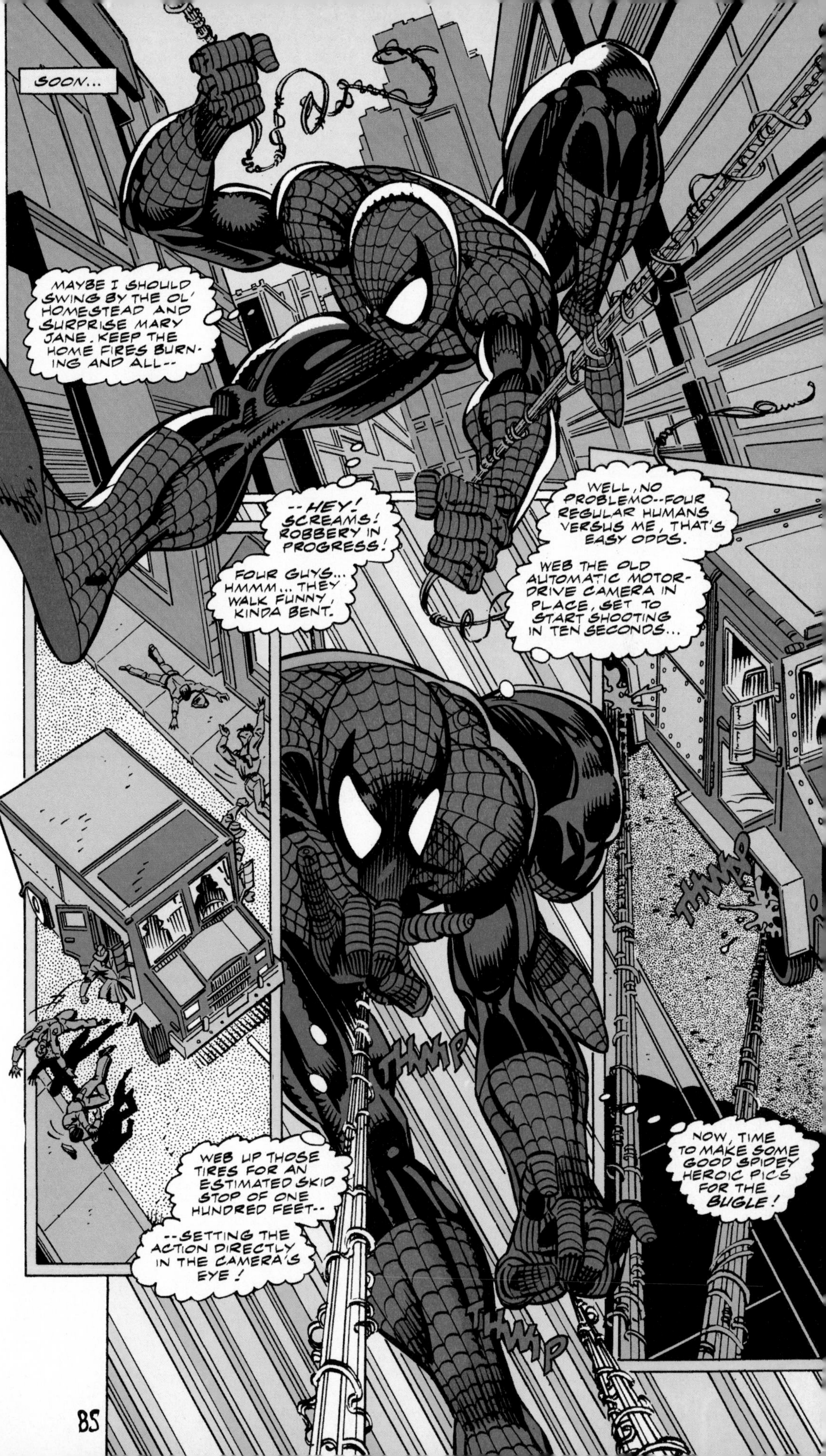
SOON...
MAYBE I SHOULD SWING BY THE OL' HOMESTEAD AND SURPRISE MARY JANE. KEEP THE HOME FIRES BURN-ING AND ALL--
--HEY! SCREAMS! ROBBERY IN PROGRESS!
FOUR GUYS... HMMM... THEY WALK FUNNY, KINDA BENT.
WELL, NO PROBLEMO--FOUR REGULAR HUMANS VERSUS ME, THAT'S EASY ODDS.
WEB THE OLD AUTOMATIC MOTOR-DRIVE CAMERA IN PLACE, SET TO START SHOOTING IN TEN SECONDS...
THWAP
THMMP
WEB UP THOSE TIRES FOR AN ESTIMATED SKID STOP OF ONE HUNDRED FEET--
--SETTING THE ACTION DIRECTLY IN THE CAMERA'S EYE!
NOW, TIME TO MAKE SOME GOOD SPIDEY HEROIC PICS FOR THE BUGLE!
THMMP

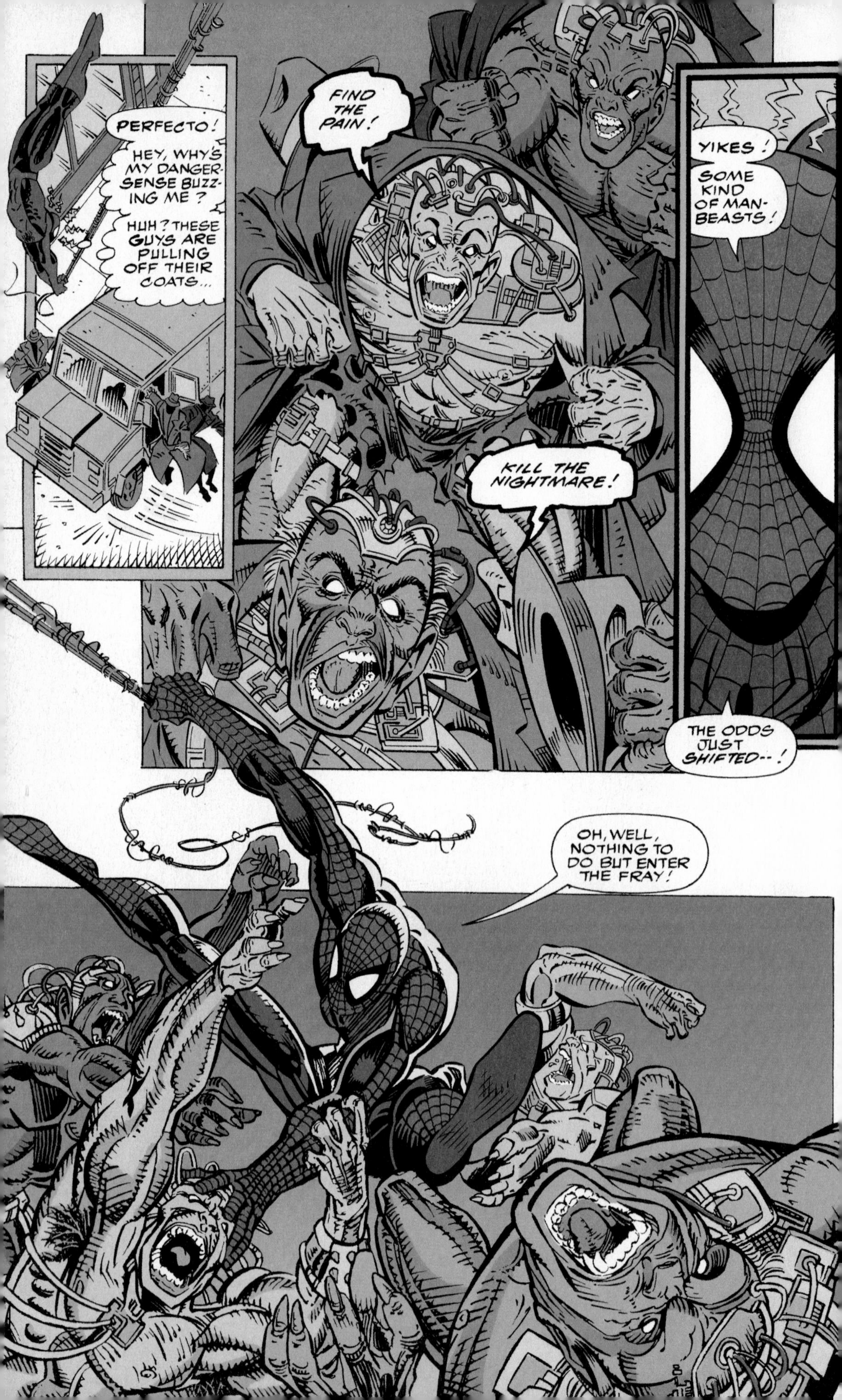
PERFECTO!
HEY, WHY'S MY DANGER-SENSE BUZZING ME?
HUH? THESE GUYS ARE PULLING OFF THEIR COATS...
FIND THE PAIN!
YIKES!
SOME KIND OF MAN-BEASTS!
KILL THE NIGHTMARE!
THE ODDS JUST SHIFTED--!
OH, WELL, NOTHING TO DO BUT ENTER THE FRAY!

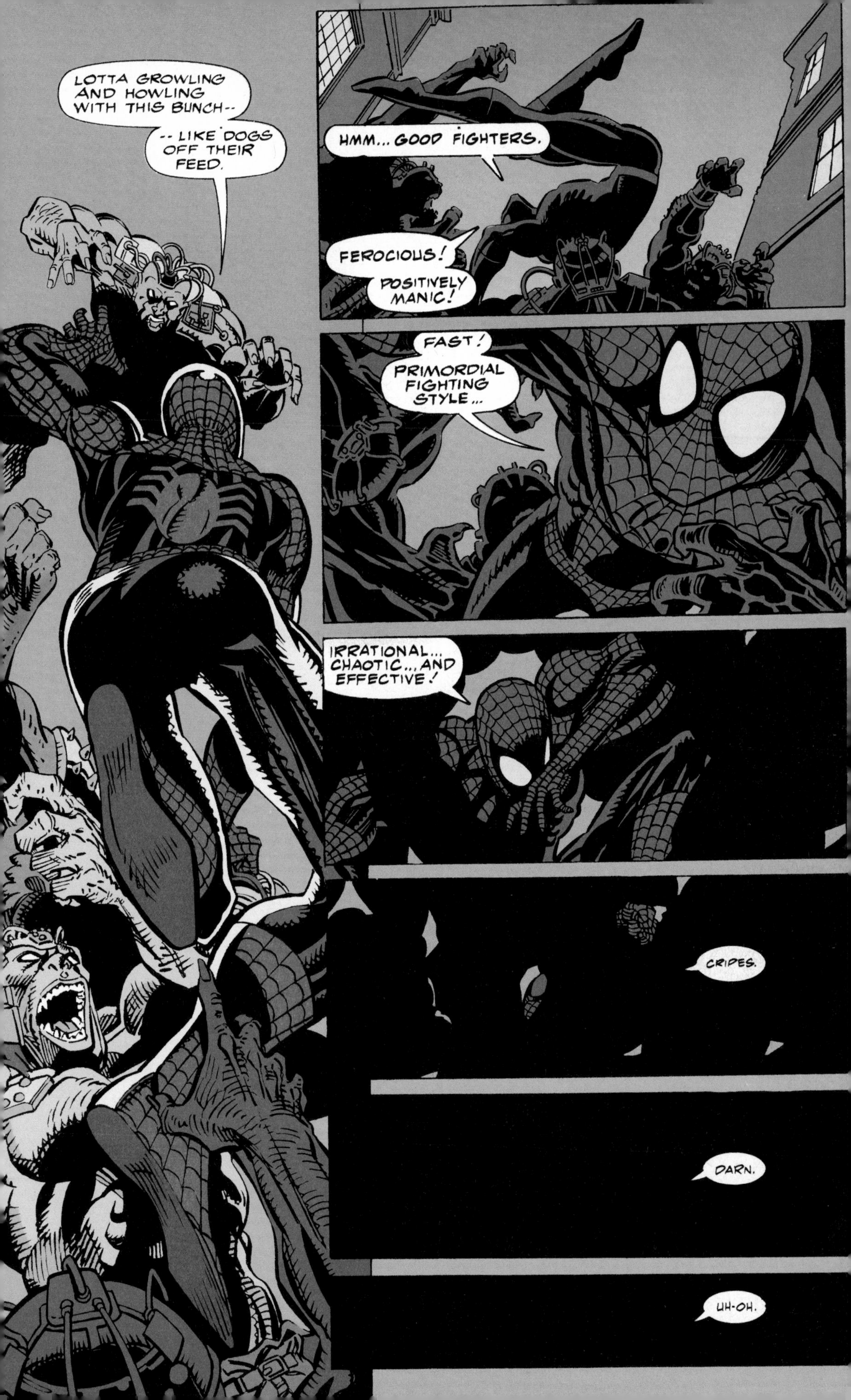
LOTTA GROWLING AND HOWLING WITH THIS BUNCH--
-- LIKE DOGS OFF THEIR FEED.
HMM... GOOD FIGHTERS.
FEROCIOUS!
POSITIVELY MANIC!
FAST!
PRIMORDIAL FIGHTING STYLE...
IRRATIONAL... CHAOTIC... AND EFFECTIVE!
CRIPES.
DARN.
UH-OH.

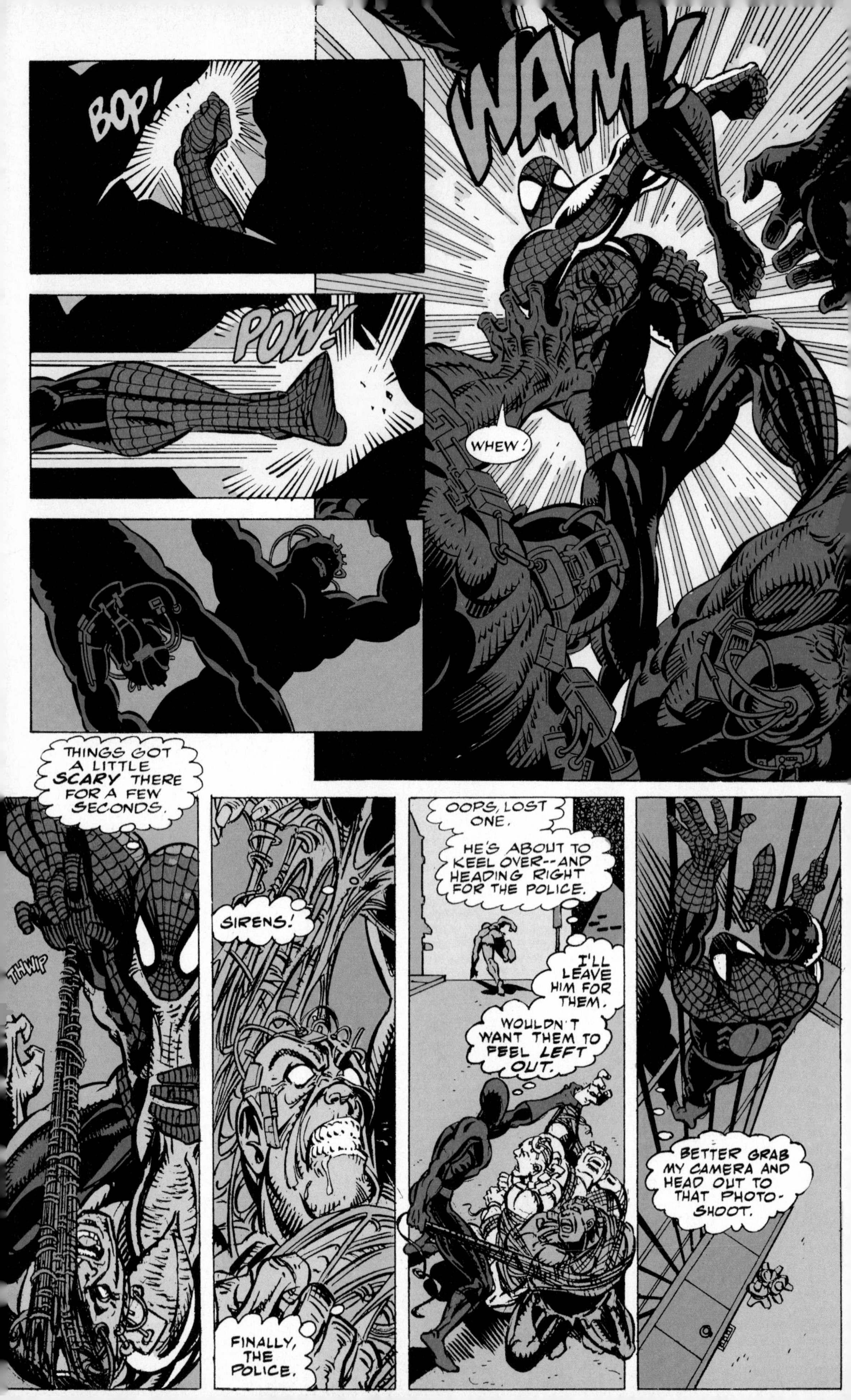
BOP!
WAM!
POW!
WHEW!
THINGS GOT A LITTLE SCARY THERE FOR A FEW SECONDS.
THWIP
SIRENS!
FINALLY, THE POLICE.
OOPS, LOST ONE.
HE'S ABOUT TO KEEL OVER--AND HEADING RIGHT FOR THE POLICE.
I'LL LEAVE HIM FOR THEM.
WOULDN'T WANT THEM TO FEEL LEFT OUT.
BETTER GRAB MY CAMERA AND HEAD OUT TO THAT PHOTO-SHOOT.

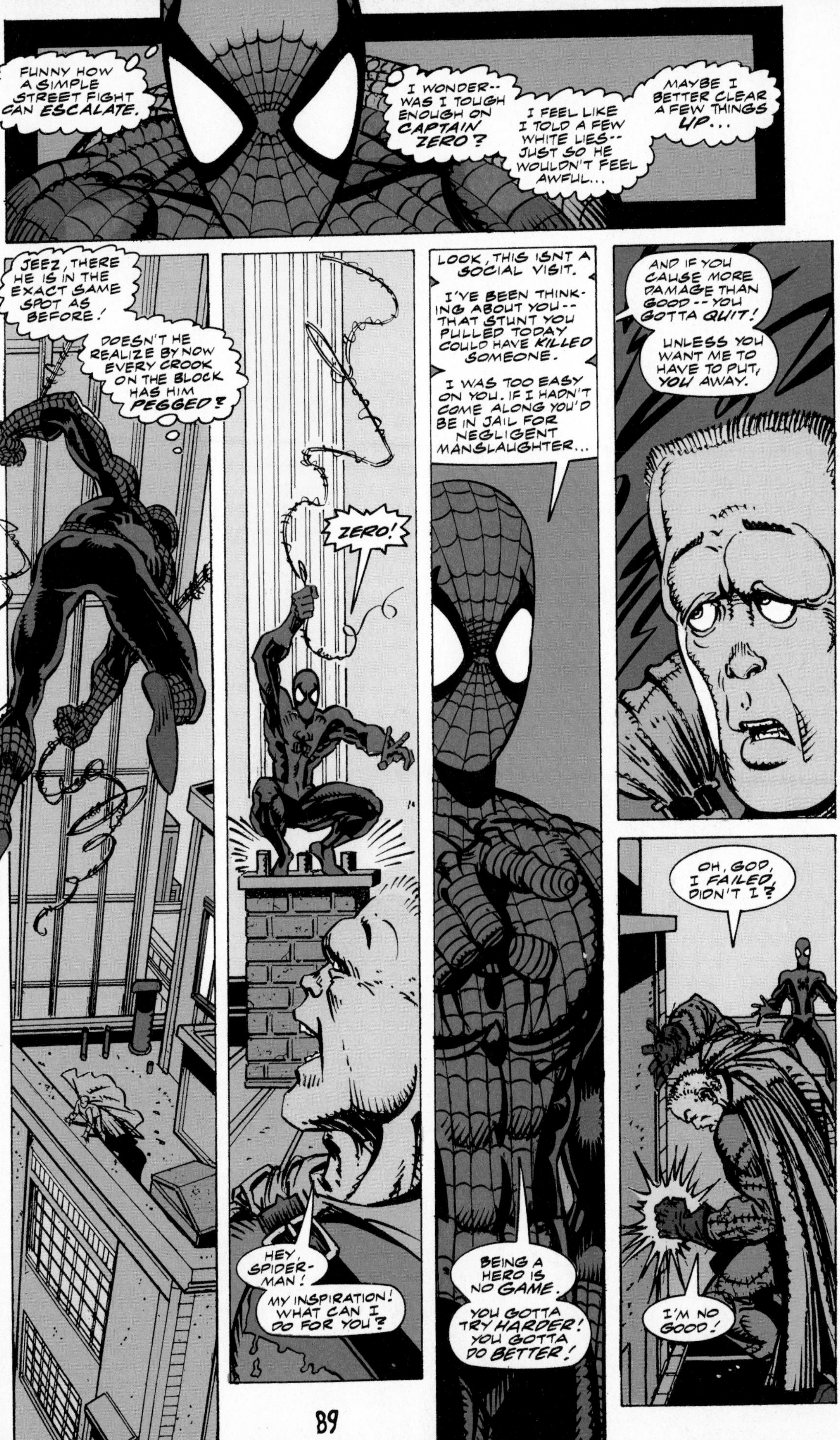

FUNNY HOW A SIMPLE STREET FIGHT CAN ESCALATE.
I WONDER-- WAS I TOUGH ENOUGH ON CAPTAIN ZERO?
I FEEL LIKE I TOLD A FEW WHITE LIES-- JUST SO HE WOULDN'T FEEL AWFUL...
MAYBE I BETTER CLEAR A FEW THINGS UP...
JEEZ, THERE HE IS IN THE EXACT SAME SPOT AS BEFORE!
DOESN'T HE REALIZE BY NOW EVERY CROOK ON THE BLOCK HAS HIM PEGGED?
ZERO!
HEY, SPIDER-MAN!
MY INSPIRATION! WHAT CAN I DO FOR YOU?
LOOK, THIS ISNT A SOCIAL VISIT.
I'VE BEEN THINKING ABOUT YOU-- THAT STUNT YOU PULLED TODAY COULD HAVE KILLED SOMEONE.
I WAS TOO EASY ON YOU. IF I HADN'T COME ALONG YOU'D BE IN JAIL FOR NEGLIGENT MANSLAUGHTER...
BEING A HERO IS NO GAME.
YOU GOTTA TRY HARDER! YOU GOTTA DO BETTER!
AND IF YOU CAUSE MORE DAMAGE THAN GOOD -- YOU GOTTA QUIT!
UNLESS YOU WANT ME TO HAVE TO PUT, YOU AWAY.
OH, GOD, I FAILED, DIDN'T I?
I'M NO GOOD!

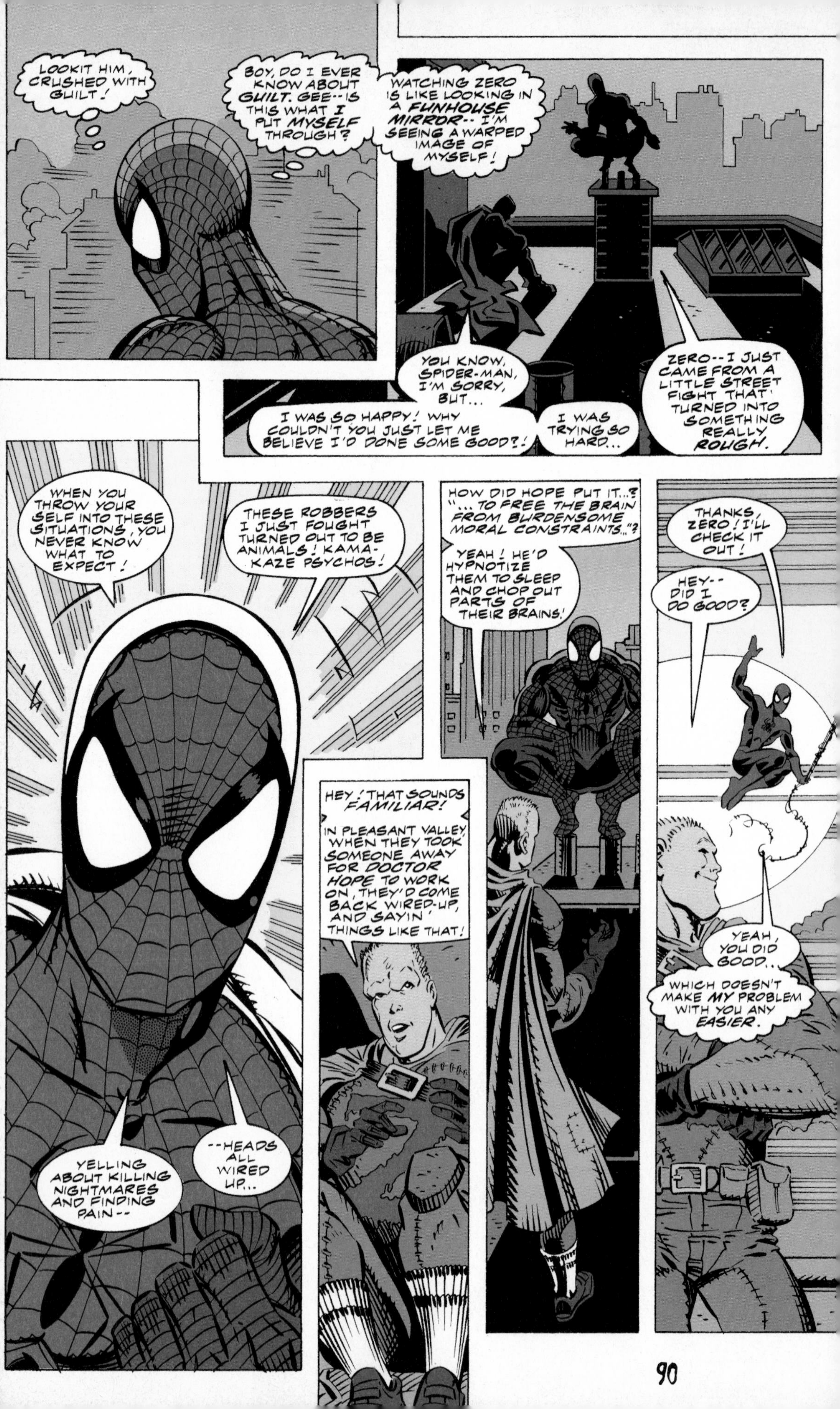

LOOKIT HIM, CRUSHED WITH GUILT!
BOY, DO I EVER KNOW ABOUT GUILT. GEE--IS THIS WHAT I PUT MYSELF THROUGH?
WATCHING ZERO IS LIKE LOOKING IN A FUNHOUSE MIRROR-- I'M SEEING A WARPED IMAGE OF MYSELF!
YOU KNOW, SPIDER-MAN, I'M SORRY, BUT...
I WAS SO HAPPY! WHY COULDN'T YOU JUST LET ME BELIEVE I'D DONE SOME GOOD?!
I WAS TRYING SO HARD...
ZERO--I JUST CAME FROM A LITTLE STREET FIGHT THAT TURNED INTO SOMETHING REALLY ROUGH.
WHEN YOU THROW YOURSELF INTO THESE SITUATIONS, YOU NEVER KNOW WHAT TO EXPECT!
THESE ROBBERS I JUST FOUGHT TURNED OUT TO BE ANIMALS! KAMAKAZE PSYCHOS!
YELLING ABOUT KILLING NIGHTMARES AND FINDING PAIN--
--HEADS ALL WIRED UP...
HEY! THAT SOUNDS FAMILIAR!
IN PLEASANT VALLEY, WHEN THEY TOOK SOMEONE AWAY FOR DOCTOR HOPE TO WORK ON, THEY'D COME BACK WIRED-UP, AND SAYIN' THINGS LIKE THAT!
HOW DID HOPE PUT IT...? "...TO FREE THE BRAIN FROM BURDENSOME MORAL CONSTRAINTS..."?
YEAH! HE'D HYPNOTIZE THEM TO SLEEP AND CHOP OUT PARTS OF THEIR BRAINS!
THANKS, ZERO! I'LL CHECK IT OUT!
HEY-- DID I DO GOOD?
YEAH, YOU DID GOOD..
WHICH DOESN'T MAKE MY PROBLEM WITH YOU ANY EASIER.

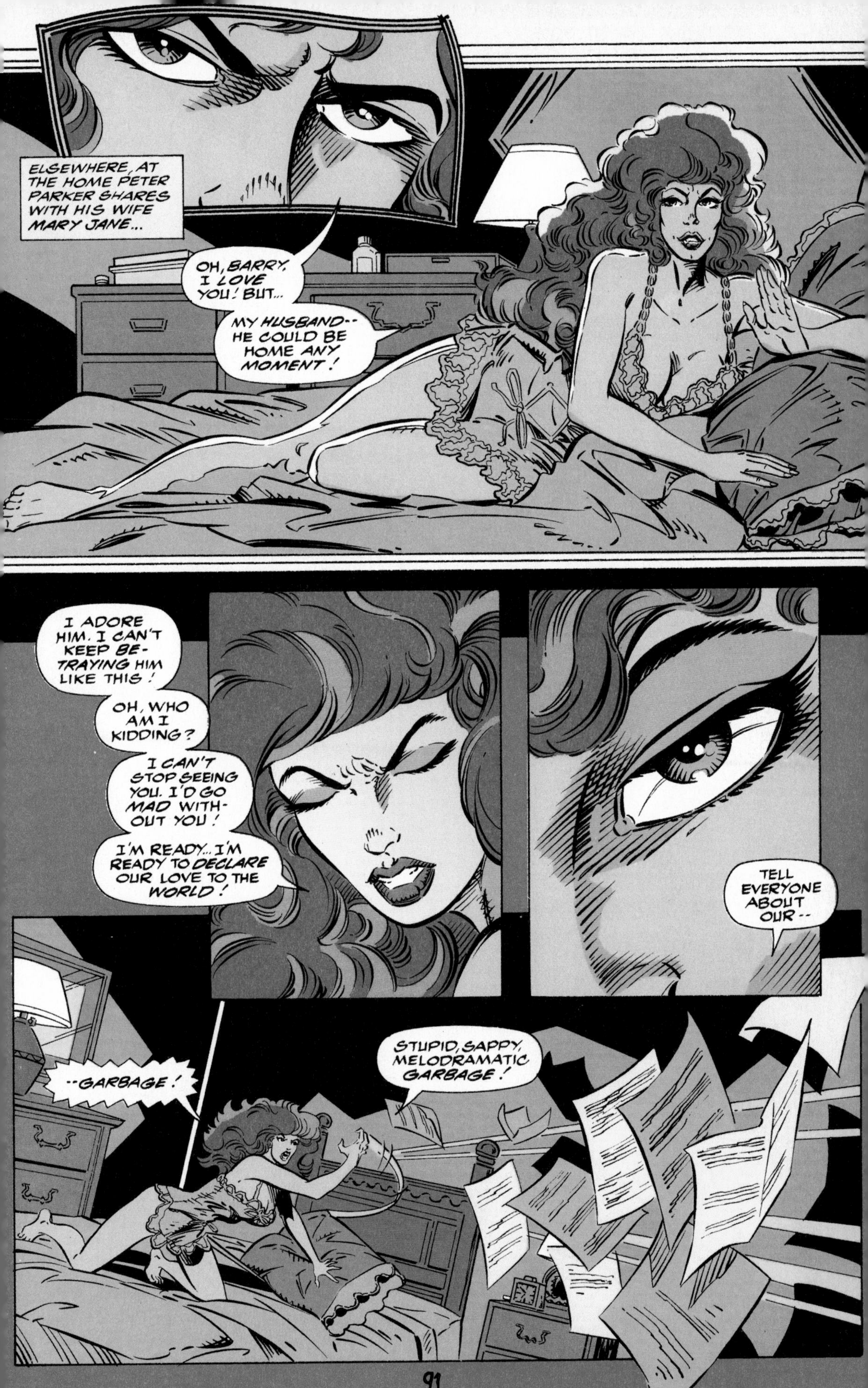
ELSEWHERE, AT THE HOME PETER PARKER SHARES WITH HIS WIFE MARY JANE...
OH, BARRY, I LOVE YOU! BUT...
MY HUSBAND-- HE COULD BE HOME ANY MOMENT!
I ADORE HIM. I CAN'T KEEP BE-TRAYING HIM LIKE THIS!
OH, WHO AM I KIDDING?
I CAN'T STOP SEEING YOU. I'D GO MAD WITH-OUT YOU!
I'M READY... I'M READY TO DECLARE OUR LOVE TO THE WORLD!
TELL EVERYONE ABOUT OUR--
--GARBAGE!
STUPID, SAPPY, MELODRAMATIC GARBAGE!

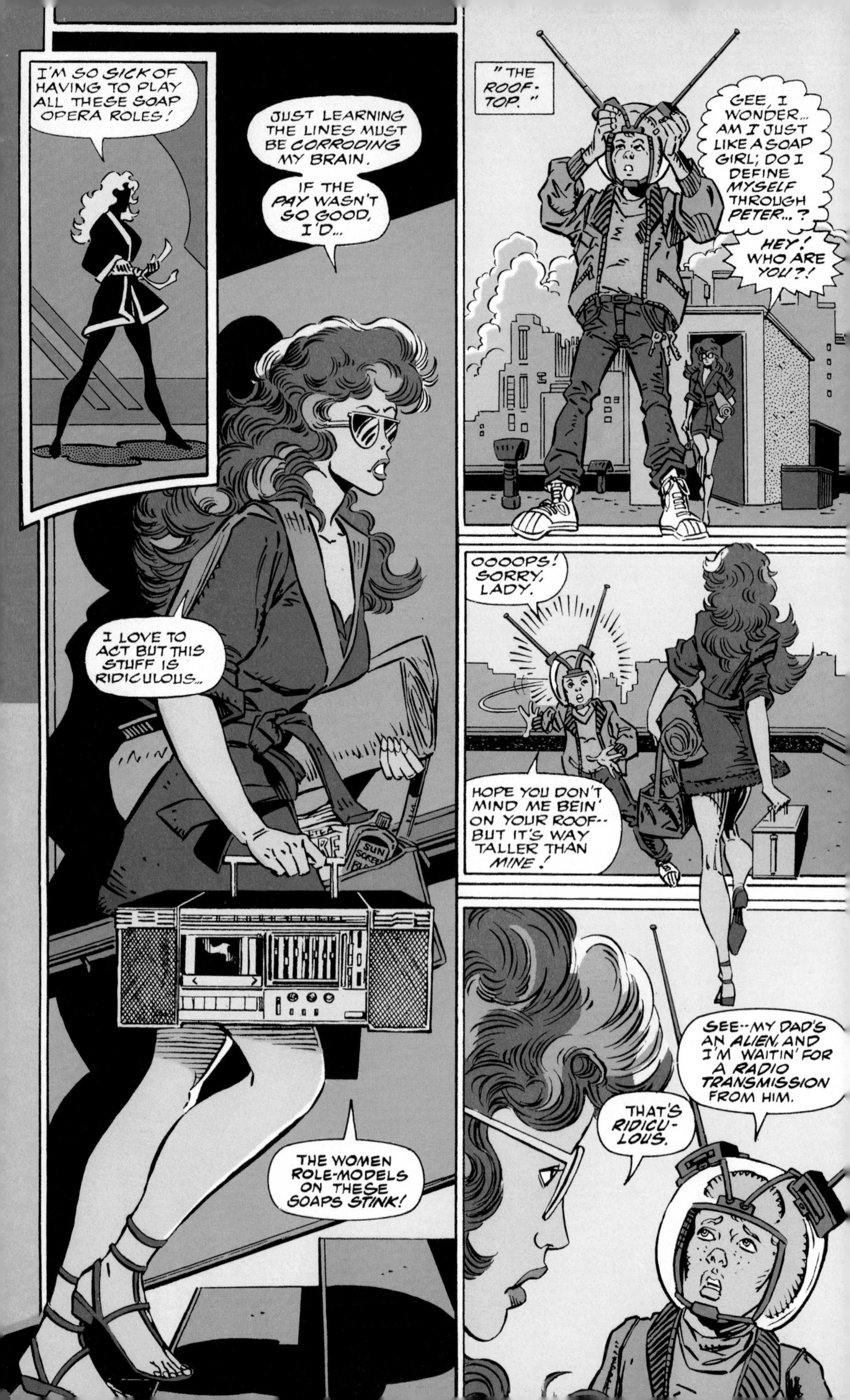
I'M SO SICK OF HAVING TO PLAY ALL THESE SOAP OPERA ROLES!
JUST LEARNING THE LINES MUST BE CORRODING MY BRAIN.
IF THE PAY WASN'T SO GOOD, I'D...
I LOVE TO ACT BUT THIS STUFF IS RIDICULOUS...
THE WOMEN ROLE-MODELS ON THESE SOAPS STINK!
"THE ROOF-TOP."
GEE, I WONDER... AM I JUST LIKE A SOAP GIRL; DO I DEFINE MYSELF THROUGH PETER...?
HEY! WHO ARE YOU?!
OOOOPS! SORRY, LADY.
HOPE YOU DON'T MIND ME BEIN' ON YOUR ROOF-- BUT IT'S WAY TALLER THAN MINE!
SEE--MY DAD'S AN ALIEN, AND I'M WAITIN' FOR A RADIO TRANSMISSION FROM HIM.
THAT'S RIDICU-LOUS.

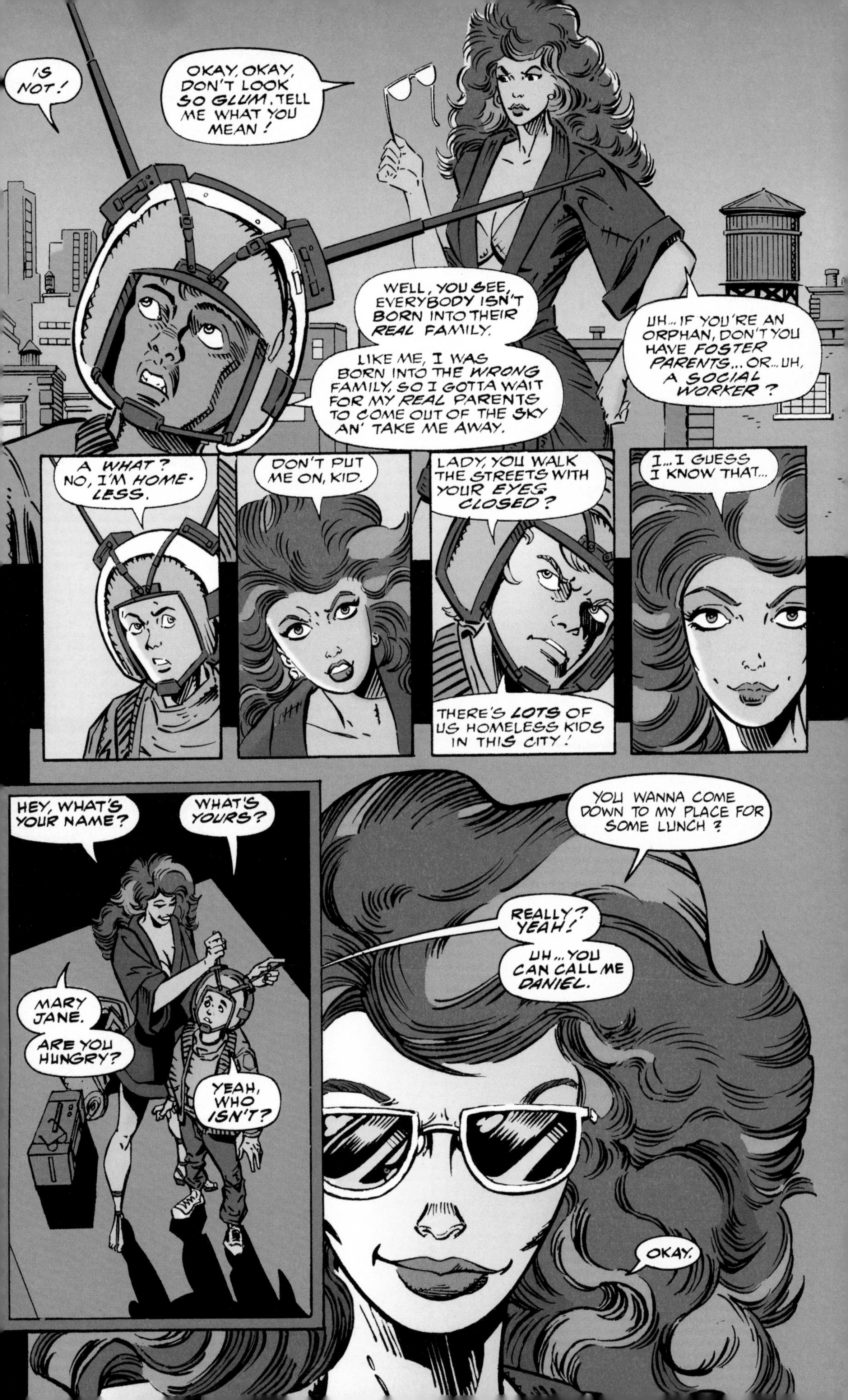
IS NOT!
OKAY, OKAY, DON'T LOOK SO GLUM. TELL ME WHAT YOU MEAN!
WELL, YOU SEE, EVERYBODY ISN'T BORN INTO THEIR REAL FAMILY.
LIKE ME, I WAS BORN INTO THE WRONG FAMILY, SO I GOTTA WAIT FOR MY REAL PARENTS TO COME OUT OF THE SKY AN' TAKE ME AWAY.
UH... IF YOU'RE AN ORPHAN, DON'T YOU HAVE FOSTER PARENTS... OR... UH, A SOCIAL WORKER?
A WHAT? NO, I'M HOME-LESS.
DON'T PUT ME ON, KID.
LADY, YOU WALK THE STREETS WITH YOUR EYES CLOSED?
THERE'S LOTS OF US HOMELESS KIDS IN THIS CITY!
I... I GUESS I KNOW THAT...
HEY, WHAT'S YOUR NAME?
WHAT'S YOURS?
MARY JANE.
ARE YOU HUNGRY?
YEAH, WHO ISN'T?
YOU WANNA COME DOWN TO MY PLACE FOR SOME LUNCH?
REALLY? YEAH!
UH... YOU CAN CALL ME DANIEL.
OKAY.

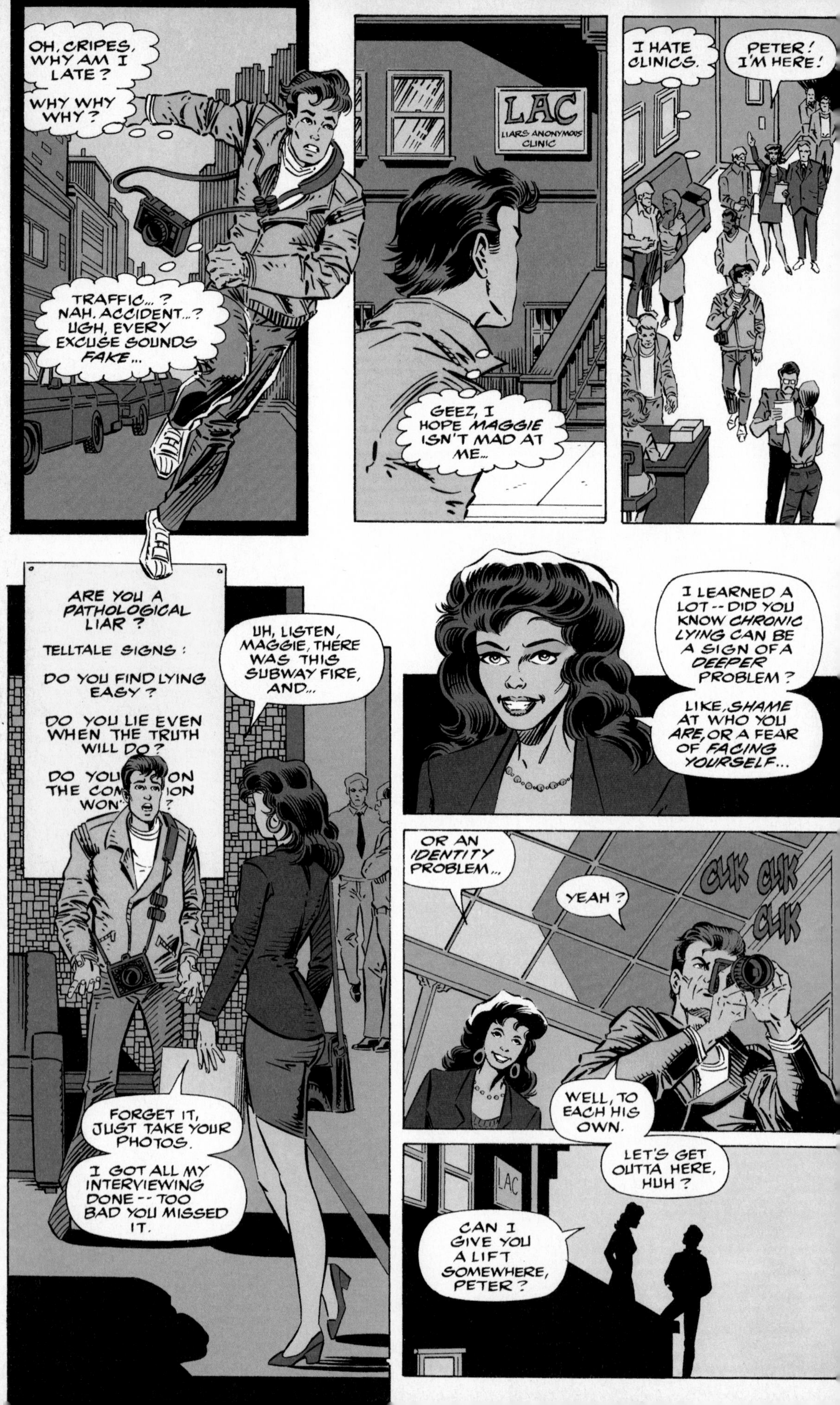

OH, CRIPES, WHY AM I LATE?
WHY WHY WHY?
TRAFFIC...? NAH. ACCIDENT...? UGH, EVERY EXCUSE SOUNDS FAKE...
LAC
LIARS ANONYMOUS CLINIC
GEEZ, I HOPE MAGGIE ISN'T MAD AT ME...
I HATE CLINICS.
PETER! I'M HERE!
ARE YOU A PATHOLOGICAL LIAR?
TELLTALE SIGNS:
DO YOU FIND LYING EASY?
DO YOU LIE EVEN WHEN THE TRUTH WILL DO?
UH, LISTEN, MAGGIE, THERE WAS THIS SUBWAY FIRE, AND...
FORGET IT, JUST TAKE YOUR PHOTOS.
I GOT ALL MY INTERVIEWING DONE -- TOO BAD YOU MISSED IT.
I LEARNED A LOT -- DID YOU KNOW CHRONIC LYING CAN BE A SIGN OF A DEEPER PROBLEM?
LIKE, SHAME AT WHO YOU ARE, OR A FEAR OF FACING YOURSELF...
OR AN IDENTITY PROBLEM...
YEAH?
CLIK CLIK CLIK
WELL, TO EACH HIS OWN.
LET'S GET OUTTA HERE, HUH?
LAC
CAN I GIVE YOU A LIFT SOMEWHERE, PETER?

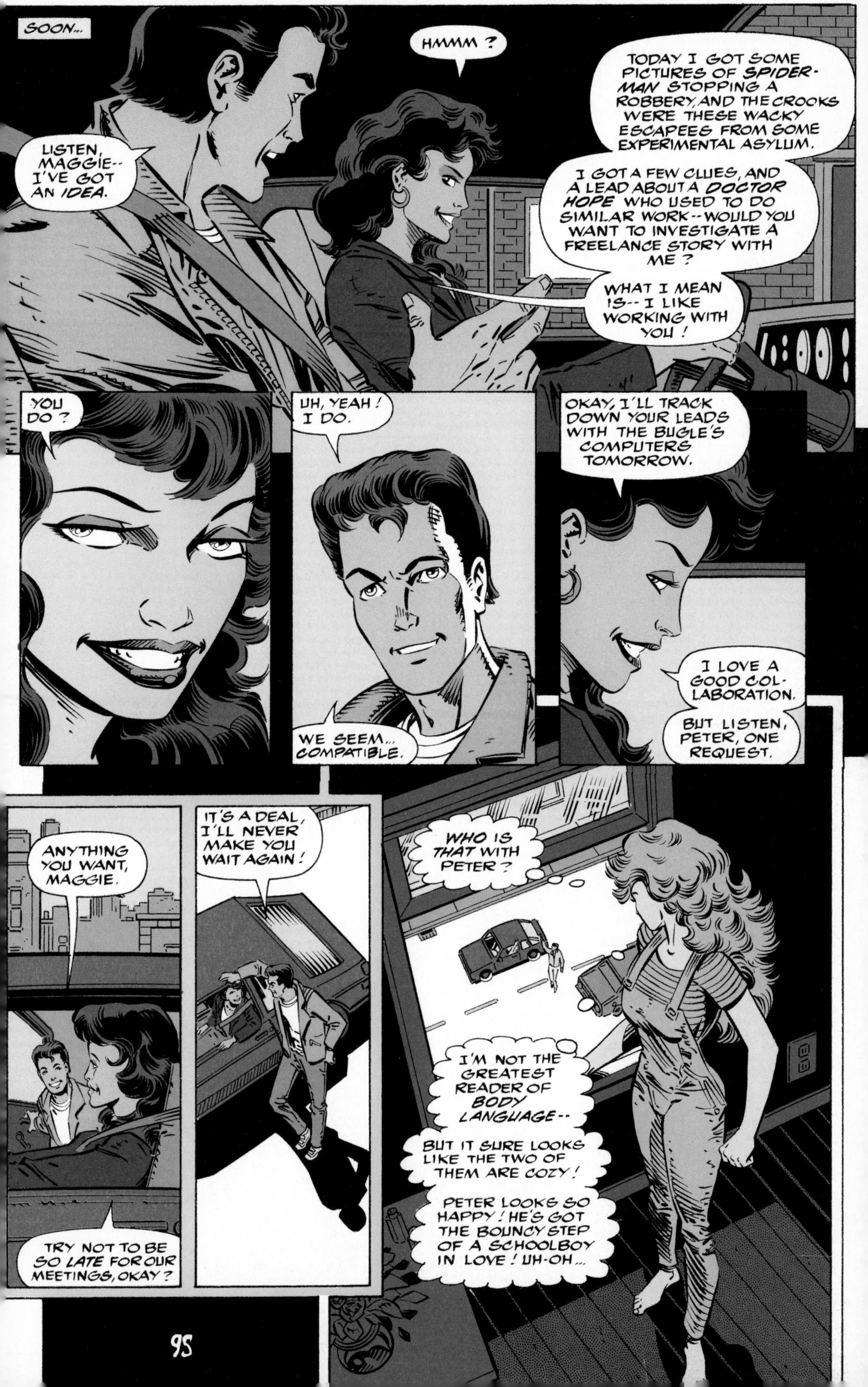
SOON...
LISTEN, MAGGIE-- I'VE GOT AN IDEA.
HMMM ?
TODAY I GOT SOME PICTURES OF SPIDER-MAN STOPPING A ROBBERY, AND THE CROOKS WERE THESE WACKY ESCAPEES FROM SOME EXPERIMENTAL ASYLUM.
I GOT A FEW CLUES, AND A LEAD ABOUT A DOCTOR HOPE WHO USED TO DO SIMILAR WORK--WOULD YOU WANT TO INVESTIGATE A FREELANCE STORY WITH ME ?
WHAT I MEAN IS-- I LIKE WORKING WITH YOU !
YOU DO ?
UH, YEAH ! I DO.
WE SEEM... COMPATIBLE.
OKAY, I'LL TRACK DOWN YOUR LEADS WITH THE BUGLE'S COMPUTERS TOMORROW.
I LOVE A GOOD COL-LABORATION.
BUT LISTEN, PETER, ONE REQUEST.
TRY NOT TO BE SO LATE FOR OUR MEETINGS, OKAY ?
ANYTHING YOU WANT, MAGGIE.
IT'S A DEAL, I'LL NEVER MAKE YOU WAIT AGAIN !
WHO IS THAT WITH PETER ?
I'M NOT THE GREATEST READER OF BODY LANGUAGE--
BUT IT SURE LOOKS LIKE THE TWO OF THEM ARE COZY !
PETER LOOKS SO HAPPY ! HE'S GOT THE BOUNCY STEP OF A SCHOOLBOY IN LOVE ! UH-OH...

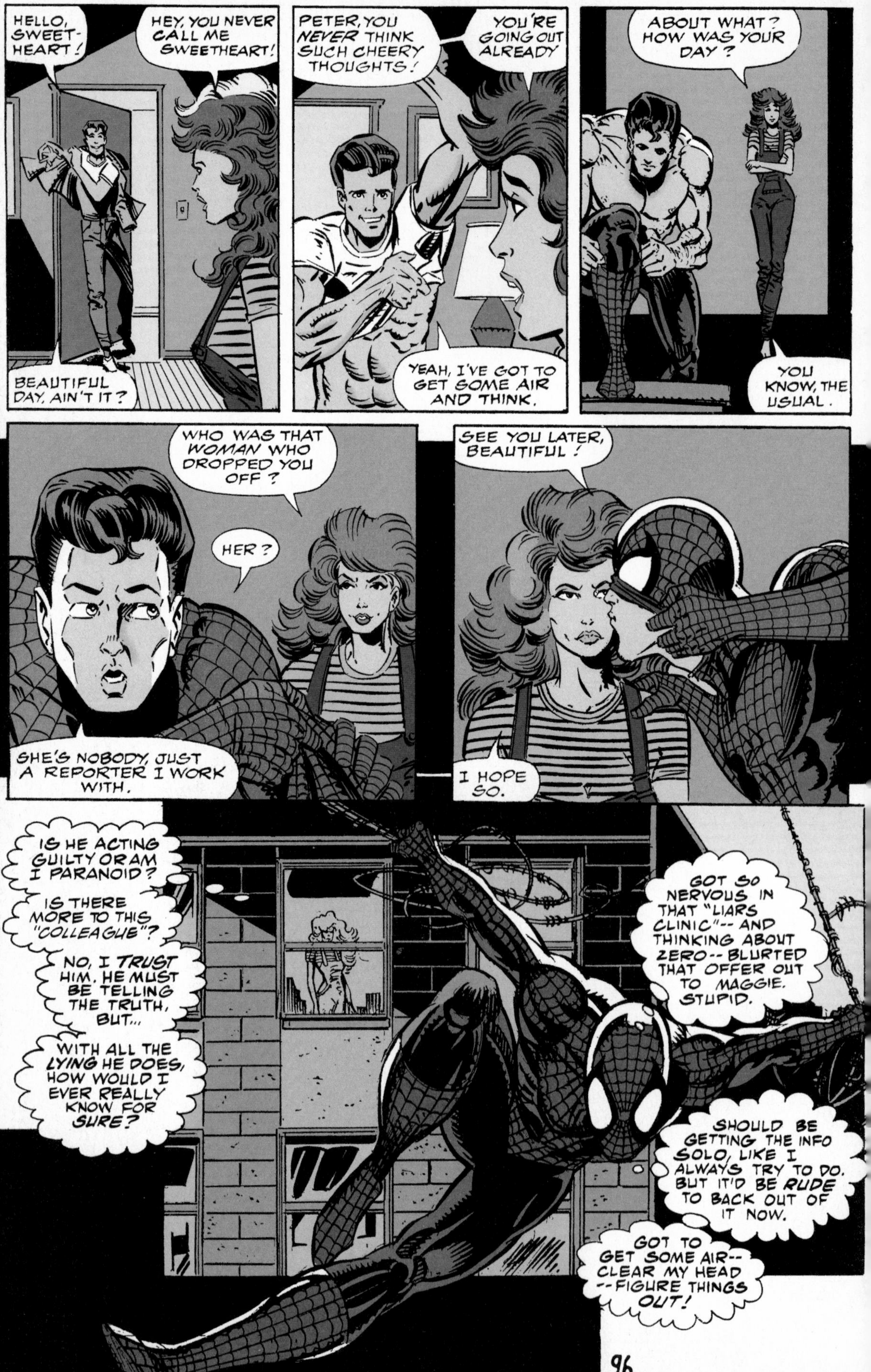

HELLO, SWEET-HEART!
HEY, YOU NEVER CALL ME SWEETHEART!
BEAUTIFUL DAY, AIN'T IT?
PETER, YOU NEVER THINK SUCH CHEERY THOUGHTS!
YOU'RE GOING OUT ALREADY
YEAH, I'VE GOT TO GET SOME AIR AND THINK.
ABOUT WHAT? HOW WAS YOUR DAY?
YOU KNOW, THE USUAL.
WHO WAS THAT WOMAN WHO DROPPED YOU OFF?
HER?
SHE'S NOBODY, JUST A REPORTER I WORK WITH.
SEE YOU LATER, BEAUTIFUL!
I HOPE SO.
IS HE ACTING GUILTY OR AM I PARANOID?
IS THERE MORE TO THIS "COLLEAGUE"?
NO, I TRUST HIM. HE MUST BE TELLING THE TRUTH, BUT...
WITH ALL THE LYING HE DOES, HOW WOULD I EVER REALLY KNOW FOR SURE?
GOT SO NERVOUS IN THAT "LIARS CLINIC"-- AND THINKING ABOUT ZERO-- BLURTED THAT OFFER OUT TO MAGGIE. STUPID.
SHOULD BE GETTING THE INFO SOLO, LIKE I ALWAYS TRY TO DO. BUT IT'D BE RUDE TO BACK OUT OF IT NOW.
GOT TO GET SOME AIR-- CLEAR MY HEAD --FIGURE THINGS OUT!

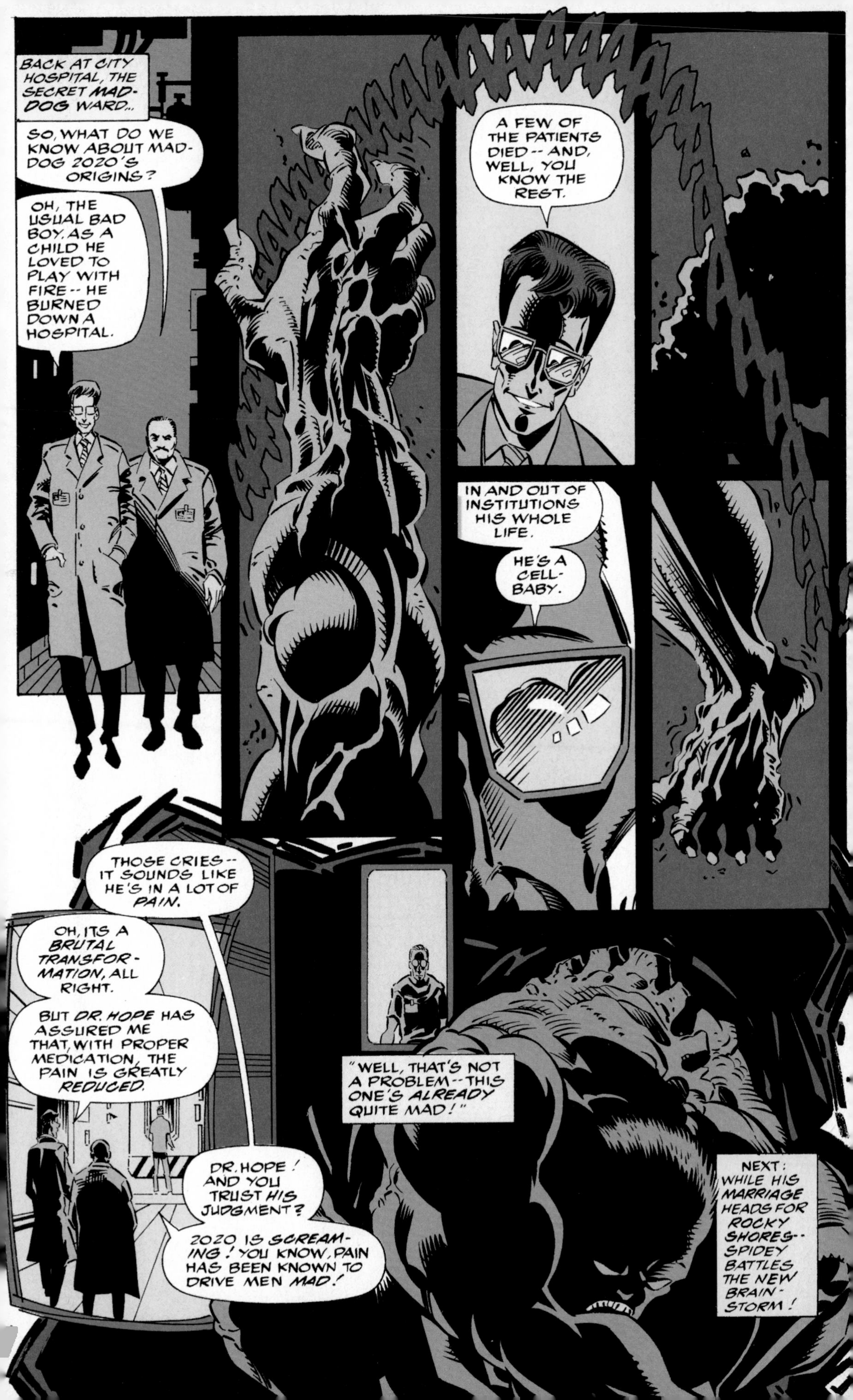
BACK AT CITY HOSPITAL, THE SECRET MAD-DOG WARD...
SO, WHAT DO WE KNOW ABOUT MAD-DOG 2020'S ORIGINS?
OH, THE USUAL BAD BOY. AS A CHILD HE LOVED TO PLAY WITH FIRE -- HE BURNED DOWN A HOSPITAL.
AAAAAAAAAAAAAAAAAAAAAAAAAAAAAAAAAAAAAAAA
A FEW OF THE PATIENTS DIED -- AND, WELL, YOU KNOW THE REST.
IN AND OUT OF INSTITUTIONS HIS WHOLE LIFE.
HE'S A CELL-BABY.
THOSE CRIES -- IT SOUNDS LIKE HE'S IN A LOT OF PAIN.
OH, ITS A BRUTAL TRANSFORMATION, ALL RIGHT.
BUT DR. HOPE HAS ASSURED ME THAT, WITH PROPER MEDICATION, THE PAIN IS GREATLY REDUCED.
DR. HOPE! AND YOU TRUST HIS JUDGMENT?
2020 IS SCREAMING! YOU KNOW, PAIN HAS BEEN KNOWN TO DRIVE MEN MAD!
"WELL, THAT'S NOT A PROBLEM -- THIS ONE'S ALREADY QUITE MAD!"
NEXT: WHILE HIS MARRIAGE HEADS FOR ROCKY SHORES -- SPIDEY BATTLES THE NEW BRAIN-STORM!

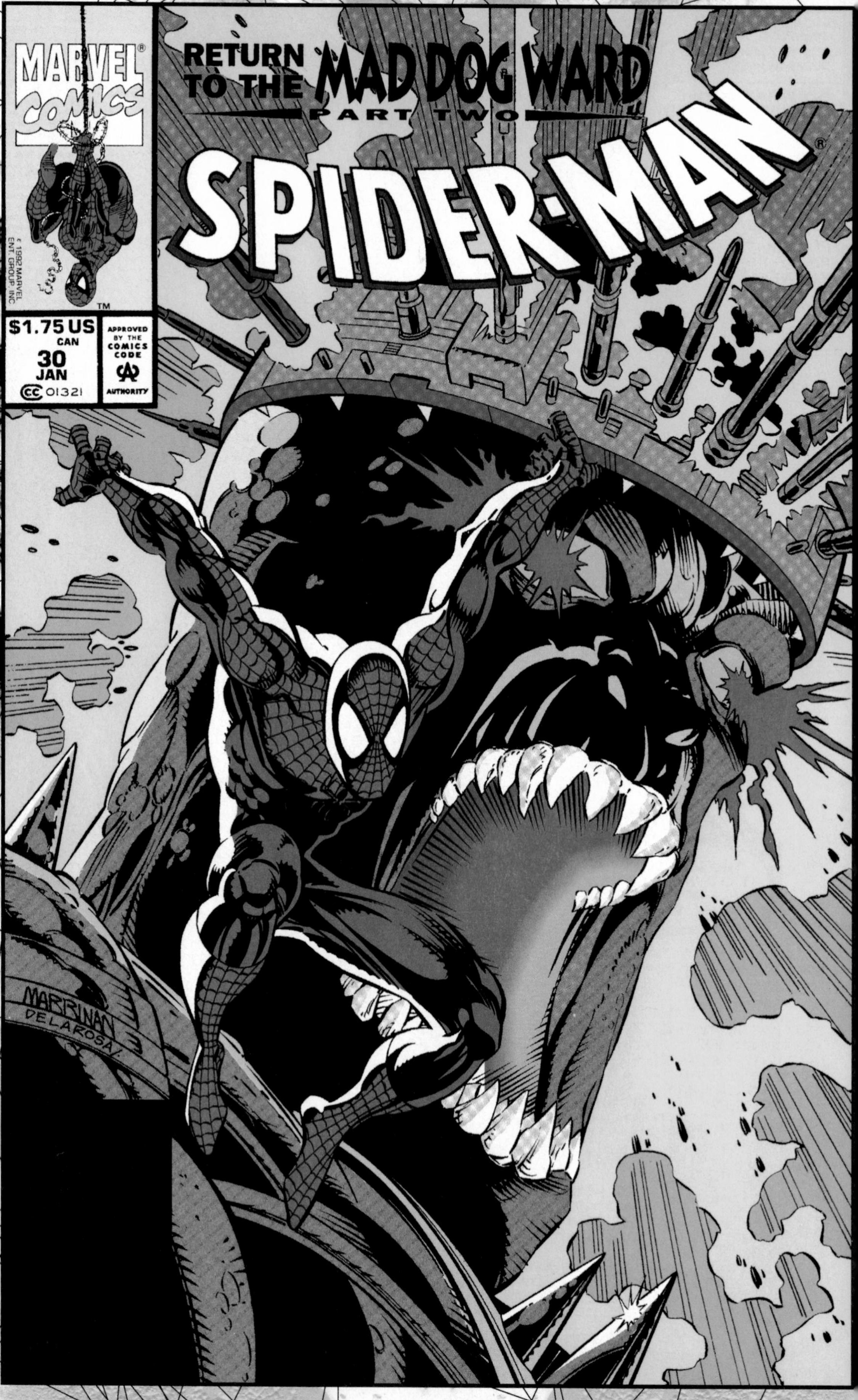
MARVEL COMICS
RETURN TO THE MAD DOG WARD
PART TWO
SPIDER-MAN
© 1992 MARVEL ENT. GROUP, INC
$1.75 US
CAN
30
JAN
CC 01321
APPROVED BY THE COMICS CODE AUTHORITY
MARRINAN
DELAROSA

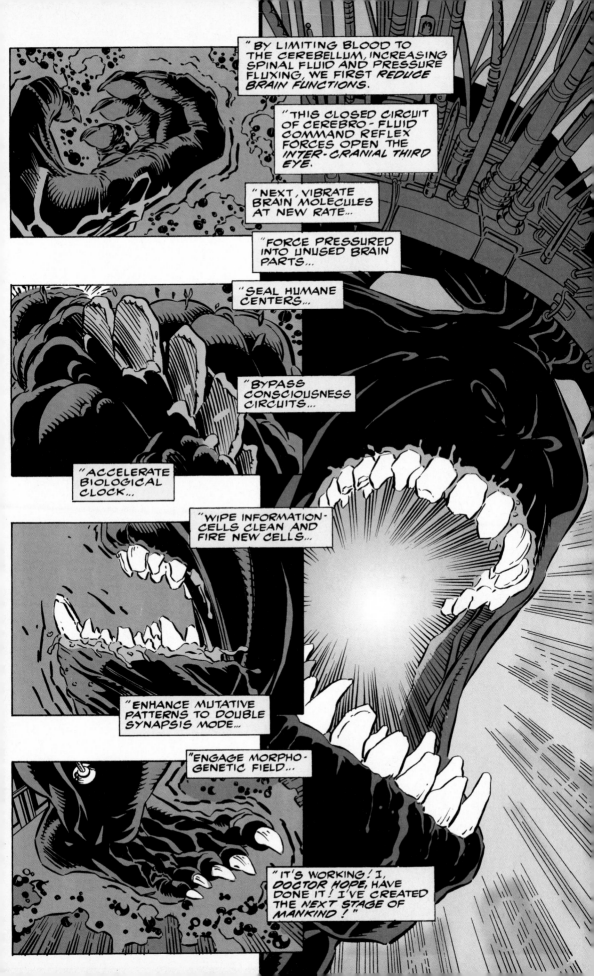

"BY LIMITING BLOOD TO THE CEREBELLUM, INCREASING SPINAL FLUID AND PRESSURE FLUXING, WE FIRST *REDUCE* BRAIN FUNCTIONS.

"THIS CLOSED CIRCUIT OF CEREBRO-FLUID COMMAND REFLEX FORCES OPEN THE *INTER-CRANIAL THIRD EYE.*

"NEXT, VIBRATE BRAIN MOLECULES AT NEW RATE...

"FORCE PRESSURED INTO UNUSED BRAIN PARTS...

"SEAL HUMANE CENTERS...

"BYPASS CONSCIOUSNESS CIRCUITS...

"ACCELERATE BIOLOGICAL CLOCK...

"WIPE INFORMATION-CELLS CLEAN AND FIRE NEW CELLS...

"ENHANCE MUTATIVE PATTERNS TO DOUBLE SYNAPSIS MODE...

"ENGAGE MORPHO-GENETIC FIELD...

"IT'S WORKING! I, *DOCTOR HOPE,* HAVE DONE IT! I'VE CREATED THE *NEXT STAGE OF MANKIND!*"

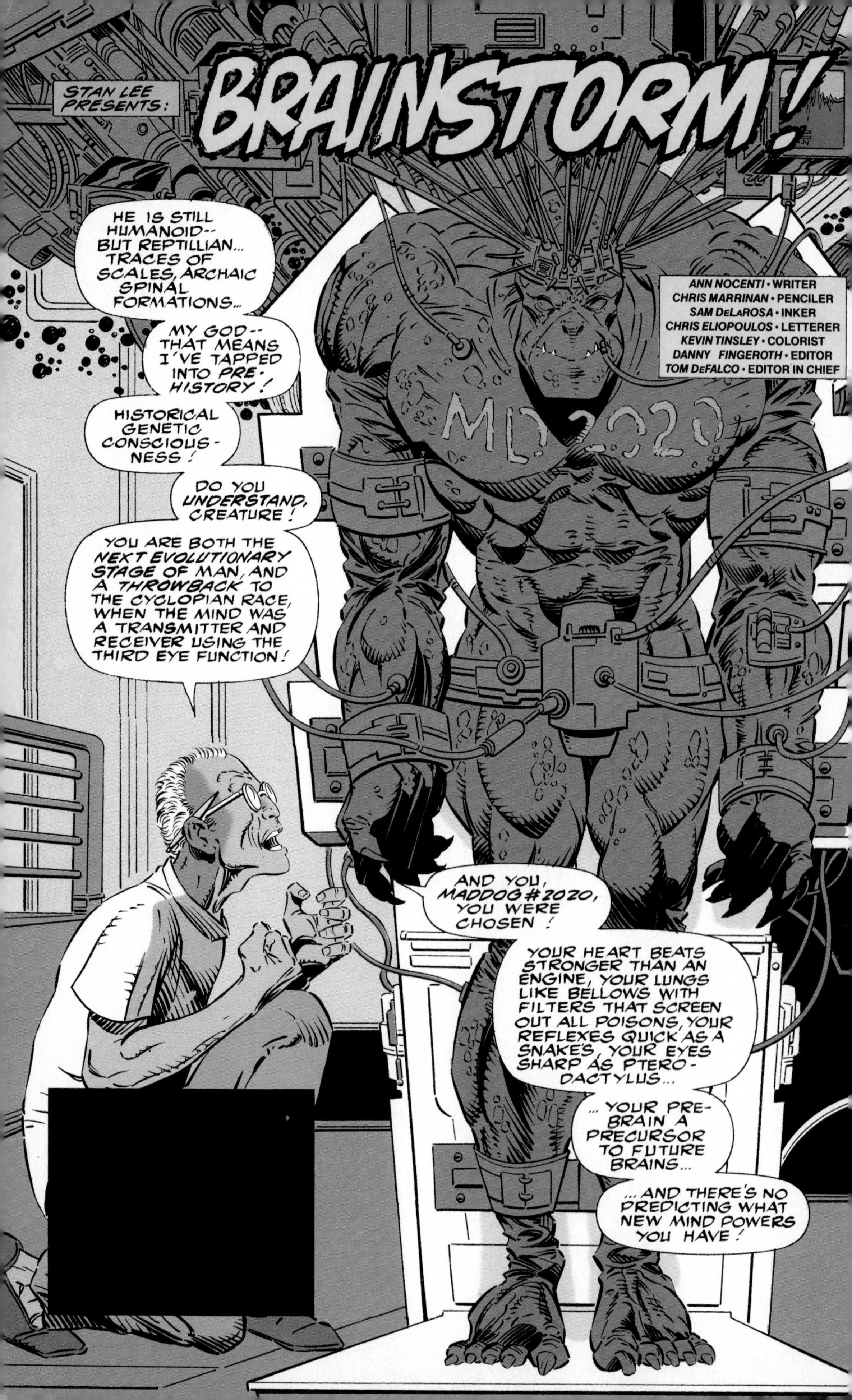

STAN LEE PRESENTS:
BRAINSTORM!
HE IS STILL HUMANOID-- BUT REPTILLIAN... TRACES OF SCALES, ARCHAIC SPINAL FORMATIONS...
MY GOD-- THAT MEANS I'VE TAPPED INTO PRE-HISTORY!
HISTORICAL GENETIC CONSCIOUSNESS!
DO YOU UNDERSTAND, CREATURE!
YOU ARE BOTH THE NEXT EVOLUTIONARY STAGE OF MAN, AND A THROWBACK TO THE CYCLOPIAN RACE, WHEN THE MIND WAS A TRANSMITTER AND RECEIVER USING THE THIRD EYE FUNCTION!
ANN NOCENTI • WRITER
CHRIS MARRINAN • PENCILER
SAM DeLaROSA • INKER
CHRIS ELIOPOULOS • LETTERER
KEVIN TINSLEY • COLORIST
DANNY FINGEROTH • EDITOR
TOM DeFALCO • EDITOR IN CHIEF
MD 2020
AND YOU, MADDOG #2020, YOU WERE CHOSEN!
YOUR HEART BEATS STRONGER THAN AN ENGINE, YOUR LUNGS LIKE BELLOWS WITH FILTERS THAT SCREEN OUT ALL POISONS, YOUR REFLEXES QUICK AS A SNAKE'S, YOUR EYES SHARP AS PTERO-DACTYLUS...
... YOUR PRE-BRAIN A PRECURSOR TO FUTURE BRAINS...
... AND THERE'S NO PREDICTING WHAT NEW MIND POWERS YOU HAVE!
[redacted]

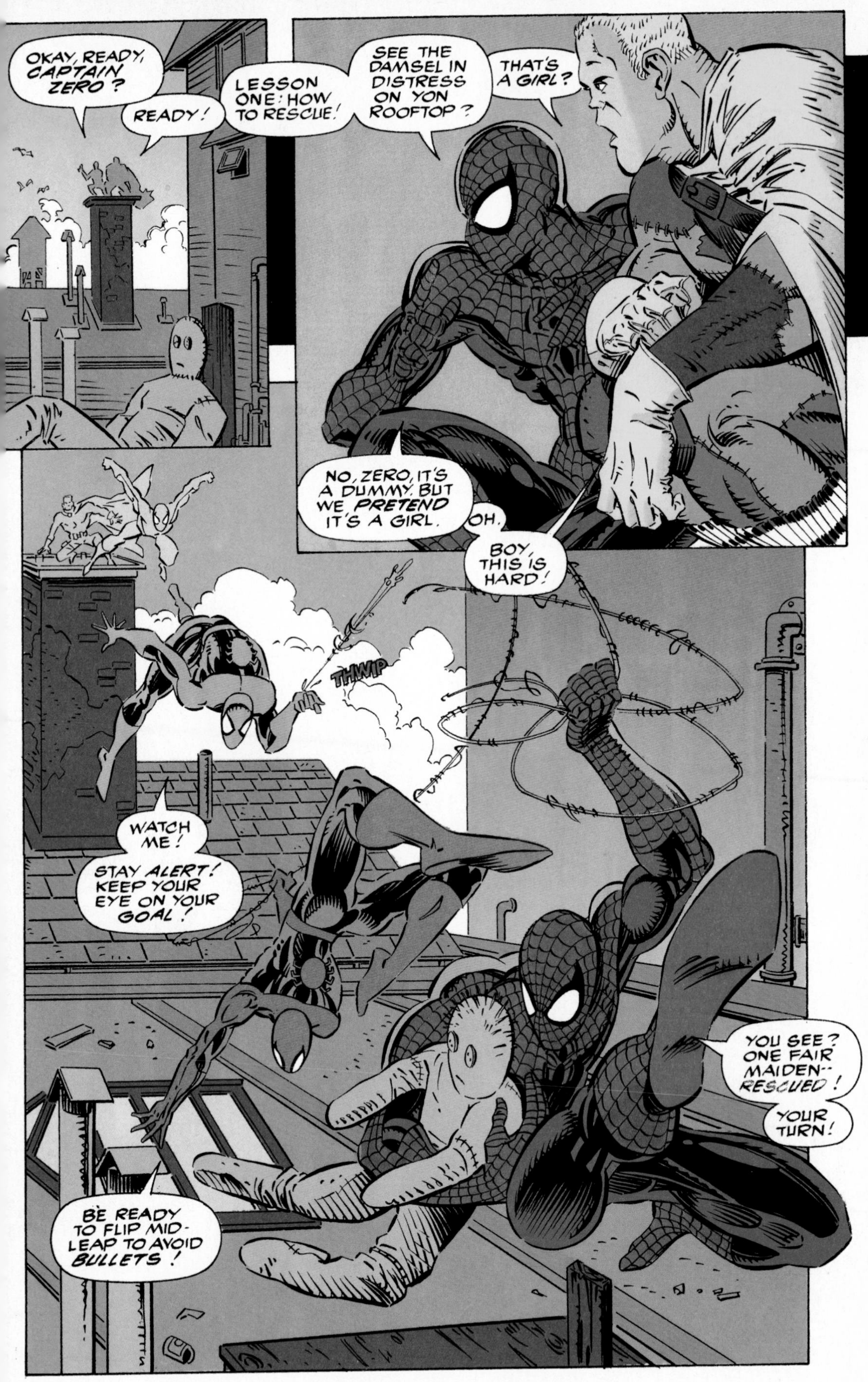

OKAY, READY, CAPTAIN ZERO?
READY!
LESSON ONE: HOW TO RESCUE!
SEE THE DAMSEL IN DISTRESS ON YON ROOFTOP?
THAT'S A GIRL?
NO, ZERO, IT'S A DUMMY. BUT WE PRETEND IT'S A GIRL.
OH.
BOY, THIS IS HARD!
THWIP
WATCH ME!
STAY ALERT! KEEP YOUR EYE ON YOUR GOAL!
BE READY TO FLIP MID-LEAP TO AVOID BULLETS!
YOU SEE? ONE FAIR MAIDEN-- RESCUED!
YOUR TURN!

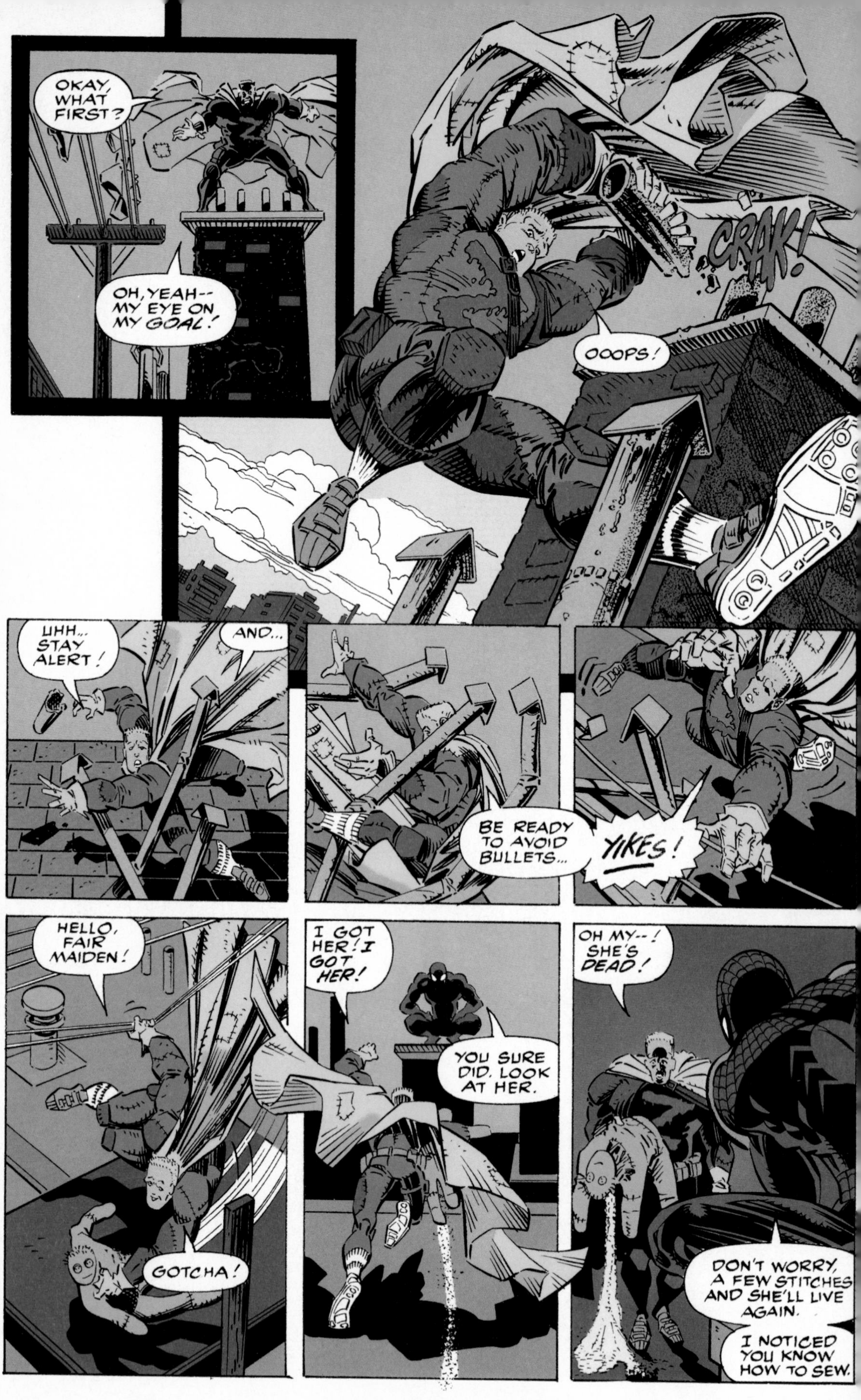
OKAY, WHAT FIRST?
OH, YEAH-- MY EYE ON MY GOAL!
CRAK!
OOOPS!
UHH... STAY ALERT!
AND...
BE READY TO AVOID BULLETS...
YIKES!
HELLO, FAIR MAIDEN!
GOTCHA!
I GOT HER! I GOT HER!
YOU SURE DID. LOOK AT HER.
OH MY--! SHE'S DEAD!
DON'T WORRY, A FEW STITCHES AND SHE'LL LIVE AGAIN.
I NOTICED YOU KNOW HOW TO SEW.

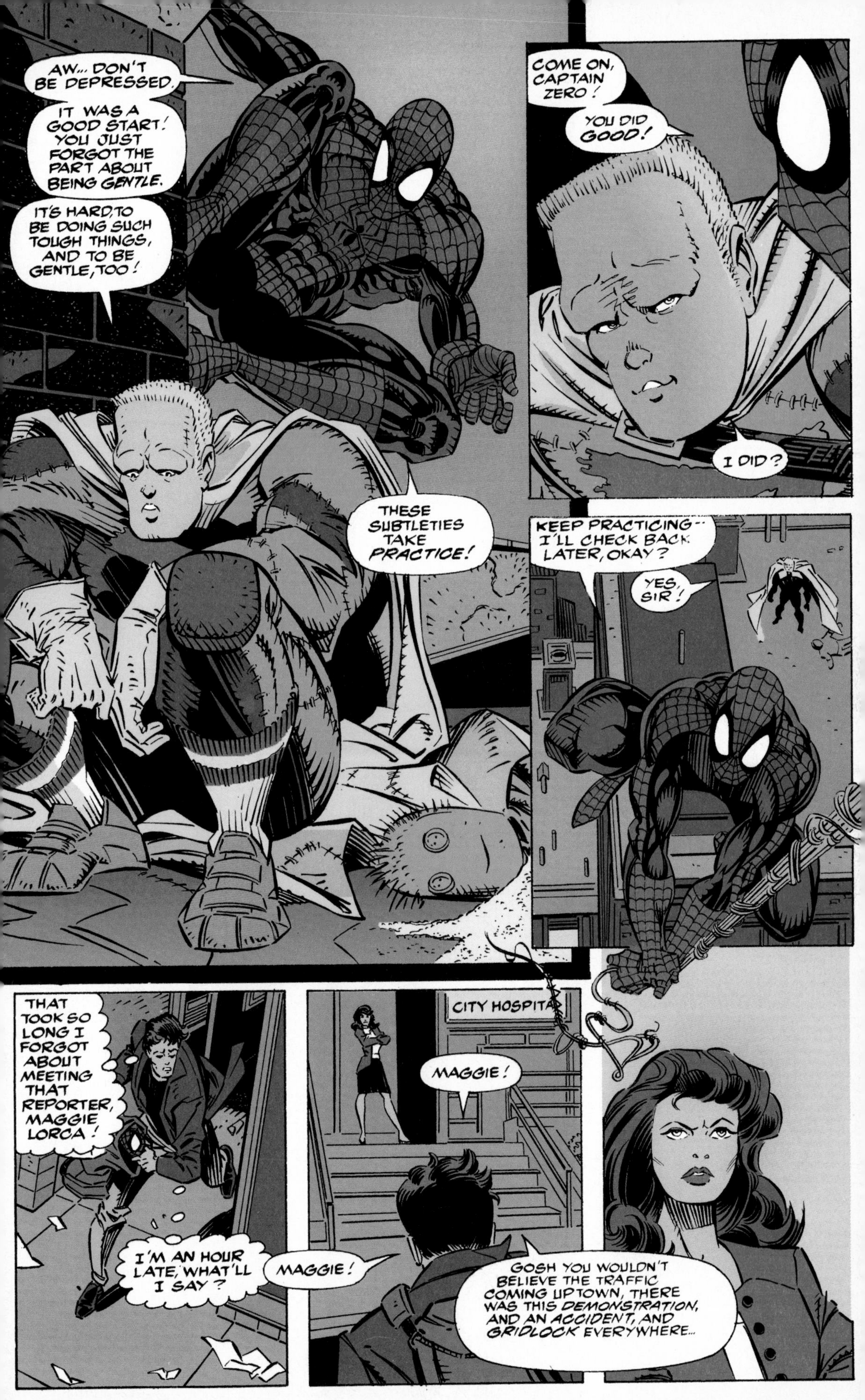
AW... DON'T BE DEPRESSED.
IT WAS A GOOD START! YOU JUST FORGOT THE PART ABOUT BEING GENTLE.
IT'S HARD, TO BE DOING SUCH TOUGH THINGS, AND TO BE GENTLE, TOO!
THESE SUBTLETIES TAKE PRACTICE!
COME ON, CAPTAIN ZERO!
YOU DID GOOD!
I DID?
KEEP PRACTICING-- I'LL CHECK BACK LATER, OKAY?
YES, SIR!
THAT TOOK SO LONG I FORGOT ABOUT MEETING THAT REPORTER, MAGGIE LORCA!
I'M AN HOUR LATE, WHAT'LL I SAY?
CITY HOSPITA
MAGGIE!
MAGGIE!
GOSH YOU WOULDN'T BELIEVE THE TRAFFIC COMING UPTOWN, THERE WAS THIS DEMONSTRATION, AND AN ACCIDENT, AND GRIDLOCK EVERYWHERE...

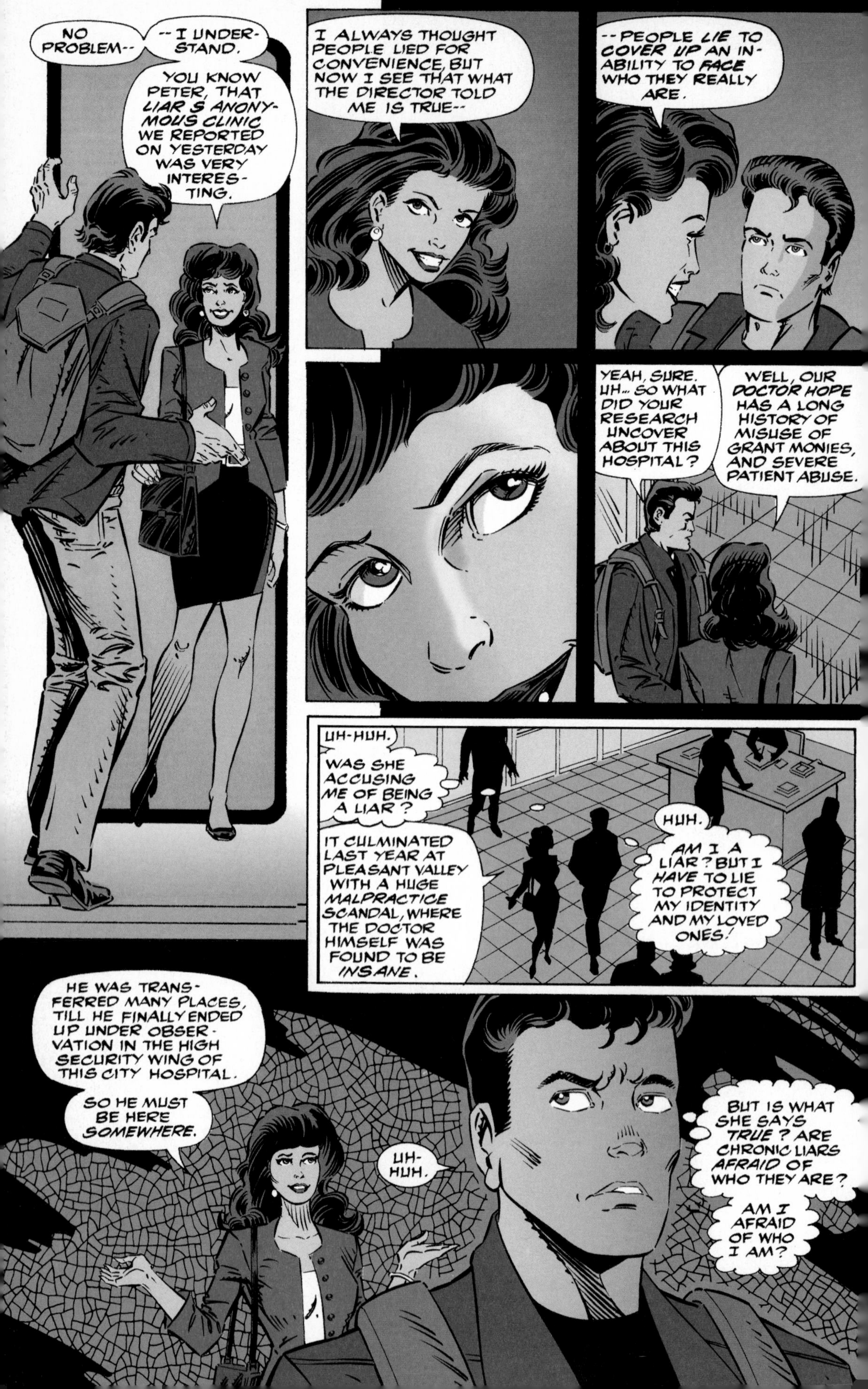
NO PROBLEM--
--I UNDERSTAND.
YOU KNOW PETER, THAT LIAR'S ANONYMOUS CLINIC WE REPORTED ON YESTERDAY WAS VERY INTERESTING.
I ALWAYS THOUGHT PEOPLE LIED FOR CONVENIENCE, BUT NOW I SEE THAT WHAT THE DIRECTOR TOLD ME IS TRUE--
--PEOPLE LIE TO COVER UP AN INABILITY TO FACE WHO THEY REALLY ARE.
YEAH, SURE. UH... SO WHAT DID YOUR RESEARCH UNCOVER ABOUT THIS HOSPITAL?
WELL, OUR DOCTOR HOPE HAS A LONG HISTORY OF MISUSE OF GRANT MONIES, AND SEVERE PATIENT ABUSE.
UH-HUH.
WAS SHE ACCUSING ME OF BEING A LIAR?
IT CULMINATED LAST YEAR AT PLEASANT VALLEY WITH A HUGE MALPRACTICE SCANDAL, WHERE THE DOCTOR HIMSELF WAS FOUND TO BE INSANE.
HUH.
AM I A LIAR? BUT I HAVE TO LIE TO PROTECT MY IDENTITY AND MY LOVED ONES!
HE WAS TRANSFERRED MANY PLACES, TILL HE FINALLY ENDED UP UNDER OBSERVATION IN THE HIGH SECURITY WING OF THIS CITY HOSPITAL.
SO HE MUST BE HERE SOMEWHERE.
UH-HUH.
BUT IS WHAT SHE SAYS TRUE? ARE CHRONIC LIARS AFRAID OF WHO THEY ARE?
AM I AFRAID OF WHO I AM?

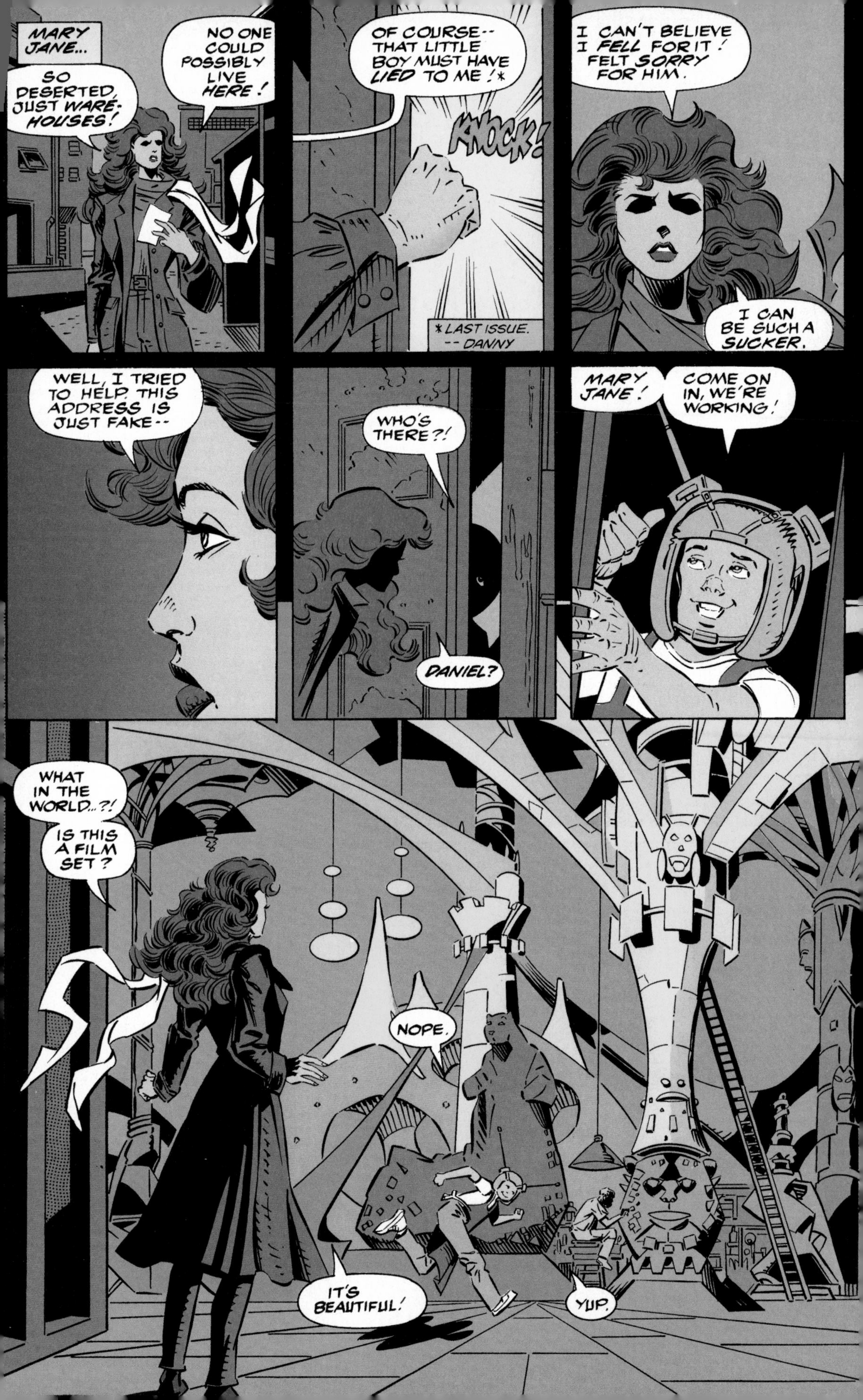

MARY JANE...
SO DESERTED, JUST WAREHOUSES!
NO ONE COULD POSSIBLY LIVE HERE!
OF COURSE-- THAT LITTLE BOY MUST HAVE LIED TO ME!*
KNOCK!
*LAST ISSUE. --DANNY
I CAN'T BELIEVE I FELL FOR IT! FELT SORRY FOR HIM.
I CAN BE SUCH A SUCKER.
WELL, I TRIED TO HELP. THIS ADDRESS IS JUST FAKE--
WHO'S THERE?!
DANIEL?
MARY JANE!
COME ON IN, WE'RE WORKING!
WHAT IN THE WORLD...?!
IS THIS A FILM SET?
NOPE.
IT'S BEAUTIFUL!
YUP.

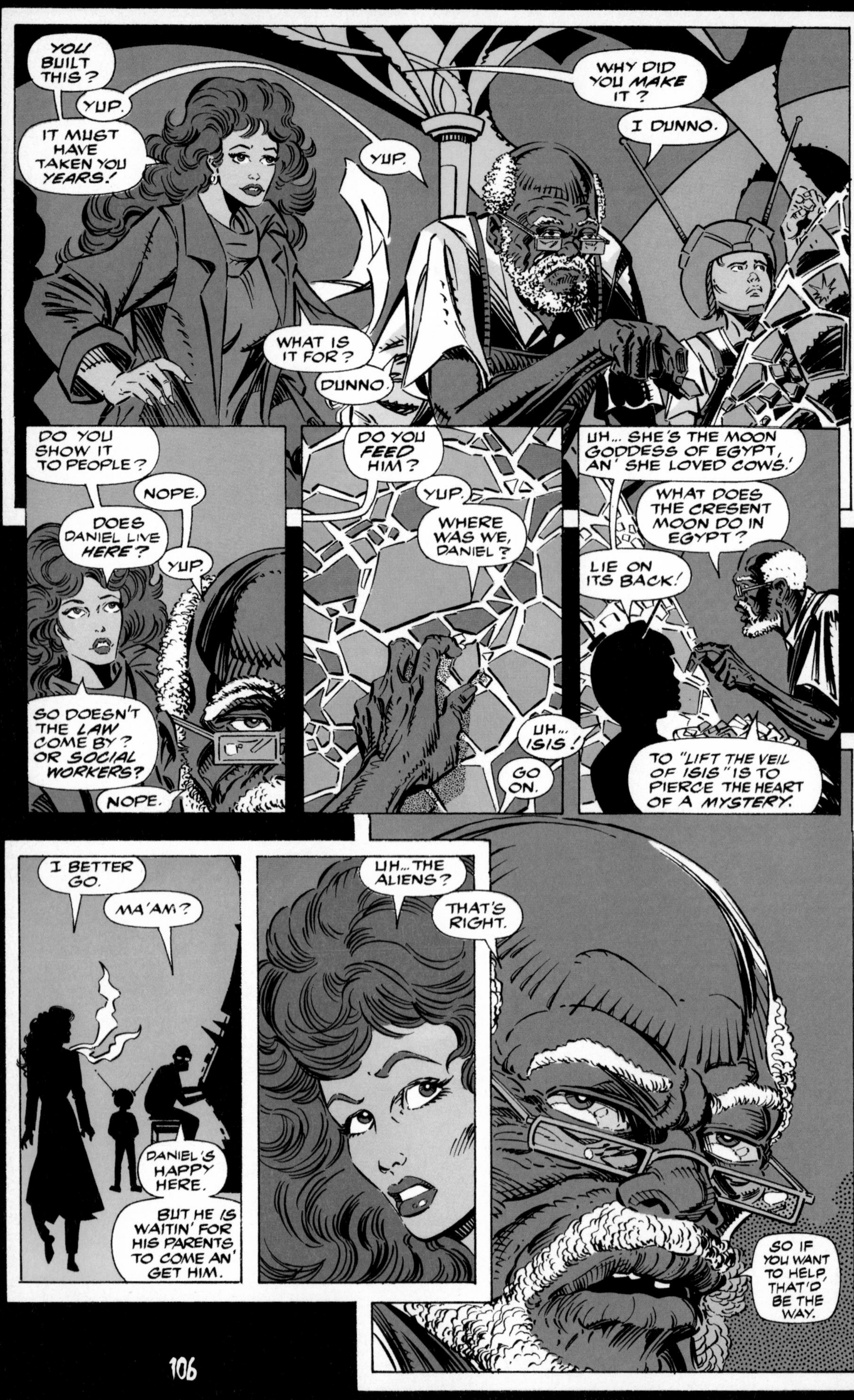

YOU BUILT THIS?
YUP.
IT MUST HAVE TAKEN YOU YEARS!
YUP.
WHY DID YOU MAKE IT?
I DUNNO.
WHAT IS IT FOR?
DUNNO.
DO YOU SHOW IT TO PEOPLE?
NOPE.
DOES DANIEL LIVE HERE?
YUP.
SO DOESN'T THE LAW COME BY? OR SOCIAL WORKERS?
NOPE.
DO YOU FEED HIM?
YUP.
WHERE WAS WE, DANIEL?
UH... ISIS!
GO ON.
UH... SHE'S THE MOON GODDESS OF EGYPT, AN' SHE LOVED COWS!
WHAT DOES THE CRESENT MOON DO IN EGYPT?
LIE ON ITS BACK!
TO "LIFT THE VEIL OF ISIS" IS TO PIERCE THE HEART OF A MYSTERY.
I BETTER GO.
MA'AM?
DANIEL'S HAPPY HERE.
BUT HE IS WAITIN' FOR HIS PARENTS TO COME AN' GET HIM.
UH... THE ALIENS?
THAT'S RIGHT.
SO IF YOU WANT TO HELP, THAT'D BE THE WAY.

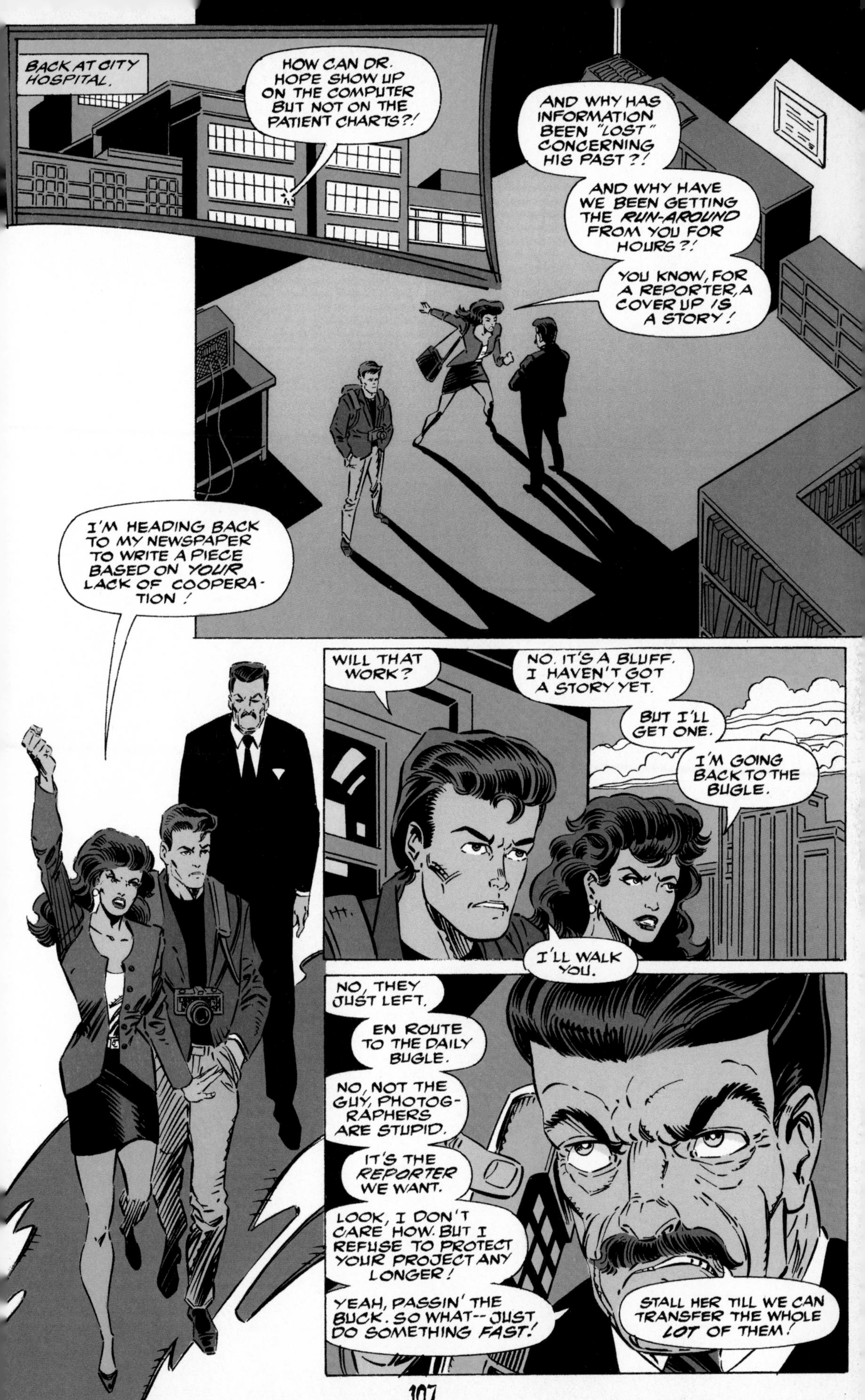
BACK AT CITY HOSPITAL.
HOW CAN DR. HOPE SHOW UP ON THE COMPUTER BUT NOT ON THE PATIENT CHARTS?!
AND WHY HAS INFORMATION BEEN "LOST" CONCERNING HIS PAST?!
AND WHY HAVE WE BEEN GETTING THE RUN-AROUND FROM YOU FOR HOURS?!
YOU KNOW, FOR A REPORTER, A COVER UP IS A STORY!
I'M HEADING BACK TO MY NEWSPAPER TO WRITE A PIECE BASED ON YOUR LACK OF COOPERATION!
WILL THAT WORK?
NO. IT'S A BLUFF. I HAVEN'T GOT A STORY YET.
BUT I'LL GET ONE.
I'M GOING BACK TO THE BUGLE.
I'LL WALK YOU.
NO, THEY JUST LEFT.
EN ROUTE TO THE DAILY BUGLE.
NO, NOT THE GUY, PHOTOGRAPHERS ARE STUPID.
IT'S THE REPORTER WE WANT.
LOOK, I DON'T CARE HOW. BUT I REFUSE TO PROTECT YOUR PROJECT ANY LONGER!
YEAH, PASSIN' THE BUCK. SO WHAT-- JUST DO SOMETHING FAST!
STALL HER TILL WE CAN TRANSFER THE WHOLE LOT OF THEM!

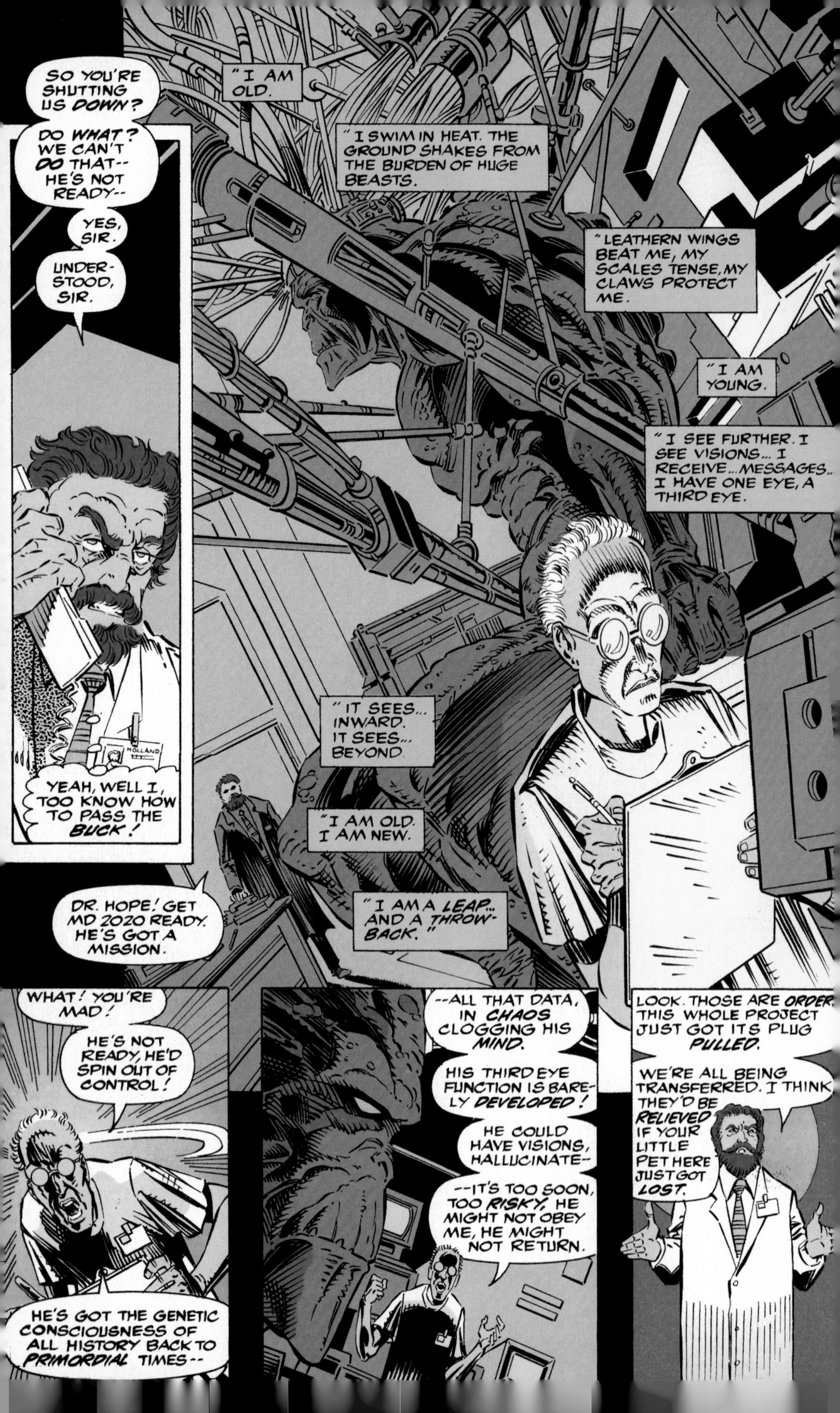

SO YOU'RE SHUTTING US DOWN?
DO WHAT? WE CAN'T DO THAT-- HE'S NOT READY--
YES, SIR.
UNDER-STOOD, SIR.
HOLLAND
YEAH, WELL I, TOO KNOW HOW TO PASS THE BUCK!
"I AM OLD.
"I SWIM IN HEAT. THE GROUND SHAKES FROM THE BURDEN OF HUGE BEASTS.
"LEATHERN WINGS BEAT ME, MY SCALES TENSE, MY CLAWS PROTECT ME.
"I AM YOUNG.
"I SEE FURTHER. I SEE VISIONS... I RECEIVE... MESSAGES.. I HAVE ONE EYE, A THIRD EYE.
"IT SEES... INWARD. IT SEES... BEYOND.
"I AM OLD. I AM NEW.
"I AM A LEAP... AND A THROW-BACK."
DR. HOPE! GET MD 2020 READY. HE'S GOT A MISSION.
WHAT! YOU'RE MAD!
HE'S NOT READY, HE'D SPIN OUT OF CONTROL!
HE'S GOT THE GENETIC CONSCIOUSNESS OF ALL HISTORY BACK TO PRIMORDIAL TIMES--
--ALL THAT DATA, IN CHAOS CLOGGING HIS MIND.
HIS THIRD EYE FUNCTION IS BARELY DEVELOPED!
HE COULD HAVE VISIONS, HALLUCINATE--
--IT'S TOO SOON, TOO RISKY, HE MIGHT NOT OBEY ME, HE MIGHT NOT RETURN.
LOOK. THOSE ARE ORDERS. THIS WHOLE PROJECT JUST GOT ITS PLUG PULLED.
WE'RE ALL BEING TRANSFERRED. I THINK THEY'D BE RELIEVED IF YOUR LITTLE PET HERE JUST GOT LOST.

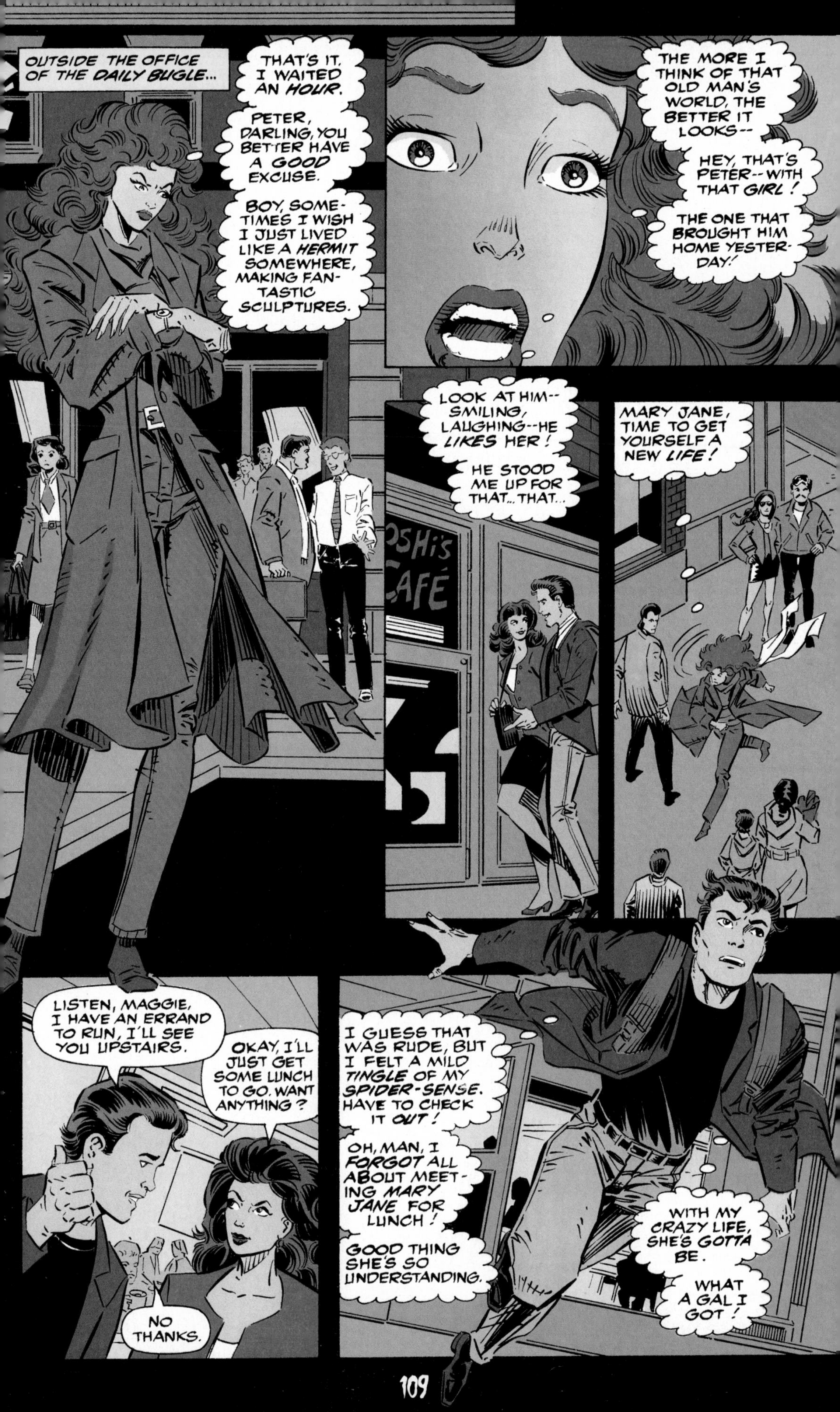

OUTSIDE THE OFFICE OF THE DAILY BUGLE...
THAT'S IT. I WAITED AN HOUR.
PETER, DARLING, YOU BETTER HAVE A GOOD EXCUSE.
BOY, SOMETIMES I WISH I JUST LIVED LIKE A HERMIT SOMEWHERE, MAKING FANTASTIC SCULPTURES.
THE MORE I THINK OF THAT OLD MAN'S WORLD, THE BETTER IT LOOKS--
HEY, THAT'S PETER--WITH THAT GIRL!
THE ONE THAT BROUGHT HIM HOME YESTERDAY!
LOOK AT HIM-- SMILING, LAUGHING--HE LIKES HER!
HE STOOD ME UP FOR THAT... THAT...
OSHI'S CAFÉ
MARY JANE, TIME TO GET YOURSELF A NEW LIFE!
LISTEN, MAGGIE, I HAVE AN ERRAND TO RUN. I'LL SEE YOU UPSTAIRS.
OKAY, I'LL JUST GET SOME LUNCH TO GO. WANT ANYTHING?
NO THANKS.
I GUESS THAT WAS RUDE, BUT I FELT A MILD TINGLE OF MY SPIDER-SENSE. HAVE TO CHECK IT OUT!
OH, MAN, I FORGOT ALL ABOUT MEETING MARY JANE FOR LUNCH!
GOOD THING SHE'S SO UNDERSTANDING.
WITH MY CRAZY LIFE, SHE'S GOTTA BE.
WHAT A GAL I GOT!

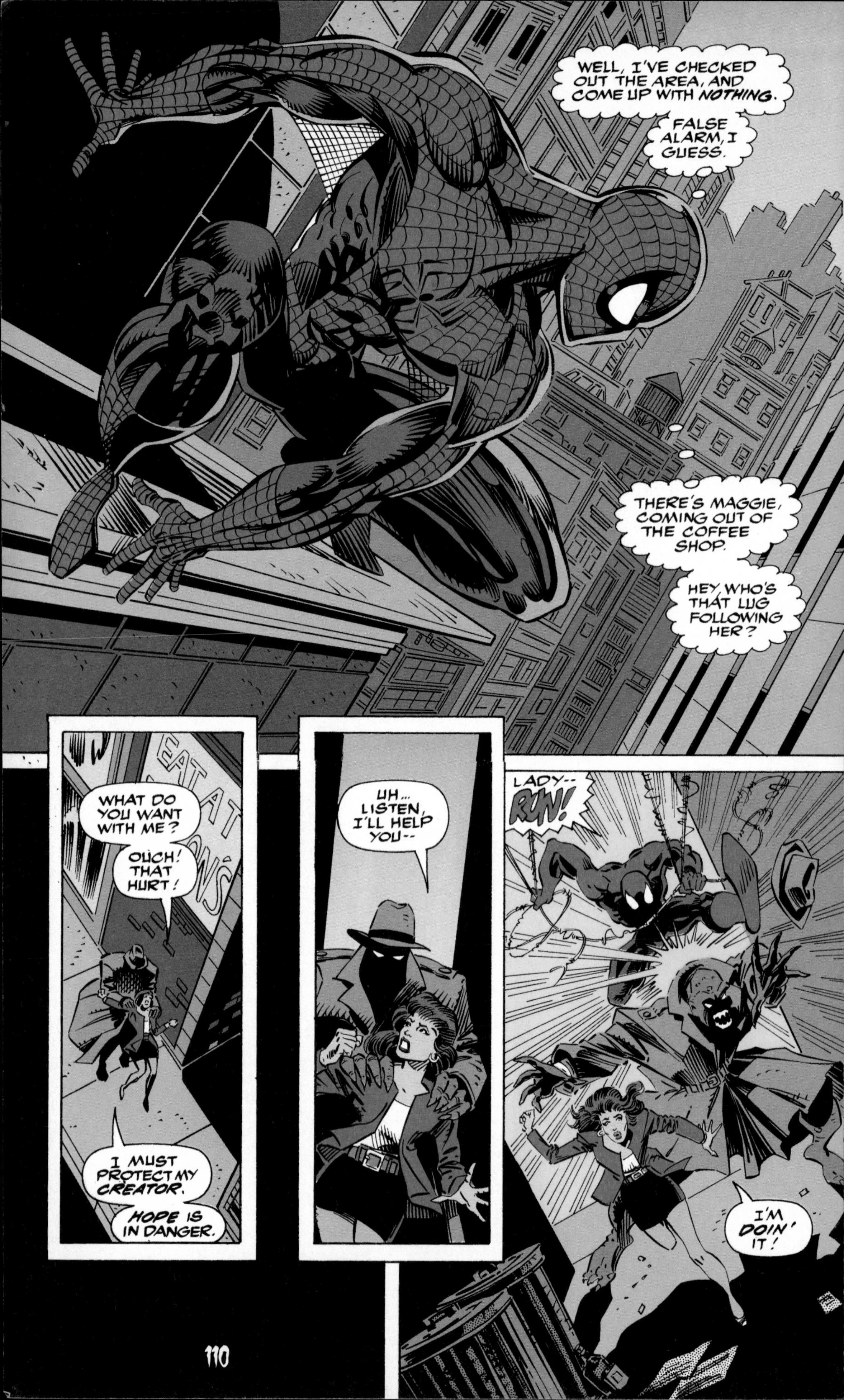
WELL, I'VE CHECKED OUT THE AREA, AND COME UP WITH NOTHING.
FALSE ALARM, I GUESS.
THERE'S MAGGIE, COMING OUT OF THE COFFEE SHOP.
HEY, WHO'S THAT LUG FOLLOWING HER?
WHAT DO YOU WANT WITH ME?
OUCH! THAT HURT!
I MUST PROTECT MY CREATOR.
HOPE IS IN DANGER.
UH... LISTEN, I'LL HELP YOU--
LADY-- RUN!
I'M DOIN' IT!

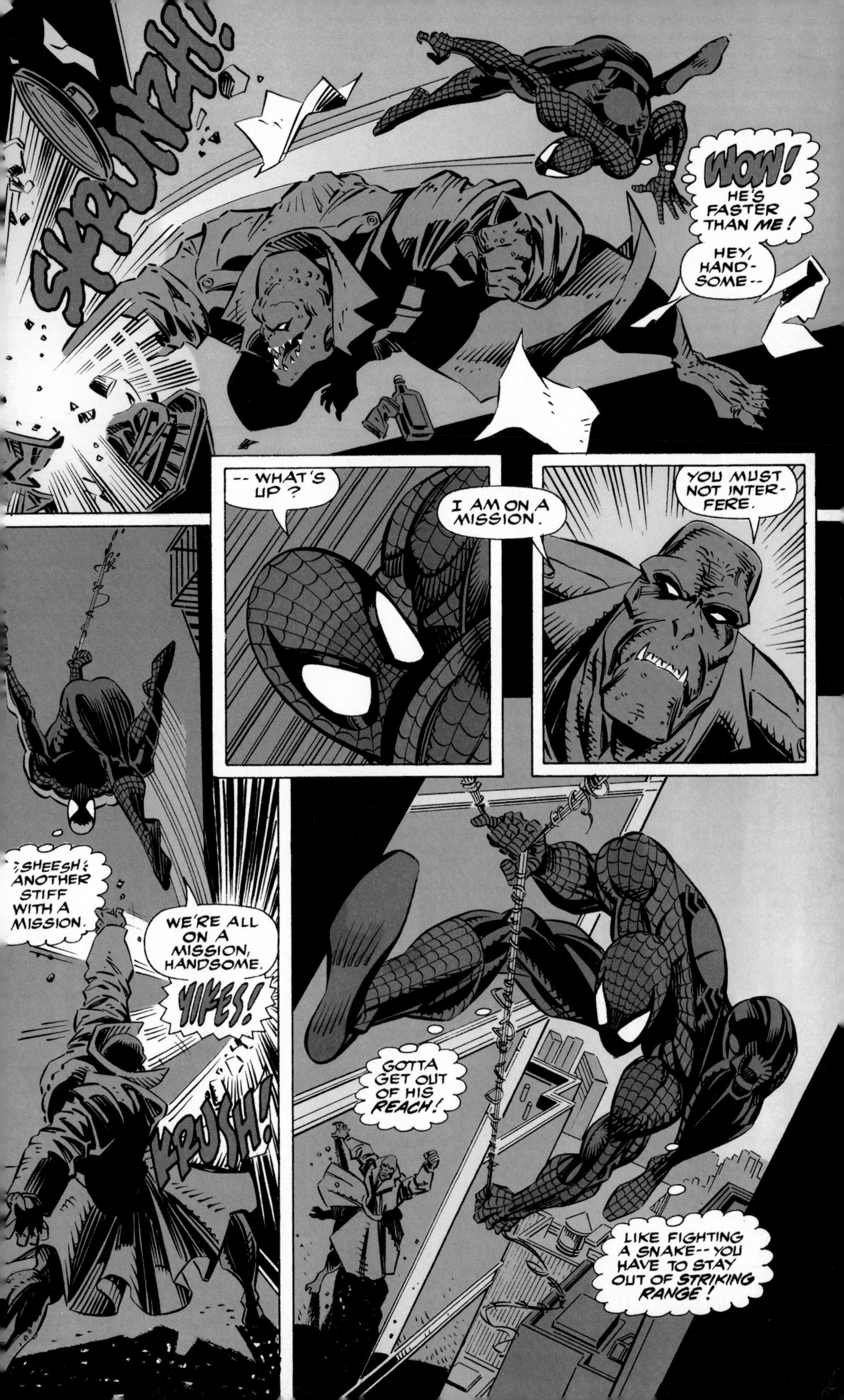
SKRUNCH!
WOW! HE'S FASTER THAN ME!
HEY, HAND-SOME--
-- WHAT'S UP?
I AM ON A MISSION.
YOU MUST NOT INTER-FERE.
SHEESH ANOTHER STIFF WITH A MISSION.
WE'RE ALL ON A MISSION, HANDSOME.
YIKES!
KRUSH!
GOTTA GET OUT OF HIS REACH!
LIKE FIGHTING A SNAKE-- YOU HAVE TO STAY OUT OF STRIKING RANGE!

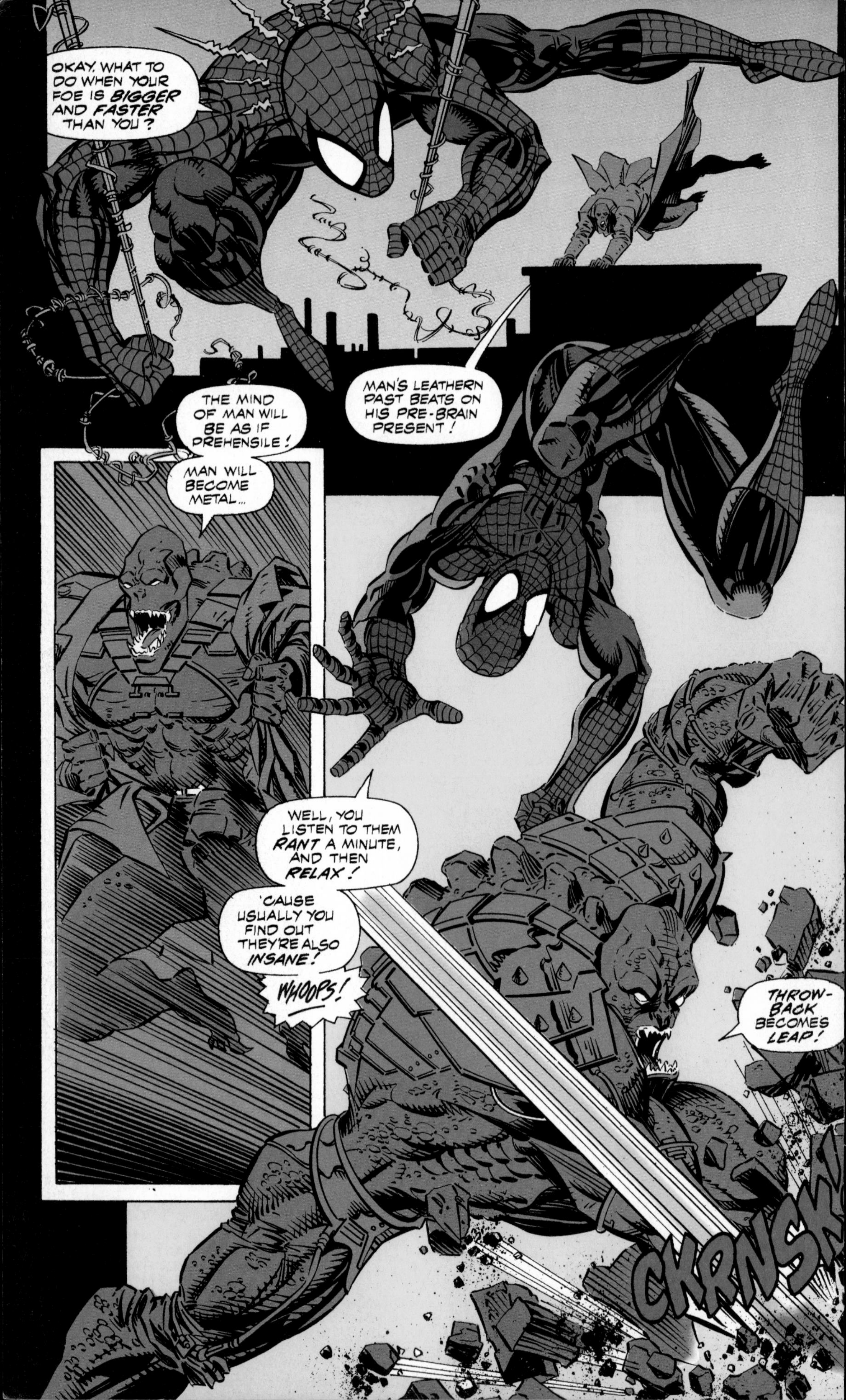
OKAY. WHAT TO DO WHEN YOUR FOE IS BIGGER AND FASTER THAN YOU?
THE MIND OF MAN WILL BE AS IF PREHENSILE!
MAN WILL BECOME METAL...
MAN'S LEATHERN PAST BEATS ON HIS PRE-BRAIN PRESENT!
WELL, YOU LISTEN TO THEM RANT A MINUTE, AND THEN RELAX!
'CAUSE USUALLY YOU FIND OUT THEY'RE ALSO INSANE!
WHOOPS!
THROW-BACK BECOMES LEAP!
CKRNSK

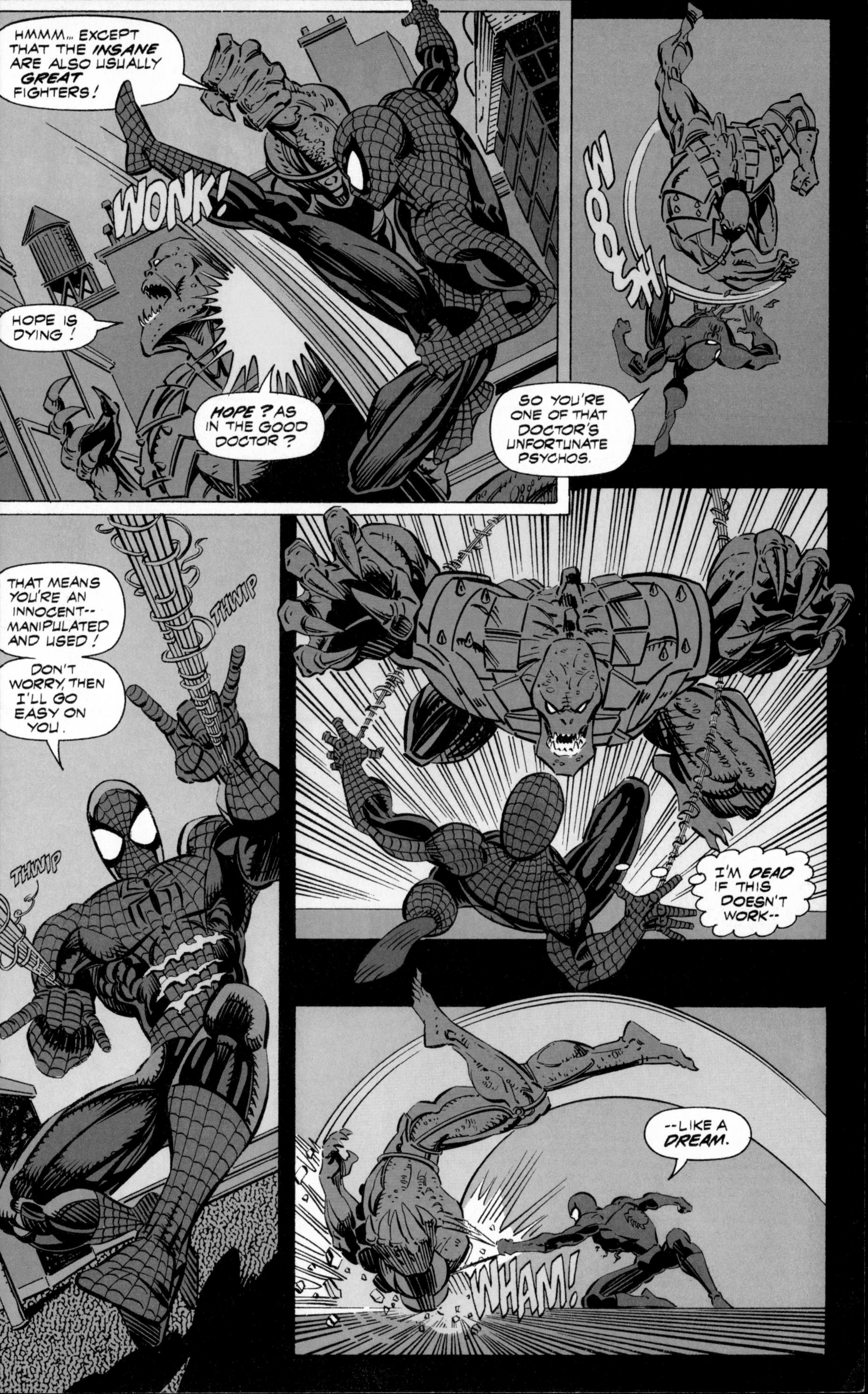
HMMM... EXCEPT THAT THE INSANE ARE ALSO USUALLY GREAT FIGHTERS!
WONK!
HOPE IS DYING!
HOPE? AS IN THE GOOD DOCTOR?
WOOSH
SO YOU'RE ONE OF THAT DOCTOR'S UNFORTUNATE PSYCHOS.
THAT MEANS YOU'RE AN INNOCENT-- MANIPULATED AND USED!
DON'T WORRY, THEN I'LL GO EASY ON YOU.
THWIP
THWIP
I'M DEAD IF THIS DOESN'T WORK--
--LIKE A DREAM.
WHAM!

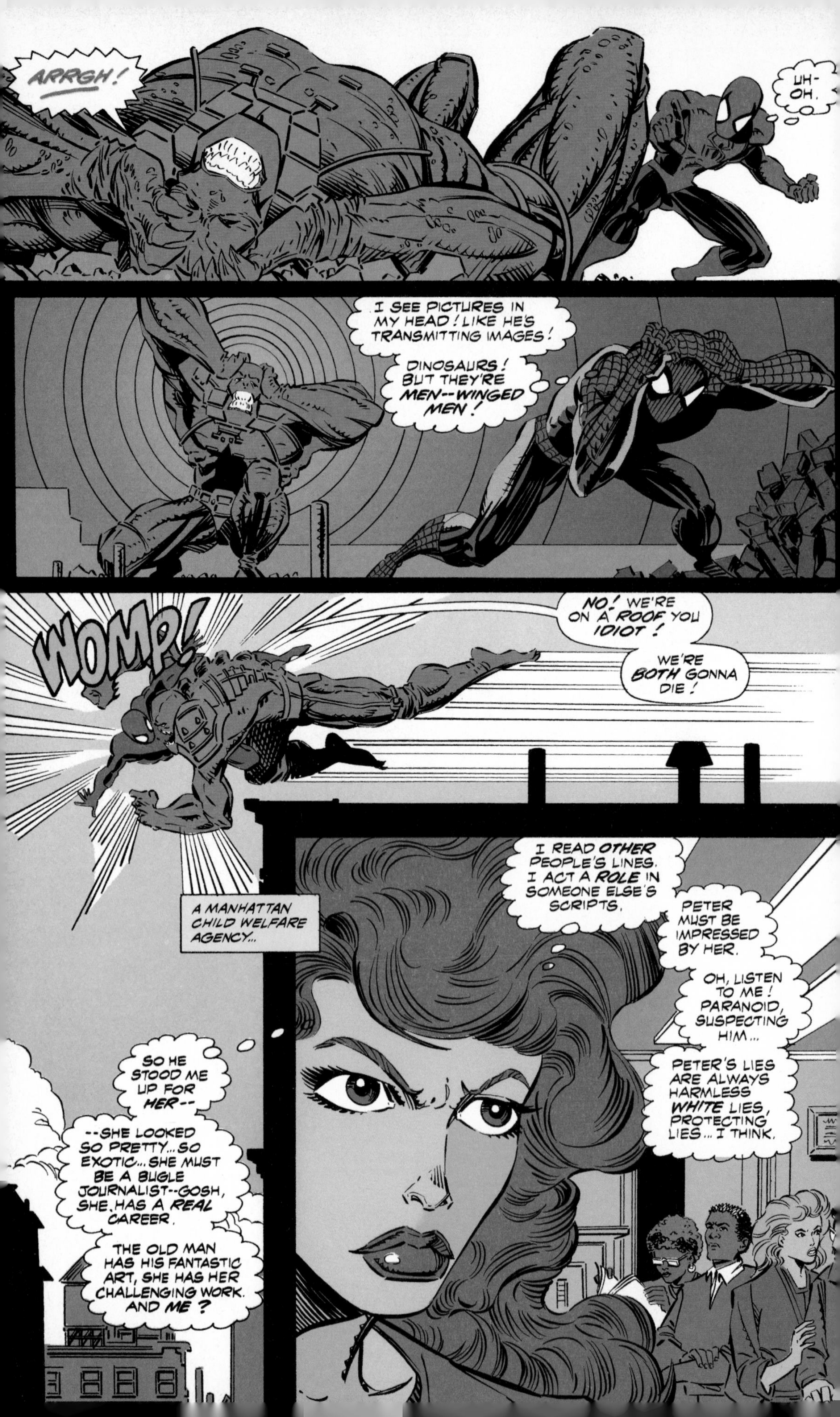
ARRGH!
UH-OH.
I SEE PICTURES IN MY HEAD! LIKE HE'S TRANSMITTING IMAGES!
DINOSAURS! BUT THEY'RE MEN--WINGED MEN!
WOMP!
NO! WE'RE ON A ROOF YOU IDIOT!
WE'RE BOTH GONNA DIE!
A MANHATTAN CHILD WELFARE AGENCY...
I READ OTHER PEOPLE'S LINES. I ACT A ROLE IN SOMEONE ELSE'S SCRIPTS.
PETER MUST BE IMPRESSED BY HER.
OH, LISTEN TO ME! PARANOID, SUSPECTING HIM...
PETER'S LIES ARE ALWAYS HARMLESS WHITE LIES, PROTECTING LIES... I THINK.
SO HE STOOD ME UP FOR HER--
--SHE LOOKED SO PRETTY... SO EXOTIC... SHE MUST BE A BUGLE JOURNALIST--GOSH, SHE HAS A REAL CAREER.
THE OLD MAN HAS HIS FANTASTIC ART, SHE HAS HER CHALLENGING WORK. AND ME?

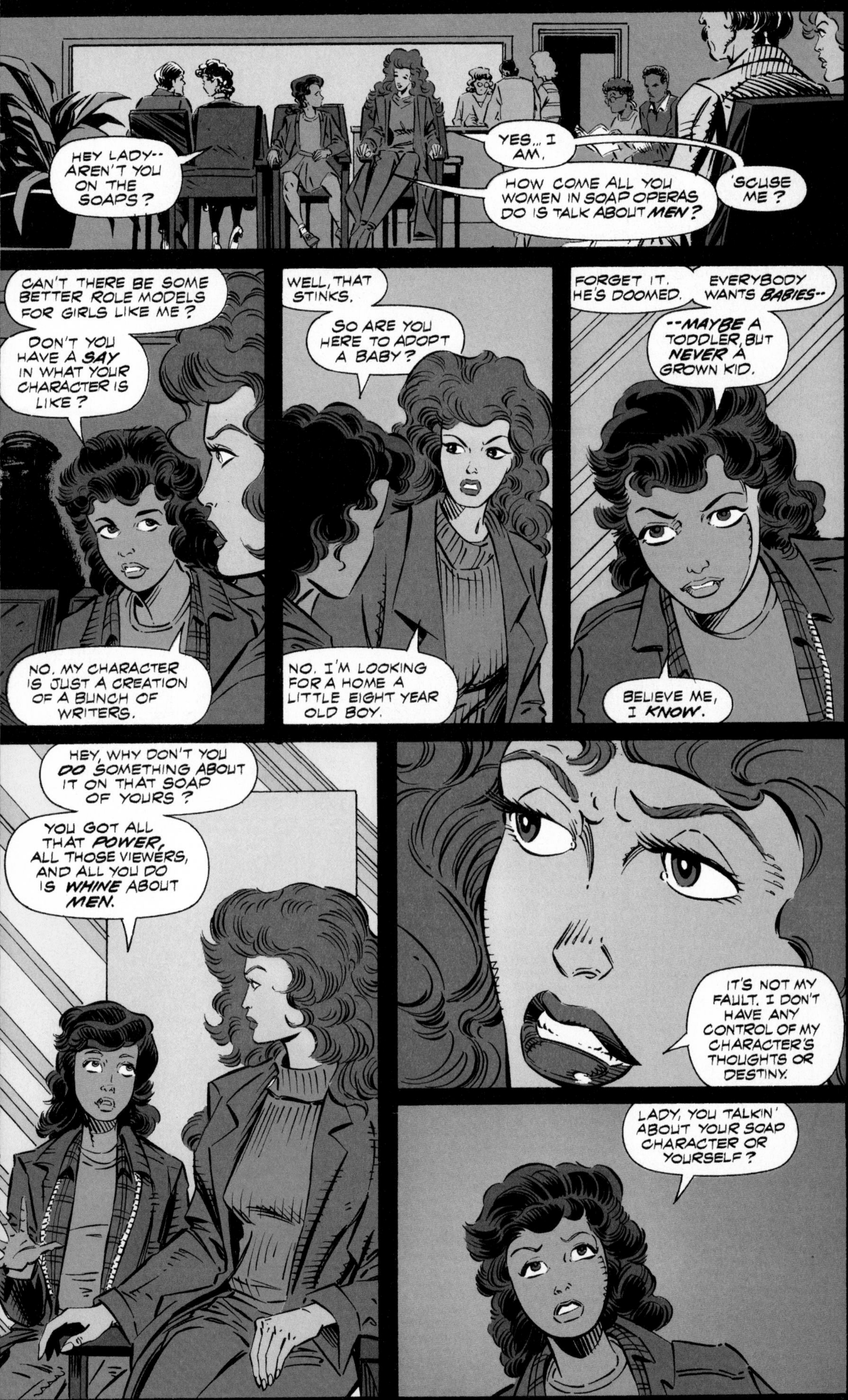

HEY LADY-- AREN'T YOU ON THE SOAPS?
YES... I AM.
HOW COME ALL YOU WOMEN IN SOAP OPERAS DO IS TALK ABOUT MEN?
'SCUSE ME?
CAN'T THERE BE SOME BETTER ROLE MODELS FOR GIRLS LIKE ME?
DON'T YOU HAVE A SAY IN WHAT YOUR CHARACTER IS LIKE?
NO. MY CHARACTER IS JUST A CREATION OF A BUNCH OF WRITERS.
WELL, THAT STINKS.
SO ARE YOU HERE TO ADOPT A BABY?
NO. I'M LOOKING FOR A HOME A LITTLE EIGHT YEAR OLD BOY.
FORGET IT. HE'S DOOMED.
EVERYBODY WANTS BABIES--
--MAYBE A TODDLER, BUT NEVER A GROWN KID.
BELIEVE ME, I KNOW.
HEY, WHY DON'T YOU DO SOMETHING ABOUT IT ON THAT SOAP OF YOURS?
YOU GOT ALL THAT POWER, ALL THOSE VIEWERS, AND ALL YOU DO IS WHINE ABOUT MEN.
IT'S NOT MY FAULT. I DON'T HAVE ANY CONTROL OF MY CHARACTER'S THOUGHTS OR DESTINY.
LADY, YOU TALKIN' ABOUT YOUR SOAP CHARACTER OR YOURSELF?

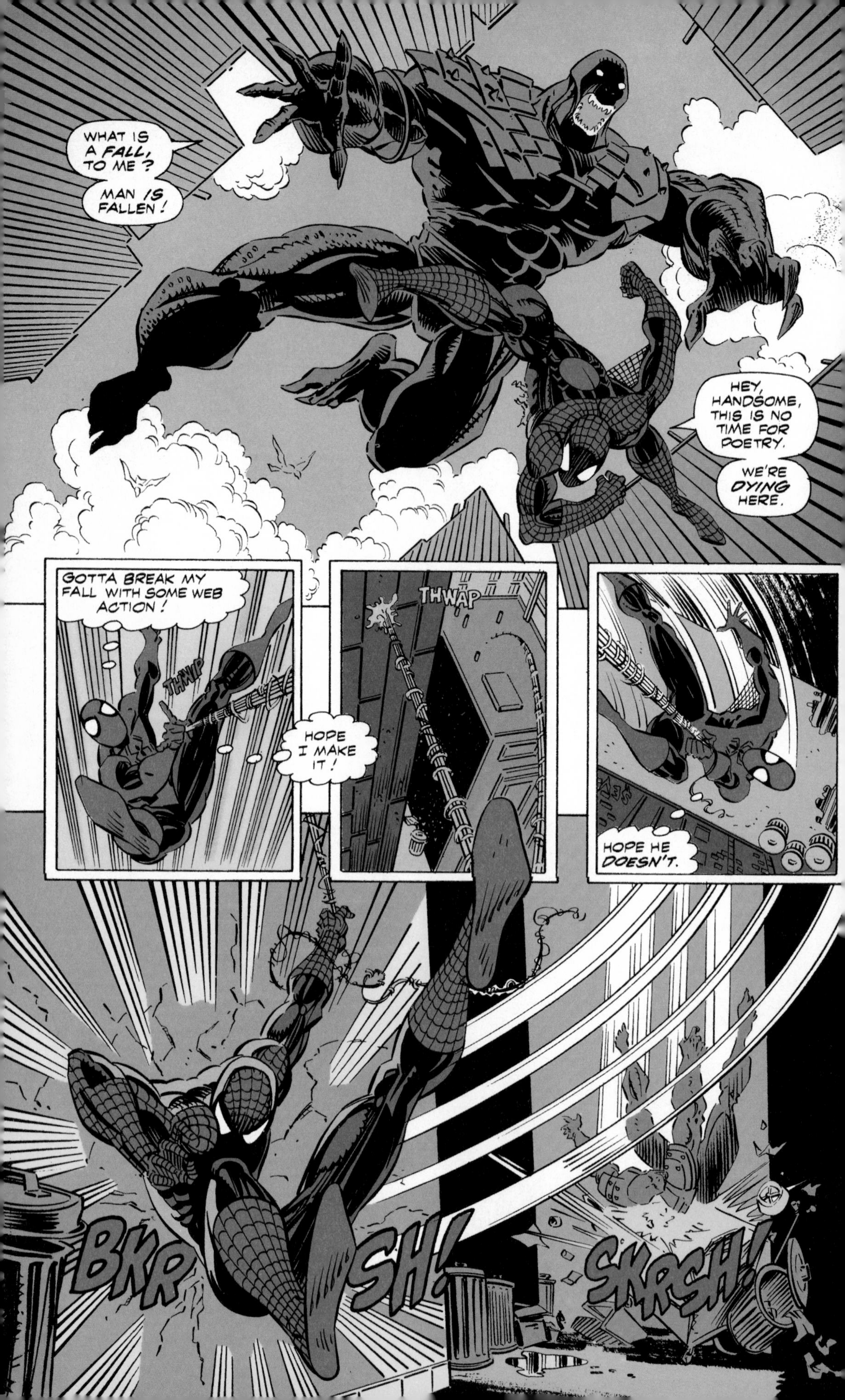

WHAT IS A FALL, TO ME?
MAN IS FALLEN!
HEY, HANDSOME, THIS IS NO TIME FOR POETRY.
WE'RE DYING HERE.
GOTTA BREAK MY FALL WITH SOME WEB ACTION!
THWIP
HOPE I MAKE IT!
THWAP
HOPE HE DOESN'T.
BKRSH!
SKRSH!

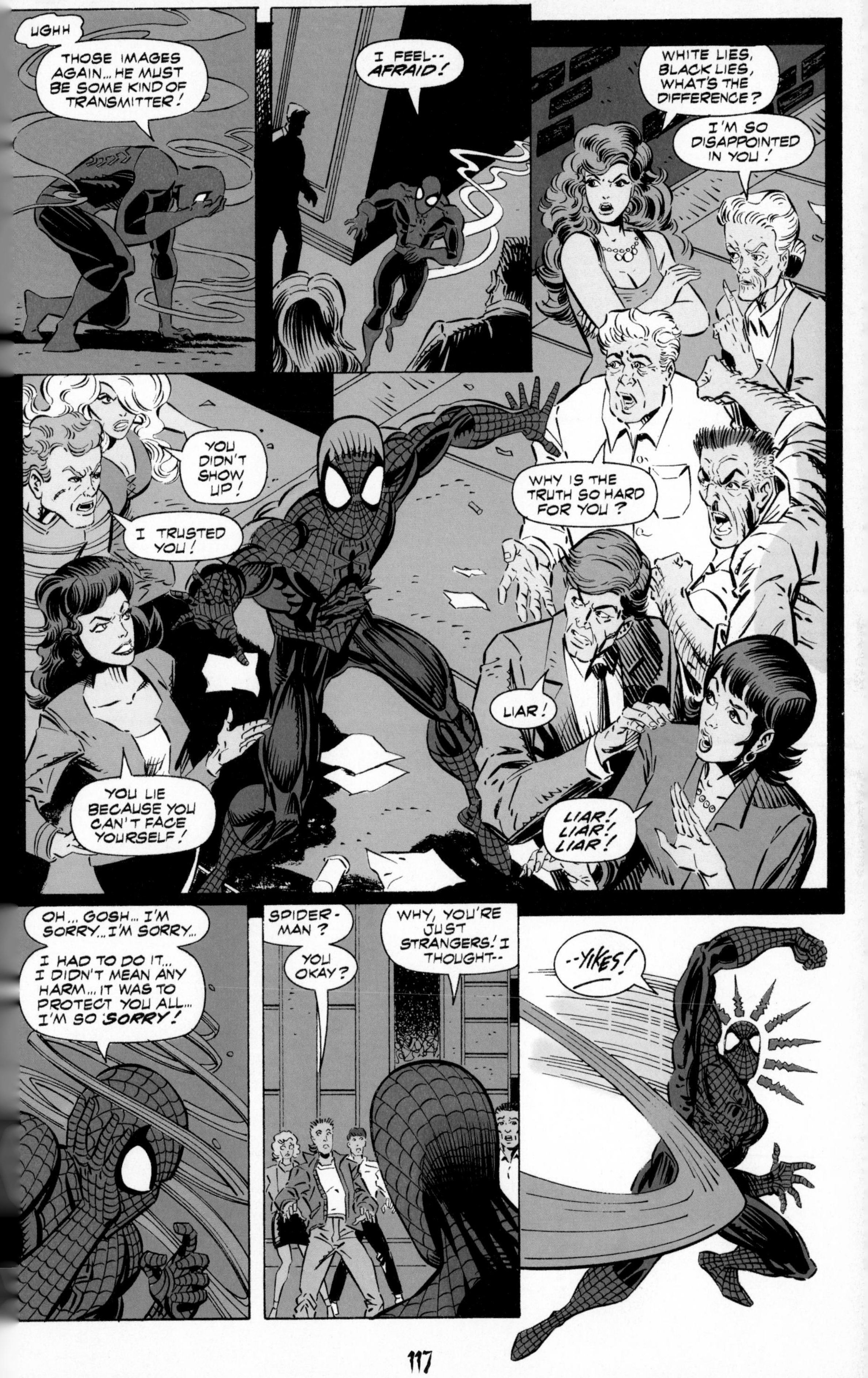
UGHH
THOSE IMAGES AGAIN... HE MUST BE SOME KIND OF TRANSMITTER!
I FEEL-- AFRAID!
WHITE LIES, BLACK LIES, WHAT'S THE DIFFERENCE?
I'M SO DISAPPOINTED IN YOU!
YOU DIDN'T SHOW UP!
I TRUSTED YOU!
WHY IS THE TRUTH SO HARD FOR YOU?
LIAR!
YOU LIE BECAUSE YOU CAN'T FACE YOURSELF!
LIAR! LIAR! LIAR!
OH... GOSH... I'M SORRY... I'M SORRY...
I HAD TO DO IT... I DIDN'T MEAN ANY HARM... IT WAS TO PROTECT YOU ALL... I'M SO SORRY!
SPIDER-MAN?
YOU OKAY?
WHY, YOU'RE JUST STRANGERS! I THOUGHT--
--YIKES!

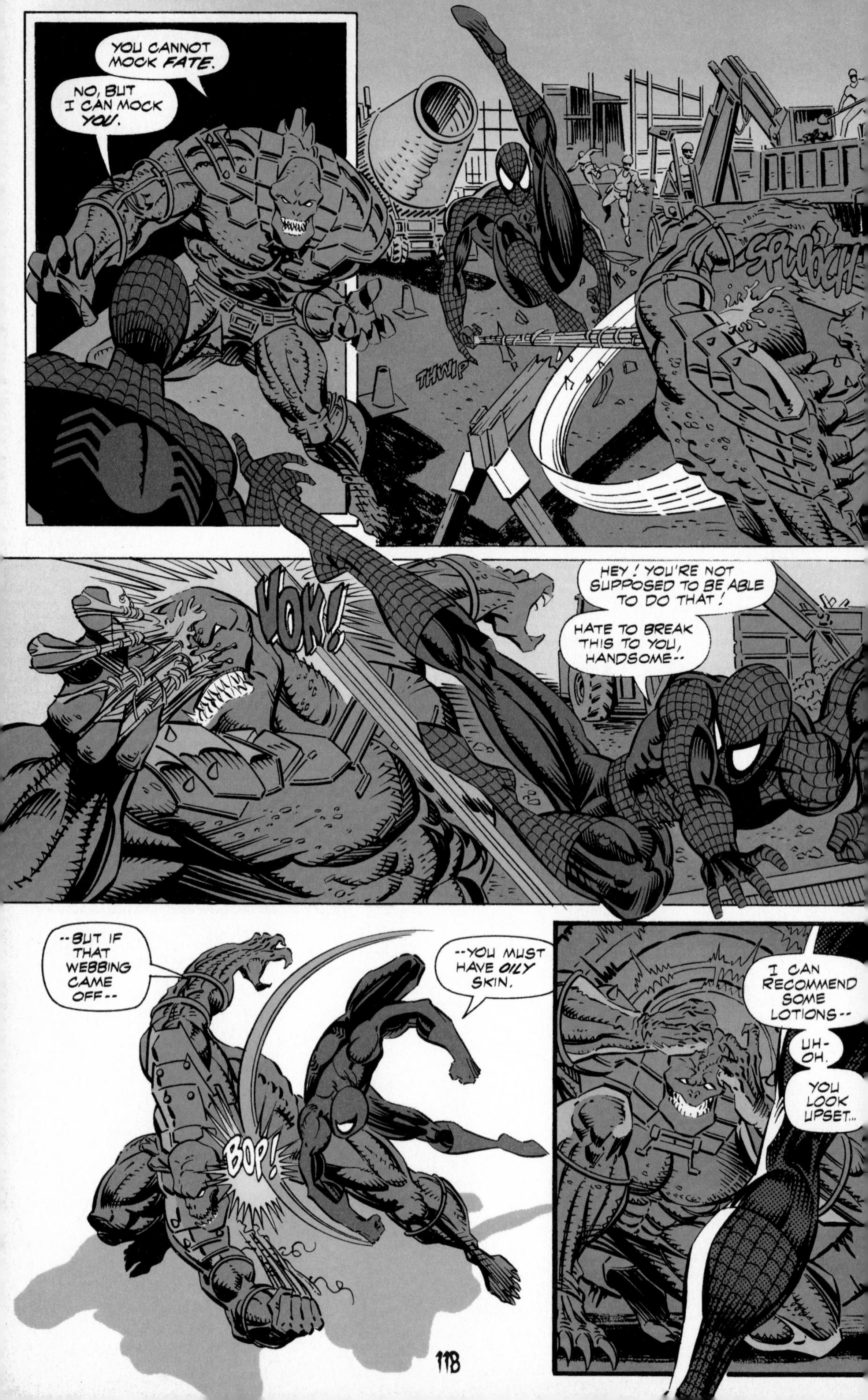

YOU CANNOT MOCK FATE.
NO, BUT I CAN MOCK YOU.
THWIP
SPLOOCH
VOK!
HEY! YOU'RE NOT SUPPOSED TO BE ABLE TO DO THAT!
HATE TO BREAK THIS TO YOU, HANDSOME--
--BUT IF THAT WEBBING CAME OFF--
--YOU MUST HAVE OILY SKIN.
BOP!
I CAN RECOMMEND SOME LOTIONS--
UH-OH.
YOU LOOK UPSET...

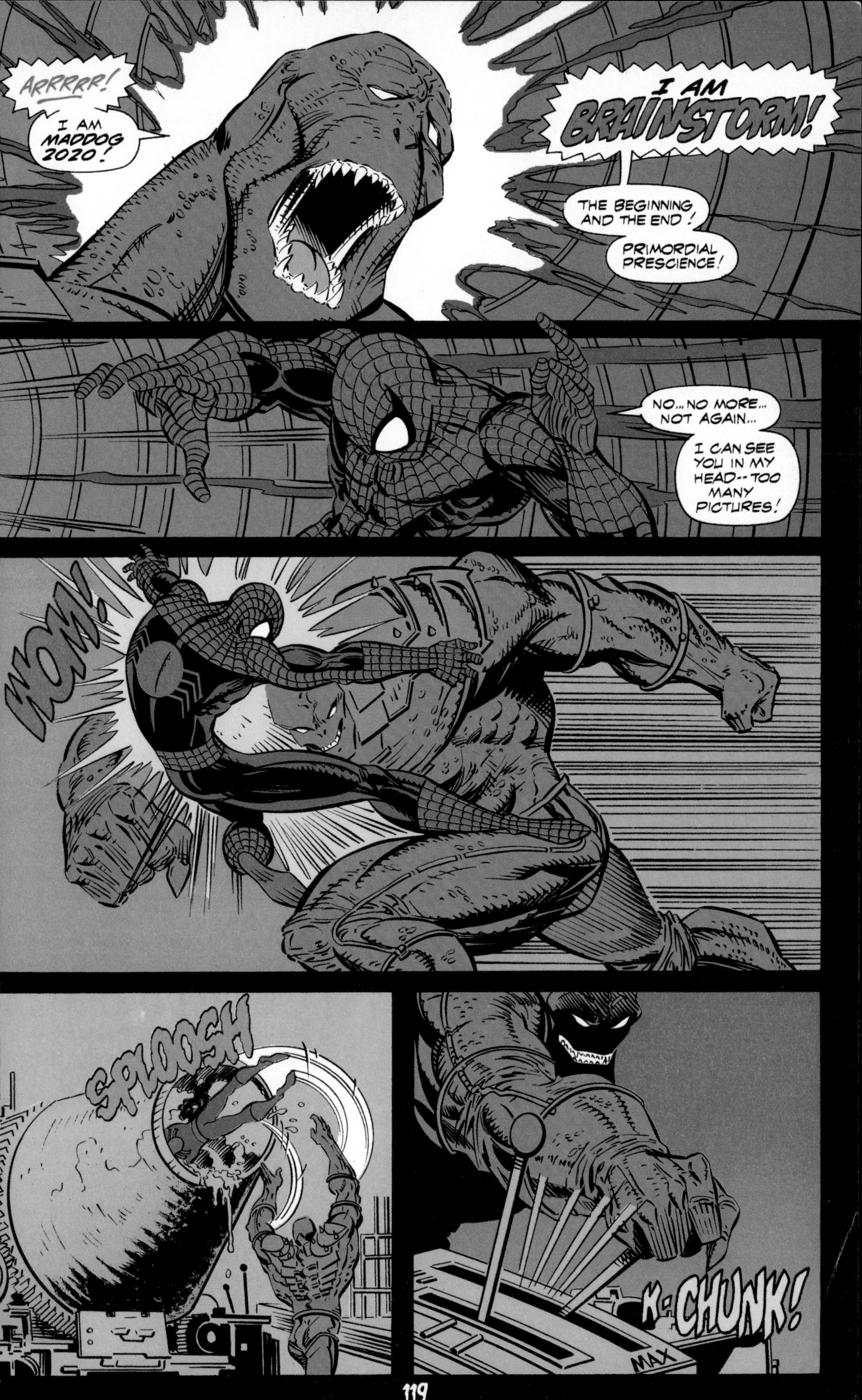
ARRRRR!
I AM MADDOG 2020!
I AM BRAINSTORM!
THE BEGINNING AND THE END!
PRIMORDIAL PRESCIENCE!
NO... NO MORE... NOT AGAIN...
I CAN SEE YOU IN MY HEAD-- TOO MANY PICTURES!
WOM!
SPLOOSH
K-CHUNK!
MAX

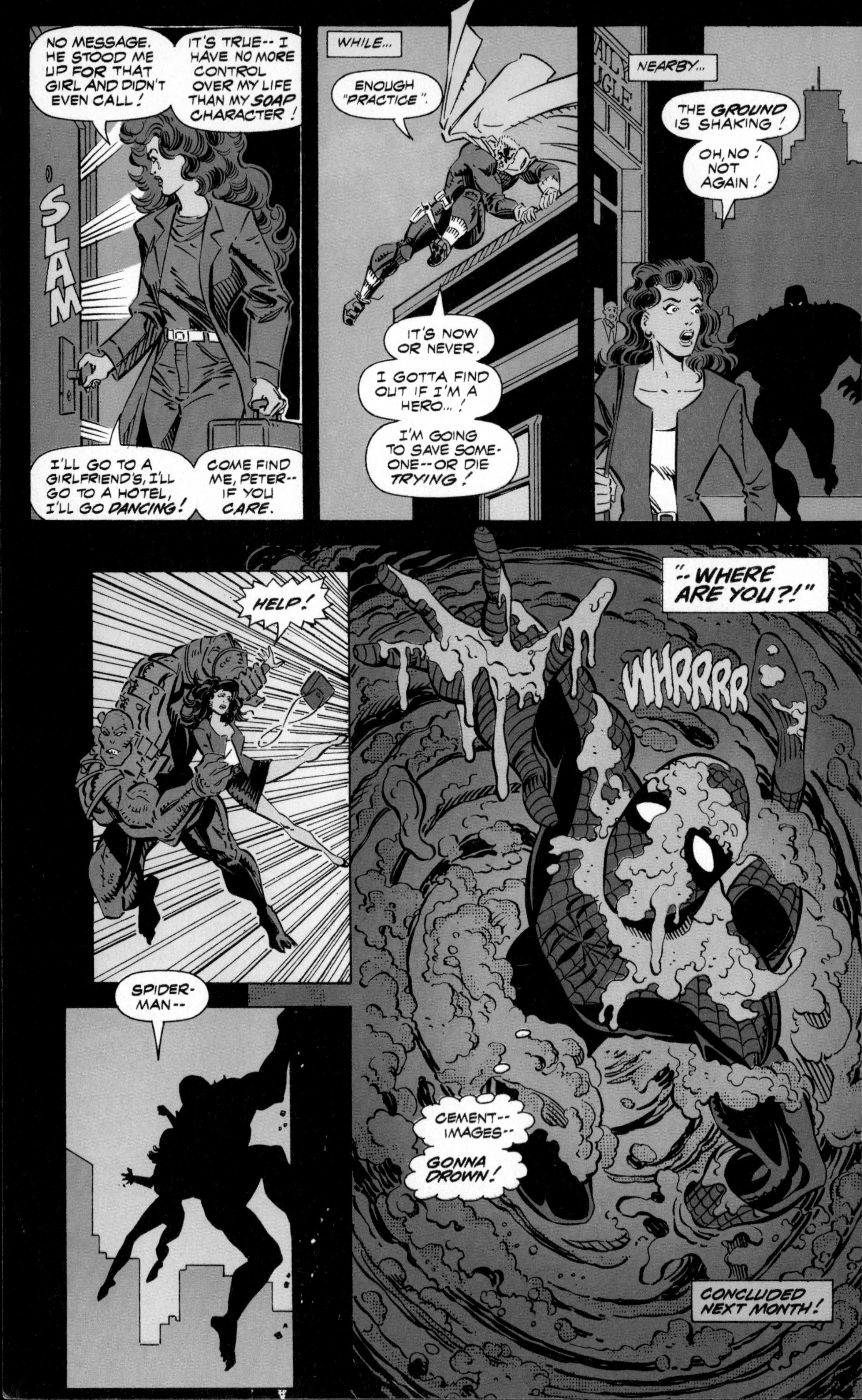
NO MESSAGE. HE STOOD ME UP FOR THAT GIRL AND DIDN'T EVEN CALL!
IT'S TRUE-- I HAVE NO MORE CONTROL OVER MY LIFE THAN MY SOAP CHARACTER!
SLAM
I'LL GO TO A GIRLFRIEND'S, I'LL GO TO A HOTEL, I'LL GO DANCING!
COME FIND ME, PETER-- IF YOU CARE.
WHILE...
ENOUGH "PRACTICE".
IT'S NOW OR NEVER.
I GOTTA FIND OUT IF I'M A HERO...!
I'M GOING TO SAVE SOME-ONE--OR DIE TRYING!
NEARBY...
THE GROUND IS SHAKING!
OH, NO! NOT AGAIN!
HELP!
SPIDER-MAN--
"--WHERE ARE YOU?!"
WHRRRR
CEMENT-- IMAGES--
GONNA DROWN!
CONCLUDED NEXT MONTH!

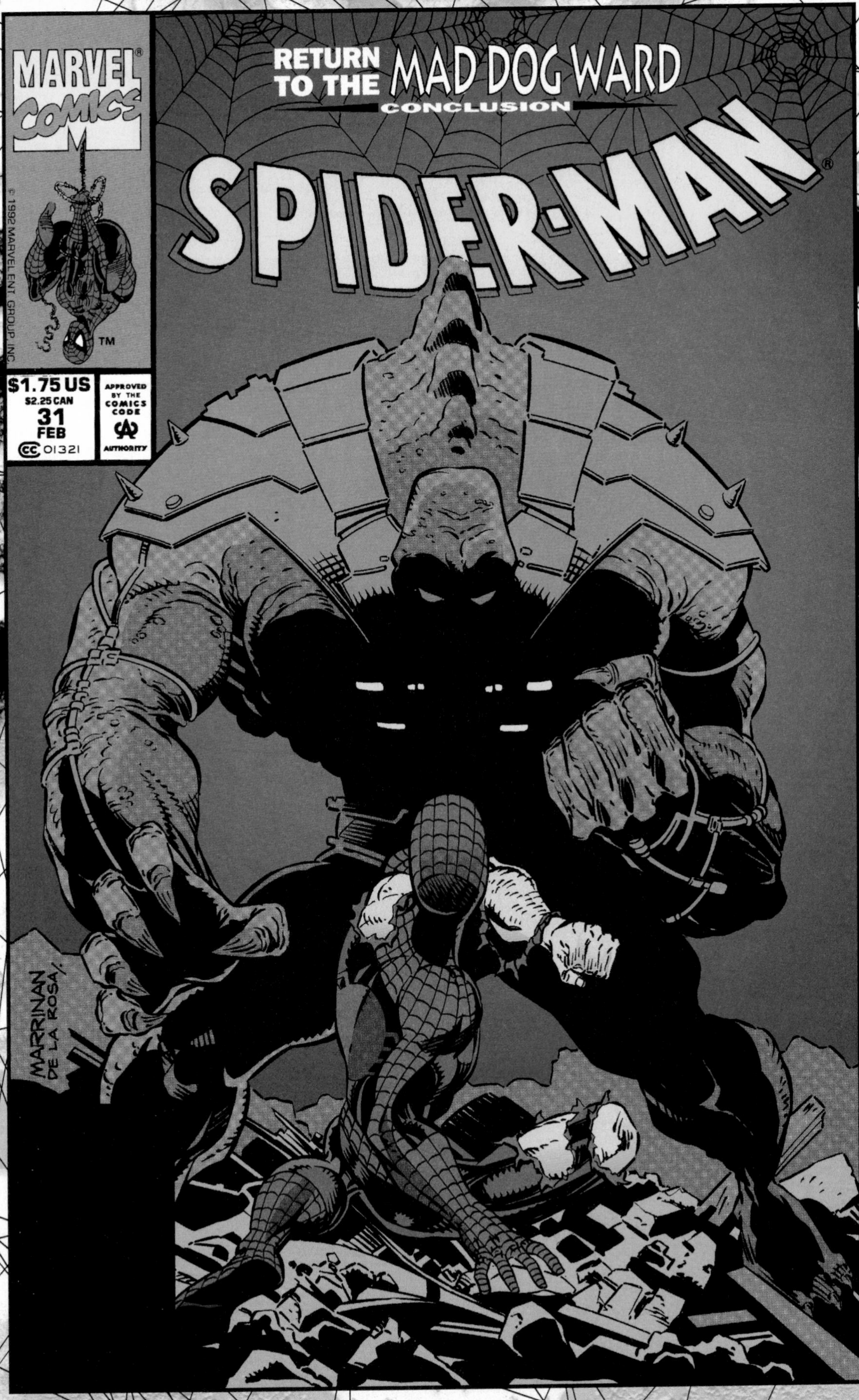
MARVEL® COMICS
RETURN TO THE MAD DOG WARD
CONCLUSION
SPIDER-MAN®
© 1992 MARVEL ENT. GROUP, INC.
TM
$1.75 US
$2.25 CAN
31
FEB
CC 01321
APPROVED BY THE COMICS CODE AUTHORITY
MARRINAN
DE LA ROSA

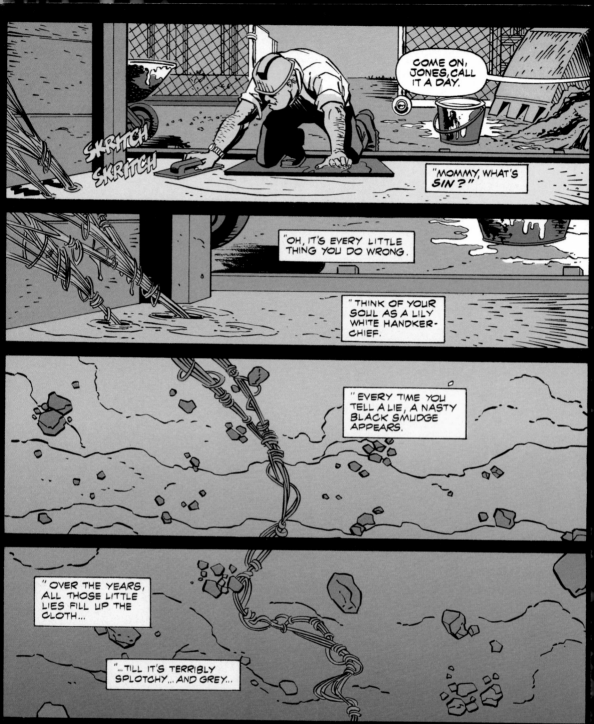

COME ON, JONES, CALL IT A DAY.

SKRITCH
SKRITCH

"MOMMY, WHAT'S *SIN*?"

"OH, IT'S EVERY LITTLE THING YOU DO WRONG.

"THINK OF YOUR SOUL AS A LILY WHITE HANDKER-CHIEF.

"EVERY TIME YOU TELL A LIE, A NASTY BLACK SMUDGE APPEARS.

"OVER THE YEARS, ALL THOSE LITTLE LIES FILL UP THE CLOTH...

"...TILL IT'S TERRIBLY SPLOTCHY... AND GREY...

"...AND FINALLY: ALL BLACK.

"AND WHEN YOUR SOUL IS BLACK, YOU BETTER DO SOME PENANCE."

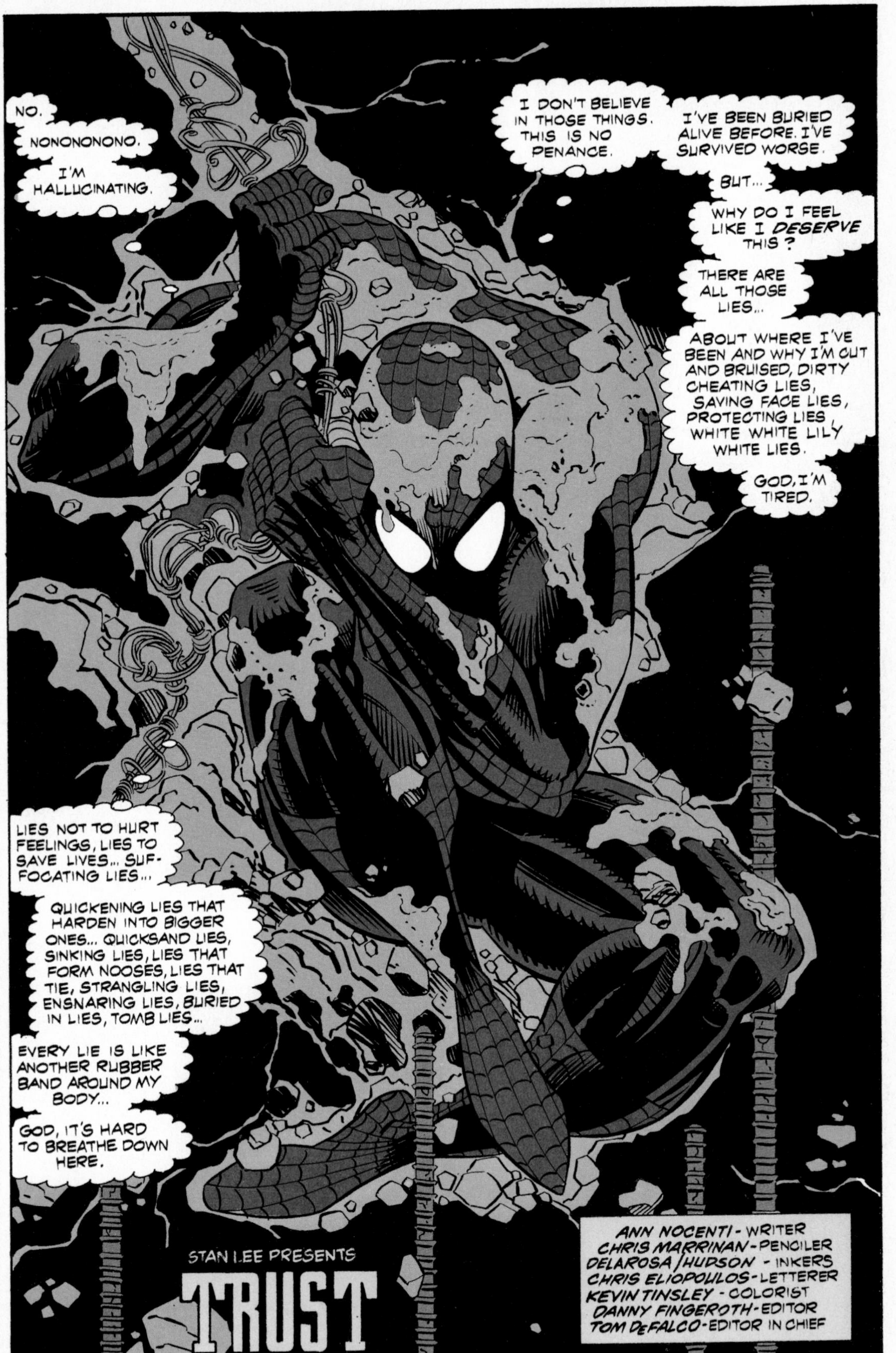
NO.
NONONONONO.
I'M HALLUCINATING.
I DON'T BELIEVE IN THOSE THINGS. THIS IS NO PENANCE.
I'VE BEEN BURIED ALIVE BEFORE. I'VE SURVIVED WORSE.
BUT...
WHY DO I FEEL LIKE I *DESERVE* THIS?
THERE ARE ALL THOSE LIES...
ABOUT WHERE I'VE BEEN AND WHY I'M CUT AND BRUISED, DIRTY CHEATING LIES, SAVING FACE LIES, PROTECTING LIES, WHITE WHITE LILY WHITE LIES.
GOD, I'M TIRED.
LIES NOT TO HURT FEELINGS, LIES TO SAVE LIVES... SUF-FOCATING LIES...
QUICKENING LIES THAT HARDEN INTO BIGGER ONES... QUICKSAND LIES, SINKING LIES, LIES THAT FORM NOOSES, LIES THAT TIE, STRANGLING LIES, ENSNARING LIES, BURIED IN LIES, TOMB LIES...
EVERY LIE IS LIKE ANOTHER RUBBER BAND AROUND MY BODY...
GOD, IT'S HARD TO BREATHE DOWN HERE.
STAN LEE PRESENTS
TRUST
ANN NOCENTI - WRITER
CHRIS MARRINAN - PENCILER
DELAROSA/HUDSON - INKERS
CHRIS ELIOPOULOS - LETTERER
KEVIN TINSLEY - COLORIST
DANNY FINGEROTH - EDITOR
TOM DEFALCO - EDITOR IN CHIEF

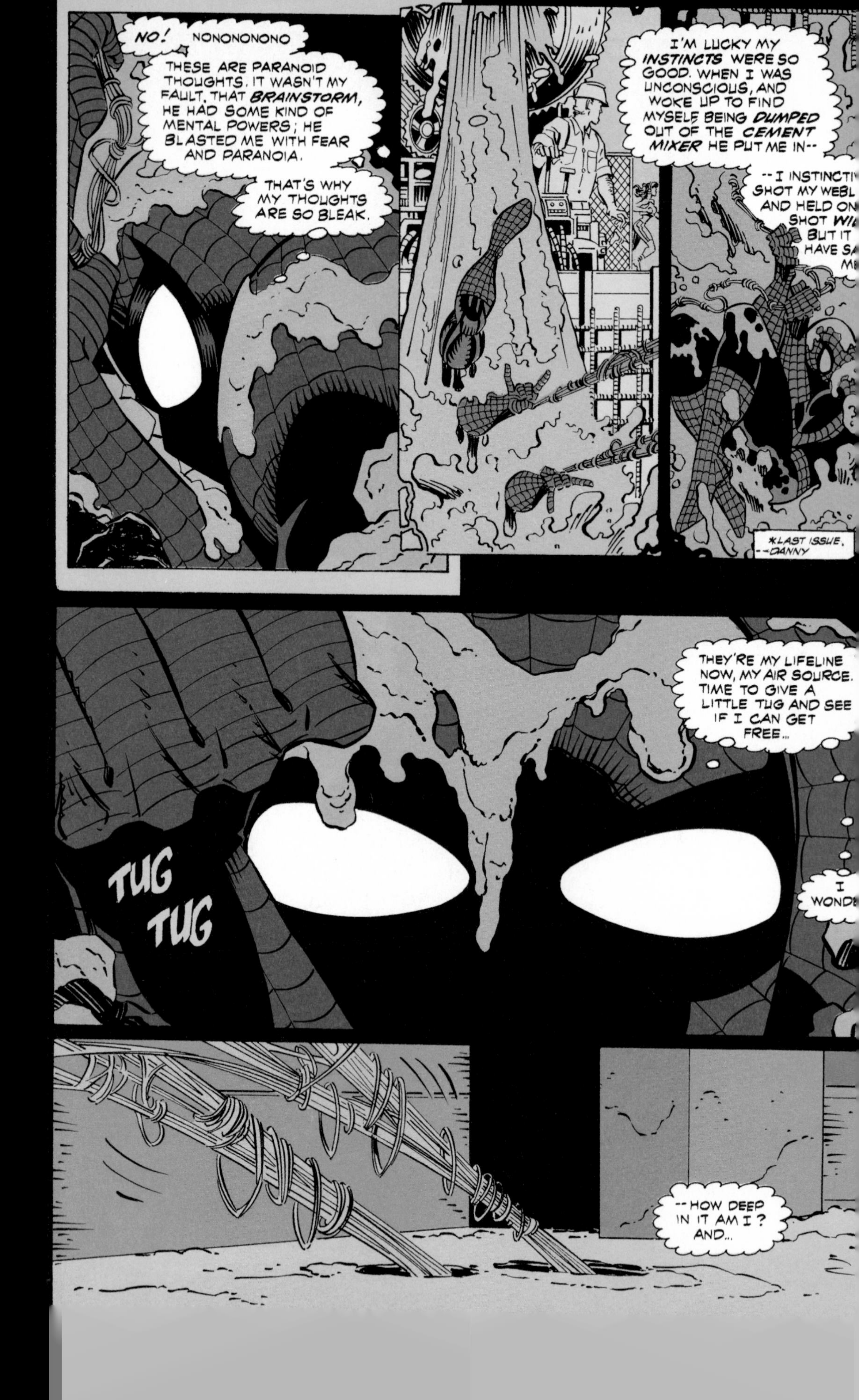
NO! NONONONONO
THESE ARE PARANOID THOUGHTS. IT WASN'T MY FAULT. THAT BRAINSTORM, HE HAD SOME KIND OF MENTAL POWERS; HE BLASTED ME WITH FEAR AND PARANOIA.
THAT'S WHY MY THOUGHTS ARE SO BLEAK.
I'M LUCKY MY INSTINCTS WERE SO GOOD. WHEN I WAS UNCONSCIOUS, AND WOKE UP TO FIND MYSELF BEING DUMPED OUT OF THE CEMENT MIXER HE PUT ME IN--
-- I INSTINCTI SHOT MY WEBL AND HELD ON SHOT WI BUT IT HAVE SA M
*LAST ISSUE. --DANNY
THEY'RE MY LIFELINE NOW, MY AIR SOURCE. TIME TO GIVE A LITTLE TUG AND SEE IF I CAN GET FREE...
TUG TUG
I WONDE
--HOW DEEP IN IT AM I? AND...

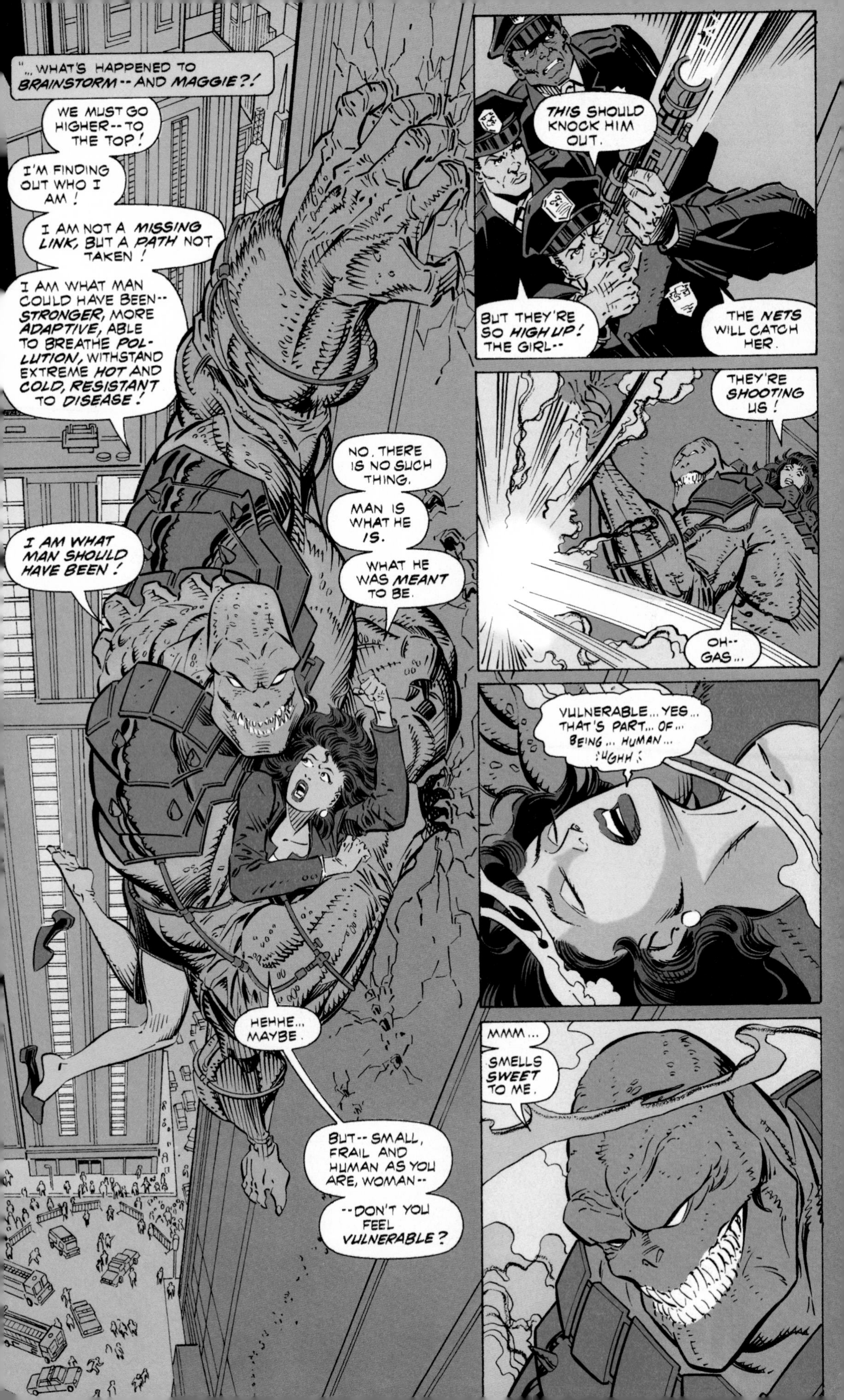
"...WHAT'S HAPPENED TO BRAINSTORM -- AND MAGGIE?!
WE MUST GO HIGHER -- TO THE TOP!
I'M FINDING OUT WHO I AM!
I AM NOT A MISSING LINK, BUT A PATH NOT TAKEN!
I AM WHAT MAN COULD HAVE BEEN -- STRONGER, MORE ADAPTIVE, ABLE TO BREATHE POL-LUTION, WITHSTAND EXTREME HOT AND COLD, RESISTANT TO DISEASE!
NO. THERE IS NO SUCH THING.
MAN IS WHAT HE IS.
WHAT HE WAS MEANT TO BE.
I AM WHAT MAN SHOULD HAVE BEEN!
HEHHE... MAYBE.
BUT -- SMALL, FRAIL AND HUMAN AS YOU ARE, WOMAN --
-- DON'T YOU FEEL VULNERABLE?
THIS SHOULD KNOCK HIM OUT.
BUT THEY'RE SO HIGH UP! THE GIRL --
THE NETS WILL CATCH HER.
THEY'RE SHOOTING US!
OH -- GAS...
VULNERABLE... YES... THAT'S PART... OF... BEING... HUMAN... UGHH
MMM...
SMELLS SWEET TO ME.

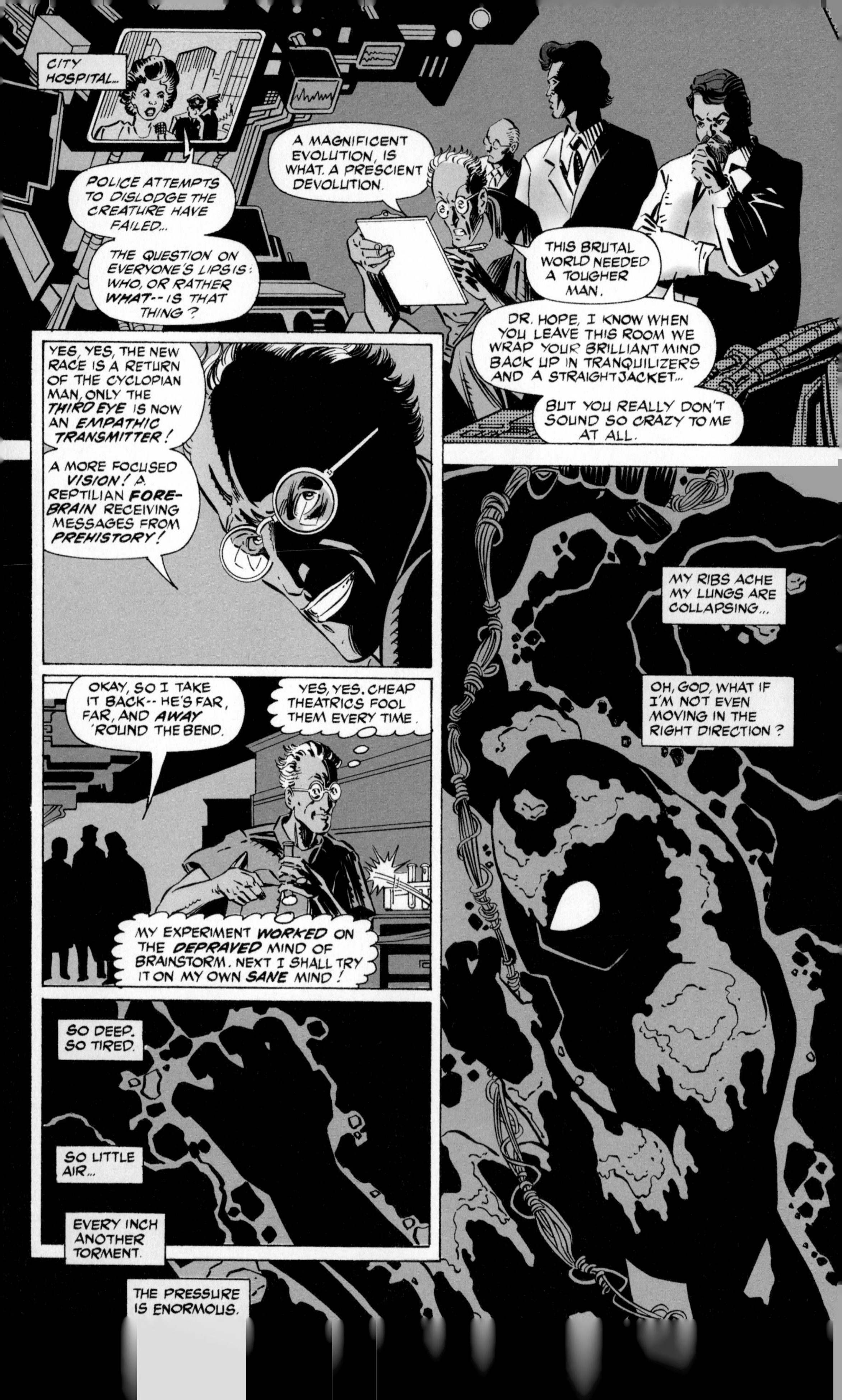

CITY HOSPITAL...
POLICE ATTEMPTS TO DISLODGE THE CREATURE HAVE FAILED...
THE QUESTION ON EVERYONE'S LIPS IS: WHO, OR RATHER WHAT-- IS THAT THING?
A MAGNIFICENT EVOLUTION, IS WHAT. A PRESCIENT DEVOLUTION.
THIS BRUTAL WORLD NEEDED A TOUGHER MAN.
DR. HOPE, I KNOW WHEN YOU LEAVE THIS ROOM WE WRAP YOUR BRILLIANT MIND BACK UP IN TRANQUILIZERS AND A STRAIGHTJACKET...
BUT YOU REALLY DON'T SOUND SO CRAZY TO ME AT ALL.
YES, YES, THE NEW RACE IS A RETURN OF THE CYCLOPIAN MAN, ONLY THE THIRD EYE IS NOW AN EMPATHIC TRANSMITTER!
A MORE FOCUSED VISION! A REPTILIAN FORE-BRAIN RECEIVING MESSAGES FROM PREHISTORY!
OKAY, SO I TAKE IT BACK-- HE'S FAR, FAR, AND AWAY 'ROUND THE BEND.
YES, YES. CHEAP THEATRICS FOOL THEM EVERY TIME.
MY EXPERIMENT WORKED ON THE DEPRAVED MIND OF BRAINSTORM. NEXT I SHALL TRY IT ON MY OWN SANE MIND!
SO DEEP. SO TIRED.
SO LITTLE AIR...
EVERY INCH ANOTHER TORMENT.
THE PRESSURE IS ENORMOUS.
MY RIBS ACHE MY LUNGS ARE COLLAPSING...
OH, GOD, WHAT IF I'M NOT EVEN MOVING IN THE RIGHT DIRECTION?

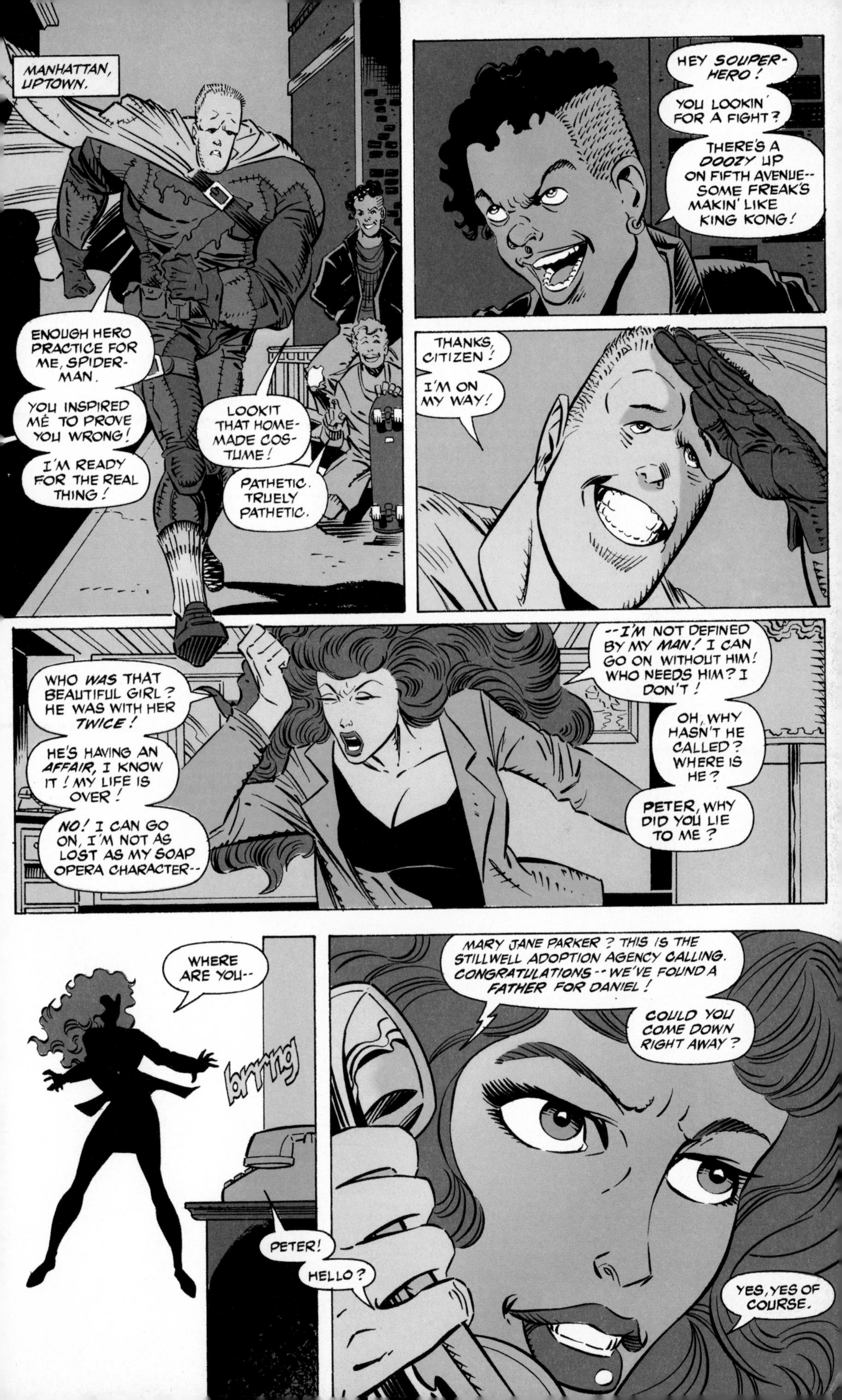
MANHATTAN, UPTOWN.
ENOUGH HERO PRACTICE FOR ME, SPIDER-MAN.
YOU INSPIRED ME TO PROVE YOU WRONG!
I'M READY FOR THE REAL THING!
LOOKIT THAT HOME-MADE COS-TUME!
PATHETIC. TRUELY PATHETIC.
HEY SOUPER-HERO!
YOU LOOKIN' FOR A FIGHT?
THERE'S A DOOZY UP ON FIFTH AVENUE-- SOME FREAK'S MAKIN' LIKE KING KONG!
THANKS, CITIZEN!
I'M ON MY WAY!
WHO WAS THAT BEAUTIFUL GIRL? HE WAS WITH HER TWICE!
HE'S HAVING AN AFFAIR, I KNOW IT! MY LIFE IS OVER!
NO! I CAN GO ON, I'M NOT AS LOST AS MY SOAP OPERA CHARACTER--
--I'M NOT DEFINED BY MY MAN! I CAN GO ON WITHOUT HIM! WHO NEEDS HIM? I DON'T!
OH, WHY HASN'T HE CALLED? WHERE IS HE?
PETER, WHY DID YOU LIE TO ME?
WHERE ARE YOU--
brrrng
PETER!
HELLO?
MARY JANE PARKER? THIS IS THE STILLWELL ADOPTION AGENCY CALLING. CONGRATULATIONS--WE'VE FOUND A FATHER FOR DANIEL!
COULD YOU COME DOWN RIGHT AWAY?
YES, YES OF COURSE.

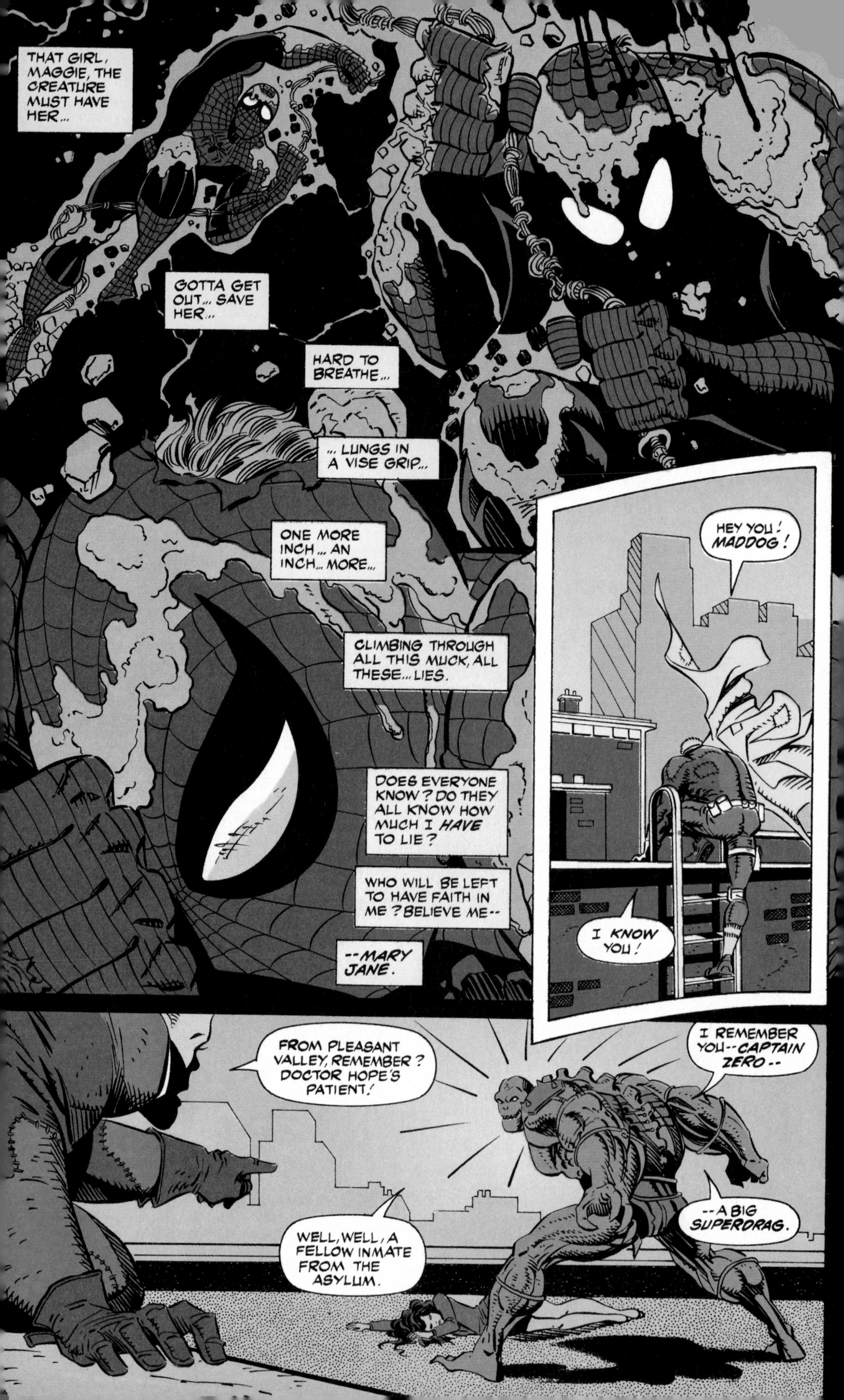
THAT GIRL, MAGGIE, THE CREATURE MUST HAVE HER...
GOTTA GET OUT... SAVE HER...
HARD TO BREATHE...
... LUNGS IN A VISE GRIP...
ONE MORE INCH... AN INCH... MORE...
CLIMBING THROUGH ALL THIS MUCK, ALL THESE... LIES.
DOES EVERYONE KNOW? DO THEY ALL KNOW HOW MUCH I HAVE TO LIE?
WHO WILL BE LEFT TO HAVE FAITH IN ME? BELIEVE ME--
--MARY JANE.
HEY YOU! MADDOG!
I KNOW YOU!
FROM PLEASANT VALLEY, REMEMBER? DOCTOR HOPE'S PATIENT!
I REMEMBER YOU--CAPTAIN ZERO--
--A BIG SUPERDRAG.
WELL, WELL, A FELLOW INMATE FROM THE ASYLUM.

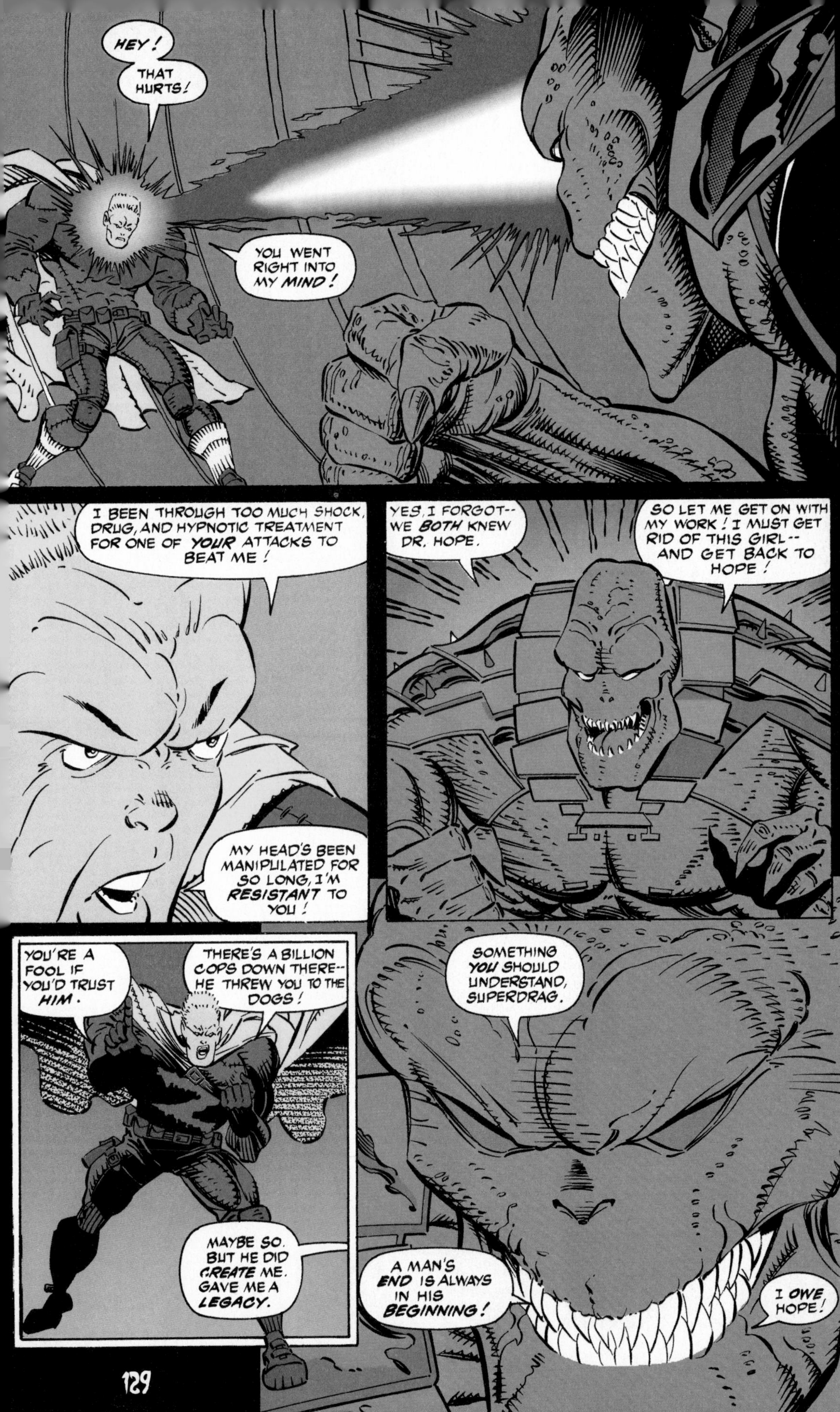
HEY!
THAT HURTS!
YOU WENT RIGHT INTO MY MIND!
I BEEN THROUGH TOO MUCH SHOCK, DRUG, AND HYPNOTIC TREATMENT FOR ONE OF YOUR ATTACKS TO BEAT ME!
MY HEAD'S BEEN MANIPULATED FOR SO LONG, I'M RESISTANT TO YOU!
YES, I FORGOT-- WE BOTH KNEW DR. HOPE.
SO LET ME GET ON WITH MY WORK! I MUST GET RID OF THIS GIRL-- AND GET BACK TO HOPE!
YOU'RE A FOOL IF YOU'D TRUST HIM.
THERE'S A BILLION COPS DOWN THERE-- HE THREW YOU TO THE DOGS!
MAYBE SO. BUT HE DID CREATE ME. GAVE ME A LEGACY.
SOMETHING YOU SHOULD UNDERSTAND, SUPERDRAG.
A MAN'S END IS ALWAYS IN HIS BEGINNING!
I OWE HOPE!

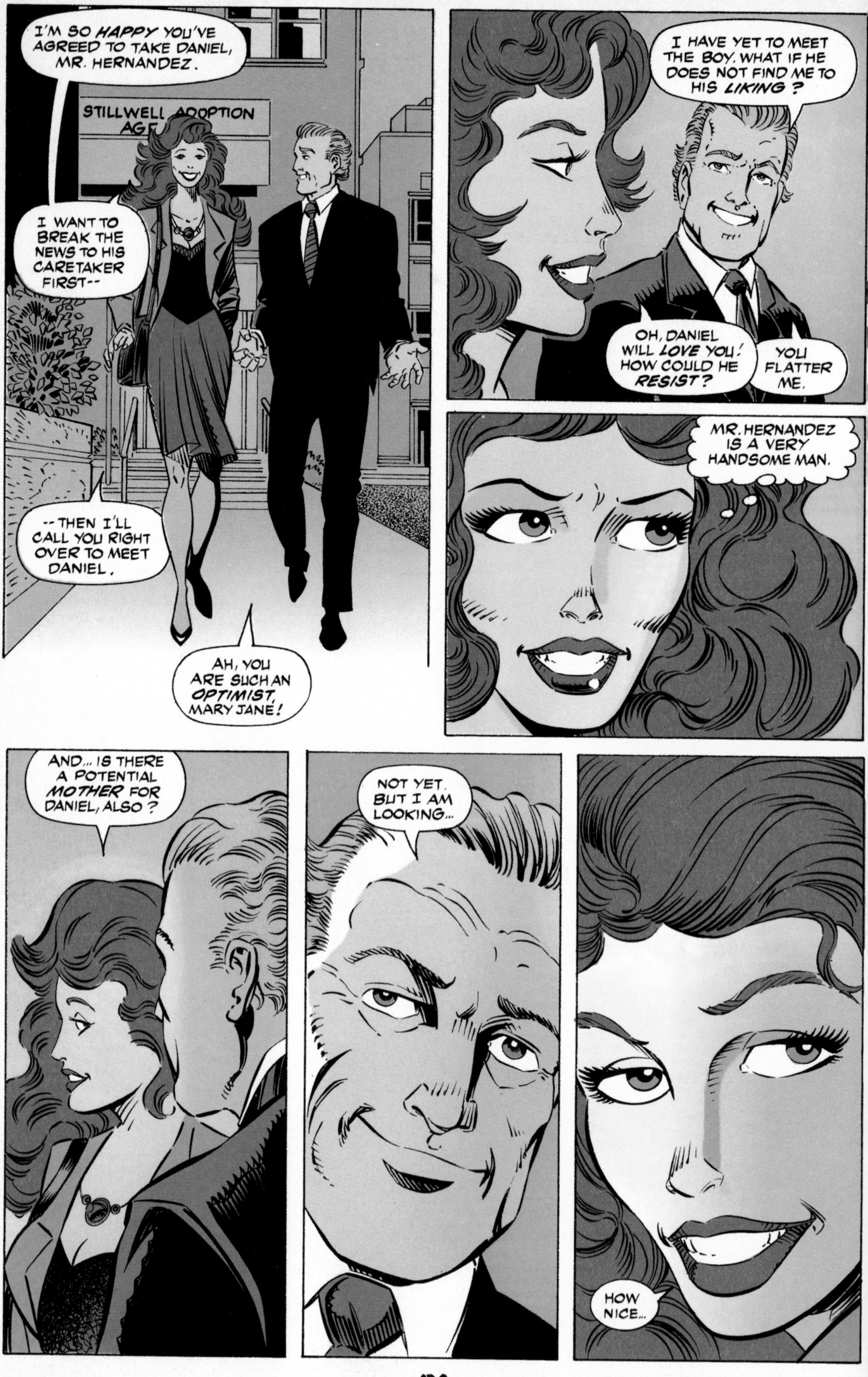
I'M SO HAPPY YOU'VE AGREED TO TAKE DANIEL, MR. HERNANDEZ.
STILLWELL ADOPTION AGE
I WANT TO BREAK THE NEWS TO HIS CARETAKER FIRST--
--THEN I'LL CALL YOU RIGHT OVER TO MEET DANIEL.
AH, YOU ARE SUCH AN OPTIMIST, MARY JANE!
I HAVE YET TO MEET THE BOY. WHAT IF HE DOES NOT FIND ME TO HIS LIKING?
OH, DANIEL WILL LOVE YOU! HOW COULD HE RESIST?
YOU FLATTER ME.
MR. HERNANDEZ IS A VERY HANDSOME MAN.
AND... IS THERE A POTENTIAL MOTHER FOR DANIEL, ALSO?
NOT YET. BUT I AM LOOKING...
HOW NICE...

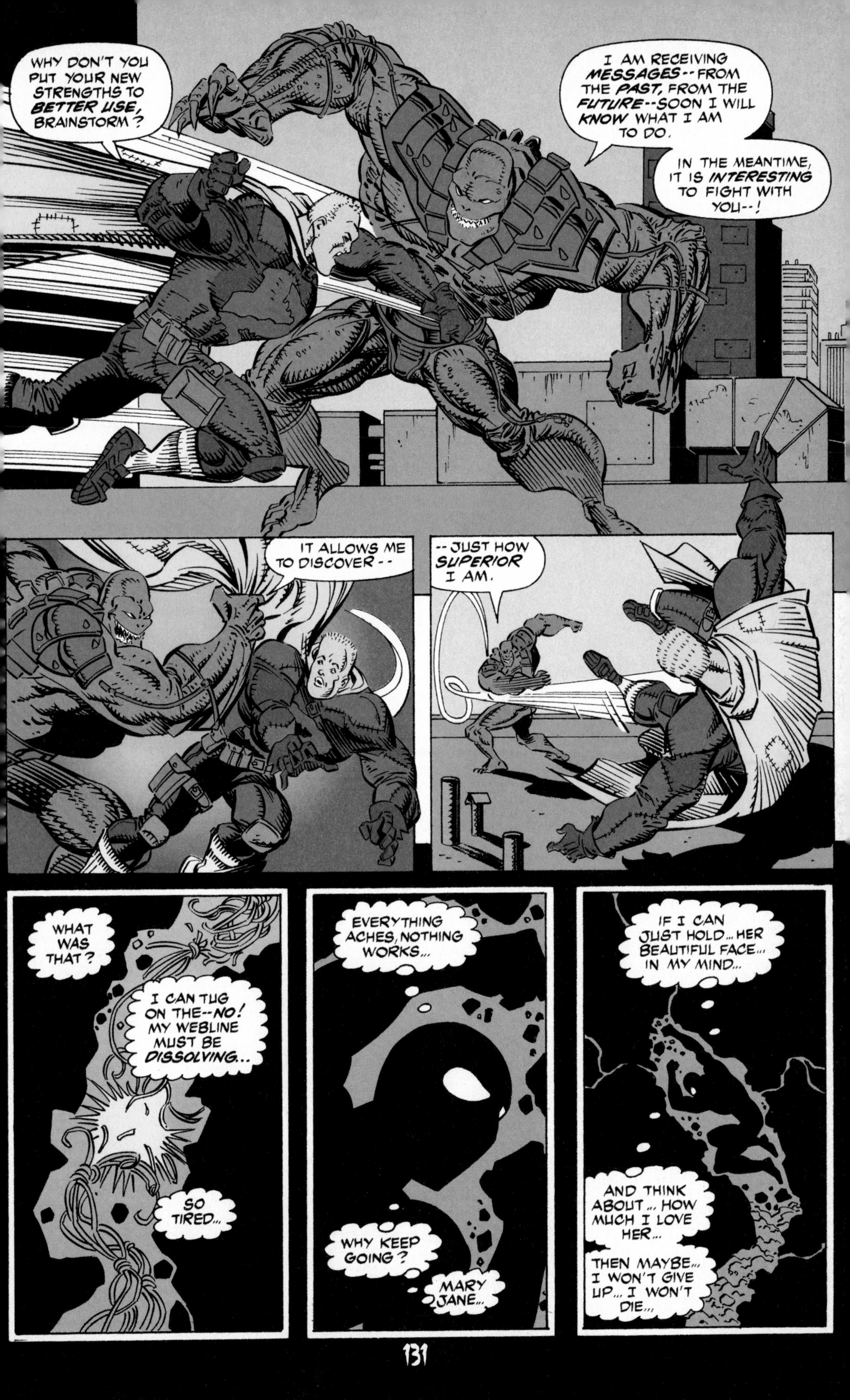
WHY DON'T YOU PUT YOUR NEW STRENGTHS TO BETTER USE, BRAINSTORM?
I AM RECEIVING MESSAGES--FROM THE PAST, FROM THE FUTURE--SOON I WILL KNOW WHAT I AM TO DO.
IN THE MEANTIME, IT IS INTERESTING TO FIGHT WITH YOU--!
IT ALLOWS ME TO DISCOVER--
--JUST HOW SUPERIOR I AM.
WHAT WAS THAT?
I CAN TUG ON THE--NO! MY WEBLINE MUST BE DISSOLVING...
SO TIRED...
EVERYTHING ACHES, NOTHING WORKS...
WHY KEEP GOING?
MARY JANE...
IF I CAN JUST HOLD... HER BEAUTIFUL FACE... IN MY MIND...
AND THINK ABOUT... HOW MUCH I LOVE HER...
THEN MAYBE... I WON'T GIVE UP... I WON'T DIE...

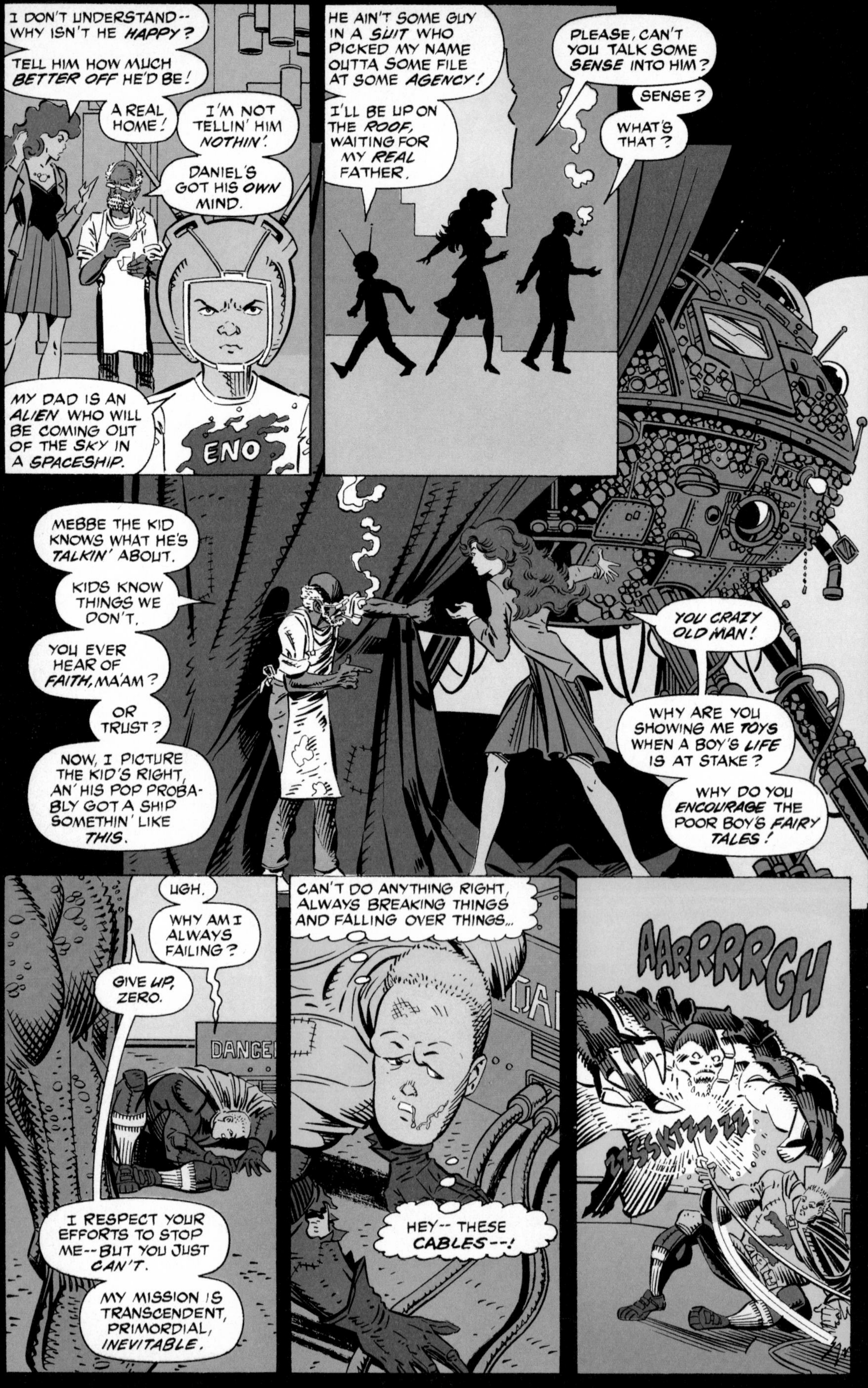

I DON'T UNDERSTAND-- WHY ISN'T HE HAPPY?
TELL HIM HOW MUCH BETTER OFF HE'D BE!
A REAL HOME!
I'M NOT TELLIN' HIM NOTHIN'.
DANIEL'S GOT HIS OWN MIND.
MY DAD IS AN ALIEN WHO WILL BE COMING OUT OF THE SKY IN A SPACESHIP.
ENO
HE AIN'T SOME GUY IN A SUIT WHO PICKED MY NAME OUTTA SOME FILE AT SOME AGENCY!
I'LL BE UP ON THE ROOF, WAITING FOR MY REAL FATHER.
PLEASE, CAN'T YOU TALK SOME SENSE INTO HIM?
SENSE?
WHAT'S THAT?
MEBBE THE KID KNOWS WHAT HE'S TALKIN' ABOUT.
KIDS KNOW THINGS WE DON'T.
YOU EVER HEAR OF FAITH, MA'AM?
OR TRUST?
NOW, I PICTURE THE KID'S RIGHT, AN' HIS POP PROBABLY GOT A SHIP SOMETHIN' LIKE THIS.
YOU CRAZY OLD MAN!
WHY ARE YOU SHOWING ME TOYS WHEN A BOY'S LIFE IS AT STAKE?
WHY DO YOU ENCOURAGE THE POOR BOY'S FAIRY TALES!
UGH.
WHY AM I ALWAYS FAILING?
GIVE UP, ZERO.
DANGER
I RESPECT YOUR EFFORTS TO STOP ME--BUT YOU JUST CAN'T.
MY MISSION IS TRANSCENDENT, PRIMORDIAL, INEVITABLE.
CAN'T DO ANYTHING RIGHT, ALWAYS BREAKING THINGS AND FALLING OVER THINGS...
HEY-- THESE CABLES--!
AARRRRGH
ZZSSKTZZZZZ

STILL NO WORD FROM PETER...

I'M GOING OUT OF MY MIND!

WHAT IF IT WASN'T THE GIRL, WHAT IF HE'S IN *TROUBLE*?

OH, PLEASE PETER!

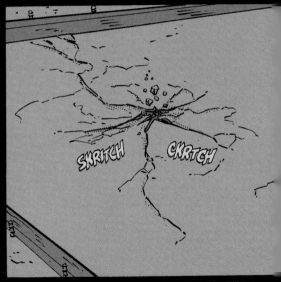

SKRITCH   CKRTCH

HAVEN'T YOU EVER HEARD OF FAITH?

THE OLD MAN'S WORDS...

DID I SIMPLY LOSE *FAITH*? IS *THAT* WHY PETER HAS VANISHED?

KRKCH   PKIKC

I LOVE YOU, PETER, AND I TRUST YOU AND I KNOW YOU'LL COME BACK TO ME!

K RAK KOW

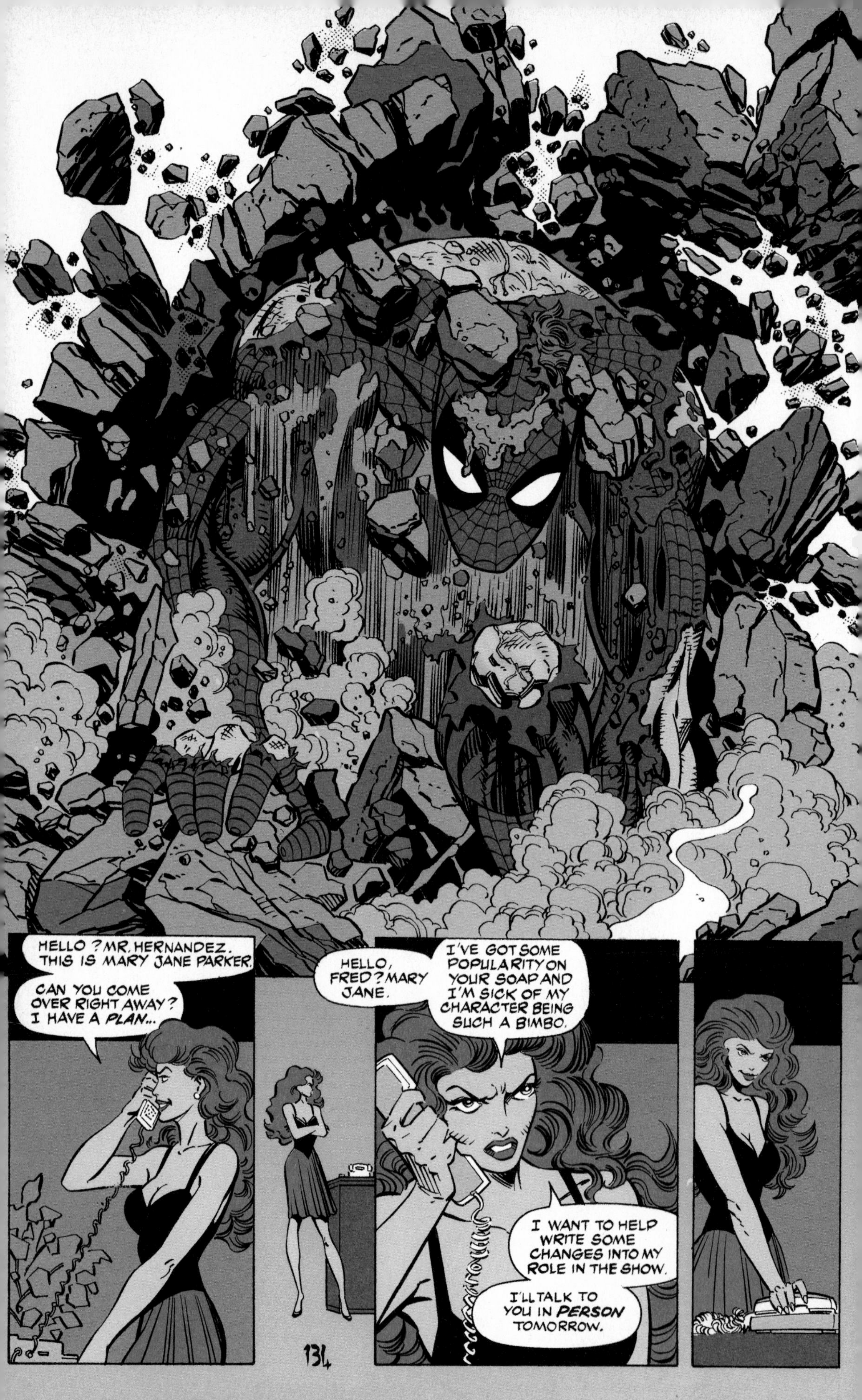
HELLO? MR. HERNANDEZ. THIS IS MARY JANE PARKER.
CAN YOU COME OVER RIGHT AWAY? I HAVE A PLAN...
HELLO, FRED? MARY JANE.
I'VE GOT SOME POPULARITY ON YOUR SOAP AND I'M SICK OF MY CHARACTER BEING SUCH A BIMBO.
I WANT TO HELP WRITE SOME CHANGES INTO MY ROLE IN THE SHOW.
I'LL TALK TO YOU IN PERSON TOMORROW.

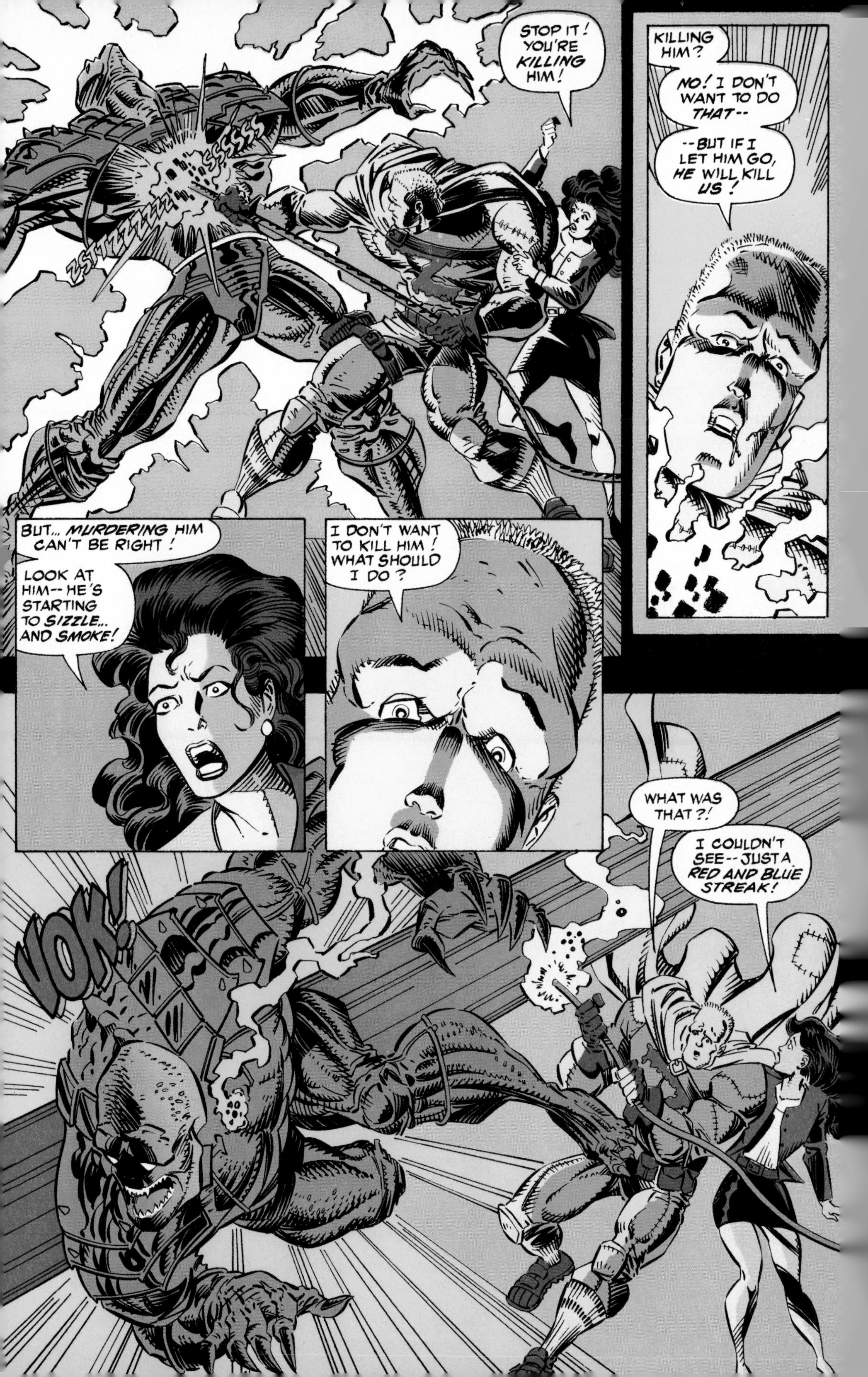
ZSTTZZZZZZ
SSSSSS
STOP IT! YOU'RE KILLING HIM!
KILLING HIM?
NO! I DON'T WANT TO DO THAT--
--BUT IF I LET HIM GO, HE WILL KILL US!
BUT... MURDERING HIM CAN'T BE RIGHT!
LOOK AT HIM-- HE'S STARTING TO SIZZLE... AND SMOKE!
I DON'T WANT TO KILL HIM! WHAT SHOULD I DO?
VOK!
WHAT WAS THAT?!
I COULDN'T SEE-- JUST A RED AND BLUE STREAK!

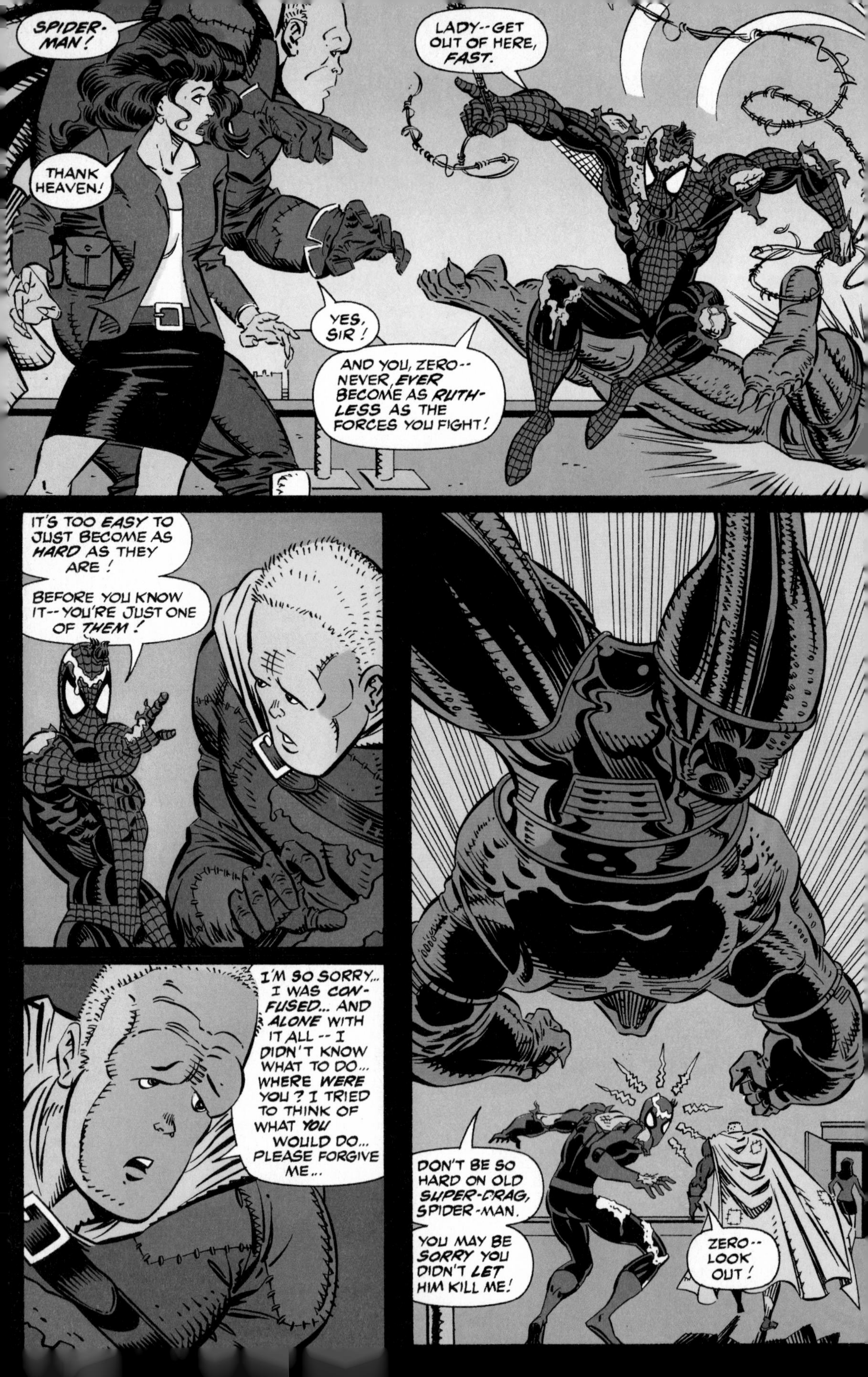
SPIDER-MAN!
THANK HEAVEN!
LADY--GET OUT OF HERE, FAST.
YES, SIR!
AND YOU, ZERO--NEVER, EVER BECOME AS RUTHLESS AS THE FORCES YOU FIGHT!
IT'S TOO EASY TO JUST BECOME AS HARD AS THEY ARE!
BEFORE YOU KNOW IT--YOU'RE JUST ONE OF THEM!
I'M SO SORRY... I WAS CONFUSED... AND ALONE WITH IT ALL--I DIDN'T KNOW WHAT TO DO... WHERE WERE YOU? I TRIED TO THINK OF WHAT YOU WOULD DO... PLEASE FORGIVE ME...
DON'T BE SO HARD ON OLD SUPER-DRAG, SPIDER-MAN.
YOU MAY BE SORRY YOU DIDN'T LET HIM KILL ME!
ZERO--LOOK OUT!

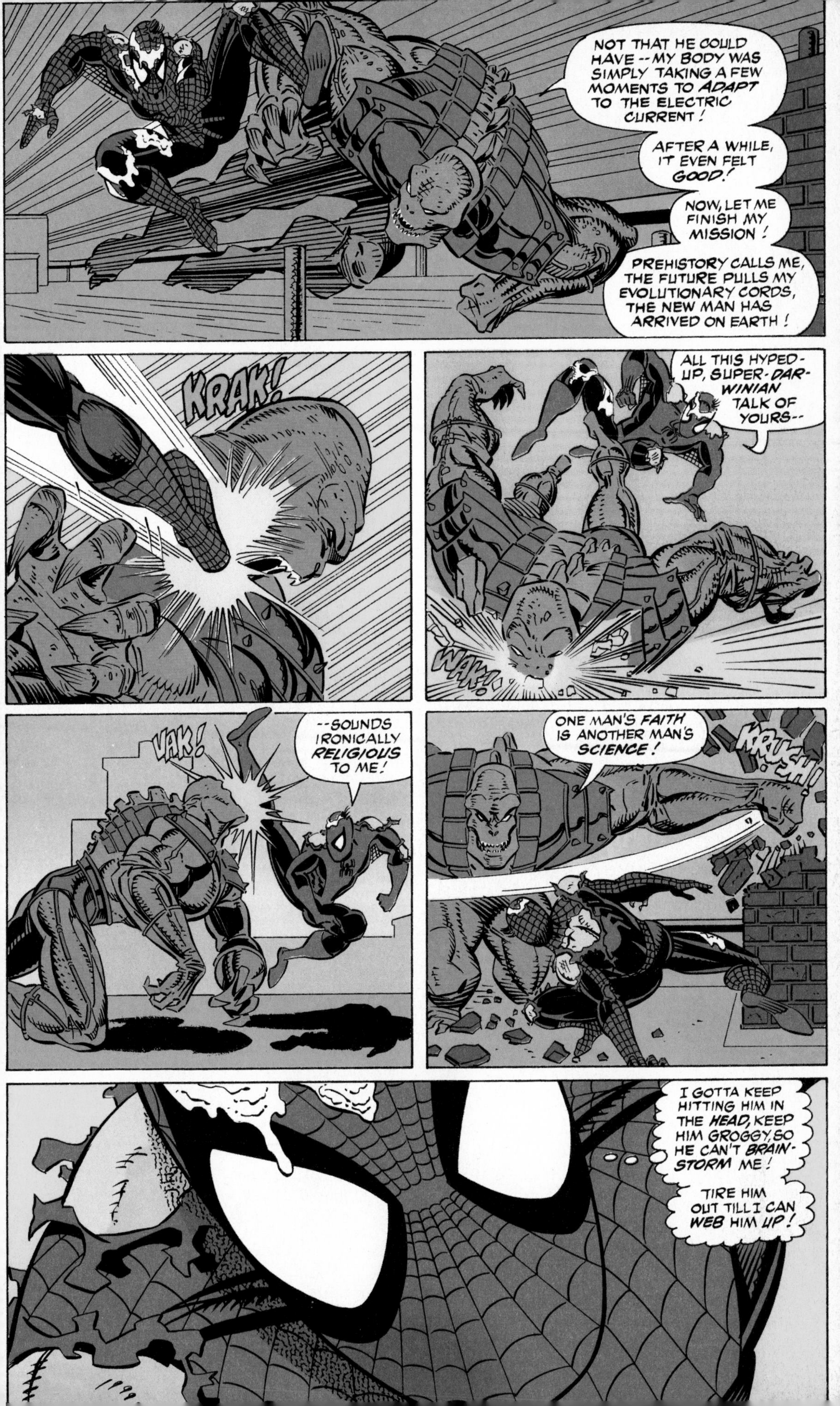
NOT THAT HE COULD HAVE -- MY BODY WAS SIMPLY TAKING A FEW MOMENTS TO ADAPT TO THE ELECTRIC CURRENT!
AFTER A WHILE, IT EVEN FELT GOOD!
NOW, LET ME FINISH MY MISSION!
PREHISTORY CALLS ME, THE FUTURE PULLS MY EVOLUTIONARY CORDS, THE NEW MAN HAS ARRIVED ON EARTH!
KRAK!
ALL THIS HYPED-UP, SUPER-DARWINIAN TALK OF YOURS--
WAK!
VAK!
--SOUNDS IRONICALLY RELIGIOUS TO ME!
ONE MAN'S FAITH IS ANOTHER MAN'S SCIENCE!
KRUSH CH!
I GOTTA KEEP HITTING HIM IN THE HEAD, KEEP HIM GROGGY, SO HE CAN'T BRAINSTORM ME!
TIRE HIM OUT TILL I CAN WEB HIM UP!

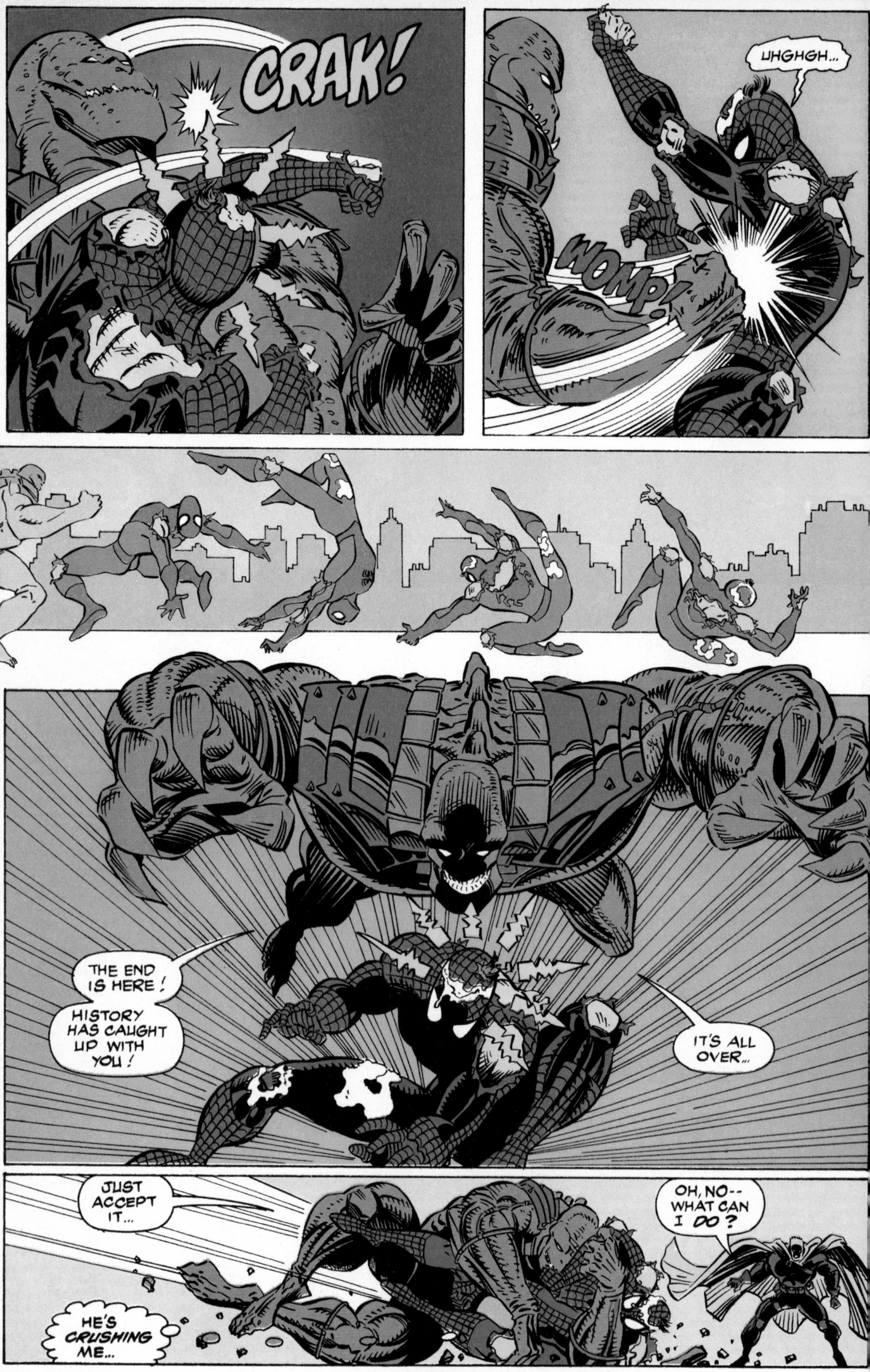
CRAK!
UHGHGH...
WOMP!
THE END IS HERE!
HISTORY HAS CAUGHT UP WITH YOU!
IT'S ALL OVER...
JUST ACCEPT IT...
HE'S CRUSHING ME...
OH, NO-- WHAT CAN I DO?

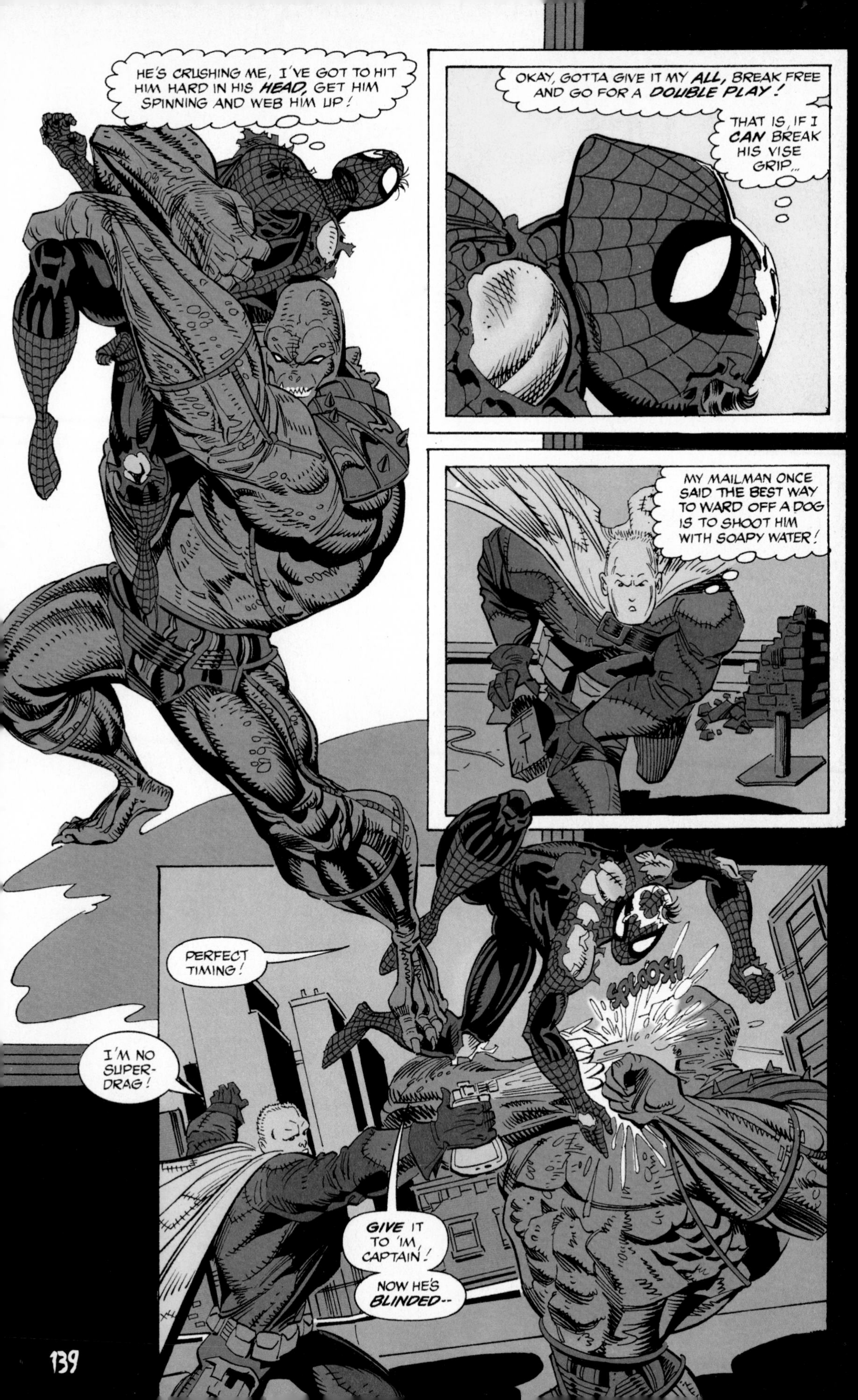
HE'S CRUSHING ME, I'VE GOT TO HIT HIM HARD IN HIS HEAD, GET HIM SPINNING AND WEB HIM UP!
OKAY, GOTTA GIVE IT MY ALL, BREAK FREE AND GO FOR A DOUBLE PLAY!
THAT IS, IF I CAN BREAK HIS VISE GRIP...
MY MAILMAN ONCE SAID THE BEST WAY TO WARD OFF A DOG IS TO SHOOT HIM WITH SOAPY WATER!
PERFECT TIMING!
I'M NO SUPER-DRAG!
SPLOOSH
GIVE IT TO 'IM, CAPTAIN!
NOW HE'S BLINDED--

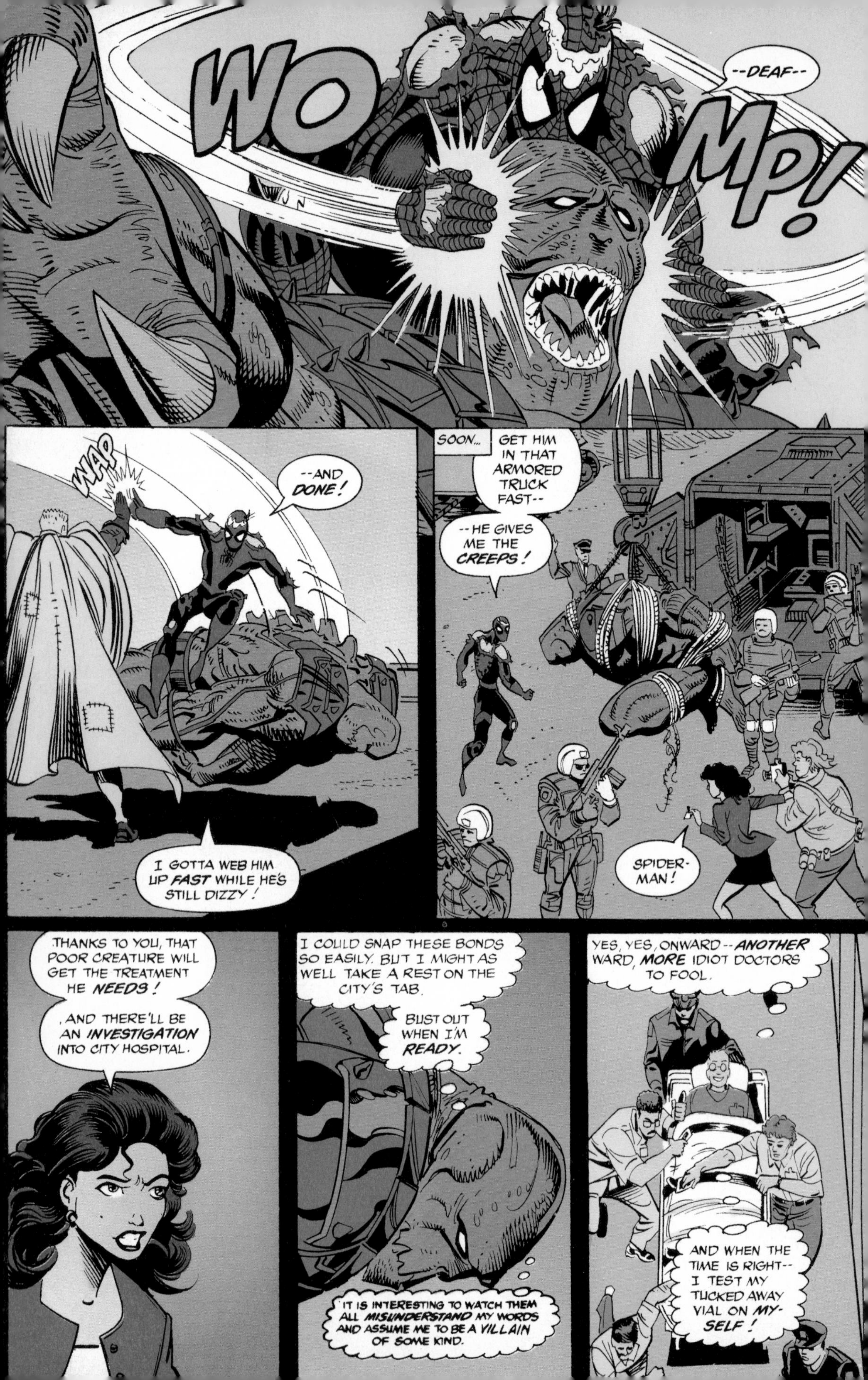

WOMP!
--DEAF--
WAP
--AND DONE!
I GOTTA WEB HIM UP FAST WHILE HE'S STILL DIZZY!
SOON...
GET HIM IN THAT ARMORED TRUCK FAST--
--HE GIVES ME THE CREEPS!
SPIDER-MAN!
THANKS TO YOU, THAT POOR CREATURE WILL GET THE TREATMENT HE NEEDS!
AND THERE'LL BE AN INVESTIGATION INTO CITY HOSPITAL.
I COULD SNAP THESE BONDS SO EASILY. BUT I MIGHT AS WELL TAKE A REST ON THE CITY'S TAB.
BUST OUT WHEN I'M READY.
IT IS INTERESTING TO WATCH THEM ALL MISUNDERSTAND MY WORDS AND ASSUME ME TO BE A VILLAIN OF SOME KIND.
YES, YES, ONWARD--ANOTHER WARD, MORE IDIOT DOCTORS TO FOOL.
AND WHEN THE TIME IS RIGHT--I TEST MY TUCKED AWAY VIAL ON MYSELF!

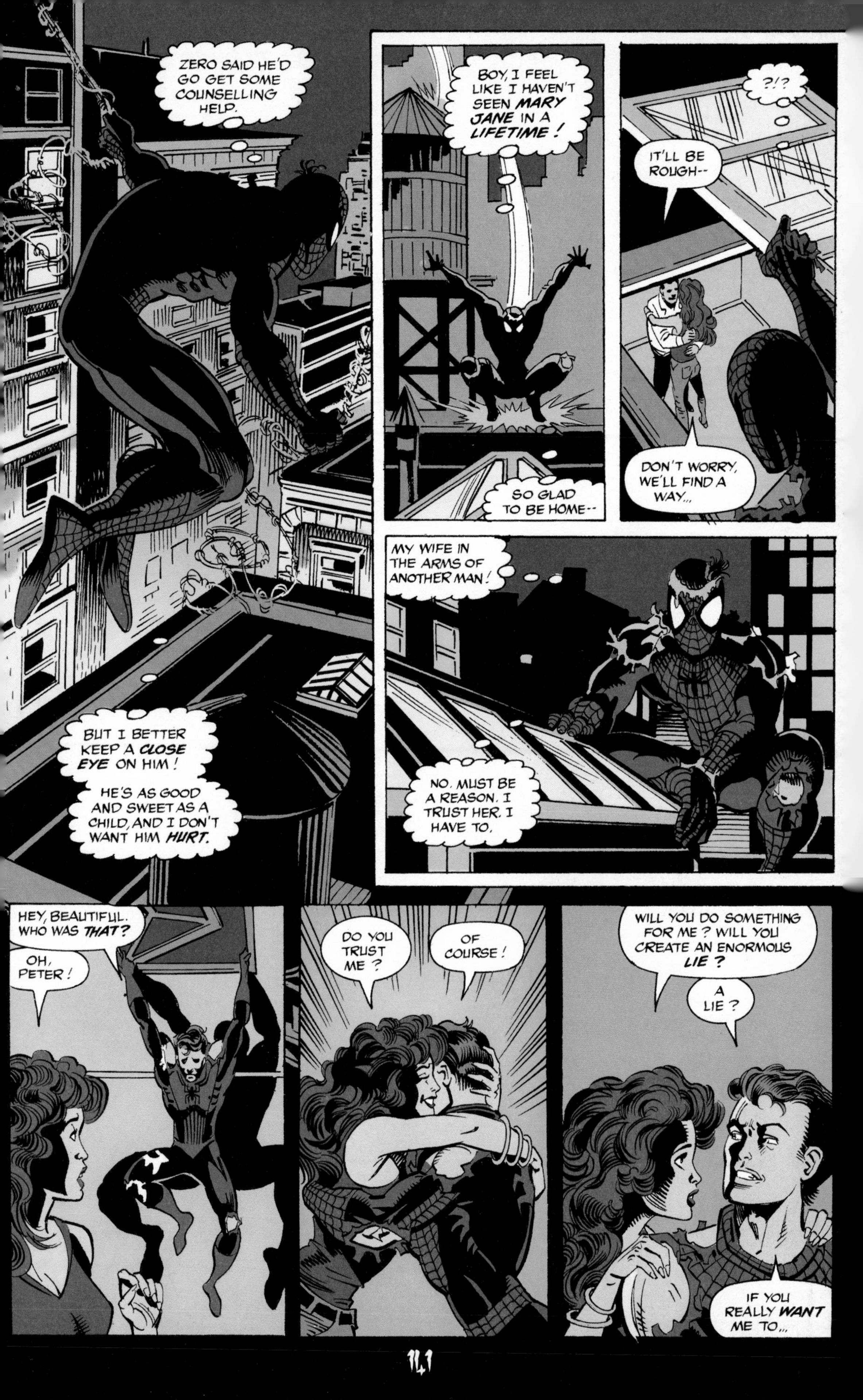
ZERO SAID HE'D GO GET SOME COUNSELLING HELP.
BUT I BETTER KEEP A CLOSE EYE ON HIM!
HE'S AS GOOD AND SWEET AS A CHILD, AND I DON'T WANT HIM HURT.
BOY, I FEEL LIKE I HAVEN'T SEEN MARY JANE IN A LIFETIME!
SO GLAD TO BE HOME--
?!?
IT'LL BE ROUGH--
DON'T WORRY, WE'LL FIND A WAY...
MY WIFE IN THE ARMS OF ANOTHER MAN!
NO. MUST BE A REASON. I TRUST HER. I HAVE TO.
HEY, BEAUTIFUL. WHO WAS THAT?
OH, PETER!
DO YOU TRUST ME?
OF COURSE!
WILL YOU DO SOMETHING FOR ME? WILL YOU CREATE AN ENORMOUS LIE?
A LIE?
IF YOU REALLY WANT ME TO...

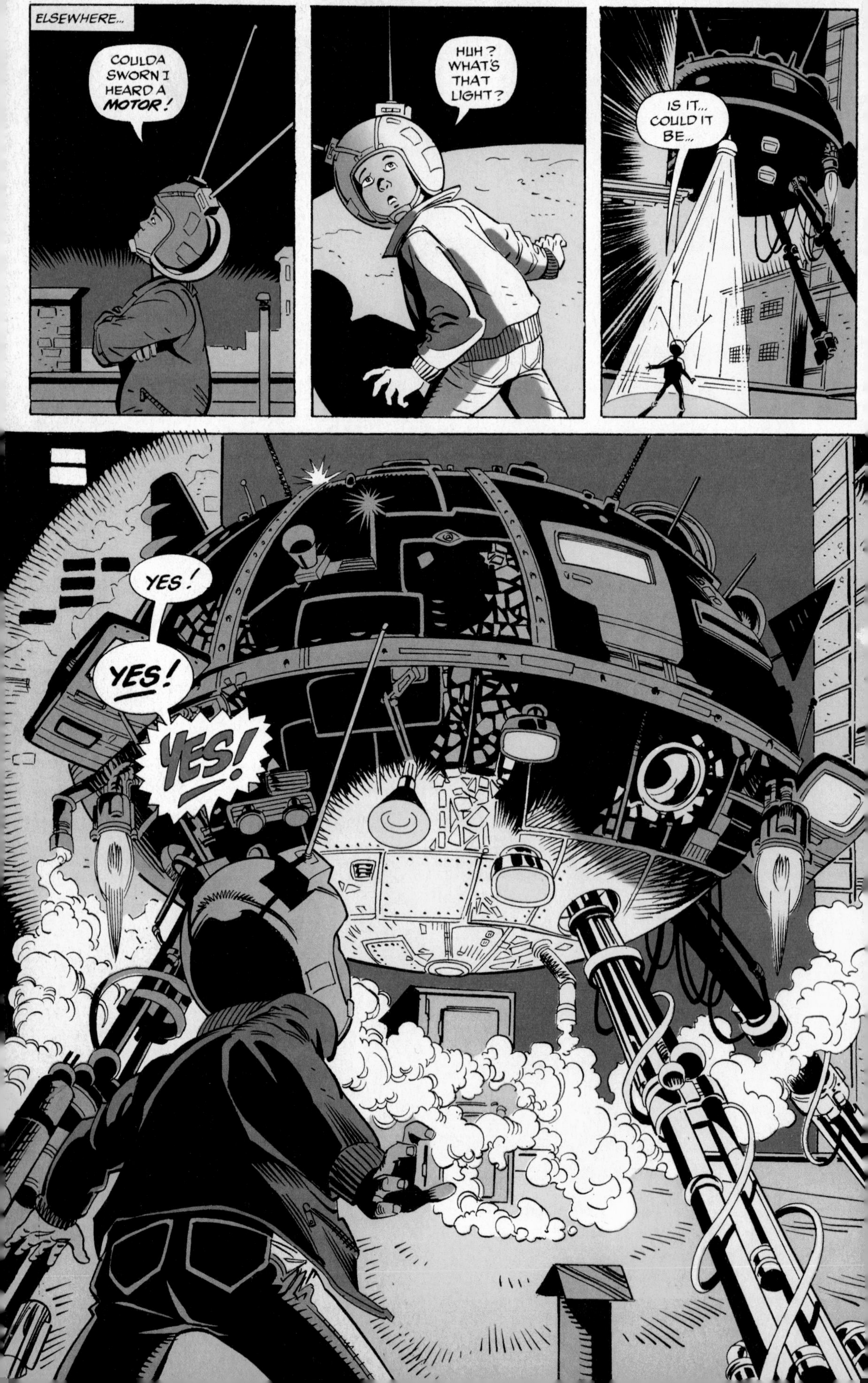

ELSEWHERE...
COULDA SWORN I HEARD A MOTOR!
HUH? WHAT'S THAT LIGHT?
IS IT... COULD IT BE...
YES!
YES!
YES!

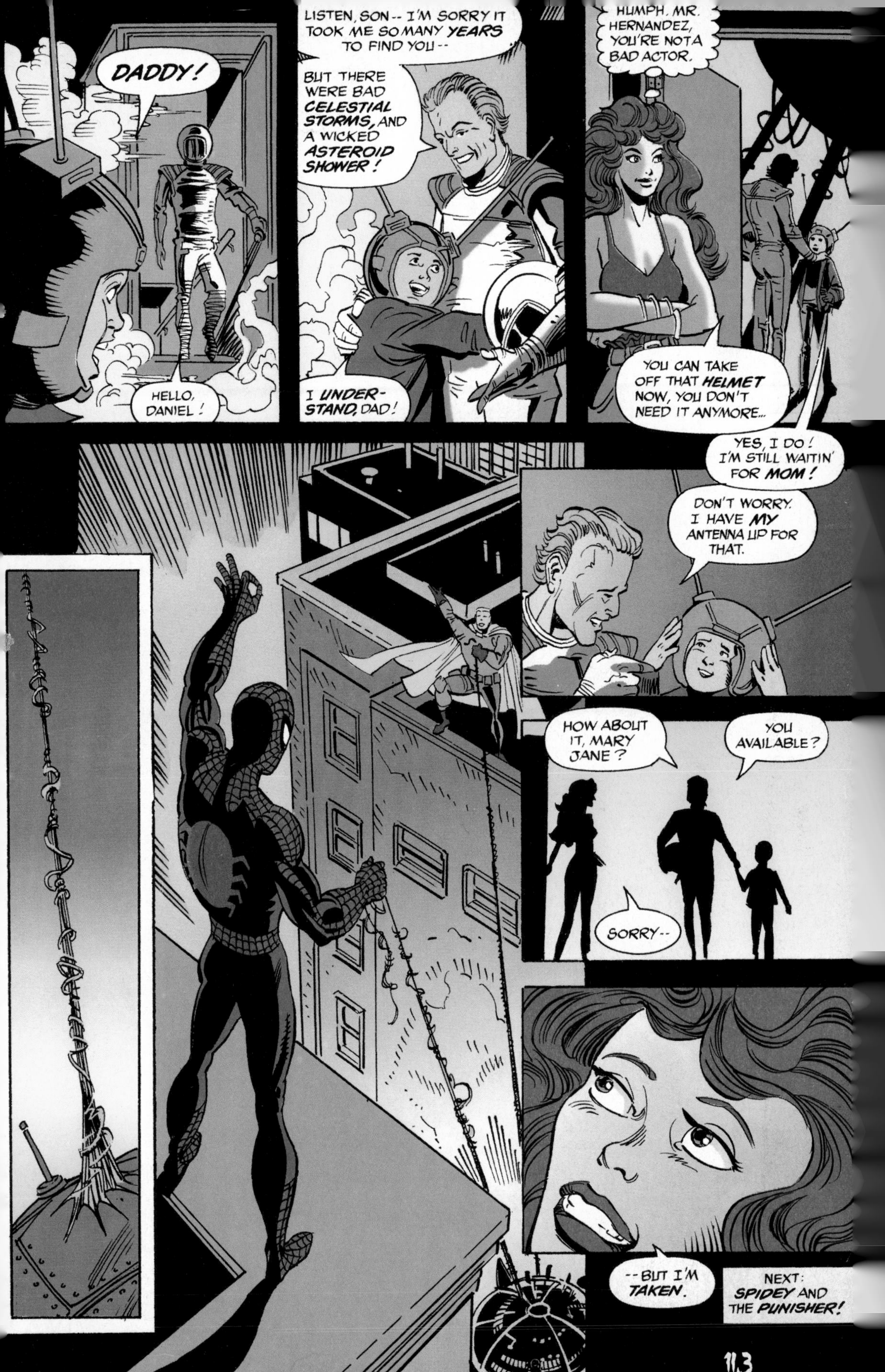
DADDY!
HELLO, DANIEL!
LISTEN, SON -- I'M SORRY IT TOOK ME SO MANY YEARS TO FIND YOU --
BUT THERE WERE BAD CELESTIAL STORMS, AND A WICKED ASTEROID SHOWER!
I UNDERSTAND, DAD!
HUMPH. MR. HERNANDEZ, YOU'RE NOT A BAD ACTOR.
YOU CAN TAKE OFF THAT HELMET NOW, YOU DON'T NEED IT ANYMORE...
YES, I DO! I'M STILL WAITIN' FOR MOM!
DON'T WORRY. I HAVE MY ANTENNA UP FOR THAT.
HOW ABOUT IT, MARY JANE?
YOU AVAILABLE?
SORRY --
-- BUT I'M TAKEN.
NEXT: SPIDEY AND THE PUNISHER!

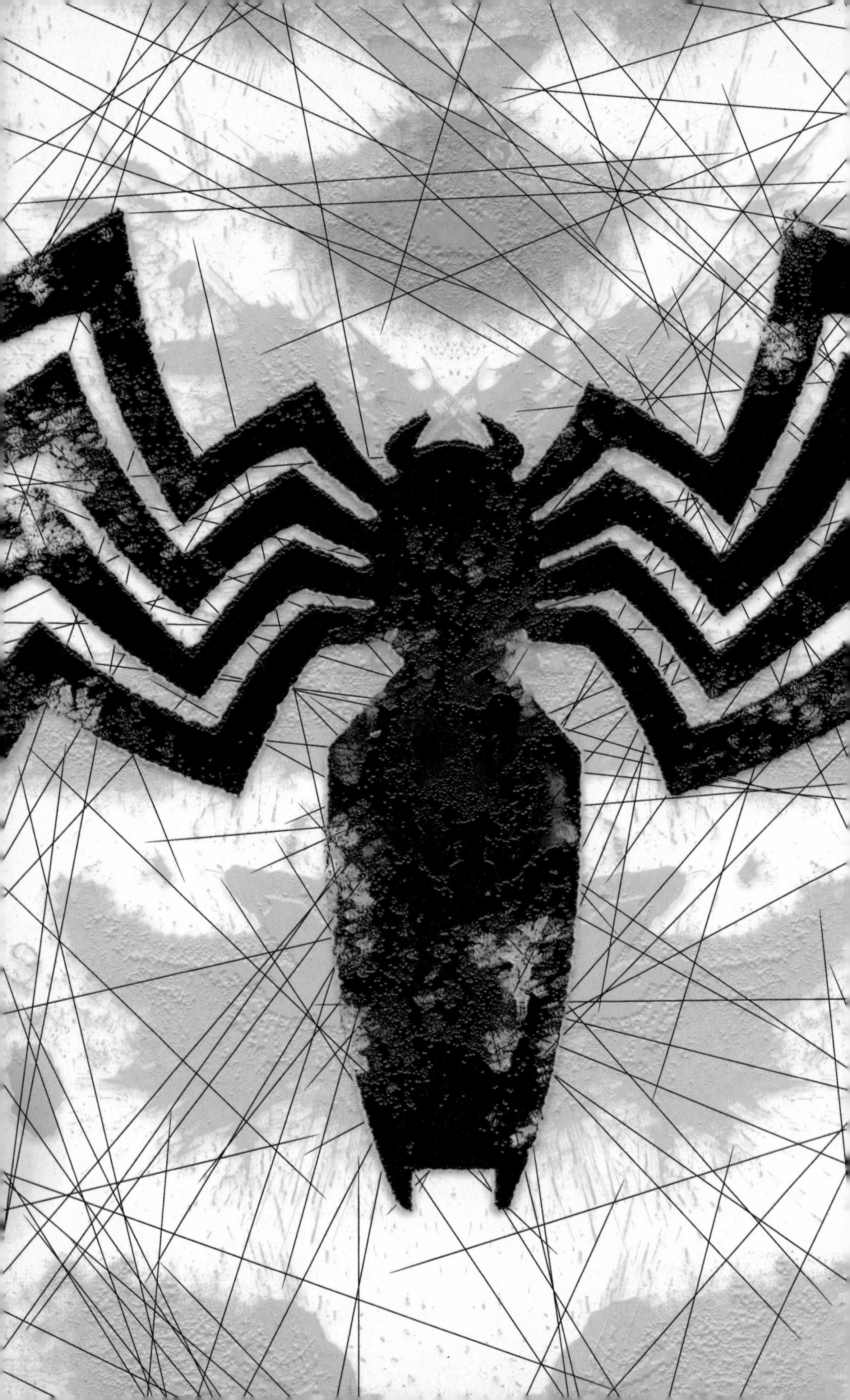